The Role of Large Enterprises in Democracy and Society

The Role of Large Enterprises in Democracy and Society

Edited by

Barbara Fryzel

and

Paul H. Dembinski

Observatoire de la Finance

palgrave
macmillan

First published 2010 by
PALGRAVE MACMILLAN

Palgrave Macmillan in the UK is an imprint of Macmillan Publishers Limited,
registered in England, company number 785998, of Houndmills, Basingstoke,
Hampshire RG21 6XS.

Palgrave Macmillan in the US is a division of St Martin's Press LLC,
175 Fifth Avenue, New York, NY 10010.

Palgrave Macmillan is the global academic imprint of the above companies
and has companies and representatives throughout the world.

Palgrave® and Macmillan® are registered trademarks in the United States,
the United Kingdom, Europe and other countries.

ISBN 978–0–230–22918–1

This book is printed on paper suitable for recycling and made from fully
managed and sustained forest sources. Logging, pulping and manufacturing
processes are expected to conform to the environmental regulations of the
country of origin.

A catalogue record for this book is available from the British Library.

A catalog record for this book is available from the Library of Congress.

10   9   8   7   6   5   4   3   2   1
19 18 17 16 15 14 13 12 11 10

Printed and bound in Great Britain by
CPI Antony Rowe, Chippenham and Eastbourne

Contents

List of Tables and Figures	vii
Preface	viii
Acknowledgements	xvi
Notes on the Contributors	xvii
List of Abbreviations	xxiv

Part I   Democracy and Corporate Lobbying

1   Private Interests and Democracy
    Jan Krzysztof Bielecki — 3

2   The Dialectics of Democracy: Common–Particular
    and Public–Private
    Rafael Alvira — 9

3   Democracy, Networks of Power and Trust in
    Eastern Europe: Considerations around the Syndrome
    of Political Personalism
    Nicolas Hayoz — 16

4   The Voices of Enterprises and Political Games:
    The Corporate World and Its Single Voice?
    Laurent Mortreuil — 39

5   The European Transparency Initiative: Monitoring
    Brussels Lobbying
    Anna Melich — 47

Part II   Corporate Power

6   Economic Power and Social Responsibility of
    Very Big Enterprises: Facts And Challenges
    Paul H. Dembinski — 67

7   Economic Power: Competition Law, Economic Evaluation
    and Policy Implications
    Vindelyn Smith-Hillman and Adam Scott — 76

8 International Companies in Places of Instability:
   The Issue of Mutual Capture   88
   Justin Welby

9 Ethical Dilemmas for Large Corporations in
   Under-developed Countries   99
   Philip Booth

**Part III   Are Corporations Really Responsive
             to Social Concerns?**

10 The Implementation of Compliance Programmes
    in Multinational Organizations   119
    Jean-Pierre Méan

11 The Implementation of CSR as a New Social Contract
    in Poland   138
    Janina Filek

12 Stakeholder Dialogue in Polish Organizations   160
    Barbara Fryzel

13 The Role of NGOs in Promoting Responsible
    Business Practice   175
    Peter Davis

Part IV   Global Issues in Corporate Social Responsibility

14 In Search for a New Balance: The Ethical Dimension
    of the Crisis   189
    *Wojciech Gasparski, Anna Lewicka-Strzalecka,
    Boleslaw Rok and Dariusz Bak*

15 Corporate Responsibility in Multi-Stakeholder
    Collaboration in Social Governance   207
    Aurore Lalucq, Michel Sauquet and Martin Vielajus

16 The Fabric of Knowledge: The Role of Large Corporations
    in Knowledge Production and Dissemination   214
    Laszlo Fekete and Zsolt Boda

17 The Role of Corporations in Shaping Employee Values
    and Behaviour   248
    Stefan Dunin-Wąsowicz

18 Big Business: A Driving Force for Civic Virtue   258
    Montserrat Herrero

Index   267

List of Tables and Figures

Tables

3.1 Four constellations of relationship or co-operation
in the private or public sphere   19

5.1 Current level of perceived transparency and the
importance of it for EU institutions   50

5.2 Current level of perceived transparency and the
importance of it for national institutions   51

5.3 Level of perceived transparency of European institutions
by several independent variables of EU support   52

7.1 The ten largest transnational corporations, 2008   81

16.1 Gross domestic expenditures on research and
development as percentage of GDP, 2000–8   221

16.2 Gross domestic expenditures on research and
development as percentage of GDP, 2000–8   223

16.3 (a) and (b) Revenues and R&D expenditures of the
European telecommunications corporations, 2000–8   232

16.4 Revenues and R&D expenditures of the major European
energy companies, 2000–8   238

16.5 Corporate and social effects of R&D strategies   241

Figures

5.1 Evolution over time of the registration of EU lobbies   60
6.1 Economic and financial weight of the world's 800 largest
enterprises compared to the 114 poorest countries   71

8.1 Peace and sustainable development   95
8.2 The roots of conflict   96

Preface

Large multinational enterprises play a critical role in the world economy as innovators, marketers, employers, standard-setters, international investors, taxpayers, generators of financial returns and organizers of work for millions of other smaller entities across the world. Through their intense interactions with the so-called 'non-market environment' (public bodies and social actors), the very large enterprises contribute greatly towards shaping their socioeconomic and political environment.

Operating with a longer perspective, endowed with greater financial resources and intellectual skills than smaller enterprises, the very large and usually global enterprises are highly sensitive to the possible outcomes of almost any regulatory or legislative process. On the other hand, policy-making, regulation or legislative work do not take place in a social and economic vacuum. These processes occur in a context that surrounds and permeates them. Large enterprises and governments interact closely. The interaction can take different forms, ranging from 'state capture' by private interests to a text-book case of the hermetic isolation of political and economic spheres.

Between what can be normally understood as the purely private sphere (in terms of ownership and property rights) and the public sphere (in terms of democratically elected representation of general interest as opposite to the interests of particular groups in the private sphere) there is civil society – an intermediate platform with the aim of providing a balance between all market and non-market actors to ensure the well-being of citizens and the sustainability of all resources. Thus, a discussion about interactions between business and governments needs to be embedded in the context of how the public voice is expressed in various forms of civil society.

The concept of stakeholders, assigning various degrees of importance to virtually all existing market actors, whether from the public or the private sphere, contributed significantly to the operational complexity of the business environment. It is a difficult and challenging managerial task to prioritize the stakeholders and to build conflict-free relations with them. This prioritization generates a goal alignment problem at the micro level of an enterprise and seems contradictory to a macro-level postulate of sustainability that in operational terms allocates equal rights and importance to all stakeholder groups. In this sense, relations between business, government and society are generally relations of potential conflict if looked at from a sectoral and segmented perspective as opposed to a systemic approach.[1] The latter assumes business, governments and civil society form particular sector- , region- and time-specific ecosystems.

From this point of view the relations specific to business and civil society will touch on issues such as providing consumers with good and affordable products and technologies, giving jobs, pensions and salaries to employees, ensuring a decent return on their investment for shareholders, and donating to local communities, to enhance good citizenship and neighbourhood relations. However, relations based on these contributions are neither linear nor straightforward, when one acknowledges that employees expect a good ratio of quality to price as far as products are concerned, and competitive salaries and meaningful jobs sustainable in the long term. In that context off-shoring contracts to low-wage countries, while being beneficial for the shareholders if it has a positive effect on the bottom line results, may be in obvious conflict with the interests of the local society that would prefer to keep employment at home. Another good example is the interaction between academia and business. While the first expects a greater engagement of the private sector in academic research which provides new knowledge and inventions, business tends to expect the research to translate into new products or services, and be interpreted directly in commercial terms. Such a point of view, however, clearly compromises the independence of research and academics as such.

Relations between the private and public sectors in a democratic setting should be intermediated by governments acting, on the one hand, as setters of the rules designed to ensure that the general interests of people are internalized and observed by all the players on the market, and, on the other, as the executors of the normative system acting through efficient checks and balances. Yet relations between governments and business are also subject to public scrutiny as the potential conflict of interests is exemplified in formal deeds – for example, in law-making – which favours particular interests.

The general contributions of business such as payment of taxes, the creation of wealth, and economic development should meet, in an ideal situation, governmental expectations related to the attraction of foreign direct investment (FDI), building the competitive advantage of the country, creating full employment and, above all, acting in full compliance with generally agreed standards. In return, governments provide the institutional setting and formal framework for enterprises, together with infrastructure related to the availability and sustainability of the labour market, research, communication or political stability. Potential conflicts of interest arise when an institutional environment depicting norms and rules that should guard the common good of the citizens, becomes a trade-off in commercial negotiations between business driven by the paradigm of productivity and cost reduction, and governments driven by political motivation to attract resources for which countries compete – namely, foreign capital. While business promotes successfully the ideology of market liberalization backed by the philosophy of lowering institutional barriers and marginalizing the role of governments, the latter, in trying to defend their electoral positions,[2] multiply various regulators, thus making the environment even less clear and more prone to pathologies such as corruption. The notions of a regulatory state and state power are discussed in the contributions by Bielecki and Alvira.

Considering the points mentioned above, one can conclude that, while the problem seems to be institutional, public discussion on governance deals with a question of distribution that is of a normative nature. Corporate social responsibility (CSR), defined in the context of voluntary deeds beyond the norm, does not therefore seem to be very well suited to solving the norm-related dilemmas.

In the apparent weakness of governments as regulators, the question then is, how and by whom should the governments be stimulated in their regulatory role? Is big business, naturally overtaking this sphere of public activities, legitimized to perform such a role, especially in view of the fact that, together with the cancellation of the rule of sovereignty as a result of globalization, the nature of government–society–business relations has also changed. Large enterprises unbound from the rigour of nationally defined interests and strengthened by their economic power become natural candidates to take a leading role in framework-setting, but they are almost too dangerous, because of their immense embeddedness in the global financial system, to be considered seriously for the role. Have we reached the point that, in order to protect the stability and safety of the global economy, large enterprises will have to be reduced?

Intrigued by a rich variety of questions related to the issues mentioned above, we have invited both academics and practitioners, between them representing various areas of activity (private enterprises, universities, government institutions), to engage in a discourse on the role of large enterprises in the contemporary world. Our aim was to create a dialogue platform, which, because of its representational diversity and multidisciplinary approach to the subject, could become a focus for public-sphere engagement in a discourse on the critical issue of overlapping private and public areas, and evolving structures of power, in the contemporary world.

The topic of the meeting, which took place in October 2007 in Krakow, was limited to interaction between large enterprises and politics in a democratic context. More specifically, the central issue of interest was to learn how enterprises cope with their 'non-market environment' and how this affects the outcomes of economic and democratic processes.

The question addressed by the conference was: how do large enterprises respond to the law, and more broadly to social concerns and expectations; how do they influence the law, and the social and economic rules; and – when necessary – how do they look for ways to accommodate the law. The issue we attempted to address appeared, on the one hand, to be topical for the functioning not only of European democracy but also of emerging world governments, and on the other, as a topic that is seldom fully understood.

The predominant trend in organization and management studies focuses either on management practice and the implementation of CSR postulates in strategic and operational terms (for example, M. E. Porter and M. R. Kramer, 'Strategy and Society: The Link Between Competitive Advantage and Corporate Social Responsibility', *Harvard Business Review*, 2006), or on regaining the balance between human being and organizations (one example being the Academy of Management (AOM) meeting planned for 2010), or on promoting good practice by the corporate sector (for example, various non-governmental organizations (NGOs), such as the Responsible Business Forum (FOB) in Poland), thus concentrating on the instrumental aspect and trying to provide operational solutions for something that has not been properly analysed at the strategic level. There seems to be a lack of a macro perspective looking into the subtle interplay of relations between the three spheres of civil society, the private sector and governments.

The corporate dimension of CSR was accommodated by the private sector through the growing number of professional consultancy services such as that provided by PricewaterhouseCoopers (PwC); anti-fraud and anti-corruption services of Ernst & Young (EY); or Green Construction services in the Building and Construction sector, also backed up by the influential public discourse on green management (AOM meeting, 2009). Yet all the areas mentioned above have roots in the same global problem, which is a changing balance of power between private business influencing millions of people and weakening governments democratically elected to represent people, yet engaging increasingly in dealings with the private sector in ways that make it often less and less clear as to whose interests are being represented. The pace of development of new market entities and the unprecedented scale of their interconnectedness implies a need for a brand new research perspective around topics specific to international business – that is, politics, corruption and corporate social responsibility (Rodriguez, P., Siegel, D., Hillman, A. and Eden, L. (2006) 'Three Lenses on the Multinational Enterprise: Politics, Corruption and Corporate Social Responsibility', *Rensselaer Working Papers in Economics*, April: 2006), backed by economic discourse on the New Economy. This book is the outcome of various analytical perspectives and different interpretations of the changing enterprise and its societal and democratic ties, and, we hope, it presents a new angle on the schools of thought in CSR discourse described above. We present interpretations first shared in Krakow and then enriched by the internalized perceptions of what was introduced and discussed. In this sense it is a sensemaking[3] exercise, with all the benefits of unrestricted methodologies and traditions of thought in the background.

Part I consists of five chapters on the topic of Democracy and Corporate Lobbying. In Chapter 1, the (postmodern in its shape) text of Jan Krzysztof Bielecki explains one of the key paradoxes of democracy, which is how to ensure that the democratic process expresses the general interests of society as opposed to the coalition of particular interests, which agree a policy programme on the basis of 'horse trading' at the expense of the rest of society. This paradox is deeply rooted in the philosophical dialectics of democracy between what is common versus what is particular, and what is public versus what is private This is discussed in Chapter 2 by Rafael Alvira, who interprets the role of enterprises from the perspective of a common good. Nicolas Hayoz, in Chapter 3, elaborates on the transformation of Eastern Europe and the rise of its young democracies as the descriptive background for the classical dichotomy between state and society. He names corruption and personalism as the key problems in societies where relationship-building between the public and the private sphere, and the resultant extensive power networks, are often part of the strategy various actors use to 'get things done'. Laurent Mortreuil introduces in Chapter 4 the discussion of the voice of enterprise as it is seen from both corporate communication and corporate behavioural standpoints, and analyses one language relative to politics that today's corporate world admits to speaking – the voice of CSR. Chapter 5 concludes Part I with a discourse on the European Transparency Initiative by Anna Melich.

Having introduced the issue of the intermingling of the public and private spheres and the often non-transparent relations between business, politics and society – with the latter often being considered a victim of corporate abuse – we examine Corporate Power in Part II.

We start with an explanatory text in Chapter 6 by Paul H. Dembinski on the sources of power of the biggest corporations in the world, followed in Chapter 7 by a thorough elaboration by Vindelyn Smith-Hillman and Adam Scott of the Competition Appeal Tribunal on measuring economic power and controlling it with the use of institutionalized instruments such as competition law and policy. The next two chapters serve to illustrate the practical aspects of corporate power. In Chapter 8, Justin Welby looks at the generic weaknesses in governance and social stability that lead to conflict, and how this makes countries endowed with natural resource wealth particularly vulnerable, using the imagination-triggering example of the Niger Delta. The case of multinational corporations operating in underdeveloped countries is examined further by Philip Booth in Chapter 9, using the Catholic perspective to interpret the ethical dilemmas they encounter.

The economic power of large corporations is implemented and executed in different ways – lobbying and extensive informal or formal pressures on key actors in the surrounding environment being the most obvious. This often results in the strengthening of social concerns from which various initiatives to curb business originate. Various forms of the specific dialogue between the business sector and society are explored in Part III, where we attempt to answer the question 'Are Corporations Really Responsive to Social Concerns?' Most obvious concerns relate to the transparency of corporate actions – for example, serious wrongdoing such as corruption and fraud, or corporate sensitivity towards the needs of stakeholders, specifically local communities. Corporate responses are varied, starting from compliance with the legally binding requirements on social responsibility to non-compulsory, voluntary engagement in solving social problems and attempting to gain a wider understanding of the social context in which a company operates. In Chapter 10, Jean-Pierre Méan discusses the issue of 'compliance' – a notion with exact operational implications for today's managers – and provides the in-depth guidelines for implementing a compliance programme within the company. This is followed by two texts tackling the practical, local perspective of Poland: Janina Filek, in Chapter 11, introducing CSR being implemented as a new social contract; and, in Chapter 12, Barbara Fryzel researching stakeholder communication strategies from the perspective of engaging stakeholders in corporate dialogue. The latter promotes a sensemaking view of the managerial processes, where involving neighbouring actors in a two-way, symmetrical dialogue may open possibilities for a deeper understanding of the goals of other members of the society, thus contributing to a better alignment of corporate and community goals. We conclude this part of the book with Chapter 13 – Peter Davis's text on the role NGOs can play in promoting responsible business practice and in a sense curbing corporate power.

Finally, in Part IV we round off the book by describing Global Issues in Corporate Social Responsibility, beginning with a discussion in Chapter 14 by Wojciech Gasparski *et al.* on the ethical dimensions of the recent global crisis. In Chapter 15, the authors elaborate on social governance performed in the context of a multi-stakeholder collaboration, while in Chapter 16 Laszlo Fekete and Zsolt Boda discuss the role large enterprises have in creating and disseminating knowledge. The roles of large enterprises in general terms do not relate solely to shaping the technical background of competitive societies – for example, by facilitating knowledge production; they also relate to more subtle and intangible features of society, such as values and behaviour based on them, as discussed in Chapter 17 by Stefan Dunin-Wąsowicz.

We began this discourse from the macro perspective, with interpretations of democracy and the workings of the public versus the private sphere, and we conclude with the final chapter in the book – Chapter 18 by Montserrat Herrero, promoting the role of enterprises as potential facilitators for the creation of civic virtues and thus seeing enterprises in the context of political philosophy with civil society, rather that in purely administrative terms.

We are hoping to stimulate further discussion, which could find its conclusions in the international research programme addressing some or all of the issues discussed in this book, which seem to be an inevitable consequence of the intellectual speculation about the role that large enterprises play in the changing social and economic setting.

Aspects of the political legitimacy of corporations would encourage questions on what encompasses 'corporate or enterprise' interests – are corporate interests broader than those of shareholders, and what and whom do enterprises represent today? In that sense, the notion of corporate citizenship may be treated as an oxymoron, while we explore the legitimacy of corporate interests, as different from private individual (citizens') interests, and from public or general interest, and contemplate advocacy as another brand of legitimacy.

Another field for potential research relates to the limits of the 'public sphere' – understood as the limits of the domain in which a democratic voice is entitled to prevail. Elaboration on what is accepted and why, what is the scope of self-regulation by sectors or professions as opposed to public regulation, and whether regulation is just a negotiation, also fall into this category.

Corporate influence on 'public opinion' is another topic we would very much like to see developed. Specifically, our point of interest sits with the question of whether the media can be seen as just another business: financing and controlling as opposed to 'normal' investment.

On the broader level of analysis interesting questions remain about the ethical nature of morality and culture as opposed to internal corporate standards. The questions for further research are how to respect the autonomy of politics – what are the required behavioural and ethical standards? Can values, standards and culture become exclusively corporate concerns?

Last, but not least, discussion around the problem of divergence between the systemic inefficiency of the state-induced regulatory system and the instrumentally-focused CSR debate, which leaves the true source of the problem – the norm setting – unsolved, implies further research is needed on global governance issues, with specific questions such as whether a global common good is possible without a world 'demos'; does CSR effort contribute to building a 'world demos'; and can private 'soft law' be a generator of hard norms – for example, environment and accounting norms.

Barbara Fryzel
Paul H. Dembinski

Notes

1. This is the view presented by Brigitte Monsou De Tantawy during her presentation at the World Business Council for Sustainable Development meeting, 'The Role of Large Enterprises in Democracy and Society', Krakow, October 2007.
2. Backed by the relations between government and civil society based on the votes contributed by the latter.
3. We interpret the term sensemaking as the set of attempts at individual or organizational level to create shared meanings and result in a common understanding of the experienced situation. People make sense of the events around them as well as of actions taken by other people. They also give sense when they attempt to promote their individual interpretations or the surrounding reality to others. This is particularly true of organizations as well, where sensemaking provides a cognitive map for its members, enabling them to position themselves within organizational policies, standards and corporate culture. See Weick, K. E. (1995) *Sensemaking in Organizations* (Thousand Oaks, Calif./London: Sage) for details.

Acknowledgements

This book is a result of a long-term co-operation among a team of authors, who shared their views and built the intellectual foundations for this project at a meeting held at Jagiellonian University in Krakow in October 2007.

We would like to thank sincerely Professor Michal du Vall, Prorector of the Jagiellonian University, who, as the Dean of the Faculty of Management and Social Communication in 2007, kindly hosted the meeting at the University.

Special thanks are owed to Professor Zbigniew Neçki, director of the Institute of Economics and Management at the time, whose support helped to organize the meeting, as well as to Professor Andrzej Matczewski for his continuous support of our efforts to develop a scientific discourse around corporate social responsibility, in both our teaching and our research.

We would also like to thank Sibilla La Spina, whose administrative skills helped greatly in organizing the meeting.

Notes on the Contributors

Rafael Alvira was educated at various universities, mainly in Madrid-Complutense and Navarra, in Spain. He is Licentiate in Philosophy and Letters (History and Philosophy), final grade Sobresaliente cum laude (University of Navarra), achieved a Doctorate in Philosophy (Sobresaliente cum laude and Class Valedictorian) at the Universidad Complutense de Madrid and a Doctorate in Philosophy at the Lateran University, Rome. He is Profesor Ordinario at the University of Navarra and the director of the Institute Empresa y Humanismo, director of the Department of Philosophy and director of the Programme of Government and Culture of the Organization. He is Profesor Extraordinario of the Mendoza University, Argentina and the University of Montevideo, Uruguay.

Dariusz Bak is a member of the Business Ethics Centre of Kozminski University and the Polish Academy of Science's Institute of Philosophy and Sociology. He is also a Lecturer at Kozminski University and Warsaw University of Technology (Faculty of Administration and Social Sciences). In his research he focuses on administration ethics and institutional solutions in business ethics, especially in the area of human resources management. His interests cover the functioning of codes of ethics.

Jan Krzysztof Bielecki started his career as an economics lecturer at Gdansk University in 1973, but lost his job in 1981 because of his anti-Communist political activities and participation in the historic strike at Gdansk Shipyard. He was the CEO of the Bank Pekao SA between 2003 and 2009, and prime minister of Poland from January to December 1991. Later he was the chief delegate of the Polish Parliament to the European Parliament and a Minister for European Integration. In December 1993, he was appointed to the board of directors of the European Bank for Reconstruction and Development in London, where, until 2003, he represented Poland and supervised EBRD activities in Poland, Romania and Albania.

Zsolt Boda is Senior Research Fellow at the Institute of Political Science, Hungarian Academy of Sciences, and Associate Professor at the Business Ethics Center of the Corvinus University of Budapest. He is visiting lecturer at the Université Pierre et Marie Curie in Paris and the European

University Viadrina in Frankfurt. His research interests and publications are concerned with international environmental policy, business ethics and global governance.

Philip Booth is Editorial and Programme Director of the Institute of Economic Affairs and Professor of Insurance and Risk Management at Cass Business School, City University. He has written extensively on regulation, social insurance and Catholic social teaching. He is a fellow of the Institute of Actuaries and of the Royal Statistical Society, and Associate Editor of the *Annals of Actuarial Science* and the *British Actuarial Journal*. He has also advised the Bank of England on financial stability issues (1998–2002). Publications include *Catholic Social Teaching and the Market Economy* and *The Road to Economic Freedom* – an edited compilation of the work of Nobel Prize winners in Economics. He is also a Visiting Fellow at the Las Casas Institute, Blackfriars Hall, Oxford University.

Peter Davis is Director of Greystones Management, which specializes in corporate responsibility, political and societal risk, and business ethics. He advises a wide range of organizations, including the Swedish International Development Agency, Anglo American, Northrop Grumman and Diageo. From 2006 to 2008, he chaired the British Conservative Party's policy group on responsible business practice. He is co-Director of the Ethical Corporation Institute and the political editor of *Ethical Corporation*.

Paul H. Dembinski, an economist and political scientist by training, is a Professor at the University of Fribourg, where he teaches International Competition and Strategy. He has served as a consultant to international bodies such as OECD and UNCTAD. He is also the initiator and executive director of the Observatoire de la Finance foundation (1996) (www. obsfin.ch). and the founder and editor of the bilingual journal *Finance & the Common Good/Bien Commun* (1998). His most recent published books include: *Enron and the World of Finance: A Case Study in Ethics* (co-editor), Basingstoke, Palgrave Macmillan, 2005; *Finance: Servant or Deceiver?* (in French: Paris, Desclée de Brouwer, 2008; and, in English, Basingstoke, Palgrave Macmillan, 2009).

Stefan Dunin-Wąsowicz holds degrees in Economics from Warsaw University, Poland, the University of Nancy, France, and the Graduate Institute of International Studies, University of Geneva, Switzerland. He is the Director and a board member of BPI Polska, a human resources consulting company. He has a leading profile in Poland, having consulted on transnational projects for more than fifty private and public sector organizations. Previously, for more than fifteen years he held senior worldwide positions in the global electronic companies, Hewlett Packard (HP) and Philips. He conducts research on industrial strategies and restructuring.

Laszlo Fekete is Associate Professor at the Business Ethics Center of the Corvinus University of Budapest. He studied History, Economic History and Sociology at Eötvös Loránd University of Budapest, the Friedrich-Schiller-Universität zu Jena, Germany, and the State University of New York at Binghamton, USA. He has an MA in Economic History and Sociology, and a PhD in Philosophy. He is associate editor of *Ethical Prospects: Economy, Society, and Environment* (Springer). His research interests include philosophical and ethical problems of business transactions, digital culture and the information society.

Janina Filek, who has been working in the Chair of Philosophy at the Economic University of Krakow, Poland, is the author of over seventy articles. Her most important book publications include *On the Freedom and Responsibility of the Economic Subject* (2002), *Introduction to Business Ethics* (2004), and *Ethical Aspects of Self-Government Activities* (Editor, 2004). From 2005–8, she was Deputy Dean of the Economy and International Relationships Department. Since 2003, as Plenipotentiary for Handicapped Persons to the University Rector, she has been working to increase accessibility for disabled students to the University's facilities. She is a member of the EBEN Poland Programme Council.

Barbara Fryzel, an economist by training with diplomas from the University of Economics in Krakow (MSc in Corporate Finance) and the Jagiellonian University (PhD in Economics, Management Sciences) is an Adjunct at the Jagiellonian University, specializing in Management and Organizational Science. She was an Honorary Research Fellow at University College London in 2006–8 and is the laureate of the fellowship programme of the Foundation for Polish Science. She is a management practitioner. During her commercial career she co-operated with many international organizations including British Petroleum plc and Royal Ahold. Her research interests focus in particular on corporate social responsibility and stakeholder management.

Wojciech Gasparski is Professor of Humanities, Director and founder of the Business Ethics Centre (a joint unit of Kozminski University and the Polish Academy of Science's Institute of Philosophy and Sociology). Immediate past Vice-Rector for Research at Kozminski University.

Professor emeritus of the Institute of Philosophy and Sociology, Polish Academy of Science, where he chaired the Academic Board and headed the Department of Praxiology as well as the Research Group for Ethics in Business and the Economy. He is the editor-in-chief of *Praxiology: The International Annual of Practical Philosophy and Methodology* (Edison, New Jersey, USA, Transaction Publishers).

Nicolas Hayoz is Associate Professor of Political Science and the Director of the Interdisciplinary Institute of Central and Eastern Europe at the University of Fribourg, Switzerland. Since 2007 he has also been Programme Director of the Regional Research Promotion Programme in the Western Balkans (RRPP). Since 2009 he has directed a research promotion programme in the Southern Caucasus – the Academic Swiss Caucasus Net (ASCN). He has conducted research projects in Russia and in Georgia (in the framework of SCOPES – Scientific Co-operation between Eastern Europe and Switzerland). His research interests include transition studies in Eastern Europe, particularly the transformation process in Russia, and political theory. Among his latest publications (together with Simon Hug) is *Tax Evasion, State Capacity and Trust* (Berne etc., Peter Lang, 2007).

Montserrat Herrero is a Professor of Political Philosophy at the University of Navarra, Spain, from which she also holds a PhD degree. Her main publications are: *Carl Schmitt und Alvaro d'Ors Briefwechsel* (Berlin, Duncker & Humblot, 2004); *Sociedad del trabajo y sociedad del conocimiento en la era de la globalización* (Knowledge Society and Work Society in a Globalized Era) (Madrid, Pearson/Prentice Hall, 2003); *El nomos y lo político: la filosofía política de Carl Schmitt* (The Nomos and the Political: The Political Philosophy of Carl Schmitt) (Pamplona, Eunsa, 1997 and 2007). She is co-editor of *Sociedad civil: la democracia y su destino* (Civil Society: The Destiny of Democracy) (Pamplona, Eunsa, 2nd edn 2008); *La experiencia social del tiempo* (Time and Society) (Pamplona, Eunsa, 2nd edn 2006); *Educación y ciudadanía en una sociedad democrática* (Education and Citizenship in a Democratic Society) (Madrid, Encuentro, 2006). She has also published several papers on topics of political philosophy.

Aurore Lalucq is an economist by training. She graduated from the University of Paris-Sorbonne and the Institute for Economic and Social Development Studies (IEDES), Paris. She has been a project manager at the Charles Léopold Mayer Foundation for Human Progress (FPH), at Lares (a University of Rennes laboratory for social sciences) and at

Ritimo (an information network for international solidarity and development). Her field of specialization is the question of pluralism in Economics. A member of the Institute for Research and Debate on Governance (IRG) since 2006, she heads the IRE (International Initiative for Rethinking the Economy).

Anna Lewicka-Strzalecka is a Professor at the Business Ethics Centre Institute of Philosophy and Sociology, the Polish Academy of Sciences and the Leon Kozminski Academy, Warsaw, Poland. She participated in the research programme entitled 'Ethics in the Polish Economy: Perception, Preferences, Norms', which was supported by the State Committee for Scientific Research. She is a member of a research team working on a research project entitled 'Understanding and Responding to Societal Demands on Corporate Responsibility' (REPONSE). The project is supported by funding under the Sixth Research Framework Programme of the European Union. She is editor-in-chief of 'Prakseologia', a Polish journal on human action theory, (PAS, Poland) and a founder and vice-chairman of the European Business Ethics Network in Poland (EBEN-Poland).

Jean-Pierre Méan was General Counsel and Chief Compliance Officer of SGS, the Swiss inspection company, from 1996 to 2008, with a break in 2002 and 2003 when he was Chief Compliance Officer for the European Bank for Development and Reconstruction (EBRD). He has been a member of the Steering Committee on the Business Principles for Countering Bribery issued under the aegis of Transparency International, and contributed to the 2008 edition of 'Fighting Corruption – International Corporate Integrity Handbook' published by the International Chamber of Commerce. He is President of the Swiss Chapter of Transparency International and a member of the Anticorruption Commission of the International Chamber of Commerce and President of the Board of Trustees of Caux-Initiatives of Change. He has been admitted to the Bar in Quebec/Canada and Switzerland.

Anna Melich is a Political Adviser on Public Opinion, Information and Communication, Culture, Multilingualism and Professional Ethics at the Bureau of European Policy Advisers (BEPA) attached to the President of the European Commission in Brussels. She has been responsible for several years for the Public Opinion Research Services of the European Commission – the Eurobarometer quantitative and qualitative surveys. Her past academic career was in the Department of Political Science of the University of Geneva, Switzerland. She has written several books and papers on European public opinion; European value systems; regional, national and European identity; political socialization; media analysis; and, more recently, professional ethics of holders of public office.

Laurent Mortreuil is CFO, Capital Markets, of the Société Générale Group, and Executive Director of UNIAPAC – the International Christian Union of Business Executives. He has published several articles and a book (*The Profit of Values*, Paris, UNIAPAC, 2008) on CSR and on Christian social tradition as applied to the entrepreneurial and financial worlds. He lectures regularly and teaches in Africa, Asia, the Americas and Europe. A graduate of the École Polytechnique and École Nationale des Ponts et Chaussées, Paris, he holds a PhD in Economic Theory from the University of Paris-Sorbonne.

Boleslaw Rok is an Associate Professor at the Business Ethics Centre, Kozminski University, Warsaw. He has been partner in several international CSR projects: for example, the Growing Inclusive Markets Forum with the UN and Dalhousie University in Halifax, Nova Scotia, Canada (from 2006); 'The CSR Navigator – Public Policies in Europe, Asia, Africa and the Americas', with Bertelsmann Stiftung (2006–7); 'Mainstreaming CSR among SMEs' (2003–7); and 'Responsible Entrepreneurship' (2003–4), DG Enterprise and Industry, European Commission, Brussels. He is a founder of the Responsible Business Forum (2000), a co-founder of Caux Round Table Poland and the European Business Ethics Network Poland.

Michel Sauquet is the Director of the Institute for Research and Debate on Governance (IRG). He is a graduate of the Institut d'Études Politiques de Paris (Sciences Po) and a Doctor of Applied Economics. He has spent a large part of his professional career, since the beginning of the 1970s, in the areas of international co-operation, intercultural dialogue, and communication for development, notably in Africa and Latin America, for various NGOs, international organizations and for the Charles Léopold Mayer Foundation. He is Vice-President of the Alliance of Independent publishers, and is currently a teacher at Sciences Po and the author of around fifteen published books.

Adam Scott is a member of the UK's Competition Appeal Tribunal and has held fellowships at the University of St Andrews since 1994. His academic interests include scenario planning, and economic and legal regulation of competition and of utilities. He has been a consultant in these fields and a senior adviser to Europe Economics. After qualifying at the Bar with an intellectual property background, he worked mainly in telecommunications, being a corporate planner in the creation and privatization of British Telecommunications plc, then heading BT's international affairs and, until 1994, chairing its apparatus business. He is a Fellow of the Institution of Engineering and Technology.

Vindelyn Smith-Hillman is a member of the UK's Competition Appeal Tribunal and the Economic Adviser at the Law Commission, having previously been an academic with lectureships at the Open University and the University of Northampton, and holding a number of external examiner positions. Prior to that she was a Senior Economist at the Bank of Jamaica in Kingston, Jamaica. She is a listed Assistant Examiner with Cambridge and London Examining Boards and an Assessor with the Government Economic Service.

Martin Vielajus is Deputy Director of the Institute for Research and Debate on Governance (IRG), and is a graduate of the International Affairs Masters of the Institut d'Études Politiques de Paris (Sciences Po). Until October 2006 he assumed a parallel function to that at the IRG as a member of the teaching executive at Sciences Po. His main fields of study are the forms and modes of action of civil society actors, and the perceptions of governance criteria in the different co-operation policies. The intercultural orientation of the IRG follows his experience at UNESCO and in several cultural institutions.

Justin Welby has been Anglican Dean of Liverpool since December 2007. He studied Law and History at Cambridge and then spent eleven years in the oil industry based in Paris and London, working in West Africa and on North Sea projects. He ended his oil industry career as Group Treasurer of Enterprise Oil plc, a large UK exploration and production company. Having studied theology at Durham, after ten years in parish work, from 2002–7 he was responsible for Coventry Cathedral's international ministry of reconciliation, which included practical direct intervention work in the Middle East and Africa. Among other activities, he has been chairman of an NHS Trust. He is the Personal and Ethical Adviser to the UK Association of Corporate Treasurers, and lectures extensively on ethics and finance. He has published a number of articles in English and French on issues of international finance, ethics and management. He is on the Committee of Reference for the Ethical Funds of F&C plc.

List of Abbreviations

AGE	European Commission's Advisory Group on Energy
ALTER-EU	The Alliance for Lobbying Transparency & Ethics Regulation
AOM	Academy of Management
ASCN	Academic Swiss Caucasus Net
ATCA	Alien Tort Claims Act (USA)
Attac	international campaigning network for social change
BBC	British Broadcasting Corporation
BEPA	Bureau of European Advisers on European Policies
BPI	Bribe Payers Index (Transparency International)
CEE	Central and Eastern Europe
CEO	chief executive officer
CEO	Corporate Europe Observatory
CONECCS	Consultation, the European Commission and Civil Society database
CPI	Corruption Perceptions Index (Transparency International)
CSR	corporate social responsibility
EBRD	European Bank for Reconstruction and Development
EC	European Commission
EIPA	European Intellectual Property Association
EITI	The Extractive Industries Transparency Initiative
EP	European Parliament
ETI	European Transparency Initiative
EU	European Union
EY	Ernst & Young
FDI	foreign direct investment
FOB	Responsible Business Forum

FPH	Charles Léopold Mayer Foundation for Human Progress
FSC	Forest Stewardship Council
GDP	gross domestic product
GHG	greenhouse gas
GRI	Global Reporting Initiative
ICN	International Competition Network
IEDES	Institute for Economic and Social Development Studies
IFC	International Finance Corporation
IPCC	Intergovernmental Panel on Climate Change
IRE	International Initiative for Rethinking the Economy
IRG	Institute for Research and Debate on Governance
IT	information technology
MEP	Member of the European Parliament
MNC	multinational corporation
NCP	National Contact Point
NGO	non-governmental organization
NSA	non-state actors
OECD	Organisation for Economic Co-operation and Development
OLAF	Anti-Fraud Office (EU)
ORTF	Office de Radiodiffusion Télévision Française (French public sector broadcasting company)
PLN	Polish zloty (zl.) (currency)
PwC	PricewaterhouseCoopers
Ritimo	An information network for international solidarity and development
R&D	research and development
RRPP	Regional Research Promotion Programme in the Western Balkans
SCOPES	Scientific Co-operation between Eastern Europe and Switzerland
SEC	Securities and Exchange Commission
SIV	structured investment vehicle

SMEs	small and medium enterprises
SMP	significant market power
SPDC	Shell Petroleum Development Company
SRI	socially responsible investment
SWOG	European Commission's Strategic Working Group of the Advisory Group on Energy
TNC	transnational corporation
TVP	Telewizja Polska (Polish public broadcasting corporation)
UNCAC	UN Convention against Corruption
UNCTAD	United Nations Conference on Trade and Development
UNESCO	United Nations Educational, Scientific and Cultural Organization
UNODC	United Nations Office on Drugs and Crime
UNIAPAC	International Christian Union of Business Executives
VBE	very big enterprise
WTO	World Trade Organization

Part I

Democracy and Corporate Lobbying

1
Private Interests and Democracy

Jan Krzysztof Bielecki

The general interest versus particular interests in democracies

A paradox exists at the heart of the democratic system: how to ensure that the democratic process expresses the general interests of society as a whole, rather than just the particular interests of an ad hoc (or even long-term) coalition of particular interests, who agree a policy programme on the basis of 'horse trading' at the expense of the rest of society?

The problem is fundamental in that it does not disappear if the 'ruling coalition' represents an absolute majority of society (that is, a 'selfish majority' as opposed to the 'selfish minority' or oligarchy that populist politicians like to talk against). Also, it does not disappear even if the ruling coalition obtains power directly via the voting process, rather than by influencing the behaviour of an already existing democratically elected government (which is what we usually think of as the behaviour of large enterprises in the democratic arena).

Jean-Jacques Rousseau was highly conscious of this problem, and was careful to define the 'general interest' or 'general will' of a nation as something separate from the sum of the particular interests – the interests of all of its citizens, not just a majority of the population. While technically correct, this formulation allowed the Jacobins to claim during the French Revolution that they represented the 'general interests' of French people, long after it had become clear that they did not have the support of anything like a majority of their compatriots. The Terror ensued, and with it the first use of the word 'terrorist' – one who uses terror directed at his or her co-citizens to pursue the 'general interest'!

3

Lenin's Bolsheviks were the heirs of the Jacobins in this area, as in so many others. Lenin claimed that he was justified in using terror to implement his policies, as they were in the interests of a 'historical majority', which would be brought into existence by the policies themselves, and that the will of this as yet non-existent majoritarian proletariat should have precedence over that of the merely 'arithmetical' majority of currently living Russians!

It is worth remembering these facts when we discuss the problem of private interests and democracy, and especially when we do so in this part of the world [Central and Eastern Europe] which has seen over 70 million victims of the two totalitarianisms of the twentieth century. It is worth remembering that the worst results of private interests being introduced into public policy are as bamboo shoots to great oak trees when compared to the disasters caused by the self-proclaimed apostles of the 'general will' and the 'general interest', especially when these have succeeded in freeing themselves of the need to take a majority of 'currently living citizens' along with them in their definition of what these general values are.

Since the French Revolution, liberal democracies have found several pragmatic solutions to the problem of how to distinguish between the 'general interest' and the 'interests of the majority'. The first and most important of these has been to define the 'general interest' as, above all, the maintenance of certain key *individual* rights, such as the right to free speech, the due process of law, a non-politicized and fair trial (the latter two rights are only ensured by a truly independent judiciary and prosecution service), the right to secure ownership of private property, the majoritarian election of certain key executive and legislative officials, and so on.

Rights of this kind, taken to define the general interest, are usually enshrined in constitutions, which can be changed only by large 'supermajorities' in parliaments and/or via referendums. Other laws must conform to such constitutions, and independent courts (sometimes special constitutional courts) ensure this. Such a system of fundamental rights, buttressed by institutionalized checks and balances on policy-making, ensures both that ideological fanatics are kept in check, and that temporary majorities representing ad hoc coalitions find it harder to behave as if their particular interests were in the 'general interest'.

Political donations, political influence and corruption

However, problems remain, and they are most visible in the areas where free speech, election financing and policy advocacy meet. If we agree that, subject to constitutional constraints, we accept the will of the electoral majority (and of the government that represents it) as the 'general will', then it is natural that groups will try to ensure that parties representing their interests form part of that majority, that they will speak in their favour, and the groups will provide the parties with the financial resources also to convince others.

Therefore, few will object to trade unions supporting a social democratic party both verbally and financially. Nor should they object to businesses supporting low-regulation, low-tax parties in the same way (though in some countries, including Poland, this is not generally allowed). But things become more complicated when a company (or a trade union) supports a party that has a policy that is in the interests of *that particular company/trade union alone*. And there are even more complications if the company/trade union supports a party that only *subsequently* 'adjusts' its policy to conform to the interests of the company/trade union concerned. Finally, there is a major problem if, in the latter case, the party concerned does not inform voters of the money it has received, or of its change of policy.

The most difficult cases to judge are intermediate ones: for example, gifts by a group of companies or by trade unions in a particular industry, to a party that supports protective tariffs for that industry. Should these be considered a normal part of democratic politics or a form of corruption?

An important issue concerns the rights of dissenting individuals who are within donating organizations. British prime minister Margaret Thatcher insisted that trade union members be required to 'opt into' their unions' contributions to the British Labour Party, on the grounds that they should not be coerced into giving money to a party they might not personally support. One could make a similar argument regarding shareholders of a company and that party's political donations. Alternatively, we could try to solve this problem by banning outright financial support of political parties by any but individual citizens, as is indeed the case in Poland. However, if we go down this road we then have the problem that some individuals are far richer than others. Should Jan Kulczyk,[1] whose assets were at one time estimated at $4 billion, be allowed to give as much as he wished in political donations in a country where the average annual wage is about $6,000 per annum? Moreover, with such wealth, Jan Kulczyk had business interests which were just as specific as those of a very large Polish corporation, as well as the ability to make donations that were of a similar size to large corporate ones. Does the distinction between individual and corporate donations make sense in such a situation?

Polish law attempts to resolve this issue by setting an upper limit on individual donations. But does this not limit an individual's rights to free speech and full participation in the political process, which, as we have seen, are often considered to be fundamental individual rights embodying the 'general interest'? Polish law attempts to circumvent this problem by limiting political donations to the participation by a political party in the very generous system of state financing. But the association is not convincing: individuals can be punished for giving 'illegal money' to parties, and there are tight constraints on institutional and individual political donations even for parties that do not accept public money. Worst of all, public financing is so generous that 'going private' does not make sense for a party that can avoid it.

The Polish system of public political financing has one great advantage: 'financing follows the vote' – that is, money is distributed between parties in proportion to the votes they received at the most recent general election. A weakness is a strong redistributive bias: while individual donations are currently capped at 14k PLN (17k PLN in 2008), state financing is drawn from general taxation (where the rich pay more) while being distributed on an 'all votes are equal' basis.

Public sector media

Broadcast media are large enterprises with the greatest impact on the political process. Public sector broadcasters are particularly problematic, particularly if they are not politically independent, as they have huge influence on electorates and no clear commercial demands that would constrain their behaviour.

This is why one of the greatest problems in our region [Central and Eastern Europe] has been the inability to ensure anything that remotely approaches independence in the public sector media. One reason for this is the shortage of politically independent people to place in charge of such media. Another is the absence of an underlying consensus on more issues than in well-established democracies (there are more things to determine when a new politico-economic system is being created, so conflicts are more fundamental and sharper).

However, one should not exaggerate the success of Western European countries in this regard, especially at times of sharp social conflict. The partiality of the French public sector broadcasting company ORTF under General Charles de Gaulle was notorious. Today, the BBC is independent of government only because it is well to the left of the whole party political spectrum in Britain. At times (for example, over the Iraq war) it has provided a more effective opposition to the Labour government than has the Conservative Party itself (and from quite different positions). It is not at all clear that this is what a public sector broadcaster funded by taxpayers' money should be doing.

In Poland, a vicious circle has developed, in which pro-government bias in the public broadcaster has led to an anti-government stance in the private media, which are keen to appeal to viewers dissatisfied by TVP (the Polish public broadcasting corporation). This in turn causes the government to fear giving up control of the public broadcaster and ending with no broadcast media support. Fuel is added to the fire because TVP is allowed to screen commercials as well as receiving a licence fee, which means that it has its own *commercial* interests to defend, which it sometimes attempts to do through political subservience to the government.

Region-specific issues

Little has been said about any special 'region-specific' problems. This is because, in spite of a commonly held view, the main problems in this subject area are not specific to the new democracies of Central and Eastern Europe. This is particularly true of the new member states of the European Union (EU).

Some post-Soviet countries have political systems which are different from those of normally functioning Western democracies. Some, such as Ukraine or Boris Yeltsin's Russia, may be described as oligarchies, in which very rich individuals and companies have far more influence over the political process than would be normal in a Western democracy. On the other hand, when the power of the oligarchs has been constrained, this has not generally led to greater democracy but rather to greater autocracy, as in the case of Vladimir Putin's Russia, with political choice for ordinary citizens being *reduced* rather than increased. This suggest that the problems of such countries run far deeper than just excessive private commercial influence on the political process.

General principles

What kinds of political donations are acceptable in a democracy, and what kinds approach corruption too closely for comfort? I do not believe that it is a matter of the wealth of the giver, the size of the donation, or the nature of the giver (company, trade union, NGO) as long as shareholders or union members are not forced to support parties financially that they do not like.

Rather, the issue is *how specific to the donor is the benefit expected by him or her?* The more specific the benefit, the less acceptable the donation. To understand this we can borrow the concept of 'externality' from economics. Markets do not work well when a deal between the seller and the buyer has strong external effects on third parties. If the external effects are positive, then too little of the good or service concerned will be produced and traded, because the buyer will not wish to spend as much money as s/he would if the full benefit of his/her expenditure went to him/her alone. Analogously, the benefits spread out more generally beyond the donor him/herself are those that result from the policies implemented by the party the donor supports, then the more the donation can be viewed as an expression of the donor's participation in a *political* rather than a *commercial* process, aimed at benefiting others more than him/herself, and thus the less objectionable is the donation, independently of all other criteria.

A major problem for political freedom therefore results from the development of the 'regulatory state', affecting increasing numbers of commercial activities in ever-greater detail. This means that more and more companies or rich individuals are likely to engage in commercial activities that are regulated in ways that affect only them and a few others, making any political donations they make suspect.

In 1944, Friedrich von Hayek wrote in *The Road to Serfdom* that a country in which more than 50 per cent of the economy was owned by the state cannot remain a democracy for long, because democratic politics cannot resolve the group conflicts that would need to be settled in the pubic sector. Modern democracies have replaced public ownership with ever more detailed public regulation. But this does not make the problem go away. Nor would banning political donations by large companies or rich individuals be a solution. The desire to influence the regulations to which business is subjected remain, as does the need of government to consult with the regulated to avoid making costly errors. The scope for undue influence will therefore always be with us, as long as regulation is excessive, no matter how such influence is exercised. The only answer is to once again roll back the state.

Editors' Note

1. Jan Kulczyk is one of the richest Polish entrepreneurs, the founder of the group of companies under the brand The Kulczyk Group. For more details see www.kulczykinvestments.com.

2
The Dialectics of Democracy: Common–Particular and Public–Private

Rafael Alvira

Democracy and the common good

It is well known that classical Greek used three words to express what we now call *people: láos, démos, ójlos*. *Ójlos* meant a group of people whose only connection was physical proximity and a common rejection of something, or protest against someone; the Romans used the term *plebs*. *Láos* is an archaic term, meaning an organized human group with an internal connection, and an internal principle of unity. The Athenians, or the Jews, were *láos*. *Démos* is an intermediate kind of word. It indicates a population which is neither *ójlos*, the masses, nor has an internal principle of articulation, precisely because *démos* was a *peaceful group of individuals*.

Of these three terms, the one that is least like what we usually understand as *people* is *démos*. We can see the people as the masses yelling in sports stadiums or at political demonstrations in the streets. We call a nation with strong cultural or historical links, such as the Poles, or the French, a 'people'. Or use the Christian term, *people of God*. But democracy taken as a political position for the peaceful coexistence of free individuals is not truly a people, given that the concept of the radical freedom of each individual as a political base means that the social bonds are minimal and external. Hence the traditional rejection by some romantic and community nationalistic movements of 'liberal democracy'.

The principle of internal unity of this liberal democracy is, simply, respect for individual freedom and peace. Without respect, democracy is de facto impossible. This principle is thus the remains of the common good which still exists in democracy. Indeed, even though this respect appears as the common will of citizens – that is, as something

9

subjective – in reality it is indisputable, unavailable for citizen freedom, and therefore, *objective*. And not all citizens accept it. Many do not want it in their hearts, and others fight it through terrorism.

The common good is not the same as the common will. *Good* is something objectively given that perfects the human being. In essence, directly or indirectly, all true good is common, as the perfection of each individual cannot be dissociated from social perfection. And what perfects human beings and what is damaging to them can be determined. It is what makes human beings truly grow or perfects them. Whatever takes something away from them, be it no more than time, is damaging.

Immanuel Kant – being here a herald of modernity – maintains that in this world nothing can be considered absolutely good except good will. Here good is subjectivized: what is good is will. But, without a doubt, a will can be called good only inasmuch as it, specifically, wants good, and, on the other hand, ethical good presupposes the will. Undoubtedly, given that human beings are free, wanting has a central value. But one may receive good things, even though one does not want them, while one may do evil objectively while having, subjectively, a good will.

The point here is that it is possible to determine the common good, because it is objective, but is impossible to know if a general common will exists. The only common will is that which can be found among people who really love one another, but this kind of relationship is not normally considered in politics, particularly in democratic politics.

The fiction of the common good

Thus, from the start, democracy has come up against the problem of not being able to accept any other common good than the above-mentioned minimum, but at the same time being incapable of achieving a universal or common good.

The consequence of this situation can only be what is already known: the best we can do is to work for the common interest of the main group of citizens, which is already *particular*. That is, there is fundamentally only one minimum *community*, of *peace* and *respect for individual freedom*–, and what exists besides this is the struggle for particular interests.

However, this conclusion is harsh, because at heart we all know that political life can only be constructed on *what is common*. This has led to the different types of *democratic community fiction*. One is the discourse of the one *nation* for all the citizens, a discourse that has lead to the problem of separatism, and that ultimately contradicts the universalistic foundation of democracy; another is the theory of *human rights;* a third is the introduction of *written constitutionalism;* and a fourth, the *supposed separation of 'state and market'* – that is, the conversion of the political and economic worlds into different spheres. Finally, we find the difference of interests that is usual in human life, but the political sphere – nowadays, the state – should be above the differences of interests, because, if this is not so, it could not arbitrate between them, and moreover, – as has already been stated – because it represents what is common *par excellence.*

Nevertheless, at the present time, this *political community* is a state fiction. On the one hand, a democratic state does not have sufficient principles to create a people; that is, a true community. And, on the other, while it is possible and necessary to distinguish the political sphere from the economic one, it is impossible to separate them.

The relationship, therefore, between these two spheres within a system that has declared them to be separate essentially and legally, cannot but be corrupt. Corruption is simply the use of what is common for private profit. Given that nowadays, supposedly following modern premises, we cannot determine objectively what is common, nor find any general will, what do really exist are necessarily only particular interests, also in politics. The result is that politics turns into economy, and the economy uses and dominates politics.

Besides, the *common–particular* pairing is not the same as the *public–private* one. The latter refers to knowledge, and the former to possession. In politics, *almost* everything that is common should be public; that is, should be known potentially by all, but not *everything,* as reality and political prudence make this impossible. In economics, what is particular, in principle, has no reason to be in the public domain. In fact, what is happening at present is that, as the area of what is truly common is reduced, and that of particular interests greatly developed, *sophistic rhetoric* has become a fundamental instrument. Politicians try to conceal their particular interests by presenting them as the *common good* – even if this concept does not have an existence in modern politics – and, as a consequence, they generate distorted views of reality, or hide them among a mass of diverse news items. On the other hand, those who are in the so-called 'economic sphere' try to present their activities in a 'transparent' manner, the *transparency* being the element that should show that they are not acting against the *common good.* It is evident these days that neither the 'political' sphere nor the 'economic' sphere can function easily as the orthodoxy of democracy had foreseen.

The dignity of democracy

A true community can only be founded under the condition of the existence of a common idea of man and society, and by means of an interior force that allows the person to overcome his or her individualistic inclinations; that is, through virtue and supernatural grace.

In other words, only religion and ethics can lay the foundations of a true community, thus simultaneously giving their noble meaning to what is particular, what is public and what is private. In this sense, the contribution of large business corporations to the common good must consist primarily in their contribution to the creation of habits of good behaviour and of a social atmosphere favourable to ethics and religion.

The modern macro and micro economic theories emphasize the relevance of rules. But these rules are purely formal and external, the only reason to observe them being ultimately convenience. Or, as history has shown, this is too weak a reason to guarantee obedience, especially in difficult times. And such moments are quite frequent in business. On the other hand, observing rules is, in general, not enough; it is necessary to work well and do good through work. In this way, companies co-operate in the emergence of a true civil society, the decent profile of what we call democracy at the present time.

In a civil society, individual freedom and the search for the common good exist simultaneously. Civil society is the political profile of the future, as it is the only one that links the common good with individual freedom: it is the dignity of democracy. But it will not be constructed principally or primarily by the state, but by the social responsibility of companies, organizations and institutions.

The role of companies in a democracy

The dimension in which companies act is not directly the one of 'general politics'. But it is one thing not to move in the same dimension, and another not to be related. One of these possible relations is real but hidden collaboration, known as corruption. In the nineteenth century, many authors who already foresaw that this would be inevitable in representative democracy, suggested the possibility of a political organicism, an 'organic or corporative democracy', where relations between the economic and political spheres would be open, public and institutionalized. But this system has not succeeded, and people clearly experienced this problem in the nineteenth century. In France, there was a common expression: '*tout est pourri*' – 'all has become rotten'.

Then, the procedure must be to consider that politics need not be contained by a political absolute – that is, the state – and that it is simply one more, admittedly fundamental, function of the working of civil society. If this civil society functions properly, then the temptation to absolutize politics will be less likely.

What is 'political' is not primarily the state, or the state's activities, but a *constitutive element* in all societies. Politics is a function within society. Every company is a unit because a political (but not a state's) element creates it. And there is a political function – governing – in every company. However, as part of a larger political whole, the company has no political/governing function, but has an obligation to perfect that political whole, which is denominated civil society, through its moral behaviour, the quality of its professional work and attention to the social whole.

It is true that it is not the business of each company to care directly for this social whole, but it is one thing not to have this task as a principal aim and a full-time occupation, and another to ignore the task and not to participate in it. Society is always a whole, and every organization must take on the responsibility of doing its part of the work the best it can, so that the whole can function as well as possible. Moreover, this is clearly of great interest to the company, and honours[1] it. An honourable person or organization is one who cares for what is his/her own and not only assists society as far as is reasonably possible for him, her or it, but, above all because she, he or it acts conscientiously in trying to find its proper role in the construction of the common good. The pure search of 'economic' profit may produce economic growth, but in the end necessarily destroys the society, and, in consequence, also the economic system.

On this issue, what is antithetical to moral nobility is *individualism*, which is so widespread today, not only among individuals but also among companies as such. But therein lies an error. Ethical nobility is not established by charity alone (though it is necessary and can be seen nowadays in donations to *non-profit organizations*); nor simply by patronage, now called sponsorship; but above all it is established in the example given by an organization and in behaviour that befits moral principles – that is, with attention to justice and the common good.

The state against civil society

The *political logic* of present Western society is based on the couple *individual totality*: individual is the person; and totality is the state. Under this logic the harmonious integration, relationship, between individuals (be they persons or companies and so on) and the 'political realm' (the state) is impossible. There is a permanent threat of conflict, and indeed social life is a succession of conflicts and truces, but there is no real *peace* – that is, there is no real society.

In Socratic philosophy, *soul* was conceived as an active principle of unity of diversity. From this point of view it can be said that the modern political society lacks soul. It undervalues, or even in some cases tries to destroy the institutions that have soul and transmit soul to society as a whole: the family, education centres (private) and the churches (religion). These are the pillars on which a common social sense and a common language are formed in a society. The state is incapable of replacing the functions of these institutions, but tries to do so. Often it 'strangles' families by means of taxes (indirect taxes affect families harshly), but mainly through the creation of social conditions and a social environment that make their lives stressful.

It acts similarly towards the churches, *laicism* being the peak of this behaviour; and in the so-called 'public' schools and universities organized very often as pure centres of teaching, but rarely as true educational centres.

Even more, the state becomes the owner of very many important companies, in this manner – as is well known– presenting unfair competition to private companies. Unfair because, on the one hand, such companies have been set up using the tax money, and on the other because the state, being the ruling power, is both judge and interested party.

The contribution of companies to the common good

Companies, mainly the large ones, can and should help the present democracy, opposing through their power and influence the incorrect and unjust development of state power. They can play a fundamental role in renewing civil society.

Companies can and should also help both the European and the Anglo-American democracies, taking care above all of the company and its role in society, not merely of the money. Money is a means, a necessity, indispensable; if a company has more, it can expand, but money is not the final end, and when the final end focuses on money, the person, the company, the economy and society as a whole is destroyed, even if a good amount of money is gained in the short term. The pragmatic point of view – very widespread among companies, mainly in America – based on the idea that it is impossible to know the future perfectly and objectively, and that – as a consequence – people may act without remembering that the final aim is the common good of society, and that this common good is essentially objective and subjective even if it is never objective when considered from a pure temporal perspective.

The role of companies, then, and specially of large companies in present-day Western democracy does not lie mainly and in the first instance in making profits to the advantage of the shareholders, nor in making money in general, nor in sponsoring or helping NGOs, but in achieving its corporate aims as perfectly as possible, taking care of the common good, providing a good, ethical example in all its works, and contributing to the creation of an ambience in society that permits family, churches and corporations to work for the common good.

Note

1. The original word is 'noble'; however, it seems to me that this word is transmitting the same idea as the English word 'honour'. 'Noble' suggests an aristocratic resonance.

Bibliography

Alvira, Rafael and Cruz, Alfredo (eds) (2003) 'Participación: Entre filosofía y política', *Anuario Filosófico*, 36(1–2).
Alvira, Rafael, Grimaldi, Nicolás and Herrero, Montserrat (eds) (2008) *Sociedad civil: la democracia y su destino*, (Pamplona: EUNSA).
Beiner, R. (1992) *What's the Matter with Liberalism?* (Berkeley, Calif.: University of California Press).
Cruz Prados, Alfredo (2006) *Ethos y polis: bases para una reconstrucción de la filosofía política* (Pamplona: EUNSA).
Habermas, Jürgen (1996) *Between Facts and Norms: Contributions to a Discourse Theory of Law and Democracy* (Cambridge: Polity Press).
Kymlicka, Will (1991) *Liberalism, Community and Culture* (Oxford: Clarendon Press).
Possenti, Vittorio (1991) *Le societá liberali al bivio: lineamenti di filosofia della societá* (Genoa: Marietti).
Rawls, John (1976) *A Theory of Justice* (Cambridge, Mass.: Harvard University Press).
Sandel, Michael J. (1997) *Democracy's Discontent: America in Search of a Public Philosophy* (Cambridge, Mass.: Harvard University Press).
Sandel, Michael J. (1998) *Liberalism and the Limits of Justice* (Cambridge University Press).
Taylor, Charles (1995) *Negative Freiheit?: zur Kritik des neuzeitlichen Individualismus* (Frankfurt am Main: Suhrkamp).
Vigna, Carmelo (ed.) (2003) *Libertà, giustizia e bene in una società plurale* (Milan: Vita e Pensiero).

3

Democracy, Networks of Power and Trust in Eastern Europe: Considerations around the Syndrome of Political Personalism

Nicolas Hayoz

The transformation process in Eastern Europe and the way that democracy in the new democracies in East–Central Europe works has given, and still gives, interesting opportunities to reconsider some basic distinctions related to the classical relationship between state and society. For rule-of-law-based democracies, the distinction between state and society is basically a question about how individual freedoms can be protected constitutionally against state intrusion. From the perspective of the constitution, both spheres have to be considered as separate. This is the political theory of the rule-of-law-orientated state issuing instructions on how to observe the social environment of the political system, and restricting its actions by constitutional means. It accepts the principle of legality of all state actions and does not interfere in private matters by respecting freedoms, particularly that of owning private property; in fact, more than any other device, private property is a restrictive factor *de*limiting state authority and drawing a line between the public and the private sectors. It is precisely this separation that provides meaning to the rule-of-law-based state. Of course, politically and sociologically, it does not make sense to speak of a separation between the state and society, or between the private and the public. On the contrary – interdependencies are the rule. Private and public overlap and condition each other. Even more, welfare states may undermine private rights in the name of equality, and in reality they do. But political interference in the economy implies the very existence of a basic distinction between state and society, or – more sociologically – between the political system and other social systems such as the economy. As is well known, the most radical attempt to overcome this distinction and to abolish private property – namely, communism – ended in disaster.[1] In this regard, the Chinese case of state capitalism admitting private property under the condition of a one-party rule has a better prospect: the regime uses a mix of private and public property in order to keep power and control over society. But the prospects for freedom are bleaker in the similar case of Russia, where a state that is too strong controls both the economy and civil society. In such contexts a politicized legal system is not able to restrain the political system from undermining rights of freedom. And a politically controlled economy is obviously also not able to function as a bulwark against political interference.

This is also what Braithwaite (1998) has in mind when he points to the importance of an equilibrium or 'checks and balances' between a strong state, strong markets and a strong civil society. Strong states, strong markets and strong civil societies are at the same time the greatest resources for building freedom and the greatest threats to it. If one of them dominates, freedom in the other two will suffer. States cannot only be too strong, but also too weak to control abuse of power in business, politics or civil society. And in countries such as the USA, the weakness of the party system is 'compensated' by a too-powerful lobbying system that is politically difficult to control. The 'economization' of politics is a risk, as well as the 'politicization' of the economy and society.

On the other hand, a look at what is happening in Central and Eastern Europe shows that not only countries from the former Soviet Union but also some of the new EU members in Eastern Europe have yet to find adequate institutional answers to handle problems related to corruption, the blurring of the difference between the private and the public, or weak state capacities.

Even more than in the West, the problem seems to have cultural aspects pointing to specific patterns of post-communist elite behaviour. And, without any doubt, the more we move towards the East, the more we are confronted with state and market structures that simply ignore the normative importance of the state/society distinction as a guarantee of individual freedom. In the case of Russia, for example, society does not seem to be something that could be thought of as being independent from state control.

On the contrary, society is seen as rather an extension of the state. Individual freedom and private interests are not really placed on the level of inviolable rights; rather, they are provided only in so far as state interests are not affected. It is precisely on the economic level that an observer gets the impression that Russia functions like a big bureaucratic corporation – 'Russia Inc.', which combines highly personalized leadership structures with organizational power and networks of power (friends, loyalties, clients).

This does not mean, however, that independent economic or political activities are not possible. They *are* possible and even admitted – the case in point is the existence of small opposition parties in Russia. But no organization gets a chance to become a real antagonist and to develop a real political opposition against the regime in the sense of becoming an alternative, a structure ready to replace the incumbent power in the case of an election. This means that beyond a certain size every organization appears to become a risk for the regime – consider, for example, the case of the imprisoned leading Russian businessman, Mikhail Khodorkovsky. In recent years, loyal economic elites have replaced those that represented a risk to the regime. Organizations in the civil society lost their autonomy and new state-driven and state-sponsored organizations have been created to contain and channel the dynamics of civil society. Generally, this amounts to a strategy of neutralization and de-politicization aimed at reducing the natural checks and balances in society as they are expressed by the plurality of interests and organizations in politics, the economy and society.

One can see, for example, that so-called 'cold societies' in the Weberian sense, that are based on the arm's length principle, such as those in Scandinavia, have a much better record with regard to fighting corruption or establishing good governance. They typically show the highest levels of trust. What is at stake here is the power structure in a given society, and obviously the structures of trust. We look at this power structure through three different but equally crucial distinctions which are usually neglected by so-called transition studies. We are not so much looking at the electoral process in order to analyse the degree of democracy in a given CEE (Central and Eastern Europe) country, but much more at specific patterns of behaviour, networks of power and trust in order to say something about the potential for change in these societies.

These three distinctions are:

1. The public/private: to what extent there is a consensus concerning the public sphere; to what extent does the distinction still make sense and provide meaning to the political sphere.
2. Distance/proximity or personalized versus depersonalized relations: to what extent do the arm's length principle or, contrarily, personalized networks dominate. This distinction points to a related one – friends or enemies (which is obviously already positioned on the side of personalized relations): in this perspective the world is populated by people who are either with you or against you. This is

obviously not the dominant distinction in democratic rule-of-law-based societies. We are living, at least in the West, in societies (so-called 'cold' societies) where indifference, the principle of arm's-length relations, universalism, or the difference between private and public are the very conditions for successful co-operation.[2]

3. Trust/distrust: to what extent do trust or distrust dominate among members of society, and between society and the state.

Obviously, these distinctions should reinforce each other. For example, a certain type of capitalism, together with an institutional design based on the rule of law, solidarity and freedom, respecting the basic distinction of public/private seem to be the necessary keys for the reproduction of trust. This chapter looks at those distinctions in a rather general but also comparative, cross-regional perspective. A tentative combination of the distinctions private/public and personalized/depersonalized would allow the establishment of four constellations of relationship or co-operation in the private or public sphere (see Table 3.1); these also correspond to different types of trust (personalized and generalized trust); also of distrust if, for example, the politicians or officials are considered to be corrupt.

In this regard, some groups of countries obviously perform much better than others. Interestingly, the 'coldest societies' (in the Weberian sense) – the Scandinavian ones – have managed to combine effective economies with much greater equality and mutual respect than have

Table 3.1 Four constellations of relationship or co-operation in the private or public sphere

		Type of dominant relationship	
		Personalized	**Depersonalized**
	Private	• Friendship; personal networks	Professional relations (for example, business, clients of companies, lawyers etc.)
		• Legal or illegal pursuit of private interests	Arm's length principle
Sector	**Public**	• Legal or illegal use of public power	Arm's length principle (ideal type: Weber's meritocratic public administration)
		• Legal or illegal networks of power	
		• Corruption	

other countries. According to Richard Layard, they have the greatest levels of trust (and happiness) of all the countries in the world.[3] With regard to corruption, the Scandinavian countries are, together with other small countries such as Switzerland and the Netherlands, among the cleanest measured by the standards of Transparency International.[4] They are generally considered to be paradigmatic cases of good governance, and the key indicator of good governance is the successful handling of corruption. Corruption can be considered here as a kind of prism through which the above-mentioned distinctions meet and reinforce each other in a negative way. There are different groups of countries coming more or less close to the Weberian ideal of 'cold' and depersonalized societies, with public administrations being based on universalism and the arm's length principle (Tanzi, 2000: 91–7). Other countries – for example, most countries from the former Soviet Union – are much closer to the opposite pole: on the side of regimes with weak institutions, strong personalism, old-boy networks, clientelism and so on. High rates of corruption are an inevitable by-product of such informal and personalized network structures.

There seems also to be a strong correlation between the effectiveness of institutions and the degree of generalized trust in these countries (see Rothstein, 2005). Such 'cold societies' typically also rely on the efficiency of assurances and institutionalized guarantees should they need them; that is, when they have to face 'treacherous' behaviour. For example, in an inclusive society such as Switzerland, the identity of the national community and the radius of trust in the country is obviously shaped by the institutional framework; by well-developed political and legal mechanisms designed specifically as trust-building institutions for the purpose of the distribution of resources (welfare state); by the degree of political participation and the integration of minorities (federalism and direct democracy); and by the protection of civil and human rights. Precisely such experiences are absent in many regions of Eastern Europe, and certainly in most of the emerging democracies in the south. Furthermore, in deeply inegalitarian societies it is hardly surprising that generalized trust is lacking (see Uslaner, 2002).

This would suggest that 'cold' societies based on a 'Protestant ethic' with a particular political culture and specific effective institutions have a better chance of fighting corruption and establishing good governance rules than the 'warm' personalized societies from the south, to which we may add those from East–Central and Eastern Europe, where good governance practices, including the implementation of effective anti-corruption rules and the establishment of a clear-cut border between the public and the private sectors, are either still not the first priority of state action or are being diluted by forms of co-operation such as personal ties and sympathies combined with clientelism. There, as Tanzi (2000: 92) puts it, the arm's length principle has been abandoned, since 'civil servants begin to make distinctions among the people they deal with according to the degree of family relationship or friendship'.

Informal politics and personalized relationships are not features that should be played off against governance principles. The question is rather to what extent personalized relationships in politics or in the economy pervert universal principles, or whether these apparently contrary principles reinforce each other positively. Thus, while it is necessary to identify the juxtaposition of apparent contrary principles such as distance and proximity, depersonalized and personalized relationships, only the analysis of concrete policy fields can tell us whether or to what extent elements of a traditional political culture, such as parochial mentalities with informal politics and old-boy networks, have negative or perverse effects on the political process, on institutions or on the daily operations of a meritocratic public administration. The same may be said in a social capital perspective. Social capital can be positive or negative. Norms of reciprocity and networks of relations can point to the needs and expectations of friends and relatives – which is the realm of the private sphere – as well as to norms of reciprocity of the public sphere. It is clear that in a rather 'warm' society the meanings and effects of personalized networks are quite different from so called *'indifferent'* and 'cold' societies, where traditional forms of social capital make a *difference* and subvert arm's-length relationships through different forms of corruption. This is not to say that in specific countries such as Switzerland or Germany one may not expect to find corruption. There may be other forms of corruption experienced, of course, than that in Third-World countries, but what matters most are forms of regulation and governance that support arm's-length relationships instead of destroying them.

What has to be seen here is the importance of institutions, laws and the structure of the political system, which can be catalysts as well as obstacles for civic life. Institutions and political choices are shaping civil society as well as markets. Their efficiency is an important condition for freedom and democracy. In the end it is about the art of politics, and about how to be effective with limited power – something authoritarian regimes in Eastern Europe do not have to worry about.

The distinction between private/public and the common good

When Alexis de Tocqueville wrote about American associations as a way of building up social capital he could not foresee today's more complicated reality of the omnipresence of lobbyists, corruption scandals related to interest groups and generalized distrust of politics.[5] Tocqueville was in line with the liberal view based on the idea that society advances best when people have the freedom to determine their own self-interest. The market was seen as the place where society advances for the common good, whereas governments should govern without interfering with private decisions. Liberalism was precisely that, about going against the idea of a state which should be more than an agency to protect individual freedom. However, when the much broader conception of politics and the state – one might say a French conception pointing back to the French Revolution – appeared – the idea of a state that should take care of the happiness of its people – this was an objective which, as we know, the totalitarian states of the twentieth century tried to realize using all means available. From the nineteenth century onwards the political system strove to be responsible for public welfare, which involved the establishment of a new distinction between public and private interests.[6]

Such developments had a parallel in the reconstruction of the modern political system as a self-referential and autonomous order which itself decides what politics is about, and which distinctions should be used in the political communication process. This already indicates that the difference between private and public interests could no longer be fixed either by normative means or in abstract terms. Politics had to decide whether private interests should also contribute to the public welfare in the sense of Adam Smith's work: the determination of which interests should be declared as public becomes a matter of political opportunism, of choice and legitimacy.

The alternative to this concept is a normative conception of society and politics in its leftist or rightist variants, with politicians who believe that they can change things, regulate markets or create a specific common good to meet specific interests. But in any case the distinction between public and private interests is a political distinction. Thus this may be a good reason to keep the distinction. But it could be that the opportunistic (that is, political) handling of the distinction, of what is 'public' and what is 'private', is also a part of the problems that political systems have when they are confronted with the question of how to regulate the activities of interest groups and political parties that present and promote their interests as public ones. Today, any private interest can be declared a public interest, and public interests always favour certain groups over others. A look at how modern welfare states or certain EU policies work gives plenty of evidence of the paradoxical aspect of the distinction between public and private.

Modern rule-of-law-based democracies have solved the problem typically through democratic procedures involving conflicts and compromises, by which private interests are being transformed in a common good. Therefore the quality of such procedures, with their corresponding checks and balances, matters.[7] Thus a distinction has to be made between the way that the terms private and public are being used in the political communication process, on the one hand, and, on the other, on a more structural level, the private/public distinction as a necessary condition of a modern rule-of-law-based liberal state, where it is a part of its constitutional architecture, of its own political theory. In this sense, the private/public distinction points to the meaning of the political in society; to the distinction between the political sphere and other social spheres (see Sales, 1991).

The correlate of such an arrangement is, of course, the existence of an adequate structure of private interests in society that are constitutionally guaranteed by associational freedoms. Since Tocqueville, such a protected freedom of association is considered as being a fundamental stronghold against the tyranny of the majority. A multitude of interests, including protected minority interests, would work to discourage an oppressive majority interest. This is exactly the contrary of what happened in France where the general interest had to be defended against the intrusion of private interests, which still have to face the question of legitimacy lobbying. This may be not a big problem under democratic (and even under specific French) conditions. But it is a problem in several Eastern European countries that are clearly not on the side of democracy and where private interests can be restricted opportunistically by the logic of an abstract and ominous 'general interest', which is nothing more than a form of 'state interest' advanced by the regime to defend its power against the opposition coming from the economy or civil society.

One may see in that context to what extent the visibility of strong and democratic state institutions help in building up trust in other parts of society is related to the construction of a common good. The prevention of the abuse of trust and power is certainly among the most important functions of institutions in a complex web of countervailing powers. Therefore, in a modern and complex society, the common good is as much the, however aggregated, result of one sphere of action – markets, for example – ('self-interest') or of civil society (volunteering), as it is the result of effective state institutions. This can be, on the contrary, also seen when studying the situation in Eastern Europe, where many countries have not yet found adequate institutional answers to handle problems related to corruption, to the blurring of the difference between private and public, or to weak state capacity. Even more than in the West, the problem seems to have cultural aspects pointing to specific patterns of post-communist elite behaviour. And, without any doubt, the more we move towards the East, the more we are confronted with state and market structures that simply ignore the normative importance of the state/society distinction as a guarantee of individual freedom.

Proximity versus arm's-length relations

Particularly in the context of Eastern Europe, the distinction private/public has to be combined with the distinction proximity/distance implying the principle of arm's-length relations. Related to this second distinction is the distinction termed personalized/depersonalized. Obviously, depersonalized relations and public space are ideally expected to coincide in modern society. And obviously, in the above-mentioned distinctions, modernity can certainly not be located on the side of personalized or the proximity side of those distinctions. This does not mean that modern society is based only on depersonalized contacts. On the contrary, modernity requires specific distinctions, particularly the possibility of making a distinction between private and public communications or spaces, and between personalized and depersonalized relations. In fact, society would not be possible without personal relations – everyday contacts based on personal interaction; as such, however, such relations have to be reproduced in a sea of depersonalized relations.

   A functionally differentiated society with highly complex systems for the solution of specific political, economic or scientific problems could not be understood simply on the basis of personal interactions. And it is precisely in modern society where personal relations may become a problem; for example, as old-boy networks or clientelism in the political or the economic system, where they might be identified as corrupt behaviour. It requires established democracies and markets in order to discover that too many 'good connections' may undermine democratic and market rules if they avoid or short-circuit established and legal procedures to gain an advantage.

In so-called 'hundred friends countries' such as Russia, it may thus be unavoidable to nourish a portfolio of friends, networks, connections and so on in order to 'get things done' (see Rose, 1999). But what seems to be a survival strategy at the individual level takes the form of a power-keeping strategy at the level of the rulers. Networks of power and friends in the right positions are important resources in a country where elections at the national level as well as in most cases at the regional level are not about transferring power but about retaining it. This comes at a huge price, since it widens the already existing broad gap between the rulers and the ruled. In fact, the public knows very well about the practices of the political and economic elites. Its distrust towards the authorities shows that it is aware of the instrumentalization of public positions for private purposes or profit – almost the classic definition of corruption – as well as of the use of private resources for political power.

Therefore, returning to the relevance of the distinction personalized versus depersonalized relations, it would not make sense to affirm, under the impression of the observation of widespread corruption and personalized networks, that a country is not really modern or a part of modern society. Worldwide-operating modern society with its dominant structure and functional differentiation allows and produces many regional experiments in relation to the above-mentioned distinctions, or with capitalism, or with the degree of state involvement in the economy. If certain countries play with authoritarianism or even communism against what they call liberal modernity, that does not put them on the side of a different modernity. On the contrary, they are part of the same modern society, but are able to block or control certain achievements of that modernity, such as democracy, with political opposition, or the so-called private sphere with its businesses, organizations and associations.

On the other hand, differences with regard to corruption, modernization, personalization, social and economic disparities or democratization cannot be the decisive factors that put a country into a type of society other than the modern one. Of course, for certain countries it may be helpful, at least on the political level, not to be considered as part of the 'West', since that would imply an obligation to respect a certain number of rules – for example, democracy or human rights. The same may be said with regard to the economic integration of countries in a globalized world economy that do not participate in certain organizations, or to insist on the coexistence of different forms of capitalism. But even insisting on differences is communication in the context of a globalized world society. This is also what we have in mind when observing that modern society is a depersonalized society with depersonalized decisions and impersonal roles in most social spheres. This could also be read as a framework of rules for reducing and dividing the power of rulers and their personal advisers.[8]

Let us return to the arm's length principle and see to what extent it can be considered an important part of the 'checks and balances system' in politics, particularly along the state/society border. What is the arm's length principle about? Well-known in business transactions, it postulates that the independence and equal footing of the parties to a transaction should be guaranteed, or that 'the transactions between affiliated firms must be made purely on a commercial basis, with both firms attempting to maximize their advantage, and neither firm accommodating or favouring the other in any way.'[9] Equitable agreements should be possible despite the existence of shared interests: for example, between employer and employee, or through familial ties. As a public policy principle applied in the political, economic or legal system, the arm's length principle is related to the checks and balances between the different constitutional powers. It is also applied, for example, to public funding of the arts, where it is expressed by autonomous art councils keeping their distance from politics and bureaucracy precisely because the allocating funds they receive from the government should be distributed according to criteria established by the arts community.[10]

The promotion of the arts or of science may be an important objectives for public policies in the political system, but the attribution of funds to specific projects has to be decided by criteria that are other than political, by professional expertise coming from the systems that should be fostered. In that sense, the arm's length principle established through independent bodies of expertise and evaluation expresses the separation between the social systems. On the other hand, it expresses not only independencies but also dependencies between the different functional systems – for example, politics, the legal system and the arts system, since the arts system needs to be funded from the politics or legal decisions made by the legal system (= dependencies), operations that have to assure the reproduction of art according to professional rules of the arts system.

One can see here to what extent the arm's length principle is part of modernity. It contributes to the principle of the functional differentiation of society, which implies that large social systems such as politics, economics, the legal system, the sciences or the arts are fulfilling their function according to their own criteria. They are autonomous in the reproduction of their structures. But at the same time they are also dependent on each other, from the fact that society continues – that the economy is creating the necessary values in order to enable the political system to 'spend' and distribute money. Principles such as that of arm's length are part of the devices in modern society that protect the autonomy of the different social spheres against 'alien' interference, be it politics with its specific interests, economic interests or interests related to clientelism, familialism, or other forms of favouritism. They are part of the organized checks and balances in place in society to control and regulate power and interest motivated interferences from one social sphere to others. And in fact in liberal democracies the existence of performant social systems such as the economy is already a 'check' against the inclination of political power to interfere in its social environment.

One may see here also to what extent a culture of arm's length relations cannot be created from scratch. It needs to be based on a system of values, a corresponding ideology of public administration and a multiplicity of socialization agencies producing efficient social control mechanisms. A rule-of-law-orientated meritocratic public administration, which is missing in many Eastern European countries, could not exist without a corresponding culture of public service. Much has been written about oversized and over-regulated state bureaucracies. In many of the new EU member states, business is much more regulated than in other economies. According to Marian Tupy, the armies of bureaucrats in central Europe have ample opportunities to extract bribes from private firms. And he concludes correctly that corruption in Central Europe is systemic: 'it cannot be eradicated through better procurement controls, as is currently being attempted. Instead, corruption has to be tackled by reducing the size and the scope of the state and with it the opportunities for self-enrichment among the political elites.'[11]

Coming back to the problem of 'interference', one may observe that the very existence of a functionally differentiated modern society with autonomous and separated systems makes it illusory to believe that the political system could interfere directly in its environment. Of course, interference in the form of regulations and restrictions does exist – the welfare state is a prominent example of state intervention through taxation and redistribution policies. Such 'interventions' may have consequences and provoke reactions in the economic systems that have not been planned by the political system – for example, in the form of blocked labour markets, or exit strategies such as tax evasion or infor-mal markets. But even an extreme politicization or instrumentalization of society by the political power – as communist power tried to real-ize in the name of socialism – could not call into question functional differentiation.

On the contrary, the de-differentiation 'tried out' by Soviet commu-nism was one of the reason for its breakdown. A socialist 'system' trying to retain control of the economy by assigning 'political prices' – and not prices fixed economically (that is, financially on the markets of a glo-balized economy) – revealed itself to be an illusion. Society cannot *not* be 'organized' and even less from the top of a party structure. But neverthe-less the communist experiment was de-differentiation of society coming at huge cost when considering the damage caused by communism at all levels in the countries where it was able to establish its regimes.

And today, after the end of communism, when certain countries try to 'nationalize' parts of their 'national economy', or when quasi-authoritarian regimes try to control the production of strategic assets such as petrol and gas, they can do it only under the conditions of world market prices. However, at the regional level it can be seen how specific political structures such as clans, families or – as is the case in Russia – the 'bureaucratic-authoritarian' system, try to control the economy or other important systems such as science or the legal sys-tem through personalization, through networks of friends and loyalties which, combined with hierarchic organizational power, raise the ques-tion of inclusion from and exclusion in the system: who is a part of it, who has access to which resources on which level and so on. This pro-duces de-differentiation of another kind, related to money, to annuities that have to be distributed, particularly in 'petrostates', in which rev-enues from gas and oil help to finance a feudal system where privileges, annuities and an organization's power are distributed in exchange for political loyalty.[12]

Corruption is a necessary side-effect of such an 'organized' system of mutual dependencies. In that way, political regimes orientated towards power and privileges can take the profit from functional differentia-tion and a globalized economy and finance the modernization of their country and their elites. It is clear that such structures are also huge obstacles for the democratic transformation of such a country, since the power structure in the country is not willing to give up its exclu-sive access to strategic resources, as the case of Russia shows. Such power structures based on organization and networks can exploit functional differentiation through their personalized networks: having friends in the right positions can be helpful and even indispensable if you want 'to get things done'. Old–new distinctions, such as friends and enemies or loyal and disloyal concealing the established differences of the functional systems; for example, the distinction legal/illegal, which can be handled in an opportunistic manner in the absence of a rule-of-law-based state.

Obviously, such a system cannot survive without corruption, and it is evident that here corruption inevitably means de-differentiation.[13] Of course it is de-differentiation only for those who are not part of the corresponding networks. For those participating in the networks, the question is about having friends in order to gain access to, or to maintain control over, assets.[14]

Trust versus distrust

Let us turn now to trust versus distrust, the third distinction, which, as mentioned earlier, is also involved in the other distinctions. Trust, depersonalization and the arm's length principle go together – at least in rule-of-law-based democracies. The question of trust allows us to look at the distinction personalized/depersonalized from a different point of view. Modern structures of trust need to be depersonalized to make complex relations possible. This is quite feasible since, on the one hand, society has 'socialized' the personal risk of a relationship of trust, and, on the other, we are living, as already noted, in a depersonalized modern society.

Generally speaking, this is what the literature on trust describes as extended or generalized trust among strangers (see, for example, Uslaner, 2002; Rothstein, 2005; Reiser, 1999). Some authors present this form of trust as moralistic, since it is not based primarily on personal experiences but can be considered as 'the belief that others share your fundamental moral values and therefore should be treated as you would wish to be treated by them'(see Uslaner, 2002: 18; see also Levi, 1998). Generalized trust, then, is about sharing basic values with regard to reliable and honest behaviour, it is about norms of reciprocity, about the expectation of reciprocity. This is in fact a definition of social capital, which points to these specific values shared by the members of a community and allowing them to co-operate. Obviously, these values cannot be the values of a criminal gang, which also needs a great deal of social capital in order to be efficient. Rather, they point, again, to universalistic moral values in society, to virtues such as truth-telling, meeting obligations and reciprocity (Fukuyama, 2000: 99).

One could reply that these values are shared by most families in the world. But in this case one speaks of personal trust, not of trust among strangers, which – and that is the point here – depends on the conditions of trust *outside* the family systems (kinship) or of personal networks between friends. According to the 'radius of trust' in a particular society, one could distinguish, with Fukuyama (1995) between 'low trust societies', with familialism and personalism representing one pole, and 'high trust societies' representing the other pole, approximating what could be called Max Weber's ideal of arm's-length relations, of trust in public life, or trust among the members of organizations – such as state bureaucracies, social security systems, political parties, interest groups or companies. This distinction overlaps to a certain degree with the distinction between 'warm' and 'cold' societies: to be more precise, it points to the importance of traditional values in modern or modernizing societies.

The radius of trust depends on the degree to which people share common values when it comes to solve collective problems by co-operating with each other. Political, economic and legal institutions have, through their symbolic efficiency, created cultural settings in which allows generalized trust to develop between people. Here it can be seen how generalized trust reinforced by values and institutions works against corrupt behaviour. On the other hand, it should also be clear that without the continuous reproduction by the social system and its institutions of values such as freedom, justice, solidarity, equality and others, and the social confirmation of virtues such as honesty, faithfulness or empathy, generalized trust would not make much sense (see Rothstein, 2000 and Uslaner, 2002).

In this short account of some important aspects of the relationship between trust and political and legal institutions we have already focused on the importance of the availability of complementary contract enforcement by the state. This 'third-party enforcement' is in fact one of the most important conditions of generalized trust (Reiser, 1999: 5). One could hardly imagine a modern economy working properly without a contract law guaranteeing creditors the enforcement of their claims. The availability of impartial enforcement by a legitimate state cannot be underestimated: not only does it extend the social reach of the legal system, it also contributes to the reproduction and the increase of generalized trust, which is also precisely what political and legal institutions need in order to run efficiently and to facilitate third-party enforcement. Third-party enforcement alone without generalized trust would certainly not work (see Reiser, 1999). The availability and the symbolic presence of efficient third-party enforcement, which implies confidence in the institutions and government officials, constitute the background of daily interactions in business, in politics or in relations between state officials and citizens.

Third-party enforcement supports and routinizes extended trust. It can be mobilized for the protection of contracts as well as for the protection of citizens' rights *against* government officials. The problem of risk and distrust reappears only exceptionally – for example, when debtors are not paying. And private actors are confronted by the people behind the institutions (usually only in the case of corruption or other abuses of power by officials) with the fact that they are not always trustworthy. But this can be reduced to 'cases' which can be handled by the political and judiciary system, and of course also by the media. To take a more political case, we could point here to a situation such as in Bosnia-Herzegovina, where the efforts of the international community to build a strong central state making impartial third-party enforcement available among all communities was aimed at increasing trust between the ethnic groups involved. Such efforts enhance the chances of reform programmes and should work to improve the economic situation by facilitating exchanges. Here, low levels of generalized trust go together with low confidence in the political and judiciary institutions, which remain inefficient and corrupted, thus reinforcing vicious cycles such as maladministration → mistrust → corruption → maladministration.[15] Such problems show again that markets and civil society, and the corresponding forms of generalized trust in them, are not possible without a trustworthy state which, in protecting the conditions of citizenship and entrepreneurship, is also protecting the very conditions of trust.

On the other hand, vicious cycles with their tendency to inflate scandals about the extent of corruption reduce confidence in institutions even more. This is normally not the case in stable democracies, since political scandals there generally seem to prove that the institutions of distrust are working and that they are able to punish the illegal behaviour of 'betrayers'. This means also that trust implies distrust. Most political and legal institutions in stable democracies, including private trust agencies, function as institutions of distrust that also aim to avoid and detect breaches of trust.[16] The idea of the separation of powers is an example of institutionalization of distrust. Strong institutions which are checking each other are among the most important factors enabling generalized trust.

Let us return now to the above-mentioned relations between scandals, corruption and trust/distrust. Stable democracies are expected to be able to handle cases of betrayal of trust. But what if the system cannot handle them? Governments, their institutions and policies are expected to be responsive, to solve the problems: in this way, they are supposed to earn trust. Citizens expect governments to establish an efficient public administration, to adopt anti-corruption policies, to establish agencies to supervise the work of the police and officials, to protect their freedoms, to adopt efficient economic and social policies and so on. At least that is the way things should work. But if we move a little further to the south or the east, into so-called 'warmer' societies, and we shall discover that the arm's length principle with its meaning of keeping a distance, particularly between civil servants and their community, of avoiding personalism, and of relying on the enforcement of universalistic norms, is no longer a shared reality.

What if state bureaucracies are not working in the ways they should? What if cultural traditions are different? What if people want and need to rely on informal, highly personalized networks in order 'to get things done' (Rose 1999: 154 ff.), as in Ukraine or in Russia? This is what we have – since James Coleman – called instrumental social capital, using personal networks to achieve personal goals (see Rose, 1999, 2009). In so-called contexts of transition it is important to know how to move from personal trust to generalized trust towards strangers, which in fact implies institutional trust. What are the cultural obstacles and chances for reform in such societies?

Differences in the levels of trust in a society raise the question concerning the institutional performance of political, economic and cultural key institutions. 'Low trust' societies can be contrasted with 'high trust' societies such as some in South-East Asia, and differential potential and conditions for building up trust can be compared between societies with different historical and cultural experiences. When we look at what has happened since 2000 in Central and Eastern Europe we should ask ourselves how it is that, despite never-ending reforms, many countries in these regions are still living under conditions of a culture of distrust, or are dominated by structures of trust that are not really modern – for example, the clientelistic patterns of corruption and power networks in Russia, Ukraine or the Balkan countries. Several authors have stressed factors such as culture and geography that could explain the persistence of distrust, familialism or politics based on old and new personal networks (see Rose, 2009). One has to consider also the considerable cultural and political gap between the countries of Central Europe and countries that were part of the former Soviet Union. On the other hand, the successor states of the Soviet Union have also to be differentiated into undemocratic parts, and countries such as Russia and Ukraine oscillate between stagnation and reform, and which are at least partly paralysed by strong networks of power.

Distrust in post-communist societies is much higher in Central and Eastern Europe than in the democracies of the European Union. Empirical data about trust in political institutions in the region show low figures of trust for political institutions, especially parliaments and political parties (see Rose, 2009: 31; Shlapentokh, 2006: 253ff.).[17] Trust in institutions is particularly low in Russia, where only 7 per cent trust parliament and only 7 per cent trust parties, which is considerably lower than the standards of trust in Central Europe. A look at surveys shows that, of all the post-communist countries, the Russian public is one of the most cynical, distrustful and dissatisfied. Almost 90 per cent believe that their public officials are corrupt. The degree of political distrust towards almost all political institutions with the exception of the president is alarming. According to Larry Diamond (2008: 198ff.) 'all post-communist publics are cynical and dissatisfied – it's just that the post-Soviet ones are more so. 72 percent think 'more than half' or 'almost all' their public officials are corrupt'.[18] Widespread feelings about corruption, resentment of inefficient authorities, and feelings of economic stress could put the new democracies at risk, since these can easily become the start point of anti-liberal and anti-elitist populism. Of course, one may point here to similar problems in established 'old' democracies. But in these cases at least checks and balances should function and the political opposition, media or a critical civil society can be mobilized against an inefficient or even corrupt power, to request accountability or to replace the holders of power.

In fact, the question of success and failure of the transformation process in Eastern Europe points to a problematic link between state performance and the structures of trust in post-communist societies. Regime type, governance, corruption and networks of power and trust are closely related. Institutional inefficiency implies huge costs and usually has to be paid with economic and political backwardness (see Rothstein, 2000). The point I would like to stress here once again concerns the relationship between regime type and institutional efficiency. Typically, the most advanced countries of Eastern and Central Europe are also the ones that resemble functioning, efficient and liberal democracies based on the rule of law. The gap in terms of democracy scores between them and the eight most authoritarian countries is huge. Post-communist states can be divided roughly into three overlapping groups of states: market-orientated democracies in East-Central Europe (some eight countries); semi-consolidated democracies together with transitional regimes (at least ten countries); and quasi- or fully authoritarian regimes with the bulk coming from the former Soviet Union (at least eleven countries).[19] Typically, this distinction of different regime types finds its reasons in the legacies of communism. The degree of totalitarian control of politics, economy and society in the past helps to explain post-communist trajectories. The emergence of several distinct geographically coherent clusters is by no means a result of contingency: the transition towards rather liberal or rather illiberal democracies, or even the development of dictatorships, is path-dependent and points to experience with and the nearness to democracy, rule-of-law and the market economy. In other words, the problem points again to historical experience with arm's length principles, and of course also to the ability of each country to undergo its own *Europeanization process* and to adapt to the new rules imposed by EU enlargement. The threefold division of post-communist states also raises the question of the dynamics of change in which these states are involved, which is also related to processes of legitimation and delegitimation.

Conclusion

Personal networks are a problem-solving strategy ('to get things done'). In some post-socialist countries these go together with the lack of generalized trust, and trust in formal institutions and civic networks. Why should you trust the world beyond your family and the wider 'family' of your friends if this world is, as the case of Russia shows, perceived in 'Hobbesian' terms, full of discriminations and exclusions, inequalities, greed, crime and corruption?[20] On the other hand, from a 'top down' perspective, things are different, since for political elites, networks, personal trust and trustworthiness are means of achieving and maintaining power.

With regard to corruption, Tanzi (2000: 92) observes that the very features that make a country a less cold and indifferent place are also those that increase the difficulty of enforcing arm's-length rules so essential for modern, efficient markets and governments. He pointed to the fact that networks are also part of a social capital that help people to integrate, co-operate and express solidarity. Proximity relations and informal networks can work both ways: they can create positive social capital (co-operation, trust, catalysts of change) but also negative social capital. It has been observed that the danger with networks is that they are just a modern version of the 'old-boy network' and that they can be agencies of development as well as 'annuity-seekers', depleting the public treasury and inhibiting economic growth.[21] Again, all depends on the institutional context in which such networks are working. Networks of power or proximity in democracies can be limited, controlled and counterbalanced by effective media, institutions and social control mechanisms that ensure a strong sense of rule-of-law and law compliance. As long as mentalities based on respect for the rule of law, for the border between private and public interests, and personalized and depersonalized relations are not really established *and* positively recognized by the political power and its elites, democracy and trust will suffer. One may say that the phenomenon of personalized networks of power and corruption can also be identified in established Western economies. The point is that institutional restrictions and political culture are not the same. Even though the degree of distrust towards politics in Western Europe is also a reason for concern, the established checks and balances and the legal framework are able to control deviant behaviour and punish corruption.

We have seen that corruption and personalism are persistent syndromes in Eastern Europe, even among the new EU members, and particularly in Bulgaria and Romania. For a whole group of the most authoritarian countries (at least eight countries) there is at present no hope of progress on the path to democracy, to good governance and to effective anti-corruption policies. Things are a little different for the group between these countries and the new EU members. For example, in the Balkans, even though the reform process is slow, the democracy promotion programmes of the EU give these countries a chance to realize postponed reforms in order to liberalize their economies. Liberalization leads to less rather than more corruption. And even in the new EU member states, where reform fatigue and the established power networks of the old communist elites were responsible for populism, the message is clear. Without better governance, without effective checks and balances, and without reforming oversized state bureaucracies, corruption and informal network structures will continue to be a burden, a powerful shadow in the background hindering the reform process and keeping distrust of politics at a high level.

Notes

1. On this theme, see Pipes (1999: 211ff.), who examines the relationship between property and freedom.
2. For the principle of arm's-length relationships, which is based on universalism and on the values described by the Weberian type of ideal bureaucracy, see Tanzi (2000: 91–7) and below.

3. See *Financial Times*, 12 March 2009, p. 17.
4. The Corruption Perceptions Index 2008 of Transparency International puts Denmark, New Zealand and Sweden in Rank 1 with a CPI score of over 9 (maximum and best value = 10). They are followed by Singapore (CPI 9.2), Finland and Switzerland (CPI 9) ranked at 4 and 5, respectively. Norway shares rank 14 with Germany (CP 7.9), whereas countries such as the USA (CPI 7.3) and France (CPI 6.9) are ranked at 18 and 23, respectively. The cleanest CEE countries follow, with Slovenia (CPI 6.7) and Estonia (CP 6.6.), ranked 26 and 27, respectively. The next group of CEE countries are to be found between ranks 47 (Hungary) and 58 (Poland, Lithuania), with Latvia and Slovakia between them (CPI between 4.6 and 5.1). The newest members of the EU, Romania and Bulgaria, are further behind (ranked at 70 and 72, respectively, with CPI 3.6 and 3.8) along with countries from the Western Balkans (for example, Albania and Serbia, both ranked at 85, with CPI 3.4. They are followed far behind by the bulk of the countries from the former Soviet Union (excluding the Baltic states), which present the darkest record: Ukraine is ranked 134 (CPI 2.5), Russia, 147 (CPI 2.1) and Belarus, 151 (CPI 2.0). Interestingly, differences exist among the southern Caucasus countries, where Azerbaijan shares the poor CPI score with its neighbours in the north (CPI 1.9, rank 158), but Armenia reaches a rank of 109 (CPI 2.9) and Georgia, being rather successful with its reforms, is ranked 67 (CPI 3.9). With the exception of the case of Georgia, these figures are consistent with the surveys carried out by Freedom House, which presents for the Non-Baltic Former Soviet states an average value of 6.10 (Russia having 6.25 and Georgia 5.0) on a scale of 1 to 7, with 7 being the worst. The differences between this group of countries and the other CEE countries are huge and reflect the differences in the democracy scores between the most authoritarian CEE countries and the rest. See www.freedomhouse.org and www.transparency.org/news_room/in_focus/2008/cpi2008/cpi_2008_table.
5. See Tocqueville (2008) Vol. 2, book 2, ch. 5 on the importance of political associations for public life.
6. Albert Hirschman (1982: 63, 125) has shown to what extent the separation of the private and the public, implying also the separation of a private economy from state control, has been a invention and an ideology established in Western societies, whereas in many other regions of the world a confusion between, or even ignorance of, the public and the private prevailed. In many countries, particularly in Eastern Europe, forms of 'patrimonialism' – the use of political power to gain access to wealth – still exist and may even be considered as normal ways to handle public service without conceiving it necessarily in terms of corruption.
7. Politicians are well aware of that necessity to discover the contours of a common good on the basis of procedures and not by referring to some pre-existing or abstractly defined criteria of such a common good. On this theme, see Moritz Leuenberger, Eigeninteresse und Gemeinwohl in der Politik', *Neue Zürcher Zeitung*, 12 June 2008, p. 15.
8. On this theme see, in the context of good and bad power, Mulgan (2006: 172ff.).
9. On this see http://www.businessdictionary.com/definition/arm-s-length-principle.html and http://en.wikipedia.org/wiki/Arm's_length_principle.

10. See http://www.budobs.org/public-grants/public-grants/grant-paper-2001. html.
11. See Marian Tupy, 'Poland Must Wind Back Power of the State', *Financial Times*, 22 October 2007.
12. See Andrey Piontkovsky, 'The Middle Class: Putin's Willing Serfs', Transitions Online Special Report: Russia Votes, November 2007, p. 20. Available at: http://www.tol.org/client/article/20835-the-russian-patient.html.
13. In an interview with William Rasch (2000: 204) Niklas Luhmann observes that 'corruption is also a dedifferentiation. You have a network of relations, of favours, and of legitimate or illegitimate manoeuvring of resources that is dominant in society, then you decide, within this network, whether you should use legal or illegal means, or whether you should favour this one or that one, or whether the big families of the country use their own network to integrate their firms or not.'
14. It can easily be seen that such friendships are instrumental or utilitarian. Particularly among the ruling elites in transition and/or quasi-authoritarian regimes in Eastern Europe, such friendships do not necessarily point to the same types of communities as those described by anthropologists. See Kaser, 2001.
15. See Della Porta (2000) for a very convincing account of such cycles.
16. See, for this account of institutionalizing distrust in democracy and more generally in society, Braithwaite (1998).
17. See also the data in the Freedom House report, *Nations in Transit 2008*. Available at: www.freedomhouse.org.
18. See also Diamond, 2008: 64ff.; Rose, 2009: 60ff., 153ff. and 173ff. See also www.levada.ru/press/2007040901.html and the Freedom House report, *Nations in Transit 2008* (as Nt 16 above).
19. See www.freedomhouse.org.
20. In this regard, Russia is no different from the cases presented by Eric Uslaner (2002) referring, among others, to Edward Banfield's study about the Italian village of Montegrano: in a society such as Russia, with huge inequalities, it should not be a surprise that interpersonal trust is low and people do perceive strangers as threatening. Here also the truth is that 'where you live – your context – shapes what you think' (Uslaner, 2002, chs 2–18).
21. See Bruszt and Stark, 2000.

Bibliography

Braithwaite, J. (1998) 'Institutionalizing Distrust, Enculturating Trust', in V. Braithwaite and M. Levi (eds), *Trust and Governance* (New York: Russell Sage Foundation), pp. 343–75.
Bruszt, L. and Stark, D. (2000) 'Postcommunist Networking: Secret Agents, Mafiosi and Sociologists', *East European Constitutional Review*, Winter/Spring: 115–20.
Della Porta, D. (2000) 'Social Capital, Beliefs in Government, and Political Corruption', in S. J. Pharr and R. D. Putnam (eds), *Disaffected Democracies* (Princeton, NJ: Princeton University Press), pp. 202–30.
Diamond, L. (2008) *The Spirit of Democracy* (New York: Holt).
Fukuyama, F. (1995) *Trust. The Social Virtues and the Creation of Prosperity* (Harmondsworth: Penguin).

Fukuyama, F. (2000) 'Social Capital', in L. E. Harrison and S. P. Huntington (eds), *Culture Matters* (New York: Basic Books), pp. 98–111.

Hirschmann, A. O. (1982) *Shifting Involvements. Private Interest and Public Action* (Princeton, NJ: Princeton University Press).

Kaser, K.(2001) *Freundschaft und Feindschaft auf dem Balkan* (Vienna: Wieser).

Levi, M. (1998) 'A State of Trust', in V. Braithwaite and M. Levi (eds), *Trust and Governance* (New York: Russell Sage Foundation.

Luhmann, N. (1982) *The Differentiation of Society* (New York: Columbia University Press).

Mulgan, G. (2006) *Good and Bad Power* (London: Allen Lane).

Pipes, R. (2000) *Property and Freedom* (New York: Vintage).

Rasch, W. (2000) *Niklas Luhmann's Modernity. The Paradoxes of Differentiation* (Stanford, Calif.: Stanford University Press).

Reiser, M. (1999) 'Trust in Transition', European Bank for Reconstruction and Development, Working paper No. 39.

Rose, R. (1999) 'Getting Things Done in an Anti-Modern Society: Social Capital Networks in Russia', in P, Dasgupta and I, Serageldin (eds), *Social Capital: A Multifaceted Perspective* (Washington, DC: The World Bank), pp. 147–71.

Rose, R. (2000) 'Uses of Social Capital in Russia: Modern, Pre-modern, and Anti-modern', *Post-Soviet Affairs* 16: 33–57.

Rose, R. (2009) *Understanding Post-communist Transformation* (London: Routledge).

Rothstein, B. (2000) 'Trust, Social Dilemmas and Collective Memory', *Journal of Theoretical Politics* 12: 477–501.

Rothstein, B. (2005) *Social Traps and the Problem of Trust* (Cambridge University Press).

Sales, A. (1991) 'The Private, the Public and Civil Society: Social Realms and Power Structures'. *International Political Science Review*, 12: 295–312.

Shlapentokh, V. (2006) 'Trust in Public Institutions in Russia: The Lowest in the World', *Communist and Post-Communist Studies*, 39: 153–74.

Tanzi, V. (2000) *Policies, Institutions and the Dark Side of Economics* (Cheltenham: Edward Elgar).

Tocqueville, Alexis de (2008) *Democracy in America*, abridged with an Introduction by Michael Kammer (New York: Palgrave Macmillan).

Uslaner, E. (2002) *The Moral Foundations of Trust* (Cambridge University Press).

4
The Voices of Enterprises and Political Games: The Corporate World and Its Single Voice?

Laurent Mortreuil

The corporate world, in itself, is diverse: it obviously comprises many (very different) enterprises, but also encompasses the many structures representing its components or interests (unions, chambers, associations, think tanks, forums, the media and so on).

In the corporate world, the most genuine voice may be that coming from an enterprise, understood as a community of people organized to deliver specific goods and services. Of course, even at the level of a single enterprise, voices can be multiple and sometimes contradictory: head-office versus local entities, shareholders, boards of directors, general assemblies, executives and management, unions, corporate communication, marketing and advertising, for example, because the reasons for an enterprise (or a part of an enterprise) to take up a position are different depending on the questioner (is it marketing to consumers; presentation to the public; communicating with the media; reports to moral authorities; development of corporate culture and motivation among employees; negotiation with providers; relations with regulators or social partners; lobbying to push its own agenda; out of philanthropy and so on). In addition, the voice heard may come from an articulated discourse (communication or action) or undesired (accidents, misbehaviour or political ordeals, for example).

We will not enter into the subtleties of the various voices inside the enterprise, but rather consider the voice of the enterprise as it can be seen from corporate communication and from the behaviour of an enterprise as it wishes to be perceived. Even at this level, enterprises know how to modulate their voice. Notwithstanding all these discrepancies, there is one language relative to politics where today's corporate world admits to speaking 'with one voice': corporate social responsibility (CSR). This language uses words (corporate communication), acts (societal actions) and thoughts (the common principles of CSR), which we shall analyse below.

Current corporate communication on CSR

Investors, regulators and, in general, all the stockholders[1] have access to corporate communication. It represents the image that an enterprise (that is, its executive management) wants to give. It has multiple aspects:

- The persuasion of potential counterparts (investors, regulators, customers, providers, media, intellectuals, and so on).
- Position in and influence on their own markets.
- Culture setting, internally, among their employees.

I have studied corporate communication of ten large, emblematic international French companies plus some analysis offering a screening based on CSR criteria:

(i) In annual reports and on internet sites, CSR is taken increasingly seriously, with sometimes a greater emphasis on it than on business development and strategy.

(ii) Sustainable development is paramount, while concrete social injustices are somewhat ignored or neglected. The systemic imbalances that led to the current financial–economical–social crisis are never questioned: political involvement is very timid.

(iii) There is little influence between the 'CSR' communication and accounting: the world of figures and the 'bottom line' is set apart. There is a greater juxtaposition of the societal and environmental balance sheets, with the economic balance sheet being chosen rather than a dialogue, which illustrates the mutual benefit of taking care of the three classical CSR dimensions.

(iv) Surprisingly, perhaps because it goes without saying, the essential social contribution of any enterprise (providing goods and services, creating wealth) is systematically underestimated and usually not even mentioned.

In short, corporate social communication essentially consists of acknowledging political correctness, with little practical commitment beyond current regulation or analysts' constraints.

Societal actions from the corporate world

Being active on all five continents – Africa, the Americas, Asia, Europe and Oceania – UNIAPAC benefits from a comprehensive view from entrepreneurs or executives of their activities, and the enterprises they are leading.

Genuine good rarely exploits publicity, therefore it is no surprise that these actions receive little or no attention. Nevertheless, they are like a murmur which witnesses that, beyond their structural social contribution (producing goods and services as well as creating wealth), enterprises do intervene and have a real impact in the social arena.

Some actions are dealt with by the corporation itself (for example, health care in Africa for employees and their (extended) families) and sometimes organized worldwide (for example, micro-entrepreneurship sponsorship from Asia to Latin America).

Other actions are dealt with by philanthropic foundations funded by wealthy corporate owners, providing a two-step redistribution of wealth made possible by the development of the enterprise (for example, the anti-malaria campaign in Africa) or directly from corporate funds (for example, a think tank to bring practical ideas to the political world).

Finally, most of them come from the personal commitment of an entrepreneur or, even better, a group of entrepreneurs (micro-financing, business schools, press releases, civil society actions against crime and so on) with, in many cases, confidence in the capacity of individuals to take care of their own lives.

There is a risk of reducing CSR merely to the 'pet projects' of the CEO or the board. By insisting on the visible side of CSR commitments, enterprises may enter into competition to catch the interest of their public, to appear as the spectacularly most responsible. Even the multi-factor scoring instruments trying to be comprehensive carry the same risk: what is not measured and reported is not done, but all measurement and reporting systems have their failures. For a real, active CSR, the necessary ingredient is the personal responsibility of the people involved, beginning with the leadership.

Evolving principles of CSR

The first step: the 'economico-legal' CSR

This consists of recognizing the irreplaceable role of an enterprise as a service and product provider as well as a wealth generator. The first contribution of an enterprise to society is its offer of goods and services in an optimized way, if respecting the rules (not only laws and regulations, provided these are properly set up, but also the 'rules of the market'). Accordingly, in a perfect world, the distribution of wealth is assured (since prices – including salaries – are the results of agreed transactions) and every diversion of it towards a side activity ('social') not related to the explicit mission (producing goods and services) would be sub-optimal and would not respect the freedom of each person to manage his or her own money. It would be like a subtle tax without a democratic sanction.

The issue is that, to function correctly, this vision makes the assumption that each person's preferences are orientated towards the common good, and that each has access to all available information and is fully capable of exercising his/her own choice, which is not the case in the real world. Nevertheless, this 'first-order' vision has the merit of revealing that, in themselves, by offering goods and services and creating economic value, enterprises have a positive contribution to make to society and must keep in mind that this is what society expects from them.

The second step: from legal shareholders to stakeholders

First, prices are not perfectly fixed, and many externalities are not priced, or even 'priceable'. Therefore, the value created (and sometimes lost) by the existence and activity of any enterprise goes beyond the creation of wealth for investors. Enterprises have long realized that they have an impact on society and on public policies. A diagnostic on CSR goes through a systematic analysis of its stakeholders, including those who have no voice with which to claim their rights (for example, the future generations that will depend on the sustainability of the environment). 'An enterprise cannot limit itself to economic goals without considering the moral goals stemming from the consequences of its actions; it belongs to its essence.'[2]

But consideration for and care of stakeholders can be perverted if it is focused only on the shareholders' interests and on the use of 'labels' and other types of instruments (codes of ethics, quality certification, evaluations of environmental and social performances, balance sheets) which, if used without personal commitment at each level of an enterprise, will not prevent misconduct. The current global crisis, where most of the actors have passed all the principal CSR tests, illustrate the shortfall of formal CSR.

A third step in CSR: responsibility for the common good

The enterprise, then, is no longer considered as a place of arbitrage between conflicting interests, but as a community of people. One goes from considering only groups of stakeholders with their own goals to the commitment of each person to the common good. This is only possible when the proper culture is sustained by the management and lived by all inside, and eventually outside, the enterprise:

- Promotion takes priority over utilization.
- Values are based on respect for human dignity and not on arbitrage to serve common interests.
- Social responsibility does not merely signify that business practice is benchmarked by a code of conduct. It is also related to the personal responsibility of each actor, based on motivation.
- Management is orientated more towards individuals and their development, and less towards the erroneous competitive use of natural resources and what is wrongly called 'human resources' (since people cannot be reduced merely to being a 'resource' to be 'used').

The final goal and criteria of achievement is not only the sustainable development of the economy within the limits of the law but also participation in the construction of a fair society.

Conclusion

The voice of an enterprise appears to be twofold: on one side, the voice of official corporate communication – 'clean', well-thought-out and adapted to selected auditors; and on the other, the true actions of its members, finding and implementing concrete solutions to down-to-earth issues to which they happen to be sensitive.

When tackling the issue of connections between the political sphere and the corporate world, there is often a feeling of unease as if one (the political) should be pure and the other, of itself, guilty of satisfying only its own interests. Indeed, the short-term view, narrowed to the profit of a few, may lead to misconduct and corruption. But companies need a healthy society, which in turn needs a healthy economy. The common good is not detrimental to a well-understood interest (including financial) of the enterprises. Respecting customers and the environment is good for business, and no market would develop sustainably without trust and regulation. One would fail in trying to negotiate a 'win–win' bargain, rather than recognizing that we all need to achieve the same common good.

Notes

1. The concept of stakeholders has gradually been introduced to encompass all those (beyond the shareholders) affected by the actions of any enterprise. They are usually gathered into eight groups: customers, investors, employees, providers, peers (or competitors), governments, local communities and future generations.
2. Chomali and Majluf (2007).

Bibliography

Action Social Empresarial (2004) *Responsabilidad Social de la Empresa* (Madrid: ASE).

Asociación de Empresarios Cristianos (2000) *Solidaridad y compromiso social en la sociedad civil* (Asunción, Paraguay: ADEC).

Associação Cristã de Empresários e Gestores (2004) *Etica, Factor de Realizaçao e Progresso* (Lisbon: ACEGE).

Bilderberg Conference (2008) *Sustainable Globalization* (The Hague: VNO-NCW).

Capron, Michel and Quairel-Lanoizelet, Françoise (2007) *La Responsabilité Sociale d'Entreprise* (Paris: La Découverte).

Caravedo, Baltazar (2001) *Responsabilidad Social, una nueva forma de Gerencia* (Lima, Peru: CIUP-SASE-PERÚ 2021).

Carroll, Archie B. and Buchholtz, Ann K. (2006) *Business and Society: Ethics and Stakeholder Management* (Mason, Ohio: Thomson/South-Western).

Chomali, Fernando and Majluf, Nicolas (2007) *Etica y Responsabilidad Social de la Empresa* (Santiago, Chile: El Mercurio).

Collins, James C. and Porras, Jerry I. (1994) *Built to Last: Successful Habits of Visionary Companies* (New York: HarperBusiness, 1994).

Cortina, Adela (2000) *Ética de las Empresas* (Madrid: Editorial Trotta).

Dembinski, Paul H. (2008) *Finance servante ou finance trompeuse* (Paris: DDB).

Dherse, Jean-Loup and Minguet, Hugues (1998) *L'Ethique ou le Chaos?* (Paris: Renaissance).

Dutch Social Economic Council (2000) *Summary of Advisory Report on CSR*, December.

Entrepreneurs et Dirigeants Chrétiens, Les (2005) *L'entreprise au service de qui? Une nouvelle approche de la gouvernance* (Paris: Les EDC).

Fernández Gago, Roberto (2005) *Administración de la Responsabilidad Social Corporativa* (Madrid: Thomson Paraninfo).

Frederick, William C. (2006) *Corporation, Be Good! The Story of Corporate Social Responsibility* (Indianapolis, Ind.: Dog Ear).

Geissler, Peter (2007) *Gestión por Valores* (Mexico City: Panorama).

Griffiths, Brian (2001) *Capitalism, Morality and Markets* (London: Institute of Economic Affairs).

Harvard Business School (2003) *Harvard Business Review on Corporate Responsibility* (Boston, Mass.: Harvard Business Press).
Henriques, Adrian and Richardson, Julie (2004) *The Triple Bottom Line, Does It All Add Up? Assessing The Sustainability of Business and CSR* (London: Earthscan).
Hoffman, W. Michael, Frederick, Robert E. and Schwartz, Mark S. (2001) *Business Ethics Readings and Cases in Corporate Morality* (Boston, Mass.: McGraw-Hill).
Hude, Henri (2007) *L'Ethique des décideurs* (Paris: Renaissance).
Institute of Business Ethics (2007) *Ethical Due Diligence: An Introduction and Guide* (London: Institute of Business Ethics).
Loza Macías, Manuel (2004) *Actitudes Sociales para Transformar la Empresa* (Mexico: Confederación USEM).
Manzone, Gianni (2002) *La Responsabilita Dell'impresa: Business Ethics e Dottrina Sociale Della Chiesa in Dialogo* (Brescia: Queriniana).
Milanés García, Salvador (2004) *Responsabilidad Social de la Riqueza* (Mexico: Confederación USEM).
Moreda de Lecea, Carlos (2002) *Consideraciones Éticas Sobre Aspectos Económicos* (Mexico: Instituto Mexicano de Doctrina Social Cristina).
Naughton, Michael and Alford, Helen (2001) *Managing as if Faith Mattered* (Notre-Dame, Ind.: University of Notre Dame Press).
Paine, Lynn Sharp (2003) *Value Shift, Why Companies Must Merge Social and Financial Imperatives to Achieve Superior Performances* (New York: McGraw-Hill Professional).
Perdiguero, Tomás (2003) *La Responsabilidad Social de las Empresas en un Mundo Global* (Barcelona: Editorial Anagrama).
Piedra, Alberto M. (2004) *Natural Law: The Foundation of an Orderly Economic System* (Lanham, Md.: Lexington Books).
Ramírez Padilla, David Noel (2007) *Integridad en las Empresas* (Mexico: McGraw Hill).
Sagawa, Shirley and Segal, Eli (1999) *Common Interest, Common Good: Creating Value Through Business and Social Sector Partnerships* (Boston, Mass.: Harvard Business Press).
Servitje, Lorenzo, (2007) *La vida económica, la empresa y los empresarios* (Mexico City: Noriega).
Spence, Laura J., Habisch, André and Schmidpeter, René (2004) *Responsibility and Social Capital: The World of Small and Medium Sized Enterprises* (Basingstoke: Palgrave Macmillan).
Teixidó, Soledad and Chavarri, Reinalina (2000) *La Acción filantrópica como un elemento de la RSE – El caso chileno* (Santiago, Chile: PROhumana).
Toro, Olga Lucía and Rey, Germán (1996) *Empresa privada y responsabilidad social* (Bogota, Colombia: Centro Colombiano de Filantropía).
Ugoji, Kaodi, Dando, Nicole and Moir, Lance (2007) *Does Business Ethics Pay? – Revisited: The Value of Ethics Training* (London: Institute of Business Ethics).
Unione Cristiana Imprenditori Dirigenti (2003) *Il lavoro per l'Uomo* (Milan: UCID).
Unione Cristiana Imprenditori Dirigenti (2007) *La Coscienza Imprenditoriale nella Costruzione del Bene Comune* (Rome: UCID).
Vogel, David (2005) *The Market for Virtue: The Potential and Limits of CSR* (Washington, DC: Brookings Institution Press).

Werther, Jr., William B. and Chandler, David (2006) *Strategic Corporate Social Responsibility: Stakeholders in a Global Environment* (Thousand Oaks, Calif.: Sage).

de Woot, Philippe (2005) *Should Prometheus Be Bound? Corporate Global Responsibility* (Basingstoke: Palgrave Macmillan).

Zamagni, Stefano (2007) *L'economia del bene comune* (Rome: Città Nuova).

5
The European Transparency Initiative: Monitoring Brussels Lobbying[1]

Anna Melich

Introduction

Considering that:

- the European Commission employs 27,000 people and the European Parliament has 736 Members (MEPs) and some 4,000 civil servants;
- the European Commission (EC) has an annual budget of €110 million and a monopoly over initiating legislation that affects 495 million citizens in twenty-seven member states;
- European law accounts for 70–80 per cent of member states' legislation; and
- that more than 1,000 journalists are accredited to the European Commission press room (more than to the White House press office in the USA).

it is hardly surprising that there are at least 15,000 – some say as many as 30,000 – lobbyists in Brussels working for some 2,500 interest groups solely in order to influence European legislation or get it changed in their clients' interests.

Brussels now has the second-largest concentration of lobbies in the world after Washington, DC (where there are around 35,000).

Are Brussels lobbies different?

The majority of political analysts agree on the definition of a lobby or interest group: a group or organization that attempts to impose its point of view on (mainly legislative) institutions in order to influence the course of political decisions in its favour or to defend an external cause.

Lobbying is not something illegal – on the contrary, it is closely bound up with the development of democratic systems, as long as it takes place openly and in accordance with certain rules. There can be no interest groups, or channels for them to use, without democracy. In undemocratic systems that do not allow monitoring by citizens, it is easier for pressure and influence to be exerted on the government – and for the government to pursue its own interests – with impunity. In all modern democratic systems, on the other hand, interest groups play a vital part in terms of consultation, dialogue and expertise. Some Constitutions, such as that of Switzerland, explicitly provide for interest groups to be involved in the legislative procedure. In the USA, there is a wide range of legislation governing the activities of interest groups and lobbies.

In Brussels, the legislative procedure followed by European institutions in drawing up European Union (EU) law is a long and complicated one. The joint interests of twenty-seven member states could not be satisfied without valuable input from the associations, businesses, chambers, federations of various manufacturing sectors, professional bodies, non-governmental organizations (NGOs), think tanks and so on that are regularly consulted on all items of EU legislation.

There are both quantitative and qualitative differences between EU lobbies and purely national ones. In quantitative terms, European legislation – especially the rules on the Single Market and decisions on the Social and Structural Funds – affects much broader economic interests than does national legislation. European lobbies therefore tend to exert greater pressure in defending their own interests or those of their clients than they would at national level. They may even be tempted to use channels or means of influence that are not always transparent, or indeed legal.

In qualitative terms, European lobbies may be rather more diverse. In Brussels (where the majority are located) and other European capitals, there are countless consultancies, freelance consultants, law firms and so on whose clients expect them to provide information and consultation, and in some cases to exert pressure to get European decisions altered in their clients' favour.

Not all EU lobbies represent purely economic interests; there are also political lobbies (associations of city or town mayors, representatives of European regions and so on), religious lobbies (the various religious denominations) and humanist lobbies.

The author of a recent book (Conradt, 2008) makes the claim that even sects such as the Church of Scientology are doing a great deal to mobilize people and resources in order to achieve their goals in Brussels, and deplores the fact that humanist, secular associations are not doing the same. The French presidency of the EU, which was held from 1 July to 31 December 2008, proposed to respond to this situation by developing a 'positive secularism' policy.

In fact, almost any profession, movement, association, minority or atypical public interest that does not feel sufficiently well represented in its region or state has at one time or another entrusted its interests to a Brussels lobby. This reflects a perception on the part of European civil society that EU institutions have an important part to play in defending the interests of all the EU's citizens.

The need for transparency

In Europe, and elsewhere, all citizens wish as far as possible either to participate directly in the political, social or economic decisions that affect them, or to be transparently informed about these.

In this connection, according to the spring 2008 Eurobarometer (see http://ec.europa.eu/public_opinion/standard_en.htm), the majority of European citizens (54 per cent) feel that EU institutions are not very transparent or not transparent at all; 26 per cent feel that the opposite is true; and 20 per cent have no views on the matter (see Table 5.1).

Most respondents (84 per cent) clearly feel that it is important or very important for EU institutions to function transparently.

However, the average proportion of people in the twenty-seven EU member states who feel their own national institutions are not very transparent or not transparent at all is higher (68 per cent) than the average of those who feel the same way about EU institutions. A larger proportion (87 per cent) also feel that it is important or very important for their own national institutions to function transparently (see Table 5.2).

There were fewer 'don't knows' (8 per cent) regarding respondents' own national institutions, and the standard deviation was larger. Sixty-five per cent of Swedes and 53 per cent of Finns feel that their own institutions are very transparent, but only 8 per cent of Bulgarians and Lithuanians, and 7 per cent of Latvians, feel the same; and the views of people in the Czech Republic, Italy, Poland, Hungary and Greece are not much different.

There are more doubts (20 per cent 'don't knows' for EU 27) regarding the transparency of European institutions. The vast majority of

Table 5.1   Current level of perceived transparency and the importance of it for EU institutions

	1. Are EU institutions transparent?		2. Is transparency in EU institutions important?	
	Are	Are not	Important	Not important
Slovenia	50	25	78	11
Cyprus	48	24	95	0
Spain	41	30	91	2
Slovakia	38	46	74	19
Greece	37	60	99	1
Malta	36	31	90	1
Ireland	35	35	79	3
Romania	35	29	73	9
Lithuania	33	35	89	4
Poland	32	40	87	6
Portugal	31	46	84	9
Italy	31	50	85	11
Finland	31	62	77	20
Bulgaria	30	33	83	5
Belgium	27	63	85	10
Czech Republic	26	58	78	14
EU 27	**26**	**54**	**84**	**8**
Estonia	25	48	80	10
Luxembourg	24	65	86	6
France	23	61	86	7
Austria	22	68	80	14
United Kingdom	21	49	94	3
Sweden	21	58	94	3
Hungary	20	64	89	8
Germany	19	74	85	12
Netherlands	18	71	88	7
Latvia	14	65	71	21
Denmark	12	81	89	9

Notes: Wording of questions: 1. According to you, how transparent are the institutions of the European Union today? Would you say that they are very transparent, transparent, not very transparent or not transparent at all? 2. Would you say that it is very important, important, not very important or not important at all for you that the institutions of the European Union function in a transparent way?
Source: Eurobarometer 69, Spring 2008 (see http://ec.europa.eu/public_opinion/standard_en.htm). Fieldwork undertaken April–May 2008.

EU citizens have never had any direct dealings with them, and so do not have a clear opinion on the subject. Those who are most critical about the lack of transparency of European institutions are the Danes (81 per cent say they are 'not very transparent' or 'not transparent at all'),

Table 5.2 Current level of perceived transparency and the importance of it for national institutions

	1. Are national institutions transparent?		2. Is transparency in national institutions important?	
	Are	Are not	Important	Not important
Sweden	65	30	93	4
Finland	53	44	83	16
Slovenia	42	45	82	9
Spain	38	51	94	2
Netherlands	36	59	91	5
Cyprus	35	55	97	0
Ireland	34	45	83	3
Luxembourg	30	62	88	5
Malta	27	57	91	1
Belgium	27	68	86	11
United Kingdom	26	57	77	10
Denmark	26	72	93	5
Slovakia	26	65	80	15
EU 27	**24**	**68**	**87**	**8**
Austria	24	65	78	16
France	23	71	87	8
Germany	23	74	88	10
Portugal	22	67	85	9
Romania	20	62	79	8
Estonia	20	70	83	11
Czech Republic	17	74	83	12
Italy	17	78	86	12
Poland	16	76	91	5
Hungary	14	82	92	7
Greece	14	86	97	3
Bulgaria	8	78	86	6
Lithuania	8	79	87	6
Latvia	7	85	77	18

Notes: Wording of questions: 1. According to you, how transparent are your own country's institutions today? Would you say that they are very transparent, transparent, not very transparent or not transparent at all? 2. Would you say that it is very important, important, not very important or not important at all that your own country's institutions function in a transparent way?
Source: Eurobarometer 69, Spring 2008 (see http://ec.europa.eu/public_opinion/standard_en.htm). Fieldwork undertaken April–May 2008.

the Germans (74 per cent) and the Dutch (71 per cent). Surprisingly, only 49 per cent of UK citizens – according to the Spring 2008 Eurobarometer – feel that European institutions lack transparency, even though British media and lobbies level the most criticism at the EU.

Not surprisingly, those who are most eurosceptical or most pessimistic about the future of the EU, or think that things in the EU are going in the wrong direction, are the most critical regarding the transparency of the decisions and activities of EU institutions (see Table 5.3). However, the reverse is not true. Trusting the EU, being optimistic about its future and thinking that it is going in the right direction are necessary – but not sufficient – conditions for feeling that its institutions are transparent.

At the same time, good, average or poor knowledge of how European institutions function or what they do does not necessarily correlate with a good or bad perception of European transparency. Irrespective of their level of knowledge of the EU, respondents are always more likely to feel it is not transparent rather than the opposite. However, those who know least about it are still more likely (45 per cent) to reply that they do not know whether European institutions are transparent, compared with those who have some knowledge of the Union.

The press, as well as associations of individuals (for example, the Corporate Europe Observatory (CEO) or ones made up of alternative

Table 5.3 Level of perceived transparency of European institutions by several independent variables of EU support

Percentage EU 27	Are EU institutions transparent?			
	Are	Are not	Don't know	Total
Trust in the EU				
Tend to trust	39	45	16	100
Tend not to trust	15	70	15	100
Future of the EU				
Optimistic	36	48	16	100
Pessimistic	13	69	18	100
Things in the EU are going in the				
Right direction	40	46	14	100
Wrong direction	19	70	11	100
Neither	20	60	20	100
Objective knowledge of the EU*				
Good	29	60	11	100
Average	28	53	19	100
Poor	17	38	45	100

Note: *Indicator built up from true and false answers to a quiz about EU facts.
Source: Eurobarometer 69, Spring 2008 (see http://ec.europa.eu/public_opinion/standard_en.htm). Fieldwork undertaken April–May 2008.

NGOs (for example, ALTER-EU), together with associations such as Attac or Greenpeace, have constantly called for more transparency regarding the activities of lobbies they accuse of pursuing their own interests with the consent of the European Commission (since it regularly consults them and allows them to have dealings with EU institutions without being subject to standards or monitoring of any kind).

The CEO has an annual award for the 'worst' lobbyists – that is, those whose methods are the most obscure and misleading. In 2007, the award went to BMW, Daimler and Porsche for their attempts to get the EU to delay its CO_2 emission reduction targets. The organization was also planning to create a new category of awards for the Worst Conflict of Interest in Europe.

European Transparency Initiative

The European Commission wants to be transparent, and above all it wants to be ethical. Why is this the case?

- As explained earlier, it faces more serious ethical challenges than most other public administrations.
- It embraces numerous cultural differences, twenty-three official languages and different political traditions.
- In the past it has experienced some dysfunction that has done it a great deal of damage, even if personal enrichment was never the intention.
- The Commission is aware that 'good ethics is good economics' – a strong sense of ethics in European government will mean that less effort is put into monitoring and more into getting results.

However, just as European institutions need to be transparent towards all the Union's citizens, they can, and must, also insist on transparency and open, legal behaviour from those that deal, discuss and negotiate with them.

The present Commission has therefore implemented effective policies designed to serve the overall European interest. 'Improving transparency' was identified early as one of the EU's strategic objectives for 2005–9: 'The Union must be open to public scrutiny and accountable for its work. This requires a high level of ... transparency.'

The Commission believes that the legitimacy of any modern administration depends on compliance with the highest standards of transparency. European citizens are entitled to expect efficient, responsible, service-minded public institutions, and to expect that the powers and resources entrusted to political and public bodies will be used carefully and never be diverted for personal ends. This is why the Commission launched the European Transparency Initiative (ETI) in November 2005 (SEC(2005)1300/6).

The purpose of the initiative is to extend a series of transparency measures already adopted by the Commission, especially those put forward as part of the general reforms introduced since 1999 and in the White Paper on European Governance (COM(2006)35 final). Major progress has already been made in this area, including:

- The 'Code of Good Administrative Behaviour' adopted by the Commission. This is the quality standard for the Commission's relations with the public. The ethical standards that apply to Commission staff are set out in the Code and its implementing regulations.
- On the political level, the European Communities treaty includes specific provisions on the ethical standards to be met by members of the Commission. These provisions came into force with the adoption of the Code of Conduct for Commissioners (SEC(2004)1487/2).

In launching the ETI, the Commission has embarked on an analysis of its general conception of transparency. The idea is to identify areas for improvement and open them up for debate. The initiative thus covers a broad range of issues, including better information on the management and use of EU resources, rules of ethics applicable to European institutions, and the limits within which interest groups and civil society organizations should act.

When presenting the ETI on 9 November 2005, the Commission identified two main areas of action:

(i) Immediate measures to ensure more effective control and monitoring of the use of EU resources and to extend the field covered by its document register.
(ii) A series of measures to encourage a debate with other European institutions on the following issues:
    (a) Rules and standards of professional ethics for holders of public office in the European institutions;[2]
    (b) A review of the legislation on access to documents. The resulting inter-institutional co-operation was followed -by consultations between the relevant parties in late 2006/2007 and then by a Commission proposal; and

(c) A review of the legal framework of the Anti-Fraud Office (OLAF) to ensure that member states notify the Office systematically of the final outcome of fraud cases reported to their national authorities.

Proposed rules for monitoring lobbies

Among many other activities in numerous areas of professional ethics, the ETI proposed specific measures to monitor lobbies:

> It is of course positive that interest groups are actively submitting contributions in the context of open public consultations run by the Commission. The benefit could be further enhanced if such groups would make their contributions accessible to the general public. While they must already make available information about their structure and functioning, the Interservice Working Group report concludes that reinforced monitoring in this respect could ensure that these requirements are actually fulfilled. The analysis of the current practice also shows that it is possible to improve the transparency vis-à-vis the general public on the input given to the EU decision-making process. This issue should be dealt with in a broader debate on the Commission's consultation practices, addressing the implementation of the Commission's consultation standards, including, for instance, the rules on how to publish policy submissions received from external stakeholders.

The report proposes a number of solutions, including improving the information the Commission provides on the activities of pressure groups, compulsory registration of interest groups represented in consultative bodies, and compulsory registration of all pressure groups. If these solutions were to be adopted, it would be important to avoid placing an unnecessary administrative burden on either the interest groups or the Commission. One possibility would be to convert the CONECCS database into a compulsory registration system for all interest and pressure groups, including public affairs professionals, trade unions and so on.

Another proposal was to

> give new momentum to the self-regulatory approach by encouraging all organizations and individuals listed in a (voluntary or compulsory) register to adhere to a common code of conduct. While the

Commission could of course propose this code of conduct, it would clearly be preferable for its 'users' to take the lead. It must be noted, however, that the credibility of such a system would depend on its proper monitoring, systems for enforcement and the percentage of lobbyists active in Brussels that are effectively adhering to such a code.[3]

Register and code of conduct

On 25 May 2008, after consulting all the relevant parties, the Commission proposed to the Council and Parliament a draft code of conduct (COM (2008) 323) for 'interest representatives', including a definition of European lobbying and a proposal to set up a register of all those who lobby in Brussels.

(a) 'Interest representation' activities for which registration is expected are defined as 'activities carried out with the objective of influencing the policy formulation and decision-making processes of the European institutions'.[4]

The following are deemed to be lobbyists: professional lobbies, businesses' 'in-house' lobbyists, NGOs, think tanks, trade associations, employers' organizations, trade unions, profit-making or non-profit organizations, lawyers and consultants whose purpose is to influence Commission decisions, and associations of public authorities with a private legal status or any mixed (private/public) structure of which public authorities are a part.

This does not apply to regional, national or international public authorities, or national or European political parties.

(b) The code of conduct lays down seven clear, monitorable rules to be complied with by signatories to the code. Interest representatives shall always:
　　(i) identify themselves by name and by the entity(ies) they work for or represent;
　(ii) not misrepresent themselves as to the effect of registration to mislead third parties and/or EU staff;
　(iii) declare the interests, and where applicable the clients or the members, which they represent;
　(iv) ensure that, to the best of their knowledge, information they provide is unbiased, complete, up-to-date and not misleading;
　(v) not obtain or try to obtain information, or any decision, dishonestly;

(vi) not induce EU staff to contravene rules and standards of behaviour applicable to them; and

(vii) if employing former EU staff, respect their obligation to abide by the rules and confidentiality requirements that apply to them (a measure to combat 'revolving doors' abuses).

The register, which remains voluntary, must include details of lobbyists' turnover and their main clients' relative shares of it; an estimate of the costs connected with direct lobbying that businesses' internal representatives and professional groups carry out with EU institutions; and NGOs' and think tanks' overall budgets and breakdowns by main funding sources.

Anyone who suspects that the code has been infringed may lodge a complaint with the Commission. If the infringement is confirmed by an official procedure, corrective measures will be taken.

The Parliament wants to go a step further than the Commission

The European Parliament (EP) already has a register controlling access by lobbyists by means of a badge and a code of conduct. A total of 1,712 organizations and 2,757 individuals' names (1,590 updated) were registered in 2009. Despite such a system certainly being needed in order to control physical access by lobbyists, it is not sufficient. It is therefore quite understandable that, following the Commission's initiative, the Parliament wants to go a step further: see the report by Alexander Stubb, who, before he became Finland's Minister for Foreign Affairs, was rapporteur for the Committee on Constitutional Affairs (2007/2115(INI), adopted on 8 April 2008 (doc. A6-0105/2008)).

The Commission and the Parliament have slightly different views on two issues:

• The Commission believes the approach should initially be voluntary, with lobbyists being invited to register in order to boost the overall reputation of their profession. This is in view of the profession's favourable response during preliminary consultations. The Commission feels that a year should be enough time to decide whether such confidence is justified. The Parliament, on the other hand, believes that work should start immediately on a single, compulsory register for lobbyists wishing to have regular access to European institutions. Irrespective of its legal status, the Commission takes the view that a single register for the Commission and the Parliament (in which lobbyists must be listed in order to be acknowledged by the Commission and have access to the Parliament) is in practice compulsory for all serious lobbyists. Apart from the length of time needed to draw up a compulsory register, this is not an insurmountable point of disagreement.

- The second difference seems to be just as readily resolvable. Unlike the register set up by the Commission, the Parliament would like the single register to specify not only the names of the lobbying businesses, but also the names of the actual lobbyists. The Commission is prepared to consider such an addition, since the Parliament does indeed require this in order to regulate individuals' access to its buildings. However, the Commission does not, and will not, issue special badges to lobbyists entering its premises, and has therefore focused on the transparency of the interests represented rather than the identities of the representatives, which is in any case known when contact is made with Commission officials.

As regards funding information, the EP more or less agrees with the Commission's initial proposals. Among other things, there is agreement on the definition of the entities to be registered, on the code of conduct and the monitoring procedure, on penalties for lobbyists that infringe the code, and on the need for a financial statement.

In accordance with the Commission's proposals, the EP wished for there to be a 'one-stop shop', in the form of a single lobbying register and code of conduct for the Parliament, the Commission and the Council. Specifically, the Parliament proposed that the three institutions swiftly set up a working party to draw up such joint measures by the end of 2009. The Commission responded favourably to this proposal, and President José Manuel Barroso has appointed Vice-President Siim Kallas to handle the task.

An inter-institutional 'High Level Working Group on a Common Register and Code of Conduct for Lobbyists' was set up soon after the launching of the Commission's register. This group met on several occasions to discuss the possible shape and scope of a common register as well as issues relating to a possible common code of conduct for lobbyists. At its meeting on 22 April 2009, the High Level Working Group agreed:

- A new web page to be opened on 22 April 2009 on the inter-institutional pages of the Europa website, presenting information about and links to both institutions' current registers, and enabling the public to access information about both registers from a single starting point: http://europa.eu/lobbyists/interest_representative_registers/index_en.html.

- A draft text of a common code of conduct for lobbyists.
- A series of guidelines for the two institutions for a future *common register*, pending the Commission's review of its register and a final agreement between the institutions.
- Finally, the Parliament and Commission strongly regret that Council, as a co-legislator, has not yet been willing to join negotiations on a common register, and reiterate their invitation to Council to so do.

The Commission's lobby register and how it works

On 23 June 2008, the European Commission opened its 'lobby register', and the 2,500 known European pressure groups were invited to register online (see http://ec.europa.eu/transparency/regrin/). Most of the media, relevant parties and anti-European lobbies did not give it much credit. They predicted that few lobbyists would register, or at least that they would hesitate for a long time before doing so.

The first interest group to register in the Commission's new lobby register, on 24 June 2008, was a multinational concern: Spain's Telefónica. It wanted to show it was conscientious and had nothing to hide. Telefónica stated that it had spent €950,000 for European lobbying purposes.

By 14 November 2009 there were 2,140 interest representatives listed in the Commission's register:

- 127 professional consultancies/ law firms involved in lobbying EU institutions;
- 1,184 'in-house' lobbyists and trade associations active in lobbying;
- 602 NGOs and think tanks; and
- 227 other organizations.

Major corporations, multinational or otherwise, professional associations, trade unions and other similar bodies are using the register as a way of publicly displaying their interests, and even their economic power. They are very willing to register. The number of registrations for this 'in-house representation' lobby has grown exponentially, from zero in June 2008 to 133 in July, to 607 in February 2009, to 1,083 in September 2009 and to 1,184 in November 2009 (see Figure 5.1).

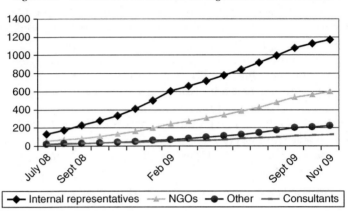

Figure 5.1 Evolution over time of the registration of EU lobbies

Since the summer of 2008, the number of registrations of NGOs and associations of these, think tanks and other similar bodies has grown more slowly, but steadily. In contrast, the registration of public affairs consultancies, law firms, freelance public affairs consultants and other similar bodies that lobby European institutions has barely got off the ground, with only 127 doing so between the date that the register opened and November 2009. There is one crucial reason for this. In order to register, they must indicate their clients' names and how much money they invest in lobbying. This puts consultants in a difficult position, both ethically (they are expected not to divulge such information about their clients) and professionally (they are reluctant to reveal how much they are paid).

Consultants would prefer simply to subscribe to the code of conduct for lobbyists that forms part of the register. They would then be penalized, or even struck off the register, if they are found to have infringed the code. They would thus be legally bound to comply with the code of conduct, without having to reveal their clients' names and payments.

The 'others' (227 as of November 2009) are academic bodies and associations of these, representatives of religions, churches and faiths, associations of public authorities and other similar bodies. Not many of these have registered. In this case, the reason is probably that such organizations do not think of themselves as lobbyists and do not allow themselves be treated in the same way as political and economic pressure groups.

Think tanks are also quite reluctant to consider themselves as lobbies and do not register willingly.

Besides, in wishing to keep the lobby register fully transparent, the Commission is exposed to the risk of hacking. One case involved a mysterious company which claimed to have a turnover forty times that of the largest firms operating in Brussels and was registered without further ado. Whether this was a case of provocation, an attempt to test the transparency of the register, or deliberate hacking, the company was swiftly unmasked as a result of outside complaints about this 'black sheep'.

First revision of the Commission's lobby register rules

After examining the experiences of the first year, the Commission considered that the voluntary approach had worked. It decided to take a further step with some improvements based on experience. Thus the Commission revised the rules of its register of interest representatives in October 2009, hoping to make rapid progress on agreeing a common register with the European Parliament. The main changes were related to the scope of the register; lawyers and think tanks; and the financial information required.

The scope of the register and specific categories of interest representatives

The review clarifies the scope of activities covered by the register, and hence to be included in making the financial estimate. The revised definition of eligible activities covers direct lobbying as well as all indirect means of lobbying such as think-tank reports, platforms, forums and campaigns. This additional guidance should facilitate the registration of a number of organizations that were still hesitant to do so.

Lawyers and think tanks

Two specific categories did not contribute fully one year after the launch of the register.

While law firms were included among the target groups from the start, they are still largely hiding behind the Bar, claiming registration is against Bar rules. The Commission is convinced that there is a way to register while respecting Bar rules. To facilitate this registration, further clarification is provided on the distinction between legal advice and lobbying. The Commission intends to pursue its contacts with the Bar associations to resolve this issue.

The review confirms the expectation that think tanks should join the register, and the revised definition further underlines that the indirect influence often pursued via events and publications organized by think tanks is to be considered a lobbying activity. To facilitate registration, a separate category for think tanks has been created within the Register, to underline their distinct character from other registrants.

Financial information required

The provision of financial information by public affairs consultancies is adapted. The experience gained in the first year demonstrated that the choice offered between expressing the relative weight of clients in brackets of either €50.000 or 10 percentage points of turnover, failed to meet the original objective. In practice, registrants choosing the percentage option have disclosed their client list, but not – as was originally intended – given adding transparency to the relative weight of those clients. This applies in particular to the large companies, with the unintended consequence that smaller companies were required to be more transparent than larger ones. The Commission is therefore replacing the current choice between brackets and percentage of turnover by client with a unique grid composed of brackets in euros of progressive size. In addition to the information already provided by the register regarding the financial resources mobilized for the purposes of interest representation, information concerning the human resources at stake is requested.

In order to decide whether the voluntary approach is definitely working, the number of registrations must continue to increase. The Commission has seen some encouraging signs, but these are not enough. If the registration of consultants and lawyers – the very lobbyists the institutions are most keen to know about – does not increase, then compulsory registration will become necessary. This will give lobbyists free access to the buildings of European institutions and enable them to be involved quite transparently in drawing up legislation.

Notes

1. The author takes full responsibility for the views expressed in this paper, which do not necessarily reflect those of the European Commission.
2. In this connection, see the comparative study of the twenty-seven EU member states, the USA and Canada, conducted on behalf of the EC by the European Institute of Public Administration: *Regulating Conflicts of Interest for Holders of Public Office in the European Union*, October 2007 (http://ec.europa.eu/dgs/policy_advisers/publications/docs/hpo_professional_ethics_en.pdf).
3. Communication to the Commission from the President, Ms Wallström, Mr Kallas, Ms Hübner and Ms Fischer Boel: 'Proposing the Launch of a European Transparency Initiative', European Commission (SEC(2005) 1300/6, p. 7.

4. The definition does not include (a) activities concerning legal and other professional advice, in so far as they relate to the exercise of the fundamental right to a fair trial of a client, including the right of defence in administrative proceedings, such as carried out by lawyers or by any other professionals involved therein; (b) activities of the social partners as actors in the social dialogue (trade unions, employers' associations, etc.). However, when such actors engage in activities falling outside the role conferred on them by the treaties, they are expected to register in order to guarantee a level playing field between all the interests represented; or (c) activities in response to the Commission's direct request, such as ad hoc or regular requests for factual information, data or expertise, invitations to public hearings, or participation in consultative committees or in any similar forums.

Bibliography

Conradt, M. (2008) *Le Cheval de Troie: Sectes et lobbies religieux à l'assaut de l'Europe* (Brussels: Editions du Grand Orient de Belgique).

Demmke C., Bovens, M., Henökl, T. and Moilanen, T. (2008) *Regulating Conflicts of Interest for Holders of Public Office in the European Union* (Maastricht: European Institute of Public Administration).

Eurobarometer 69, Fieldwork: April–May 2008.

European Commission (2004) *Code of Conduct for Commissioners* (SEC(2004) 1487/2).

European Commission (2005) *European Transparency Initiative* (ETI), (SEC(2005)1300/6).

European Commission (2006) *White Paper on a European Communication Policy*, (COM(2006) 35 final).

European Commission (2009) *European Transparency Initiative: The Register of Interest Representatives, One Year After* (COM (2009)612 final).

Melich, A. (1990) 'Problématique centre-périphérie en Espagne: intégration des groupes d'intérêt catalans à la Communauté Européenne', in D. Sidjanski and U. Ayberk (eds), *L'Europe du Sud dans la Communauté Européenne* (Paris: PUF).

Part II
Corporate Power

6
Economic Power and Social Responsibility of Very Big Enterprises: Facts and Challenges

Paul H. Dembinski

There is evidence and a broad agreement that multinational enterprises play a leading role in the world economy. However, both evidence and agreement collapse when it comes to qualifying this role in quantitative as well as qualitative terms. This chapter addresses three rather different issues but leaves aside much of the technical debate.

First, it presents some macroeconomic evidence on the aggregate weight in the world economy of the largest non-financial enterprises.

Second, it compares these enterprises to the poorest countries and discusses the deepening productivity gap.

Third, it looks at very big enterprises (VBEs) as the ultimate structuring forces of the world economy and the real drivers of globalization, and argues that self-regulation of these enterprises by corporate social responsibility (CSR)-type initiatives may well not suffice to counterbalance their long-term structuring power.

The weight of VBEs in the world economy

The focal reference of mainstream economic theory is an idealized market in which, under perfect competition, an infinite number of enterprises battle for the favours of an equally innumerable crowd of buyers. In the real-world economy, however, things are very different. In each sector or industry, a finite number of players of different sizes, products and factor-mixes pursue various strategies and have a variety of mutual relationships ranging from outright competition through various degrees of (inter)dependence to co-operation and partnership. In the context of the global open economy, major corporations play a particularly important role because of the amount of resources they control and because of the length and breadth of time and space perspectives in which they take their investment decisions. As major players in the world economy, these VBEs influence not only smaller enterprises both upstream and downstream of their value chain, but also markets and national or regional economies where their subsidiaries and partners are located.

VBEs is a useful but fuzzy concept. Below are some characteristics that help to differentiate them from the rest of the enterprise population.

Most of the VBE are *publicly listed companies*, and their shares and bonds are listed on major financial markets. In most cases, the shares of these companies belong to the most liquid on the market – that is, the least risky for financial investors. Because of this liquidity, in normal times VBEs have a preferential access to markets, which allows them to raise additional finance on more favourable terms than less liquid or non-listed companies.

The price that listed companies pay for this preferential access to finance is their supervision and regulation by market authorities. According to International Finance Corporation (IFC) data, in the year 2000 about 50,000 enterprises were listed on world stock exchanges (Dembinski, 2003: 141), but it is clear that not all qualify as VBEs.

VBEs are large enough to set up and manage worldwide networks of subsidiaries. This enables them not only to choose new sites to suit their needs, but also to optimize their global activities and skills. The often used term 'multinational enterprise' stresses this capacity of building trans-border networks. According to the United Nations Conference on Trade and Development (UNCTAD), there are about 60,000 'multinational' enterprises worldwide, which control about 500,000 affiliates across the globe. In its estimate, UNCTAD considers as 'multinational' any enterprise that has at least one affiliate. In consequence, it is obvious that not all multinationals in the UNCTAD sense are VBEs.

In an industrial society, the strength of major corporations used to derive from their ability to take full advantage of their production facilities (economies of scale) and hence charge lower prices than their smaller competitors could ever achieve. In a post-industrial society, in which marketing and service matters more than production of goods, the nature of the VBEs' advantages has changed. The strength of major corporations in a post-industrial society lies less in economies of scale on the production side rather than in their ability to manage global brands and carry out parallel activities which, even though they result in different products or services, make use of the same basic skills (economies of scope). VBEs are high-profile companies which polish and protect their images and reputations with the help of advertising and marketing campaigns. Their brand names or other identifying features enable them to interact directly with the consumers of their products and services, and in doing so they can often bypass distributors. In this way they can differentiate themselves from their competitors and dominate the markets they are in.

VBEs spend considerable proportions of their turnover on research and development (R&D) for new generations of products or services. In fact, what they are trying to do is to *control the speed of innovation*. Each business does what it can to match the speed of innovation to its own investment cycle and so optimize its profitability.

The company reports, stock markets' authorities, and listings produced by media groups – such as the famous Fortune 500, begun in 1954 – and financial data providers are the unique source of quantitative information on VBEs. Despite their apparent accessibility as a result of data processing technologies, a coherent statistical series on worldwide VBEs still does not exist. Four reasons explain this situation: (i) the diversity of reporting requirements; (ii) changes in reporting methods used by the same enterprise; (iii) lack of stability in the VBE population as a result of changes of names, mergers and acquisitions, spillovers, bankruptcies and so on; and (iv) a traditional lack of interest by statistical authorities and scholars in the economics of VBEs. On the latter point, things are beginning to change and a proper 'meso-economic' field is emerging.

Because of this lack of data for the whole group of VBEs, the empirical scope of this chapter has been narrowed to the biggest non-financial enterprises listed on a stock market. Using the Thomson Financial Database, I have been able to isolate the 800 largest enterprises worldwide according to their stock market capitalization at the end 2001.

The total turnover of the world's 800 largest non-financial enterprises is equivalent to 33 per cent of world GDP. This figure includes (i) the value-added that has been produced directly by these enterprises; and (ii) the cost of purchased inputs – that is, the value added by activities that are upstream of the buyer. As most of the VBEs use distribution networks to sell their products and services to end-users, their activity indirectly generates value added downstream which does not appear in the VBEs' books. By using a rule of thumb, according to which value added by distribution makes up about a third of the final price, then the 800 VBEs would directly or indirectly generate about half of the world's gross domestic product (GDP). The level of concentration within the group of 800 is high, and thus the 200 biggest enterprises would generate about 25 per cent of world GDP. These figures are only orders of magnitude, possibly on the high side, because they do not account for transactions that might occur within the group of 800 VBEs.

Under most of the reporting rules, companies are not required to report their value added, thus the direct contribution of VBEs to world GDP has to be calculated or estimated. Other studies (UK Government, 2003; Dembinski, 1998) have shown that value added by the major corporations represents a third of their turnover. Thus the 800 largest VBEs can reasonably be expected to generate directly 11 per cent of global GDP. The group of 800 largest enterprises, according to company reports, employs about 30 million people, which is about 1 per cent of the world's active population. The ratio of output to employment indicates that these enterprises are very high on world labour productivity tables, outperforming the average by a factor of ten.

When looking at their stock market capitalization, the same group of enterprises accounts for about 60 per cent of global stock market capitalization. As such, these enterprises receive an important share of world savings, either through their bond issues, through bank credits or through the issuing of shares. These corporations are the interface that really matters between what some people used to call 'real' and 'financial' dimensions of the world economy. When market capitalization is taken as an approximation of the capital stock used, then the productivity of capital in the biggest enterprises seems to be much lower than in the rest of the world economy.

These 800 enterprises are heavy direct investors. According to other work, namely by UNCTAD, these companies are responsible for the bulk of foreign direct investment worldwide, and for nearly all investments flowing from the North to the South. Again, because of their size and of the international spread of their activities, these enterprises are responsible for a very large proportion of world merchandise trade, which could be as high as 60 per cent (Rangan, 2001). With very few exceptions, the 800 biggest enterprises are based in the Triad countries, even if a certain proportion of their activities takes place in the South.

VBEs and the poorest countries: how deep is the gap?

This set of rough estimates of the weight that major corporations play in the world economy runs against the normal way of looking at the economy, which takes national economies as the normal unit of analysis. Figure 6.1 compares the 800 biggest enterprises to the 144 poorest countries. Because of the differing nature of the two sets of actors, it is more appropriate to speak of juxtaposition rather than a true comparison. The two sets of actors have one magnitude in common; both contribute 11 per cent to the world GDP. This being said, all the other

Figure 6.1 Economic and financial weight of the world's 800 largest enterprises compared to the 114 poorest countries

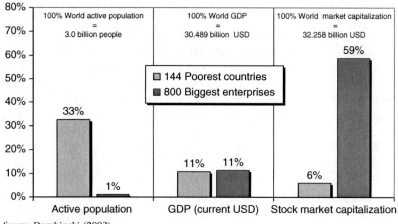

Source: Dembinski (2003).

data are at odds: employment, stock market capitalization, FDI and trade.

The quantitative evidence presented here helps to identify two sets of problems. The first is related to the productivity gap, while the second is related to the structuring power the VBEs exert on the societies of the South.

The VBEs – as is clearly shown for the 800 biggest – use a factor-mix very different from the one present in the poorest countries. The capital intensity per unit of GDP is ten times higher in the VBEs than in the poorest countries, and it is also much higher than in the rest of the economies in the North. In other words, because of their privileged access to capital markets, VBEs are able to substitute capital for labour at a much higher level than any other player in the world economy. This explains both the specific factor mix used by these companies and the speed of their technological change. Growing substitution also means that an increasing part of the value added generated by VBEs goes to capital owners – predominantly located in the North – as their remuneration. The poorest countries are in exactly opposite situations: because of a lack of local savings and the liquidity in international financial markets, local savings are siphoned off by major players, so the labour-intensive bias in their factor mix is set to remain or even to deepen. Labour-intensive countries will continue to be used by the

VBEs as places where the manufacturing activities that are labour intensive will take place, or where, because of low wages, the substitution
of labour by capital does not – for the present – make sense. In other
words, through the interface of VBEs, the labour-intensive countries
are competing against cheap and abundant capital, not against highly
qualified labour in Northern countries. In consequence, there are no
systemic reasons why the productivity gap should narrow in the future.
Left to itself, the logic of accelerating substitution of labour through
capital in the North will most probably continue in the future, and
consequently the productivity gap will widen between the North and
the South.

The second set of problems is closely linked to the previous one.
Taking into account that VBEs are major foreign direct investors, major
trade partners, and owners of global brands striving to service global
markets, these enterprises are the effective 'interdependence links' that
make different parts of the world economy work together. They are the
real builders of (inter)dependencies: but in most cases they are able to
keep an 'arbitraging' position for themselves.

Efficiency, ethics or politics? Will the structuring power of VBEs remain unbalanced by accountability?

Enterprises, especially the VBEs, have been the main conduits through
which globalization has shaped the face of the contemporary world.
During the last quarter of the twentieth century, VBEs were undoubtedly the major conduits of globalization and as such played a major role
in speeding structural changes in the world economy.

VBEs were among the first to take full advantage of the potentialities
offered by the development of information technology (IT). On the one
hand, by integrating this technology into their products, they proved
able to develop new products and new services based on the principle
of controlling feedback loops. But on the other, enterprises also rapidly
learned how to make the best use of IT in organizing and running their
own operations worldwide.

International business started well before free trade came into focus
among policy-makers. In the aftermath of the Second World War,
American VBEs were in an excellent position to establish themselves as
world leaders. However, in the following decades they had to face growing competition, including in their home markets, from Japanese and
European counterparts. The VBEs' golden age began in the 1980s, when

political context and technological potential coincided to make the management of truly global enterprises possible. In parallel, VBEs became a worldwide pressure group, having a major influence on the agendas not only of governments but also of international organizations.

The ethos of efficiency became universal, providing a supra-cultural basis on which professional and technical knowledge began to be shared among people from different cultural origins, but inspired by the same ambitions and ethos. Falling on this fertile ground, the ethos of efficiency (Dembinski, 2009) was then further spread by a growing number of business schools and inculcated in a new generation of people eager to have their share in the economic success of international business. By doing so, business schools developed a whole range of new fields of professional knowledge rooted and inspired by the ethos of efficiency. Today this knowledge has, at least partially, achieved scientific status. But the present crisis is putting this knowledge in question.

Enterprises are, by definition, social organizations capable of rapid evolution in response to changing conditions and therefore are often seen as organizational innovators. Undoubtedly, VBEs have played this role and, in this way, have contributed to the acceleration of globalization. Three main lines of organizational innovation – in the broad sense – deserve to be mentioned here: the move from product to service; the 'invention' of intangible assets as forms of capital deserving remuneration; and the growing capacity of VBEs to organize the work of others and thus avoid the commitment of their own capital (Dembinski, 2001). Each of these has fundamentally affected the modes of interaction between the VBEs and their social and economic environment, and in consequence has contributed to redesigning the set of corresponding interdependencies.

Paradoxically, the new interdependencies threaten the proper functioning of the market mechanism, and by doing so call into question the quality of allocation of resources realized worldwide under the auspices of globalization. This point is clearly illustrated by the differences in capital productivity between VBEs that have an easy and cheap access to capital and non-listed enterprises, not to speak of the poorest countries, many of which are highly indebted.

Some fields of human activity are more prone to globalization than others. It seems that less globalized activities may be condemned to bear the whole burden of adjustment to changes imposed by the more globalized layers of human activity. Therefore, the apparent interdependencies between activities at different levels of globalization tend to turn into asymmetrical relations whereby less globalized activities become dependent on more globalized ones. This is true among enterprises, where the competitive advantage of global VBEs increases the strength of their position with respect to their smaller and more local partners and suppliers, and it is also true for countries linked together by the activities of the largest enterprises. There is an analogy, but not a complete identity, between this conclusion and the reading of globalization in terms of the 'centre versus periphery' paradigm.

The transformation of interdependencies into genuine dependency relationships brings the question of power to the forefront. Power is an integral part of globalization and has to be addressed explicitly. This necessity is barely acknowledged today, and the VBEs structure the world economy (and society) in a political vacuum, where transnational regulations either do not exist or are purely functional. In this sense there is a growing and urgent need to fill the vacuum with appropriate governance solutions. This being said, when putting in place these solutions one should be careful not to give purely economic and efficiency-seeking considerations an overwhelming weight in social life. A successful international architecture could help to prevent whole societies from becoming consenting slaves of a holistic design whose ideological and anthropological roots could be called 'fully-fledged economicism'. Globalization is only one dimension of this design, one step on the road to a full market – a purely transactional civilization.

The challenge of governance has to be addressed from two extremes: one is institutional design; and the second is acknowledgement by growing numbers of people and organizations that we all have a responsibility to work for the common good, which extends far beyond the purely economic dimension. At this stage of the analysis, initiatives that aim to increase awareness among enterprises of their corporate social responsibility come to the fore. Such initiatives blossom across the whole spectrum of organizations: NGOs, enterprise associations and international organizations. These initiatives de facto pose the fundamental and normative question about the genuine nature of the enterprise: is it only an instrument for capital owners to extract profits and shareholder value, by or is it a community that has to focus on the harmonious development of all its members?

As long as the 'ethos of efficiency' prevails unchallenged, there is no reason why the gap should narrow between the North and the South. But the recent extension of CSR concerns may well lead to the consolidation of an 'ethos of humanism'. It is to early to say if these changes will suffice to change the present trend. But if it does not happen then worlds will fall apart.

Bibliography

Bartesman, E. and Beetsma, R. (2000) *Why Pay More? Corporate Tax Avoidance through Transfer Pricing in OECD Countries*, vol. 2543, CEPR Discussion paper (London: Centre for Economic Policy Research), August.

Dembinski, P. H. and Schoenenberger, A. (1998) 'Safe Landing of the Financial Balloon Is Not Impossible', *Finance & the Common Good/Bien Commun*, 1,: 35–45.

Dembinski, P. H. (2001) 'The New Global Economy: Emerging Forms of (Inter)dependence', in *Globalization – Ethical and Institutional Concerns* (Vatican City: Pontifical Academy of Social Sciences) , pp. 83–108.

Dembinski, P. H. (2003) *Economic and Financial Globalization : What the Numbers Say* (New York/Geneva: United Nations) (http://www.un.org/Pubs/whatsnew/e02344.htm).

Dembinski, P. H. (2009) *Finance: Servant or Deceiver? Financialization at the Crossroads* (Basingstoke: Palgrave Macmillan).

OECD (2002) *Measuring Globalisation: The Role of Multinationals in OECD Economies* (Paris: Organisation for Economic Co-operation and Development).

Rangan, S. (2001) *Explaining Tranquility in the Midst of Turbulence: US Multinationals' Intrafirm Trade 1966–1997*, Bureau of Labor Statistics, US Labor Department.

UK Government/Dept of Trade and Industry (2003) *The Value Added Scoreboard 2003: The Top 800 UK & Top 600 European Companies by Value Added* (London: DTI, 2003).

UNCTAD (2000) *World Investment Report 2000: Cross-border Mergers and Acquisitions and Development* (Geneva/New York: United Nations).

7
Economic Power: Competition Law, Economic Evaluation and Policy Implications

Vindelyn Smith-Hillman and Adam Scott

Introduction

A keen interest in the measurement of economic power, particularly from regulatory authorities, derives from its potentially adverse impact on resource allocation. The concept of economic power encapsulates the dual forces of market (monopoly) power and political power. It is generally associated with the large-scale accumulation of wealth and significant assets. When viewed from political, economic and ethical perspectives it is seen as a 'threat to the operation of both economy and society' (Gerber, 2001: 87). The threat derives from ills associated with the economic dependency of one firm on another, and with the potential for the poor treatment of workers. An alternative view focuses on its unfair representation that amounts to a punishment of entrepreneurial skills. In particular, Peritz (2000) perceives the animosity generated by economic power as evidence of the tension between the rhetorics of competition and property. This perception is especially unfair when economic power reflects commercial success as a result of the fruits of research and development (R&D) or economies of scale from which an economy benefits.

The demonstrated potential of economic power to affect social welfare – that is, the total well-being of an economy – lies at the heart of concerns regarding economic power. The measurement of economic power has become increasingly complex as markets have evolved and changed. Previously, firms grew organically, reliant on internal competence, and they generally maintained a fairly narrow focus on the production of a few goods or services. It is now increasingly the case that growth is pursued through mergers and acquisitions to the extent that a few very large firms dominate the global stage with a diverse range of products and services. This market transformation has introduced greater complexity into the economic evaluation of welfare, as the major international firms tend not to account for a dominant share of any single market. Against this background, the aim of this chapter is twofold: to explore perspectives on economic power and evaluate the robustness of various measures; and to examine the policy implications that arise from an evolving market structure.

Concerns regarding the effects of economic power have informed the drafting of regional and national competition laws, and established a benchmark of good/bad competitive behaviour. Competition law, complemented by regulatory guidelines, effectively sets rules governing competitive conduct by dominant firms in the private sector, and sometimes also in the public sector.

Competition law has interdisciplinary origins drawing on concepts of both law and economics. Some competition policies, such as the US antitrust policies, have generally pursued balanced application of both disciplines to the administration and enforcement of competition policy. However, European administration and enforcement has leant heavily on legal analysis. Indeed, it is only fairly recently, following the 2005 review of Article 82 TEC (now Article 102 TFEU) which guides European Union (EU) competition policy and deals with the abuse of dominance, that policy has incorporated greater economic analysis of firms' behaviour in order to reach a decision regarding the economic effects of significant market power (SMP). Practical difficulties in adopting an economics-based approach occur at two critical junctures: defining significant market power in the absence of a clear and uncontested definition of economic power, and measuring economic power given the acknowledged limitations of existing techniques.

This chapter is structured as follows; the next section discusses perspectives on economic power; the third section highlights the difficulties of its practical measurement from a competition law perspective; and the fourth section addresses policy implications that subsequently arise. The concluding section suggests some emerging themes.

Perspectives on economic power

Economic power exists within a market context and is often discussed with reference to a competitive ideal. Much has been written about the virtues of perfectly competitive markets based on the associated welfare benefit of economic efficiency. Economic efficiency describes the joint existence of three types of efficiency: *allocative efficiency*, efficiently producing what consumers demand; *technical efficiency*, where goods or services are produced at the lowest cost; and *distributional efficiency*, where goods are allocated in keeping with individuals' preferences and income constraint.

Despite the fact that economic power is associated with imperfect competition – and therefore cannot lay claim to economic efficiency in the strict economic sense, it is possible for firms with economic power to outperform a firm operating within a perfectly competitive context. For example, when compared to a firm operating within a perfectly competitive market, a monopoly undertaking may potentially deliver innovative, relatively lower priced products, based on economies of scale and investing profits in R&D.

While there is general agreement that economic power constitutes a powerful influence, there is no consensus on what constitutes an accurate portrayal. A number of definitions reflect this tension through recourse to contrasts. For example, Frost (2009) distinguishes between a firm-specific and a country-specific definition, where the former describes economic power as the 'ability to control or influence the behaviour of others through the deliberate and politically motivated use of economic assets' (Frost, 2009: 9). In contrast, a country view aligns a government with the capacity to 'use, offer, or withhold such assets even when they are in private hands' (Frost, 2009: 10). Both quotations illustrate an awareness of an interdependent relationship where economic power signals the absence of self-sufficiency. Sellers need to have a market in which to sell. If all buyers are able to, and decide to, withdraw their custom, the force associated with economic power becomes an empty threat. The apparent ability and implicit threat to withdraw may constitute an effective countervailing power.

In a similar vein, Peritz (2000) contrasts economic power with market power, where a narrower definition of market power refers to a firm's market share that is restricted to a particular location. By contrast, economic power encapsulates a large-scale accumulation of wealth, as might be signalled by large corporate size. On the basis of great wealth in a corporate group, a subsidiary is able to move into a new area and establish a prime position, ousting a previously well-established local business or businesses. A much quoted example of the formidable financial power of a company is Wal-Mart Stores, Inc. (now branded as Walmart). The company has often been accused of driving out local business as it offers a diversified range of products and services housed under a single roof, and has the capacity to cross-subsidize less successful products with the profits from lucrative ventures.

Walter Eucken (Oswalt-Eucken, 1994) identified the political power behind economic power, as demonstrated in the German case. Arms manufacturers exerted such a considerable influence in the country that they were able to block political decisions and ignore the national consensus that arms should not be exported to areas of conflict. Decisions on governmental spending in favour of granting subsidies to well-established trusts, such as Daimler-Benz (as it was known at the time), provided further evidence of the force of economic power.

Expressing similar opinions to Eucken's, Amato (1997), former chairman of the Italian Antitrust Authority, emphasized the significance of the political dimension to economic power. This aligns with the changing nature of markets as mergers between firms have repositioned firms on a global stage. Newly emergent oligopolistic firms mean that industries become dominated by a few big interdependent firms, each operating across a broad range of products and/or services. They tend not to display market power in any single product but have the capacity to displace small local firms by virtue of their size and leverage. Hence Amato identifies the conundrum as 'a big firm that does not have economic power over a market that has expanded beyond national limits may nonetheless have in the domestic political process that abusive power' (Amato, 1997: 104).

Shifting perspectives on economic power are increasingly acknowledged as various writers recognize the interplay between institutions and markets over time. Tilly (1994) identifies the current European interstate system as arising from the amalgamation of coercive and economic power between AD1000 and 1800. Economic power was held within the cities where capital was accumulated and was ultimately used to finance military activity, and this has been reinforced as modern nation states seek to extend their ambit of control. Similarly, Frost (2009) also recognizes the historical connection but applies it to the changed asset base, as the superiority of physical assets has gradually given way to intangible efficacy through sound macro policies, a stable financial climate and good governance procedures.

The European perspective on economic power reflects the influence of German economists and lawyers of the ordoliberalist school that was pre-eminent during the 1920s. The group included Ludwig Erhard, who became the economic leader of the postwar Federal Republic of Germany and played a critical role in creating the Common Market, and Friedrich Hayek who was influential in moving the political debate on from John Maynard Keynes. This group is credited with advancing discussions around the consequences of economic power and was one

of the earliest to recognize the significant power base of cartel organizations and its inherent capacity to have an adverse impact on national
welfare. Their interest derives from the German experience under Nazi
rule, when the law became a tool of political power used to attain economic power. Against this background they recommended the prohibi-
tion of monopoly enterprises or the careful monitoring of those already
in existence.

In summary, therefore, economic power derives from having a global
presence and arises from a firm, typically a multinational corporation,
extending its spatial reach beyond the local domain. Economic power
may be evidenced through market power at the domestic level but this
is not an essential condition defining its presence. By virtue of its global links, it is able to enhance performance at the level of local firms
regardless of the sphere in which it operates. It has deeper pockets to
withstand the vagaries of a local market to which small businesses may
be vulnerable, or indeed even a firm with a considerable domestic presence, as both lack a global network. The benefit of a global platform
provides a subsidiary with access to a substantial range of human, technical and indeed political resources. Nevertheless, some industries, such
as the telecommunications and motor vehicle sectors, are currently
experiencing budgetary pressures.

The measurement of economic power

Economic power derives from having a global presence and therefore its
measurement moves the focus beyond domestic market considerations
and requires the evaluation of the full range of a firm's operations. In
particular, Peritz's (2000) perspective of economic power suggests the
wholesale inclusion of all of a firm's assets, extending to those of its
subsidiaries. Global operations signal the critical role of multinational
corporations (MNCs), or indeed transnational corporations (TNCs),
since they own and control assets across a range of countries and are
characterized by their international operations.

Global Policy Forum (www.globalpolicy.org) identifies the top ten
transnational corporations, as shown in Table 7.1.

According to the *World Investment Report* (UNCTAD, 2008), in 2006
Wal-Mart had 146 foreign affiliates with foreign assets valued at
US$110,199 million; ExxonMobil had 278 and held foreign assets
valued at US$154,993 million; and Royal Dutch Shell had 518 foreign
affiliates, with foreign assets valued at US$161,122 million. The control
and ownership of foreign assets provides some indication of the breadth

Table 7.1 The ten largest transnational corporations, 2008

Rank	Company	Revenues (US$m)	Profits (US$m)
1	Wal-Mart Stores	378,799	12,731
2	Exxon Mobil	372,824	40,610
3	Royal Dutch Shell	355,782	31,331
4	BP	291,438	20,845
5	Toyota Motor	230,201	15,042
6	Chevron	210,783	18,688
7	ING Group	201,516	12,649
8	Total	187,280	18,042
9	General Motors	182,347	−38,732
10	Conoco Phillips	178,558	11,891

Source: http://www.globalpolicy.org/component/content/article/221-transnational-corporation.

of product coverage. The extent of TNC trade is illustrated through the evidence that companies, such as General Motors (with 115 foreign affiliates), account for approximately a third of world trade through transactions among different entities within the same body (Anderson and Cavanagh, 2000). However, notwithstanding indicators attesting to the number of foreign subsidiaries, it is widely acknowledged that TNCs operate within complex structures of networked holdings, as exemplified by Italian and Japanese groups, which make it difficult to get an accurate perspective of the extent of their group activities (see Hurley and Scott, 2008, on issues of parental power and responsibility within groups).

To some extent, economic power may be inferred from profitability, whereby excessive profits over some recognized industry average return signal a firm's ability to extract monopoly rents. Two scenarios are indicated: firms have the ability to set their own price which is considerably above the average cost; and/or firms operate at such an efficient level that potential rivals are unable to compete. The fact that other competitors have not entered the market to share above-average profit rates suggests that there is some barrier preventing entrance. They may, for example, face an inhibiting level of entrance costs. The efficiency argument generally arises from economies of scale, as oligopolistic firms are able to exploit the advantages of large size through negotiating cost reductions with their suppliers, or having an enhanced ability to engage in cost-saving production strategies. Alternatively, barriers may exist through government subsidies or special permits, as Eucken demonstrated in the case of Germany. Or, as demonstrated in the case of Wal-Mart, benefiting from government zoning laws. Finally, dominant firms could be engaging in anti-competitive conduct such as predatory pricing – that is, setting prices below average cost – which makes it difficult for new firms to enter the market at a competitive price.

On the other hand, what appears to be a profitable firm may be an illusion – as has recently been demonstrated in the banking sector. For example, Australia's largest investment bank, Macquarie Bank, recorded a 52.0 per cent reduction in profit from AU\$1.8 billion to AU\$871 million at the end of the financial year 2009 relative to the previous year (http://www.gmanews.tv/print/159406). In 2008, one of the most prestigious US banking establishments, Lehman Brothers, became a casualty of the subprime mortgage loans affair. Its exposure was thought to have been in the region of US\$300 billion (£167 billion), one of the largest, following a strategy of aggressive property-related investments in what is now thought to be effectively worthless stock (Voluntary Petition to the US Bankruptcy Court, Southern District of New York, 14 September 2008) (*Guardian, 2008*).

There are also the well-documented cases of financial impropriety as captured through the experience of WorldCom and Enron. Prior to the demise of WorldCom in 2002/3 it was the global leader of the telecommunications industry, responsible for 50 per cent of US internet traffic and 50 per cent of global e-mails. By falsifying balance sheets it was able to hide US\$3.8 billion in expenses. Meanwhile Enron was a leading player in the gas and energy industries and in its heyday was the company perceived as having the most innovative business strategy. In fact it had exploited a loophole in the US generally accepted accounting principles. By the end of 2002 this culminated in repayment debt obligations in excess of US\$9 billion and a public downgrading in Moody's credit rating (Cherubini, 2008).

But even in the absence of financial impropriety there are well-documented limitations associated with using profit as an indicator of financial power, underpinning one facet of economic power. For example, Geroski (1991) identified the limitation associated with its interpretation – that is, the extent to which profitability should be interpreted as backward- or forward-looking. In the case of a backward-looking perspective, profits were merely indicative of past trends; however, a forward-looking perspective was made with reference to what might conceivably occur in the long run if, for example, other competitors were to enter the market.

In the absence of an unequivocal definition of economic power, market power has been substituted as a viable proxy. How can measures used to ascertain market power be further developed to provide a clearer indication of economic power? A partial solution has seen the introduction of SMP into the analytical process of EU competition policy generally and into the regulation of the communications market in particular. In the latter, SMP is detailed in Articles 14(2) and 14(3) of the Framework Directive 2002/21/EC. This extends the scope of market power to encapsulate a broader perspective such that SMP reflects 'a position of economic strength affording it the power to behave to an appreciable extent independently of competitors, customers and ultimately consumers'. This has had an impact on the approach to market analysis by extending the scope of the relevant market and adopting a more dynamic approach as against static evaluation.

Policy implications

Competition policy is embodied not simply in competition law but also in a governance framework and in priorities that in fact determine the implementation of policy and enforcement of the law. These priorities may be distinct from the policy espoused in legislating and in creating regulatory institutions. Policy-makers have responded to the global challenge of an evolving oligopolistic market structure by maintaining an active presence in debate (see, for example, the International Competition Network (ICN) at www.internationalcompetitionnetwork. org). Increased co-operation between competition authorities has fostered a joined-up approach to common problems experienced. In particular, as the market structure has transformed into global oligopolistic operations, a global approach is more likely to identify problems than is an individual country approach.

From as early as the 1950s, J. K. Galbraith identified the limitations of traditional market power measures within competition policy. Amato (1997: 107) speaks of the prevention of economic power 'oligopoly is the proof that something has irreversibly slipped through the filter' using traditional market power measures and citing the need for a broader concept of economic power. Competition authorities increasingly have to deal with the issues raised by economic power on both sides of the Atlantic.

The European Commission competition authority's perspective on economic power was captured in the Michelin case: see Bellamy and Child (2008). The Court of Justice took into account the full breadth of the company's operations beyond that immediately represented by the case. This approach was also evident in a later case involving Van Den Bergh Foods Ltd, the Court of First Instance included in its evaluation the evidence that it was a well-known brand and part of a multinational corporation. But this is not necessarily an uncontentious view, as demonstrated in the subsequent Hoffmann–La Roche Ltd vitamins case. The Court of Justice took a narrower market power view, excluding resources that were not employed in the production or supply of goods.

The difficulty in the administration of competition law within the European Union context arises from differing perspectives as to what constitutes the relevant market. The focus is generally on the product market, whereby dominance, typically measured through market share, has to be proved in order to pursue a claim that an abuse of the dominant position has taken place. However, in relation to economic power, where MNCs operate on a global scale, there is the increased likelihood of subsidiaries operating below the market share threshold but none the less being able to pose a sufficient threat to local firms through an enhanced resource base. However, the adoption of an SMP measure provides some insurance against this risk.

Peritz (2000) subsequently questions the extent to which MNCs should be penalized for economic success. Their economic success potentially becomes subject to censure, and risks becoming the target of competition investigations given their breadth of product coverage. There are concerns regarding the potential for adverse long-term economic welfare implications if MNCs do not have the incentive to produce. This position is held by some fringe groups, such as the US-based 'Citizens Against Government Waste'. In particular, they suggest that a European competition vendetta exists against US business. However, EU and US evidence refute this policy inclination. For example, in 2000, the merger of AOL and Time Warner was allowed by the EU, albeit following some concessions on the companies' part. Further, the US Department of Justice opposed the merging of Oracle and Peoplesoft, but the EU subsequently waved it through in 2004. An alternative view highlights the evidence that global entities also carry less easily quantifiable costs, such as a loss of the sense of community and a loss of confidence in the food supply chain.

Considerations of economic power and the critical role played by MNCs questions the perspective held by Friedman (1970). It was his belief that firms should not be concerned with the public interest as this moved valuable and scarce resources away from the business of making profits for shareholders. Champlin and Knoedler (2003) provide a historical evaluation tracing the role of the public interest in US corporation law, and demonstrate that before the first half of the nineteenth century there was state legislature explicitly requiring a direct expression of public interest within the corporate form. However, as the modern corporation grew in size and gained increasing political clout, the 'specific obligation by business enterprise to serve the public interest ... became a historical artefact' (Champlin and Knoedler, 2003: 307).

Within the European context, the public interest dimension may be inferred through the objective of EC competition policy which includes the promotion of EU integration (see Smith-Hillman, 2006: 36). Since the objective of a united Europe is enhanced regional welfare, this suggests that there is also an interest in ensuring that firms operate in a manner befitting increased opportunities for job creation, innovation and increased choice among goods and services at competitive prices. In reality, this is a fraught process with no guaranteed preferred outcome. For example, in the case of mergers, decisions by competition authorities are often predicated on evidence of market concentration within a particular product range. If market concentration exceeds an identified threshold, or turnover value, the request to merge may be denied. However, an MNC with economic power may escape detection on the basis of this measure as it falls below the threshold in that market. The incorporation of the SMP concept within EU policy deliberations goes some way towards reducing this risk.

Conclusion

There is evidence of the more concentrated global reach of MNCs. It is estimated that, of the 100 largest economies in the world, fifty-one were global corporations and only forty-nine were countries (Anderson and Cavanagh, 2000). The growing wealth, distribution network and with it the political power to influence policy decision-making raises complex issues. In particular, to what extent should governments intervene?

The ordoliberals would seek to contain economic power, highlighting its corrosive nature, as evidenced during 1920s Germany and equally apparent today. Anderson and Cavanagh (2000) accuse the top 200 MNCs of being 'net job destroyers' and, contrary to the belief that MNCs foster job creation and increase choice in goods and services – in fact they contribute to a decline in economic welfare. This is the view held by anti-Wal-Mart protestors, who campaign against the establishment of Wal-Mart stores in their area (see Ortega, 1999). Similar groups have also formed in the UK in response to the growing economic clout of Tesco. In the ninety years since it was established, this supermarket chain has transformed from selling largely grocery and related items to increasingly diversified activities spanning a wide range of products and increased geographical spread. It has followed a similar trajectory to that of Wal-Mart in playing a leading role in facilitating the economic decline of local communities as small local stores close in its wake, and jobs are lost, unable to compete with the combined MNC resource base.

The demonstrated need for governments to act decisively has gained growing, if reluctant, momentum in the wake of the credit crisis. The economic power of financial institutions was evident through the extent of their global operations and their capacity to influence decision-making at the highest level.

There are lessons to be learnt from the failure to regulate. In particular, the adverse effects of inaction have global macroeconomic consequences, as demonstrated by the decline in economic growth throughout Western economies alongside the rise in global unemployment that has under-pinned the recession throughout the developed world. The call for gov-ernment action is conflicted by its potential to replace private power; hence the question, 'Where lie the bounds of power?' (Amato, 1997).

Bibliography

Amato, G. (1997) *Antitrust and the Bounds of Power: The Dilemma of Liberal Democracy in the History of the Market* (Oxford: Hart).

Anderson, S. and Cavanagh, J. (2000) 'Top 200: The Rise of Global Corporate Power', at http://www.globalpolicy.org/component/content/article/221-transnational-corporations.

Bellamy, C. and Child, G. (2008) *European Community Law of Competition*, 6th edn (eds P. Roth and V. Rose), (Oxford University Press).

Champlin, D. and Knoedler, J. (2003) 'Corporations, Workers and the Public Interest', *Journal of Economic Issues*, 37(2): 305–13.

Cherubini, U. (2008) 'Accounting Data, Transparency and Credit Spreads', in N. Wagner (ed.), *Credit Risk: Models, Derivatives and Management* (London: CRC/Taylor & Francis), pp. 115–38.

Ethical Corporation (2005) 'Not Soft on Microsoft'. Available at http://www.ethicalcorp.com/content.asp?ContentID=3661; accessed 27 July 2009.

European Regulators Group (2003) 'ERG Working Paper on the SMP concept for the New Regulatory Framework – May 2003'. Available at http://www.erg.ec.europa.eu; accessed 27 July 2009.

Friedman, M. (1970) 'The Social Responsibility of Business Is to Increase its Profits', *New York Times Magazine*, September: 32–3 and 122–6.

Frost, B. (2009) 'What Is Economic Power?', *Joint Forces Quarterly*, 53 (2nd Quarter): 8–11.

Gerber, D. (2001) *Law and Competition in Twentieth Century Europe: Protecting Prometheus* (Oxford University Press).

Geroski, P. (1991) *Technology and National Competitiveness*, ed. Jorge Niosi (Montreal and Kingston, Ontario: McGill—Queen's University Press).

GMA NEWS.TV (2009) 'Macquarie Bank Profits Collapse 52 percent'. Available at http://www.gmanews.tv/print/159406; accessed 1 July 2009.

Guardian (2008) 'Banking Crisis: Lehman Brothers Files for Bankruptcy Protection'. Available at http://www.guardian.co.uk/business/2008/sep/15/lehmanbrothers.creditcrunch; accessed 27 July 2009.

Hurley, S. and Scott, A. (2008) 'The Concept of an Undertaking and the Responsibility of Parent Companies for the Actions of Subsidiaries in the EU and UK', *Competition Law Journal*; 301–23.

Ortega, B. (1999) *In Sam We Trust: The Untold Story of Sam Walton and How Wal-Mart is Devouring the World* (London: Kogan Page).

Oswalt-Eucken, I. (1994) 'Freedom and Economic Power: Neglected Aspects of Walter Euken's Work', *Journal of Economic Studies*, 21(4): 38–45.

Peritz, R. (2000) *Competition Policy in America: History, Rhetoric, Law* (Oxford University Press).

Smith-Hillman, A. (2006) 'EC Approach to Governance as Applied to the Modernisation of EC Competition Policy', *European Business Review*, 18(1): 33–49.

Tilly, C. (1994) 'Entanglements of European Cities and States', in C. Tilly and W. Blockmans (eds) *Cities and the Rise of States in Europe AD 1000 to 1800* (Boulder, Col.: Westview Press).

UNCTAD (2008) *World Investment Report, 2008*. Available at http://www.unctad.org; accessed 1 July 2009.

8
International Companies in Places of Instability: The Issue of Mutual Capture

Justin Welby

Introduction

In the late eighteenth and early nineteenth centuries the British more or less accidentally acquired one of the largest empires in history, the jewel of which, India, was run by a private company until 1857. The East India Company (or 'John Company' as it was popularly known) had begun in 1600 as a group of London merchants trading initially with Java and other parts of modern Indonesia, and when this failed because of Dutch opposition, with India. The aim was profit, not conquest, and to this extent they were no different from the modern multinationals. The causes of the expansion of the Empire are complex, but one element is significant for us. The collapse of the official government (the Moghul Empire) and the fracturing of its area of suzerainty led to immense violence and instability across the subcontinent. The area controlled by the British tended to be governed efficiently, but on its borders there was either anarchy or threat. The solution was to control those areas and create security along the borders. But as soon as the new area was settled (often ruthlessly) the same pattern appeared, and so it was necessary to go yet further afield. Empire was acquired in the service of commerce, and then commerce to finance Empire, and there was no logical end so long as the British offered more security than the surrounding area.

There are two reasons for telling this (rather over-simplified) story. First, it illustrates a dilemma for international companies, and second, it demonstrates that the dilemma is not new.

The dilemma is essentially an outworking of the principle of unintended consequences. The nature of the complexity of societies means that all actions on a scale that affects communities will lead to some results that are not acceptable or desired. Societies in direct conflict, or proximate pre- or post-conflict, are especially complex, in that the volatile character of war and violence is mixed into the normal complexity of social existence. Where extractive industries are concerned, the natural resource curse is likely to result in weak governance at a local level, and usually even nationally. There are no examples of this level of complexity being overcome, even if it is theoretically possible.

In this chapter I intend to split the issue into three parts. First, I shall look at the generic weaknesses in governance and social stability that lead to conflict, and the way in which this makes countries endowed with natural resource wealth especially vulnerable. Second, I shall describe briefly the problems in the Niger Delta. And finally, I shall attempt to draw some conclusions in terms of socially responsible investment (SRI) in areas of instability.

Imported wealth or natural resources accelerate indigenous weakness

Multinational companies are usually a source of focused and well-organized wealth when they are working in countries with extensive problems of poverty. Especially where the guest company is extracting minerals or hydrocarbons, its influence is likely to have a negative effect on local governance in a number of ways:[1]

- *Investment pressure.* Almost all the mineral resources of Sub-Saharan Africa have been developed with international capital, at least initially. In most of the continent this has led to distortions in the local economy that weaken the capacity of indigenous industry to remain competitive. In the nineteenth century, the area to become Nigeria was (and still could be) one of the world's principal suppliers of palm oil, but the discovery of crude oil in 1956 in Ogoniland and the subsequent over-valuation of the naira in the 1970s have all but eliminated most home developed agriculture and industry commercially. The pressure to invest may also lead to the incurring of large international debts, rendering the country's economy very vulnerable to externally imposed shocks as a result of international financial crises, or sharp variations in oil price. Oil is a particular danger. The calculation of net present value and the high discount rates often applied to what are seen as inherently risky areas of investment, mean that returns deferred are worth little in current terms. The calculation of return thus demands accelerated production and the rapid recovery of costs.

These triple pressures of external investment, rapid cost recovery (often through intra company charging) and the necessity of maintaining production at a high level, make the passage of time one of the most severe costs of investment. The company and the government risk being caught in a devil's partnership that encourages the speeding up of decisions by corruption, and delays for reasons of democracy, local accountability, subsidiarity, environmental or community protection, to name but a few, become primarily economic and not ethical factors with an outcome based on consequentialism, not virtue.

• *Patronage cultures.* Following the Congress of Berlin in 1878, the European powers divided up Africa according to their convenience and without reference to the indigenous sociology and governance. If respected at all, this was as a result of accidents of conquest rather than intention. This inherent weakness of natural borders combines with a strong patronage culture in which those who take office, even when elected, are closely bound to a network that expects reward. Europe is little different, but usually under the camouflage of parties and honours – for example, a seat in the House of Lords in the UK Parliament may be the reward for loyalty, and in France mayors are expected to bring home the bacon if they achieve high national office. However, in many African countries such expectations are accentuated by tribalism and ethnic pressure. Nigeria as we know it today was created from two British protectorates in 1914 by Lord Lugard, to enable the more prosperous, predominantly Christian, south to finance the economically weaker, Muslim, north. The state that emerged in 1960 at the declaration of independence was thus artificial, and led to civil war in the late 1960s, and internal struggle on many occasions since. To this day the north is subsidized by oil, which diminishes self-respect, marginalizes its own energy and skills, and turns politics into a competition for access to revenue.

The result is that the natural systems of governance have fault lines running through them that are easy to exploit, deliberately or as a result of other factors.

• *Elite domination.* Countries suffering from instability, and especially those with large natural resources, are most easily controlled by ruling elites, usually aligned with militias. The small number of companies and financial institutions capable of participating in the business of exploitation of reserves are able to relate closely to those in a position to grant access. Combined with the natural tendency towards hierarchical societies that remains typical of significant parts of Sub-Saharan Africa, the existence of oil and other natural resources encourages rapid exploitation to maintain the domination of a small and often interrelated elite.

The widespread use of militias and the existence of mercenary forces in the service of warlords also provides a narrow funnel of influence rather than the more widespread base of power found in functional democracies.

- *Poor governance.* Strategic planning, especially of the use of natural resources, springs from a capacity for systems of governance to operate the political structures, balancing the requirements of public approval with long-term benefit. Political structures that are weak will tend towards short-termism. They will suffer from a lack of confidence and the capacity to restrain the operations of corporate entities with powerful international links and the support of their host governments.

A working example: the Niger Delta

This is obviously a very simplified view of the problem of the vulnerability of governance, but it provides a background to what I shall now address, namely the Niger Delta.

Much of the material that follows is drawn from the work of Dr Stephen Davis, a former colleague at the International Centre for Reconciliation (now called the Community of the Cross of Nails, or CCN) at Coventry Cathedral in the UK. The material on the Niger Delta is taken from an unpublished research event held in Coventry, UK.[2]

The general context

Oil was first discovered in the Niger Delta in 1956, near Port Harcourt in the region of the Ogoni people.[3] This area is today the sixth-largest producer of crude oil in the world, with a production potential of about 2.5 million barrels per day, and is well on the way to becoming one of the world's largest exporters of liquid natural gas. The geography is low-lying swamp or near-swamp, and the historical industries were fishing and farming. In the nineteenth century, it was especially important for palm oil. The area is ethnically diverse, with historical divisions.

The Delta was a trading point with the Portuguese from the fifteenth century, and was colonized in the nineteenth century by the British. Independence was achieved in 1960, as part of the Federal republic of Nigeria. In the late 1960s it was fought over during the Nigerian civil war.

Despite more than fifty years of oil production, the area remains enmeshed in the most severe poverty, which has increased since the early 1990s. Transparency International consistently rates it as one of the most corrupt parts of the world.[4] Elections are often seen as being prearranged, and governance at the local level is poor to non-existent. Violence is endemic; many politicians are involved with militias; and kidnapping for political, financial or combined reasons is a regular feature. Oil bunkering (the stealing and selling of illegally produced oil) is a part of militia activity, and the network of militias is fluid and dynamic.[5] Bunkering has at times run to more than 500,000 barrels per day, and provides income to the cartels controlling it of several billion US dollars each year.[6]

The largest single foreign holder of production interests is Royal Dutch Shell, through its subsidiary company Shell Petroleum Development Company (SPDC). Other major holders are Exxon Mobil, Agip, Chevron Texaco, Elf and, with a small participation, Statoil.

Despite the large population of the Delta (up to 20 million in the whole region), the levels of poverty remain extreme and environmental degradation is notorious. Streams and creeks are polluted, fishing has diminished, and gas flaring on a huge scale has led to acid rain. These factors combine with the over-valuation of the currency – the Nigerian naira – and the crowding-out effect of the oil-based economy to add to the causes of the collapse of the non-oil economy.

The Coventry Report sets out the immense complexity of the relationships among the different groups in the Delta and analysed in great depth the causes – principally, corruption, oil theft and poor governance. Corruption is on a breathtaking scale, estimated at US$400–500 billion since the first oil production.

The oil companies are clearly and deeply implicated in the corruption, but generally speaking the evidence is more at the local than the international level. 'Simply put, the ills of corrupt government and an increasingly corrupt society pervaded the Nigerian operations of the major international oil companies.'[7] The overseas head offices were unable to cope with the conflicting demands for greater transparency and SRI coming from their domestic European or American shareholder base, influenced by NGO and ethical investment pressures, and with the lack of effective and detailed control of the activities of local subsidiaries. The low point was the murder of the 'Ogoni 9' in 1995. Such was the breakdown of trust between companies and communities that it was, and is, widely believed in the Delta that Shell, at its head office, was implicated in these deaths, and a legal case relating to these accusations is being heard in the USA at the time of writing.

Oil company response and failure

The response of the oil industry is a powerful example of the unintended consequences suggested at the beginning of this chapter.

First, they have struggled and usually *failed to control local subsidiaries*, and in particular their interaction with communities. The issues of distance and cost control are central to the failure. The staff interacting with communities are normally on temporary contracts and low paid, with neither assurance of continued work nor security of income and pension. The temptations of corruption are hard to resist, and difficult to condemn. The work is done in the field, often with community leaders, in difficult-to-reach areas. Corruption in the hierarchy of the companies at the local level further weakens controls. Honest staff, whether local or expatriate, are often intimidated and marginalized, which prevents them from modifying the culture.

Second, the headquarters' response has been ineffective, or unwilling to recognize the problem. Social audits do not reveal the depth of the issues, and there is a sense of the inevitability of conflict and internal denial. Individual executives may recognize the issues and work hard to change the system, but the general response is one of fatalistic acceptance, intermittently replaced by bursts of fruitless energy.

Third, and most significant, development packages are ineffective. Two recent examples demonstrate the issue. The SPDC found that a large proportion of the schools and clinics built with several hundred million dollars of development aid were not being staffed and equipped by the local government and thus, even when the money donated had not gone astray, very little had helped local communities. Agip (the Italian oil company) found in an internal survey that little of its spending on community development had been effective.

The infantilization of local government

Despite the failures of community development plans and spending, the corruption of many of those involved in the industry and the inability of distant headquarters to control effectively the detailed operations of subsidiaries, the oil companies of the Delta still have the strongest internal capacity for the delivery of complex and demanding projects.

Their capacity is obviously aimed principally at the exploration, development, production, transport and distribution of hydrocarbons in all forms, in a very forbidding and difficult situation. Capacity is of equal value in planning and building roads, or in the process of sustainable community development. There is an obvious and all too frequent contrast between the relatively efficient process in which the oil companies undertake community development, and the work of local government, which often was not carried out at all, even when funded. One of the consequences is the sense that the oil companies ought to be responsible for community development, thus effectively letting official channels of state governance escape without blame, or at least pushing the issue higher up the government chain, thus removing local accountability and responsibility. Local government can be infantilized, rather than encouraged to mature and use the considerable talents and gifts that exist across the Delta among the political class.

This was also the case with the East India Company. Oil companies carry out community development either to protect their interests or out of genuine altruistic motives of SRI. But their commercial activities lead to more instability and corruption, in which they are further caught up, and removes the capacity and responsibility from local government as they seek to compensate by supplying even more community development, and thus encouraging more infantilization. It is a circle of decline.

Approaches to solutions

Summary of the issue

So far, I have sought to show two things. First, that countries with issues of instability have a number of factors that make them especially prone to weaknesses of governance; and that such weakness is almost invariably made worse when the countries involved are rich in natural resources. Second, that there is a tendency to have a mutual process of capture between the companies' local operations and the relevant levels of government, which multinationals are almost incapable of addressing, and usually refuse to admit this. The mutual capture is that the local operations to some degree succumb to corrupt governance systems, and that the relatively efficient delivery of community development draws the company into unwillingly replacing local government, removing its moral accountability and creating unreasonable expectations.

Empowerment and its problems

The classical response to the dilemma described above is a combination of capacity building for local government and sustainable community development. The diagram in Figure 8.1, designed by Dr Stephen Davis, demonstrates the intended outcomes in the Niger Delta.

The vertical axis measures the intensity of conflict and the horizontal axis the passage of time. The process leads to a diminution of violence through civil society engaging in the transformation of government and commercial activities to the benefit of the region.

Transformation of this kind relies entirely on wide support by stakeholders in the area, from national governments and international organizations, down to the most local level. In the case of the Niger Delta, numerous efforts aimed at restoring peace have failed because of the incapacity of the major stakeholders to change their behaviour. This in turn is likely to be linked to the asymmetrical reward structures for doing so. The elite stands to lose a great deal very quickly, while the mass of the people will gain less individually, and their gain will be over a prolonged period. The incentive will always remain for those with power through membership of the elite, through the legitimate or illegitimate possession of arms, through employment by a multinational

Figure 8.1 Peace and sustainable development

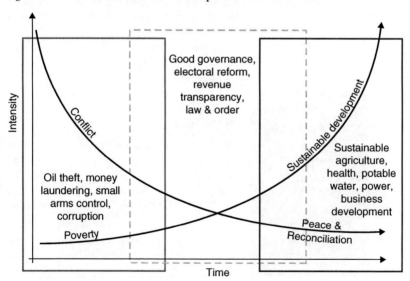

Source: Davis (2002).

company, or through local power to maximize their short-term reward at the cost of the long-term benefit of the people.

The second diagram below, also from Dr Davis, sets out the problem graphically.

Governments, international aid organizations and companies tend to work at the top two levels, whereas it is the third level – the roots – that causes instability and the problems of mutual capture.

However, unless we wish to return to a form of neo-colonialism, and even more disempowering of governments in affected areas, the roots level is something to be dealt with by domestic governance, not principally in most circumstances requiring international action, let alone the actions of multinational companies. The latter are part of the solution, but not the leaders of the solution.

I suggest that a condition precedent to the sort of sustainable development postulated in Figure 8.1 is a transformed view of responsibility and active commitment by companies to empower communities. For this to happen, the asymmetric reward structure discussed above needs to be better balanced.

First, there must be a rejection of corruption at high levels of government, regardless of economic benefit. There is a utopian aspect to such a prescription, but it cannot be avoided. In a pastoral interview some years ago in the Church of England parish where I was then working, someone described themselves to me as a little bit pregnant. To be a little bit corrupt is equal nonsense, a system either is or is not. Corruption at

Figure 8.2 The roots of conflict

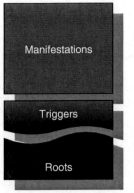

Manifestations
Riots, protests, military engagement, militia assaults, killings, property destruction

Triggers
Community development allocation, police action, boundary disputes

Roots
Ethnic differences, poverty, high unemployment, corruption, resource revenue distribution

Source: Davis (2005).

high levels can only be dealt with by international action, including the removal of visas and the confiscation of assets. Nigeria has improved its position through the rigorous action of certain incorruptible financial crime investigators, who have arrested and charged at least ten out of thirty-six state governors. Strong action has an impact.

Second, at the other end of the spectrum, there must be a change in the balance of economic benefit to local communities. The simplest approach is that there should be an equitable system that puts funds, by way of royalties from natural resources or the activities of international companies, transparently to use for the benefit of the community, and that this is done in a sustainable fashion. Such royalties make a direct link between the economic activity and the return to the local people affected by the operations. Alongside this must be a participation in operational decisions. The individuals involved from the local community must be changed often enough to avoid corruption, or at least to minimize it.

Third, development must be carried out by local government and not by private contractors, perhaps with assistance to build capacity, on the basis of widely owned and agreed programmes, with clear quality assurance. The sense of dependence on outside forces for development needs to be broken. Rewards to local government leaders can be based on outcomes in terms of roads, hospitals, schools and, above all, sustainable economic activity.

International companies will complain that such structures and extra tax would make operations impossible to carry out efficiently, or even at all. But the present system in many parts of the world is one that destroys such companies and their corporate culture as surely as it destroys local communities. There must be a point where investment or commerce that cannot be done well should not be done at all. Far from damaging local communities, over the longer term this will make it possible for more to recover a sense of their own destiny, to be those for whom development is sustainable, owned and in partnership with others, not merely a conditional gift.

The question for international investors in areas of instability is essentially whether SRI is a luxury, which is pleasant to have but not essential to investment, or the sine qua non of investment. An approach that insists on transparency, on subsidiarity, on creating solidarity among local communities, and which is based on the idea of the common good and the universal destination of goods, is immensely challenging. Its alternative is the over-centralized, corrupting and ultimately conflict-enhancing approaches that surround us today.

Notes

1. For a detailed economic discussion, see Sachs and Warner(2001) and Alexeev and Conrad (2005).
2. 'The Potential for Peace and Reconciliation in the Niger Delta' (ICR Report), February 2009. The ICR Report is a lengthy and authoritative review of the conflicts and confrontations in the Niger Delta, with possible outcomes.
3. It was in this area that Ken Saro-Wiwa, a noted human rights activist was arrested and executed by the regime of General Abacha in 1995.
4. http://report.globalintegrity.org/.
5. ICR Report, pp. 128 ff.
6. ICR Report, p. 166.
7. ICR Report, p. 208.

Bibliography

Alexeev, M. V. and Conrad, R. F. (2005) 'The Elusive Curse of Oil'. Available at: http://ssrn.com/abstract=806224.

Davis, S. (2002) Unpublished chart designed by Canon Dr Stephen Davis, subsequently Director of Reconciliation at Coventry Cathedral.

Davis, S. (2005) Unpublished chart designed by Canon Dr Stephen Davis, subsequently Director of Reconciliation at Coventry Cathedral.

ICR Report (2009) 'The Potential for Peace and Reconciliation in the Niger Delta', February.

Sachs, J. D. and Warner, A. M. (2001) 'The Curse of Natural Resources', *European Economic Review*, 45(4–5): 827–38.

9
Ethical Dilemmas for Large Corporations in Under-developed Countries[1]

Philip Booth

Introduction

The purpose of this chapter is to identify moral and ethical dilemmas that large corporations might encounter when operating in under-developed countries – particularly when those countries have a poor institutional environment. The chapter is not designed to condemn what some might regard as unethical behaviour; and it is also not designed to excuse unethical behaviour by large corporations on utilitarian grounds. The first objective is to provide an economic context for actions that businesses may take, which some might dismiss as being unethical because of their first-round economic consequences. Second, the chapter highlights genuine ethical dilemmas that are not necessarily easily resolved, and which do not arise as a result of the actions of the firms themselves but rather as a result of the environment in which they are operating. The chapter is written largely from a Roman Catholic perspective. However, the Catholic aspects of the chapter generally relate to principles and ideas that are shared by all Christians.

Much of the modern discourse on corporate social responsibility (CSR) and business ethics is not especially helpful for our purpose. It can be very woolly, often exhibiting an incomplete understanding of the economic system, entrepreneurship, corporate governance[2] and, perhaps more alarmingly, of the meaning of responsibility and ethics.[3] It is dangerous for Christians simply to absorb terms such as 'corporate social responsibility' because they are phrases with which they empathize. Business ethicists, like businesses, prefer to use phrases to describe their wares that have a marketing impact.

The Church welcomes business

It is worth beginning by pointing out that Christians should, in general, welcome business. In recent years, the Catholic Church has been more explicitly welcoming of a 'business economy'. The provision of goods through a business economy accords with the principle of subsidiarity, and with the belief in the dignity of the human person. The Church's support for the free business economy is perhaps best summed up by the following statement from the Papal encyclical of John Paul II (1991) – *Centesimus annus* (CA 42) – which answers the rhetorical question of whether the market economy is the most appropriate economic system:

> If by 'capitalism' is meant an economic system which recognizes the fundamental and positive role of business, the market, private property and the resulting responsibility for the means of production, as well as free human creativity in the economic sector, then the answer is certainly in the affirmative, even though it would perhaps be more appropriate to speak of a 'business economy', 'market economy' or simply 'free economy'.

The market is regarded by the Church as being an important means of attaining prosperity. Pontifical Council for Justice and Peace (2005, para. 347) sums up the arguments succinctly. It states that free and competitive markets have proved capable of ensuring that material needs are met, and that they encourage conservation of resources while giving a central place to a person's desires and preferences. Business is also regarded as an integral social and entrepreneurial activity (see also CA, para. 32).

The acceptance of the market is qualified and it is held that the market economy is not an end in itself but rather serves other ends – such as the provision of goods and services that meet important human needs. Nevertheless, a grudging acceptance of the market economy is mistaken. A business economy brings many benefits, not simply material economic ones. But the market economy needs to work within a framework of law and regulation; that law and regulation does not necessarily have to be provided by government, but some aspects of it often will be. As stated in the Catholic Catechism: 'The activity of a market ... presupposes sure guarantees of individual freedom and private property ... as well as a stable currency and efficient public services. Hence the principal task of the state is to guarantee this security, so that those who work and produce can enjoy the fruits of their labours and thus feel encouraged to work efficiently and honestly' (Catechism, 1994: 2431). Perhaps the most acute dilemmas for businesses in under-developed countries arise when the basic framework of law and stable currencies do not exist. This creates dilemmas directly, because a business has to decide how to act when property rights are not protected by law or are only protected on the payment of bribes and so on. It also creates dilemmas indirectly, because the general background of under-development will create problems of poverty that may make it difficult for businesses to reconcile effective business decision-making with enhancing the dignity of those with whom the business contracts. On the other hand, in the absence of an effective institutional background in which business in general can thrive, large multinational corporations are able to provide certain advantages to an under-developed country.

Institutional framework in under-developed countries

The reasons why poor countries are poor are, of course, matters of legitimate academic dispute. The contributions of large enterprises to the economies of poor countries are also matters of dispute. I will argue here that under-developed countries are poor, in general, because the basic institutional background for a market economy, as described in the quotation from the Catechism given above, is absent. The absence of a sound legal system also provides opportunities for abuse, of course.

It is becoming increasingly clear, both from studying countries that have developed (for example, in Asia) and those that have not, that the basic preconditions for development are: good governance, including the enforcement of private property; freedom of contract; enforcement of contracts; the rule of law; the authority of law; and the absence of corruption.[4] This list is not exhaustive, of course.[5] It appears that, if these preconditions are present, development and growth will generally follow. This is not surprising. Economic activity, employment, saving and capital accumulation will not take place unless there is freedom of contract and the enforcement of property rights.

The problem of the absence of formalization and security of property rights is discussed in great detail by de Soto (2000). He argues that in under-developed countries much capital is 'dead capital' that is not recognized by the legal system. The absence of both secure and formal property rights prevents proper business contracts from developing, leads to reduced opportunities for entrepreneurship, prevents capital secured on property from being invested in businesses, leads to corrupt legal and governmental systems, and leads to 'private law enforcement' or 'mafia gangs' becoming dominant. In such a situation, issues such as land reform, the provision of capital through aid and so on become irrelevant to development. Unless legal systems are reformed to properly recognize freely acquired property, capital investment and land endowments for the poor will have no meaning and will not contribute to development. It should be mentioned that private property does not necessarily imply individualized property, and there is dispute among those who sympathize with de Soto's position regarding the mechanisms by which property rights should be formalized – with some economists preferring a more evolutionary approach.

Exchange relationships are clearly necessary to enable an economy to develop beyond subsistence level. If contracts are not enforceable in the courts or recognized by legal systems, or if corruption or violence leads them to be enforced perversely, then exchange relationships cannot develop. Similarly, if property rights are not enforced justly or are not recognized, only very limited capital investment can take place.[6]

The problems of developing exchange relationships, small businesses and entrepreneurship are well illustrated both by de Soto's findings and from regular reports by the World Bank and the Economist Intelligence Unit. For example, de Soto showed how, on average, 15 per cent of turnover in Peruvian manufacturing businesses was paid out in bribes at the turn of the twenty-first century. For a business to become legal and register its property in Lima it took over 300 working days at a cost of thirty-two times the monthly minimum wage. A person living in a housing settlement where title was not formally registered would have had to go through 728 individual bureaucratic steps to register their title with the city of Lima authority alone.[7]

Most under-developed countries have similar problems. For example, in Heritage Foundation (2009) it is stated, with respect to India: 'Protection of property for local investors is weak ... Corruption is perceived as significant ... especially in government procurement of telecommunications, power and defense contracts.' For Nigeria, it is stated: 'Corruption is perceived as pervasive ... is endemic at all levels of government and society ... One of the world's least efficient property registration systems makes acquiring and maintaining rights to real property difficult.'

Gwartney and Lawson (2004) show the relationship between economic freedom and growth. One particular statistic is compelling.

A hundred countries were studied between 1980 and 2000, and their legal systems rated according to the criteria established by the Fraser Institute's *Economic Freedom of the World* index. The top twenty-four countries had an average GDP per capita of US$25,716 at the end of the period and average economic growth of 2.5 per cent. The bottom twenty-one countries had an average income of US$3,094 per capita and average economic growth of 0.33 per cent. The criteria used to rank legal systems were: consistency of legal structure, protection of property rights, enforcement of contracts, independence of judiciary and rule of law principles. This suggests that development is impossible without the basic legal structures necessary for free economic activity.

Multinational corporations in under-developed countries

An important facet of globalization is the operation of multinational corporations. Multinationals can bring huge benefits to developing countries; and they generally offer better terms and conditions of employment than do domestic employers. In a now rather dated, but still significant, study (see Irwin, 2003) the general population in Vietnam were found to have a disposable income of US$205 per annum in 1998, whereas people working in foreign-owned businesses earned US$420 per annum. Poverty rates for those working in multinationals were only a quarter of the level of the general population. Basically, wages are strongly related to productivity, and productivity is very poor in under-developed countries, largely as a result of their domestic policies. Multinationals are one vehicle for improving productivity.

Multinationals are also hugely important for promoting technology and capital transfer. When operating in developing countries they provide a stable financial and economic infrastructure – long-term contracts and so on – even in environments where contract enforcement is weak. They promote competition for labour and they enable a country to take advantage of its comparative advantage by allowing specialization within a production process where the legal and financial conditions do not allow indigenous companies to trade easily with overseas countries.

Indeed, in under-developed countries, it can take an entity with the infrastructure possessed by a multinational to establish a viable business. If we see abuses of the natural law by multinationals that may go unpunished by governments then that is a matter for serious concern, but genuine dilemmas that often face multinational companies – for example, whether to give bribes to the government, are not largely of their own making. They arise because they are working in countries that do not have the proper system of law and protection of property rights that a free economy needs. It is only with such a system that it is possible to have the variety of economic opportunities that reduces the likelihood of exploitation.

Some perceived problems of a business economy: the roles of owners and agents

Businesses, while showing a profit in an economic sense, can offend the dignity of those working for or supplying them. While profit is recognized as a legitimate signal that resources are employed in a worthwhile manner, the pursuit of profit at all costs is not acceptable. Pontifical Council for Justice and Peace (2005) states in its *Compendium* that a business should be a community of solidarity and, by its activities, promote the common good (paras 340, 341) – both of these are natural features of business in a normal environment subject to the rule of law. However, it then adds, rather out of context, though not insignificantly, that businesses must 'protect the natural environment'. We take up this theme below.

The *Compendium* also states (para. 348) that the profit of an enterprise, though legitimate, must not be an enterprise's sole objective: also important is the orientation of a business towards social usefulness, so that the market is of service to the common good. This cautious welcome to the role of business in a free economy leaves many dilemmas, for both businesses and policy-makers.

In considering this issue, it is first necessary to distinguish between the respective roles of management and shareholders. Their relative roles, from both an economic and philosophical perspective, are discussed in Sternberg (2004). Shareholders own the business property and employ management to manage that property to satisfy the shareholders' objectives.[8] The managers are employees and it is not their role to manage the assets of the business in a way that is contrary to the desires of the owners – even if managers believe that they are promoting the common good by doing so.[9]

This can be illustrated by way of an analogy. If a family left the country for six months and asked a letting agency to let out their property, it would not be the job of an employee of the letting agency to decide that the common good could be aided by housing homeless people at a low rent – contrary to the contractual agreements between the agency and the family. In the case of business managers, it is not their role, unless sanctioned by the board, acting within the powers given to it by shareholders, to, say, install enhanced insulation in all factories at a significant net cost to the business because of the managers' personal belief that the net social benefits make this worthwhile. The managers may give advice to the board, express an opinion or choose to work for another company that has a different attitude, but their roles are to be stewards of the property of the investors in the company. Indeed, if the investors are pensioners, or widows and orphans benefiting from an insurance fund, they may be in greater need than those who might benefit from any 'social action' undertaken by managers of their own volition under the guise of a CSR policy.

None of this permits either managers or owners to act in a way that is contrary to the moral law. The interpretation of that moral law may have grey areas in certain fields, but it would clearly be wrong for a manager in business, for example, to bribe contractors, treat workers unjustly, or, to take an extreme case, force female employees to have abortions in order to raise their value to the corporation. There are other offences against the moral law mentioned in the Catechism, such as price manipulation to take advantage of the ignorance of others (see Catechism, 1994, para. 2409, for example) where the responsibilities of business managers might go beyond those of civil and criminal law. If managers feel pressurized to take decisions that Christian teaching would deem to be immoral, they should reconsider their positions.

Business dilemmas

For shareholders and boards of directors, there are dilemmas about how businesses should behave when legitimate objectives appear to conflict, given that economic backgrounds and legal frameworks can be far from ideal. Some of these areas will be recognized as legitimate areas for judgement by Christians. For example, the precise relationships between the wages of different workers within a business will depend on a number of different factors, such as the contribution of the individual to the value of the business, the wage scale that the business uses to reward loyalty, the difficulties of recruiting workers with particular skills and so on. But, while it is reasonable for Christians within business to take heed of warnings from the Catholic Church and other Churches about the essential social mission of business, we should be careful before jumping to hasty conclusions when overriding decisions based on the profit motive.

To Westerners, it may seem obvious that multinational businesses should pay all employees a 'just wage', as judged by Western standards, pay a 'fair price' for primary products, and refuse to employ child labour. However, overriding price signals in the hope of achieving wider social goals may in fact compromise businesses' contribution to the common good. Obliging businesses to pay higher than the market price for primary products may draw in a greater supply and lead to unsold products. Obliging businesses to pay higher than the market price for labour can lead to unemployment, to the substitution of labour by capital, to reduced competition within labour markets, and also lead to 'insider–outsider' markets, where the privileged have jobs and others do not. The employment of child labour is sometimes necessary for families in under-developed countries to ensure a reasonable standard of living and to help finance part-time school fees (see Kis-Katos and Schulze, 2005).[10] If we do not follow the profit signal – which is an important signal of the social value of our economic activities – how do we know whether a business is making a social contribution or not?[11]

The dilemma a business faces here is not unlike the dilemmas faced by central planners within governments. It is because of the impossibility of resolving such dilemmas in a central planning system that a free economy is favoured. We can easily see the first-round effects of our actions (such as raising the wage of a poor employee), but the second-round effects of such an action (including potential employees remaining unemployed) may be hidden. Many of these dilemmas arise as a result of governments not undertaking their functions properly. If the economic and business environment is unfavourable as a result of misguided government policy, opportunities for exploitation may be increased. The ultimate wrong in such cases lies with poor government, though firms still have to face up to the added responsibilities that come as a result of poor public oversight (see below).

It is difficult to lay down a precise way in which these dilemmas can be resolved. Those who own firms, and their representatives, should be sensitive to such problems and should treat their employees and suppliers humanely and sensitively. With such an outlook, it should be possible to balance concern for the individuals connected with the enterprise with the intrinsic function of the enterprise itself. This is not an entirely satisfactory solution because it does not propose specific ways of dealing with defined problems – it is therefore out of tune with a society where people like to be governed by codes of conduct and detailed rules. In the following sections we examine specific dilemmas faced by businesses in further detail.

'Excessive' wages, 'unjust' wages and 'unjust' prices

Popular criticisms of capitalism often focus on excessive wages and profits of a few people in business and 'unjustly' low wages for others. The Catholic Church has frequently expressed concern about extreme inequality, while recognizing that some inequality is part of the natural order (see Charles, 1998: 18, 26; Pontifical Council for Justice and Peace, 2005, para. 362; *Populorum progressio* (*PP*) 57 and *Sollicitudo rei socialis* (*SRS*) 12, for example).[12] I shall focus on four different aspects of inequality. The first is the very high levels of wages that are earned by senior executives in business. The second is the very low levels of wages, at least by Western standards, received by some employees. The third is the low level of product prices received by primary product producers. The fourth is the high level of prices that Western firms can charge for goods based on intellectual property.

'Unjustly' high and 'unjustly' low wages

From an economic point of view, there are various ways of thinking about the wage hierarchy in a business, and none leads to the conclusion that any particular degree of inequality within the wage structure of the firm is immoral *per se*. Departing from economic principles in determining the wage structure may well produce more harm than good.

A well-managed company should try to ensure that its wage structure reflects the contribution of employees to the value of the firm. Consider the case where the CEO of a firm is paid £5m per year, whereas his value to the firm is £10m per year. If the CEO has a value of £6m to another company, and that company is willing to pay £6m to secure his services, the individual may change jobs, perhaps moving to a company where he adds less value. There is an overall welfare loss from this transaction as the employee is moving to an activity where his talents are worth less. Certainly, nobody at the bottom end of the wage scale gains from the decision to pay the CEO only £5m in the name of 'justice'.

Similarly, at the bottom end of the wage scale, if a company decides to pay an individual more than s/he is worth to the company, given his/her productivity, the company is likely to employ fewer such individuals, thus leaving some of them unemployed. Such a company is also likely to use less labour and more capital. Ironically, a company that decides to employ fewer people at a higher wage is likely to be praised by commentators (see the chapter by Woods in Booth, 2007) because the fact that the company has employed fewer people and more capital will not be perceptible, whereas the low wages of a company that decides to take on all the labour it can at the prevailing wage will be discernable.

There is a genuine dilemma here for business. Businesses may well, in fact, undermine not just the market economy but also the economic prospects of the low paid if they pay salaries to employees that do not reflect value added to the business. However, outsiders, including 'ethical investors', may look more favourably upon the moral position of a business that has a more 'equal' wage distribution. There are some companies that, as a matter of policy and established culture, do have more equal wage structures and relatively pyramidal and stable employment environments. This can be done, among other reasons, to help recruit labour that has particular (often risk averse) characteristics. I would argue that these are business decisions that are not necessarily less or more moral than decisions to pay wages that reflect direct supply and demand conditions in the market. Investors who believe that they are taking an 'ethical' position should be careful to understand both the 'seen' and 'unseen' effects of distorting wage structures.

There are some exceptions, however, where we might not accept that the market wage is equivalent to a 'just' wage or a morally acceptable one (see, for example, Charles, 1998, vol. II: 430). It has been articulated by Papal encyclicals from *Rerum novarum* (1891) onwards that an employer must not exploit a worker's weakness. Thus freedom of contract can be the basis of a just wage, but is not necessarily so. Weakness can arise from various situations, such as the ignorance of an employee about the treatment of others in an organization, or ignorance of alternative employment opportunities. Alternatively, a weak bargaining position might arise from the existence of monopsony[13] combined with the inability of potential employees to relocate and look for employment in other areas. In such cases, a firm should try to ensure that wages reflect the contribution of individuals to the enterprise, and not exploit their circumstances. This is simply part of the requirement to manage the enterprise and relationships with employees in a just and fair manner.

This does not necessarily mean that, where there is a large pool of unemployed people, the enterprise cannot choose to pay lower wages and employ more workers (and perhaps employ less capital) than the enterprise would in another area where employment conditions are tighter. If enterprises did not choose to vary wages in this manner, unemployment would rise and periods of unemployment would lengthen. It also does not mean that two people doing identical jobs cannot be paid different amounts if market conditions merit this. If one employer pays the same wages in (say) India as in the UK, it would potentially damage indigenous enterprises and prevent the emergence of more companies that would provide increased employment opportunities. However, the employer should not systematically exploit the ignorance or weakness of employees.

Catholic teaching has generally regarded a wage as just only if it is above the level of subsistence and provides a dignified livelihood (see, for example, Catechism, 2004, para. 2434, which mentions various Papal documents and biblical references). Exceptions are suggested if the livelihood of a business is in peril from paying higher wages. This approach does create a genuine dilemma for economists. There may well be situations where the market wage, even if there is neither monopoly nor monopsony, is insufficient to provide a dignified living.[14] But a decision to pay labour more than the market wage may have a number of detrimental effects. As has already been mentioned, less labour is likely to be employed; labour might be replaced with capital; and high-quality labour may well be drawn from other firms, which are then left in a position of having to employ less productive labour. Indeed, this may well lead to resentment and calls for the regulation of the 'poaching' of labour.

We do not resolve this dilemma here, except to comment that, in such situations, it is important that employers look to their wider responsibilities and are satisfied in good conscience that they are not exploiting the weakness of counterparties to their contracts. It may reasonably be asked, however, why the productivity of labour is so low that a living wage is not justified by an individual's productivity. Very often, the answer lies in dysfunctional governments that create a poor business environment. Without a good business environment, a market economy cannot generate competition in the labour market that leads to the high levels of productivity that are ultimately the basis of high wages.[15] But it should also be noted that the Catechism states, 'Agreement between the parties is not sufficient to justify morally the amount to be received in wages' (para. 2434). Perhaps this precise phraseology is significant. There may be occasions when the just wage is different from the agreed wage, but we cannot necessarily say what the just wage is in such circumstances. It is therefore important that employers are aware of their responsibilities to treat employees appropriately and strive to meet those responsibilities. The correct attitude towards God and one's neighbour is more important than a, perhaps fruitless, attempt to determine a figure for the 'just' wage.

'Unjustly' low prices?

When a person who is self-employed is selling products that are being purchased by a business, the purchaser cannot be immune from similar arguments to those surrounding the discussion of the just wage. This has been discussed widely in the context of the 'fair trade' movement, particularly with regard to the coffee market.[16] While it may not be said that it is unreasonable for a business to pay low prices if these are justified by supply and demand conditions, the agreed price cannot necessarily be regarded as a just price if there is monopoly or monopsony power in the market or if the purchaser is deliberately taking advantage of a seller's ignorance and weakness. In this situation, while a low price is not necessarily an indicator of injustice or immoral business practices, the systematic exploitation of suppliers who have limited information about alternative opportunities would be inappropriate.[17]

The Papal encyclical *Laborem exercens* (LE 17) outlines a role for 'indirect employers'. Though this phrase was mainly explained in terms of the role of regulators and legislators, it is also reasonable to suppose that consumers have a responsibility as indirect employers.[18] This could involve consumers choosing not to purchase from firms that act unethically in labour markets or in purchasing from suppliers. The issues here are complex too. The disastrous consequences for thousands of desperately poor children in Bangladesh who were thrown out of work after the threat of US trade sanctions over child labour have been well reported.[19] Again, this dilemma cannot be resolved definitively, except to say that consumers must bear some responsibility for their purchasing decisions.

'Unjustly' high prices?

A further dilemma for business concerns the protection of intellectual property, which confers a monopoly advantage on a producer. The generally accepted Catholic understanding of private property regards such rights as not being inviolable but as generally essential for the common good. Thus, if it is felt that the common good is not promoted by the protection of intellectual property through patents and copyrights, there should be no presumption of absolute protection. Interestingly, the law in most developed countries tends to take such a pragmatic position – intellectual property rights are protected by law but not to an unlimited or absolute extent. Most developed countries also favour reinforcing the protection of property rights through international free trade agreements.

The *Compendium* (2005) states (in relation to biotechnology):

> Entrepreneurs and directors of public agencies involved in the research, production and selling of products derived from new biotechnologies must take into account not only legitimate profit but also the common good. This principle, which holds for every type of economic activity, becomes particularly important for activities that deal with the food supply, medicine, health care and the environment. (para. 478)

It also states that, '*Equitable commercial exchange, without the burden of unjust stipulations,* is to be facilitated' (para. 475; italics in original) and that this requires the transfer of technology to developing countries.

As has been noted, the law relating to intellectual property has developed pragmatically within developed countries and there is no unanimity, even among staunch proponents of private property, as to the legitimate position of intellectual property rights.[20] Patent protection generally prevents developing countries from producing medicines and technologies at minimal cost through the copying of products. Contract provisions and world trade rules allow companies to block the re-importation of medicines sold at cheaper prices in developing countries than in developed countries. The economics of these complex issues, in so far as they relate to pharmaceuticals, is described very lucidly in Lilico (2006). We do not discuss the issue further except to comment that it would be naïve to assume that the cause of the poor would be served by simply allowing copying at cost in low-income countries.

In this area, as in many others discussed in this chapter, clear guidance about specific forms of behaviour cannot be given. Assuming that the principle of private intellectual property is accepted, it is clear that companies cannot be expected simply to give away their intellectual property rights – otherwise research and development in new products would suffer. Even where the preferential option for the poor is accepted, and the lack of availability of patented drugs leads to suffering, the principle of private intellectual property can serve the common good. The responsibility to help the poor in such situations must lie more widely than with business producers of the technological products themselves. At the same time, a Christian approach to business should not simply involve maximizing the monopoly profit potentially available from the exploitation of intellectual property when there is clear suffering. Patent law confers monopoly rights, and moral responsibilities accompany these rights. Similarly, developed countries, acting individually or as a group, should not try to negotiate trade rules in a way that simply maximizes the value of patents to industries in their own countries.[21] This is another genuine dilemma for business, where only a well-informed conscience can provide the necessary guidance about how to act in specific situations.

The environment, property rights and corruption

Presciently, in paragraph 342, Pontifical Council for Justice and Peace (2005) points out that businesses take on greater levels of responsibility in states that are not properly governed. This statement is legitimate and also helpful in focusing on the underlying problem where businesses are in a position to exploit the property rights of others and environmental resources, particularly in less-developed countries. If businesses are not working within a proper juridical framework that involves the protection of property rights, the enforcement of contracts and a stable economic environment, they have added responsibilities.[22] In such circumstances it would surely not be moral for a business to take property without compensation or to pollute the natural environment without compensation, even if the civil law of a particular country allowed it. Business people should show restraint and/or ensure just compensation when they use or acquire the property of others, even if the law of the relevant country does not compel them to do so. However, there are still grey areas where businesses must make judgements about how to behave: for example, many activities (such as open-cast mining) cause environmental harm that might well be tolerated in countries with good governance systems because the benefits are greater than the costs. It is certainly not immoral, as such, to pursue such activities in a less-developed country with a poor system of legal protection. However, the Christian business should ensure, in the absence of proper legal protection of property rights, that all those who would justly receive compensation for the loss of their property or amenity in a well functioning and just legal system are properly treated when these restraints are absent.

A particularly difficult dilemma might be how businesses in countries with poor legal environments act when faced with opportunities for bribery and corruption. There may be some difficult situations in practice here. For example, if a lorry loaded with perishable goods is crossing the border of a poor country, is it morally correct to bribe a customs officer to allow the goods to cross? There may be an element of the 'lesser of two evils' in this situation, but one should be careful not to 'pursue evil so that good might come from it.'

It would be moving from the realms of the economist to that of the moral philosopher to discuss these issues much further. Catholic teaching suggests that we are only permitted to break those positive laws that directly violate natural law (we are, for example, under no obligation to obey a law that commands us to promote abortion). There may be circumstances, such as the one above, where no serious evil comes from breaking what could be regarded as an unjust law, and to obey the law may contribute to an evil. However, this should not be done lightly, and for a multinational corporation to simply adapt to a culture of corruption and join in with it is a very serious matter. Where corruption is not against the law, of course, slightly different considerations might pertain. In fact, business networks can provide good examples of the just operation of private rules systems in the absence of well-functioning public law.

Conclusion

Those acting within businesses should clearly strive not to break the moral law. They need to be particularly careful when their enterprises are not circumscribed within an appropriate juridical framework, or when operating in environments where property rights are not enforced and corruption is rife. With regard to economic and social relationships, it can be dangerous to set rules and regulations – or even to develop codes of practice – for business operations. Such an approach can entrench established firms in the market by raising the costs of entry to new business; it can also allow managers to set business objectives at the expense of owners; and it removes the ability to take both moral and economic decisions from the very people who are in the best position to make such judgements. There is no substitute for a business owner having a properly informed conscience which acts as an appropriate restraint in the thousands of day-to-day decisions that a business person takes each year. The business person should exhibit an *attitude of solidarity* in relationships with others – particularly those who are most vulnerable – whether consumers, suppliers or employees.

Notes

1. The author takes full responsibility for the views expressed in this chapter, which do not necessarily reflect those of the European Commission.

A substantial part of this chapter was first published as 'Modern Business and Moral and Ethical Dilemmas in a Globalized World', in Ian R. Harper and Samuel Gregg (eds), *Christian Theology and Market Economics*. Reprinted with the kind permission of Edward Elgar Publishing.

2. See Sternberg (2004) for a very clear explanation of the meaning of corporate governance and of the dangers of undermining corporate governance by the pursuit of poorly understood notions of 'social responsibility'.

3. These points are well illustrated in the UK Government's report: 'Corporate Social Responsibility: A Government Update' (available from www.csr.gov. uk, undated; accessed 31 August 2007). The report has senior industry figures highlighting the importance of CSR for 'engaging business in regenerating our communities', 'contributing to sustainable development' but above all it states, '[the Government] has linked corporate social responsibility with competitiveness and ... a trading advantage in global markets'. These goals may well conflict. Moreover, the first goal raises the question of whether the objective of business should not be to regenerate communities through wealth creation (there are other institutions and non-business corporations that play more direct roles); the second goal raises the question of why the government has not set up a juridical framework with property rights and environmental amenities being protected appropriately so that business activity is naturally sustainable; the third goal has no ethical content at all: if firms feel that certain forms of behaviour lead to raised profits, this is simply a restatement of the shareholder value approach to managing business. What is notable about the CSR agenda is how it provides a wider role for governments, bureaucrats and business managers in a firm, thus blurring lines of accountability and responsibility, while ignoring a rigorous discussion of ethics and morality.

4. This section borrows heavily from Booth (2007).

5. One could add fiscal prudence and sound money, for example.

6. It is sometimes difficult for people in the West to understand the importance of this point. If contracts one makes as a consumer, employee, business person or employer are not enforceable (including contracts for borrowing and saving) business life simply cannot take place. Similarly, if one cannot enforce property rights in one's own house, land or business premises, capital investment will just grind to a halt.

7. This position has improved slightly in Peru, but many countries are beset by these sorts or problems.

8. As Sternberg states, there are many corporations that are not businesses. These bodies are complementary in a market economy to those corporate bodies that *are* businesses and whose aim is to maximize their business value. We do not concern ourselves with non-business corporations here.

9. There is a huge literature on what is known as the principal–agent problem. Though corporations may be an efficient form of business organization, it is difficult to ensure that the agents (managers) follow the objectives of the principals (shareholders), because of the divorce between ownership and control. Many of the proposals of the corporate social responsibility lobby exacerbate this problem.

10. Indeed, the Catholic Church does take a very pragmatic line on child labour (see *Compendium*, para. 245).

11. There are times when profit does not measure the full social contribution of business, because of the existence of monopolies, externalities and so on. These specific economic problems are normally best alleviated by the promotion of competition and the wider application of property rights (although externalities can sometimes be better dealt with by regulation and taxes or user charges). Nevertheless, despite the comments below about the operation of business in countries with poor legal systems, 'profit' is normally the best indicator that a business has of its economic contribution.

12. However, the empirical evidence advanced in the *Compendium*, *PP* and *SRS* is questioned in Booth, 2007: 65.

13. For example, a single employer that is dominant in the labour market of a particular locality.

14. Leaving aside for the moment the definition of a dignified living.

15. This has become a generally accepted point in economics. There are good discussions of this in Wolf (2004), de Soto (2000), and Gwartney and Lawson (2004).

16. See Booth and Whetstone (2007) for an analysis of 'fair trade' and the references contained in the paper.

17. For example, if one farmer was paid (say) £200 per tonne for a particular raw material and the buyer then visited another farm whose owner is illiterate, ignorant of alternative opportunities and desperate for food, it could be regarded as unjust to pay that farmer £100 per tonne, even if that were the agreed price.

18. See also the excellent discussion in Lamoureux (2005).

19. See Kis-Katos and Schulze (2005).

20. For example, Prof. Terence Keeley, Vice-Chancellor of the University of Buckingham, is a prominent advocate of abolishing all patent protection.

21. This is not to say that trade rules should not be compatible with maintaining patent protection but rather that countries should not act as a cartel in negotiations to exploit their advantage.

22. In fact, the precise statement is ambiguous. ' (I)n which national States show limits in their capacity to govern the rapid processes of change that effect [*sic*] international economic and financial responsibilities.' This could refer to a situation in which all governments are increasingly finding it difficult, for good or ill, to control economic activity that has a global context or a situation where particular governments are generally inadequate.

Bibliography

Booth, P. M. (ed.) (2007) *Catholic Social Teaching and the Market Economy*, Hobart Paperback 34 (London: Institute of Economic Affairs).

Booth, P. M. and Whetstone, L. (2007) 'Half a Cheer for Fair Trade', *Economic Affairs*, 27(2): 29–38.

Catechism (1994) *Catechism of the Catholic Church* (London: Geoffrey Chapman.

Charles, R. (1998) *Christian Social Witness and Teaching: The Catholic Tradition from Genesis to Centesimus Annus* (Leominster, UK: Gracewing).

de Soto, H. (2000) *The Mystery of Capital: Why Capitalism Triumphs in the West and Fails Everywhere Else* (London: Black Swan).

Gwartney, J. and Lawson, R. (2004) 'What Have We Learned from the Measurement of Economic Freedom?', in M. A. Wynne, H. Rosenblum and R. L. Formaini (eds), *The Legacy of Milton and Rose Friedman's "Free to Choose"* (Dallas, Tex.: Federal Reserve Bank of Dallas).

Heritage Foundation (2009) *2009 Index of Economic Freedom* (Washington, DC: Heritage Foundation).

Irwin, D. (2003) *Free Trade Under Fire* (Princeton, NJ: Princeton University Press).

Kis-Katos, K. and Schulze, G. (2005) 'The Regulation of Child Labour', *Economic Affairs*, 25(3): 24–30.

Lamoureux, P. A. (2005) 'Commentary on *Laborem exercens* (On Human Work)', in K. R. Himes (ed), *Modern Catholic Social Teaching: Commentaries and Interpretations* (Washington, DC, Georgetown University Press).

Lilico, A.(2006) 'Six Issues in Pharmaceuticals', *Economic Affairs*, 26(3): 33–8.

Pontifical Council for Justice and Peace (2005) *Compendium of the Social Doctrine of the Church* (London: Burns & Oates).

Sternberg, E. (2004) *Corporate Governance: Accountability in the Marketplace*, Hobart Paper 147 (London: Institute of Economic Affairs).

Wolf, M. (2004) *Why Globalization Works*, (Yale University Press, USA, 2004)

List of Papal encyclicals

The following documents can be downloaded from the Vatican website: http://www.vatican.va/phome_en.htm, free of charge.

John Paul II (1991) *Centesimus annus.*
John Paul II (1981) *Laborem exercens.*
Paul VI (1967) *Populorum progressio.*
Leo XIII (1891) *Rerum novarum.*
Pius XI (1931) *Quadragesimo anno.*
John Paul II (1987) *Sollicitudo rei socialis.*

Part III

Are Corporations Really Responsive to Social Concerns?

10
The Implementation of Compliance Programmes in Multinational Organizations

Jean-Pierre Méan

Despite the term compliance being used in the English language since the mid-seventeenth century, it is only recently that it has acquired its current meaning of observing certain rules arising from legal provisions, or from the provisions of a self-imposed code of conduct. This new connotation has been developed primarily in the USA, as evidenced by the embarrassment which its translation into other languages than English causes. Indeed, in many languages, the English word 'compliance' is used, for lack of a better word, to express a concept not yet fully assimilated and understood.

Even in English, the term 'compliance' covers different realities. In banking, the term refers to the observance of rules aiming at preserving the integrity of the banking system and avoiding its abuse for the purpose of money laundering or personal gain. In the USA, compliance also applies to programmes aimed at preventing and detecting criminal conduct, and otherwise promoting an ethical and compliant corporate culture in order to alleviate the criminal culpability of companies. In other countries, compliance generally refers to self-regulation by companies aiming at minimizing legal and reputational risks in a multinational environment.

In order to better understand how the implementation of compliance programmes in multinational companies can contribute to the role that large enterprises can play in democracy and society, it is necessary, before presenting the elements of a successful compliance programme, first to address the distinctive features of multinational organizations and the legal challenges they face.

The distinctive features of multinational organizations

Multinational (or transnational) companies are often mentioned in discussions on international trade and relations, but there is no clear definition of what they are.

How international must a company be in order to qualify as a multinational? Typically, large multinational companies realize the major part or their turnover in countries other than their country of origin, and are active through branches (or more often through subsidiaries) in a large number of countries – rarely less than ten and often up to a hundred or more. They are faced with a large variety of cultural attitudes, some of which are difficult to reconcile with their cultural terms of reference. A particular pitfall for multinational companies is taking advantage of a less constraining legal environment in some of their host countries, or using their economic muscle to extract advantages they would not be able to obtain on their home ground. However, this kind of behaviour is increasingly held in check by public opinion, at least for large quoted companies, which are expected to behave according to the high standards of behaviour professed (but not always observed) in the so-called developed world.

This evolution is accentuated by changes in the management model. In the 1980s, many multinational companies tended to be run loosely from the centre, with a large degree of autonomy given to national subsidiaries. Today, however, most multinational companies are administered centrally along business sector lines. The role of national management is often limited to handling day-to-day operations and liaising with national authorities. This centralization of management calls for uniform standards and for a uniform corporate culture, as it is not feasible to centrally manage an organization while applying varying standards of behaviour to different sections. In selecting a uniform standard, management then has little choice but to select the strictest standard as it is the only one that may be implemented in all the countries of operation, including the country(ies) in which the standard originated. Implementing best practices or the highest standard worldwide thus means that, in many countries of operation, the company will have to comply with rules that have little or no application locally.

In addition to this geographical challenge, multinational companies have to face another arising from the sectors in which they are active, some of which are more difficult or more exposed than others. In many countries, dealing directly with governments as contractual partners presents a high risk of being exposed to corrupt demands (or a high temptation to make corrupt offers); implementing the company-wide standard with respect to corruption in such sectors of activity will therefore require additional effort and diligence.

Such efforts are rendered more difficult because multinational companies are global actors in a world that is only imperfectly global. As there is no global authority to set and enforce universal rules, multinational companies have to both set and enforce these themselves, often under pressure from public opinion and the media. To be thus judge and participant in their own court is a difficult balancing act which not all companies always manage successfully.

The changing environment of international business

In addition to the endogenous factors arising from their nature, multinational companies also have to face challenges from changes in their environment.

The legal challenge as the example of anticorruption legislation

The first challenge confronting multinational companies is the legal one arising from new international legislation in a field that was previously unregulated, as is the case with the corruption of foreign public officials. The first example of such legislation was the *US Foreign Corrupt Practices Act*,[1] enacted in 1977 following investigations by the US Securities and Exchange Commission which resulted in more than 400 US companies admitting to having made payments in excess of US$300 million to foreign government officials, politicians and political parties, ranging 'from bribery of high foreign officials in order to secure some type of favourable action by a foreign government to so-called facilitating payments that allegedly were made to ensure that government functionaries discharge certain ministrial [*sic*] or clerical duties'.[2]

Over a period of twenty years, the USA was the only country effectively prosecuting the bribing of foreign civil servants. However, efforts to transpose this piece of legislation to the international level were successful, with the adoption in 1997 of the *OECD Convention on Combating Bribery of Foreign Public Officials in International Business Transactions* (OECD Anti-Bribery Convention),[3] which came into force on 15 February 1999 after the required number of ratifications had been obtained. All OECD members and several non-OECD members[4] (that is, practically the whole so-called developed world and several emerging countries) have ratified the Convention and enacted national legislation to fulfil its requirements. Companies based in these countries now have to ensure that the standards set by the OECD Convention with respect to bribery are implemented in their worldwide operations.

Other international instruments have followed, such as the *Council of Europe Criminal and Civil Law Conventions on Corruption*[5] and the *UN Convention against Corruption* (UNCAC)[6] which extends to 140 signatories,[7] of which the majority have deposited their instrument of ratification.

The media challenge

In addition to the judicial process, companies suspected of misconduct are subject to media exposure, which can have extreme consequences in less time than it takes for the judicial process even to start.

The fate of the major accounting company Arthur Andersen is a good illustration of this. In 2001, the company had revenues of US$9.3 billion and employed 85,000 staff in 390 offices in 94 countries.[8] In October 2001, the US Securities and Exchange Commission began its investigations into the Enron Corporation's questionable accounting practices. In the weeks that followed, associates of Arthur Andersen's Houston office destroyed documents related to Enron's audit, which led to the indictment (that is, a statement issued by a grand jury that there was sufficient evidence that a crime had been committed to justify having a trial) in March 2002 of Arthur Andersen for obstruction of justice.[9] The reputational damage arising from this first step in the legal process was so severe that it accelerated the negotiations for the takeover of Arthur Andersen's network by its competitors, essentially Deloitte and Ernst & Young. When Arthur Andersen was convicted of obstruction of justice in June 2002, it had already practically ceased to exist as an international auditing firm. However, the legal process continued and the conviction was overturned by the US Supreme Court in 2005.[10] At that point, there remained only about 200 of the 85,000 staff of Arthur Andersen, who were mainly handling outstanding legal matters.

The media exposure was sufficient to deal the death blow to Arthur Andersen in a matter of months. It took several years for the judicial process to finally exonerate them, much too late to resuscitate them.

The ethical challenge

The third challenge that has to be addressed is that of the consequences of tolerating unethical behaviour in an organization. While the cohesion of small, closed organizations is secured by various kinds of solidarities (such as belonging to the same family or ethnic group; living in the same community; or being part of an old boys' network of some sort), this is not the case in large multinational companies. In these, a lack of loyalty to the company is not resented as a breach of solidarity to the same extent. It is then easy for an unethical culture to develop, especially if unethical behaviour is tolerated or tacitly (or even explicitly) encouraged, for example, by expecting staff to reach their targets by any possible mean). Once management has set a wrong behaviour pattern, it is an illusion to believe that this pattern will only be used for the benefit of the company and not against it. When staff members are under pressure to pay bribes in order to secure business, they will be tempted to take advantage of the system for their own benefit and that will be rendered particularly easy because bribe payments are made without proper records so as not to leave any evidence of the payment. Staff tempted to keep part of the bribe for themselves will have no difficulty in justifying themselves to their own conscience by focusing on the risk they are taking on behalf of their employer and by their management's own endorsement of unethical conduct. Indeed it is not difficult to forget any commitment to integrity when dealing with people who show none themselves. Displaying an ethical culture in a company towards the outside world thus not only encourages the right behaviour – it also sets a standard for behaviour in the organization itself.

Model compliance programmes

The United States Federal Sentencing Guidelines[11]

The concept of the criminal liability of companies or other organizations is relatively new in criminal law. It is based on the idea that over and above the liability of the individuals directly involved in criminal misconduct within an organization, the company itself should be assigned liability if its organization or structure is such that it has failed to prevent, or has encouraged, this misconduct. As a matter of efficiency, the fear of a pecuniary punishment of the company will act as an incentive for all those interested in the company – shareholders, board and management – to put in place appropriate measures to prevent the occurrence of criminal conduct. Where such conduct has occurred, the desire to minimize the penalty will be an incentive to report it and take corrective action.

The sentencing of organizations is addressed in chapter 8 of the *United States Federal Sentencing Guidelines*. Part B.2 of that chapter describes how an effective compliance programme must be structured in order to alleviate the culpability of the company. The programme must aim at preventing and detecting criminal conduct and at promoting an ethical and compliant organizational culture. Its elements include, in substance:

- Standards and procedures to prevent and detect criminal conduct.
- Active management of the programme: oversight by the board of directors; inclusion of the programme in the mandate of senior management; appointment of a senior manager with overall responsibility; and delegation of the operational responsibility to specific individuals who have adequate resources and a direct access to the board of directors or a board committee.
- Screening of management personnel.
- Communication of the programme (including training) to employees and agents.
- Monitoring and auditing.
- Periodical evaluation.
- A helpline and whistle-blowing mechanism.
- Promotion and enforcement of the programme through appropriate incentives and disciplinary measures.
- Corrective measures to prevent the occurrence of criminal conduct.
- Periodical risk assessment.

Business Principles for Countering Bribery[12]

The *Business Principles for Countering Bribery* have been issued by a Steering Committee under the aegis of Transparency International,[13] (an NGO engaged in fighting corruption), and Social Accountability International[14] (an organization devoted to promoting human rights for workers around the world). The members of the Steering Committee include representatives of business, academia, trade unions and non-governmental bodies.

While the *Business Principles* address the specific issue of corruption, the framework they provide is equally applicable to a broader compliance programme. According to the *Business Principles*, the programme should articulate 'values, policies and procedures to be used to prevent bribery from occurring in all activities under its effective control' (Section 3.1). It should 'be tailored to reflect an enterprise's business circumstances and culture' (Section 3.2) and 'be consistent with all laws relevant to countering bribery' (Section 3.3). It should also be developed 'in consultation with employees, trade unions or other employee representative bodies' (Section 3.4).

According to the *Business Principles*, the elements of a programme are as follows:

- The scope of the programme should be clearly defined.
- In terms of organization and responsibilities, the board of directors should provide leadership, resources and support, while the CEO is 'responsible for ensuring that the Programme is carried out consistently'.
- The programme should apply to all entities under the enterprise's control, and the enterprise should encourage the implementation of an equivalent programme by its business partners, including joint ventures, consortia, agents and other intermediaries, and contractors and suppliers. Before entering into such business relationships, the enterprise should conduct appropriate due diligence.
- Human resources practices should reflect commitment to the programme; compliance should be made mandatory for all employees and it should be made clear to employees that they will not suffer any adverse consequences for refusing to pay bribes.
- Employees, directors, agents and important contractors and suppliers should receive training on the programme.
- Employees should be able to seek guidance and report suspected violations (whistle-blowing) without fearing any form of reprisal.
- The enterprise should communicate its programme both internally and externally.
- The enterprise should have an effective system of internal controls to counter bribery. It should properly and fairly document all financial transactions and should not maintain off-the-books accounts.
- The programme should be monitored, and periodically reviewed and assessed.
- The board of directors should consider whether to commission external verification or assurance of the enterprise's anti-bribery policies and systems.

Recapping the elements of a programme

The *United States Federal Sentencing Guidelines* and the *Business Principles for Countering Bribery* have a lot in common without one having been copied from the other. This is not surprising, as the elements they include are all necessary elements for setting up a programme of this kind, or of practically any kind for that purpose, in a company.

Formulated and regrouped in a slightly different way, these elements address the following issues:

- Issuing the policy, setting the rules and defining the individuals and entities covered by the programme.
- Determining the levels of responsibility.
- Communicating the programme internally and externally.
- Exercising due diligence in the selection of employees and of business partners.
- Adapting human resources policies.
- Organizing training.
- Providing guidance and receiving reports.
- Conducting investigations.
- Sanctioning misconduct and taking corrective measures.
- Monitoring, reviewing and periodically assessing the programme.

Implementing a compliance programme

Before going into the details of a programme, it is worthwhile spending some time on the debate between the *rules-based approach* (prevalent in the United States) and the *values-based approach* (prevalent in Europe).

The supporters of the rules-based approach are essentially concerned with defining clear rules that set a definite line of demarcation between desired conduct and misconduct. This approach mirrors the approach of criminal law, where clear boundaries are important for the purpose of both prevention (one has to know precisely what behaviour is criminal) and repression (the prosecutor needs to know which evidence is relevant).

By contrast, the values-based approach recognizes that there is a grey area between right and wrong, and that decisions in that area depend on the circumstances and cannot therefore be based on rules alone. It is thus important to define certain values that will help the individual to make the right decision. The values-based approach is an ethical rather than a legalistic one.

To illustrate both approaches, those favouring a rules-based approach will, for example, define precise limits applying to gifts made or received, while those favouring a values-based approach will, while also setting certain limits, insist on the likelihood that a gift may unduly influence the recipient.

It is not surprising that the values-based approach dominates in Europe, where codes of conduct are essentially conceived as self-regulation tools of the corporate world, while in the USA the main goal of compliance is, according to the *Federal Sentencing Guidelines,* to avoid or alleviate corporate criminal liability. In order to be effective, a compliance programme will have to incorporate both aspects. However, while setting rules is unlikely to make much of an impression if the underlying thinking is not assimilated, a good understanding of the values involved should enable staff to make correct decisions even if they do not remember the applicable rule. Indeed, those equipped with a solid ethical compass may not always make the right decision while operating in a grey area, but they will have no difficulty in confronting difficult situations. In contrast, knowledge of the rules will not prevent major failures of integrity in cases not covered by any (recognizable) rule. This is amply demonstrated by the current crisis, where the elaborate compliance rules applicable to banks did little or nothing to prevent misconduct on a grand scale.

Each company selecting a values-based approach should reflect on which *values* are, or should become, part of its corporate culture. The value cited most often is integrity, which is expressed by concepts such as trust and principled behaviour. Trust (that is, being trustworthy, and abstaining from lying and deceiving) is an essential cornerstone on which to build a culture of integrity, which in turn generates trust. Principled behaviour – that is, acting according to principles, treating like cases alike, and being consistent, is the basis of fairness. Honesty and responsibility are further expressions of integrity.

For practical purposes, the following tests are helpful in deciding whether a course of action is the right one:

- Does it imply doing anything illegal or unethical?
- Would it withstand the scrutiny of the public eye? Would it be embarrassing if it were exposed in the media?
- Will it involve being untruthful at any point?
- Does it have a genuine, legitimate business purpose?
- Does it imply using corporate property for personal benefit?

A hesitation in replying to any of these questions should encourage further thinking and requesting guidance.

Issuing the policy

The policy is a statement of what is expected from those to whom it applies with respect to matters covered by it. Each company should decide which matters it wants to include in a code of conduct on the basis of its business, countries of operation and other circumstances specific to it. Typically, those matters include the following:

- conflicts of interest;
- favouritism;
- the payment of bribes;
- gifts and entertainment;
- protection of the environment;
- employee relations (no discrimination, mobbing, bullying or sexual harassment);
- workplace safety;
- integrity of financial records (proper records and vouchers, no off-the-books accounts);
- confidentiality of company and client information as well as of personal data;
- insider trading;
- procurement practices;
- antitrust; and
- compliance with laws.

Most of these matters are covered by legislation, but not uniformly in all countries. Furthermore, public opinion in so-called developed countries tends to set a rather high standard for these topics, which are considered to pertain to ethics at least as much as to law. Multinational companies are thus expected to behave in accordance with these standards in all countries where they do business. It is therefore desirable to set a standard applicable throughout the company.

The policy or code of conduct should apply throughout all units controlled by the company and, to the extent that it is feasible, in joint ventures or in companies in which the company has a substantial interest. In these latter cases, where the company does not have a controlling interest, it should, prior to its involvement, obtain assurances that its standards will be complied with and that it will have a workable option to withdraw if they are not.

The code of conduct should apply to all staff as well as to the board of directors and agents or advisers hired by the company, and to subcontractors or regular suppliers in their dealings for or with the company.

The code of conduct should enunciate basic principles, formulated in simple non-legalistic terms which can be understood by staff at all levels. It should be short (five to ten pages of text). Lengthy texts will discourage readers and may create confusion rather than clarity. It does not take many words to enunciate principles, and adding more words will hardly help those who do not understand a simple formulation. Their lack of misunderstanding will generally have deeper roots than words alone can cure. The layout should be reader friendly, possibly with illustrations or photographs.

The levels of responsibility

Involvement of the board of directors and of senior management is essential. They should express their support for the programme and make clear that they will remain involved. Promoting and maintaining integrity in an organization cannot be delegated, but is the task of each and every individual. Leaders must teach by example. Compliance programmes that are not fully and visibly supported by management will amount to little more than an alibi and will fail.

The *board of directors* should endorse the programme and it, or the audit committee or another committee of the board should exercise an oversight on compliance matters and decide important issues or those that cannot be settled in other ways.

The *CEO* and senior management should have ultimate responsibility for making sure that the programme is implemented throughout the company.

A *compliance officer* should be appointed, not to discharge the management of its compliance responsibility but to support it in exercising this. This officer should be a senior manager, reporting preferably directly to the CEO. S/he should have direct access to the chairman of the board or of the board committee dealing with compliance matters and report periodically to either or both of them. The compliance officer needs a great independence of mind and this may be limited if s/he has other career objectives. It is therefore not a position that is well suited to managers at the beginning of their career. A certain degree of maturity will also be an asset to form a balanced judgement in critical cases. Not all companies need a full-time compliance officer; in smaller companies, the function is often entrusted to the General Counsel or, less often, to the head of human resources or the head of internal audit.

While the compliance officer does not have the executive authority over the compliance programme (this lies with the CEO, senior management and all staff), s/he is the person who will spearhead initiatives and provide an organizational framework. The compliance officer will be involved in formulating the policy or code of conduct. S/he will make sure that it is properly communicated, organize the training, monitor the due diligence on business partners, receive reports, conduct or supervise investigations and propose sanctions or corrective action. S/he will propose policies or guidelines that may be necessary in order to implement the programme as well as changes to the programme that may appear to be needed. Last but not least, the compliance officer will be the compliance advocate in cases where compliance imperatives and business goals diverge.

Communicating the programme internally and externally

Communicating the programme internally implies, first, distributing a copy of the code of conduct to all staff and other individuals covered by it. This should be done under cover of a message from the chairman and the CEO (or from the CEO and the chief compliance officer) stressing their support of the code.

Distributing a code of conduct throughout a multinational company will require translation into the languages of the countries where the company does business. It is not unusual for codes of conduct to need to be translated into twenty to thirty languages. Translations have to be monitored carefully, as the matters addressed in a code of conduct are not necessarily topics with which translators in all countries are familiar.

For record purposes, it is essential that each recipient acknowledges receipt of the code and commits to abide by it, thus making the code a part of the employment contract. In order to facilitate this step, it will be necessary to present the code to the unions, or better still, to involve them in the drafting of the code. After the first distribution throughout the company, the code can be handed out as part of his/her employment contract whenever an employee is hired.

Further to the distribution of the code, the programme should be advertised on the company's intranet and internet. The relevant web page(s) should have links to texts of the code of conduct in all the languages in which it is available and should describe the other elements of the programme, including training materials, where to obtain guidance, how to make reports, and the contact details of the compliance officer and his/her team.

Exercising due diligence in the selection of employees and business partners

All companies should have a procedure in place to check the background of *prospective employees*, to make sure that they do not have a criminal record. Particular attention should obviously be applied when screening personnel for a compliance function or for a position exposed to integrity issues.

Due diligence in the selection of *business partners* has a more specific compliance angle. While they may be acting (or may be seen to be acting) on behalf of the company, the company itself has only limited control over them. Therefore a specific due diligence must be conducted on business partners including subcontractors, regular suppliers, joint venture partners and agents, consultants, lobbyists or other external service providers. The due diligence will need to be tailored to the circumstances, but should include a thorough check of the background of the business partner and any involvement he/she may have had in practices not acceptable under the company's code of conduct. Business partners should undertake to abide by the company's code of conduct in their dealings with or on behalf of the company. This may seem intrusive, but dealing with business partners using child labour could severely damage a company's reputation. The same holds for intermediaries who would pay bribes to secure contracts for the company. In those cases, the acts of the business partner or intermediary would be viewed as acts of the company, if not legally, at least in the media and in public opinion. Should a business partner engage in unacceptable practices despite a commitment to the contrary, the company should have the contractual right to terminate the relationship immediately.

Adapting human resources policies

Human resources policies need to be adapted to reflect the importance given to the code of conduct, and to balance conflicts between the profit motive and compliance with the code. Staff should be protected not only against reprisals for denouncing violations of the code but also for adverse consequences (such as the absence of promotion or a lower bonus) for complying with it. This is in practice difficult to realize, as some staff may easily be tempted to blame their lack of business success on their strict compliance with the company's integrity standards. However, it is possible to obtain a good idea of an individual's integrity by an anonymous 360-degree assessment by peers, subordinates and superiors. Performance assessments should always include an integrity component, and the reaching of financial targets should be weighted by an integrity factor.

Human resources policies should also provide for rotation of individuals in exposed situations and for a time-bar on hiring when this hiring constitutes, or can be perceived as constituting, a reward for a favourable attitude in another position, such as a case when companies hire former public officials with whom they have had dealings when they occupied a public office.

Organizing training

Even the most attentive reading of a code of conduct is not sufficient to assimilate the values and ideas it conveys. For this to happen, it is necessary to explain what is meant by it and to illustrate it with examples from the daily business dealings of staff.

E-training is an appropriate induction to a code of conduct. It can convey the rules and test whether staff are able to relate them to concrete situations. However, the leadership component is missing in e-training, even if it includes a clip of the CEO stating his/her commitment to the programme. It is therefore recommended that each manager conducts a refresher session with his/her team at intervals of 12–18 months. This will require some preparation and specific training for the managers. This training for managers will require in turn the preparation of trainers to deliver it. These trainers should best be selected as representative of the company geographically, functionally and from a business point of view. In addition to delivering training for managers, they will become champions of integrity while continuing in their current job.

The training material should be specific to the company, and different training material may have to be provided depending on the business sector or function of the staff being trained (though it does no harm for staff to be confronted with ethical dilemmas that arise in other parts of the company). In principle, all staff should be trained, but it is possible to provide for a lighter form of training for support staff.

Providing guidance and receiving reports

All staff should be able to obtain guidance from the compliance officer or his/her team on a confidential basis. This is important because staff may hesitate before engaging on a course of action, whether on their own initiative or under instructions from a superior. They may also hesitate when confronted by, or witnessing what they believe may constitute a violation of the company's code of conduct that they should report. Staff should not be penalized for such hesitation, but should be encouraged to seek advice whenever they are in doubt. Developing a counselling practice will also be very helpful for the compliance officer and his/her team to gain an insight into practical problems arising in the company and to take consistent decisions and, where necessary, issue guidelines.

Staff should also be able to report suspected violations of the code of conduct. Several avenues should be open for reports, such as alerting one's superior, human resources staff, an internal auditor or a corporate lawyer. However, in order to ensure a professional handling of reports, the preferred route should be the compliance officer or his/her staff, who should receive specific training if they have no experience in that area.

The routes through which to make reports should include a hotline, a dedicated e-mail address and a dedicated fax number, as well as the possibility to make reports online on the internet or intranet site of the company. The preferred routes outside the USA are online reports and e-mail messages. Hotlines are widely used in the USA, but less so in other countries. These should best be operated by a third party for reasons of both efficiency and cost. Only very large companies can afford to operate a hotline 24 hours a day, seven days a week, as would be necessary in a group of companies operating across all time zones. Hotline providers must also have expertise in handling calls and obtaining translation services when needed.

One of the issues often discussed in relation to reports is whether anonymous reports should be accepted. They should not be encouraged, but they should not be ignored if they are made and include information that can be checked independently. An anonymous report cannot be accepted as evidence because of the impossibility of cross-examining the reporting party. However, it can be helpful as a finger pointing in a direction where evidence will be found.

Investigations are nevertheless greatly facilitated if the reporting party discloses his/her identity. S/he should then have the possibility of requesting that the matter remains confidential. In these cases, the reporting party should be consulted if the investigation cannot progress without disclosing his/her identity or disclosing facts or circumstances that will permit the identification of him/her.

Even when confidentiality is not specifically requested, knowledge of the identities of the parties involved and of the circumstances should be limited to those involved in investigating the case, in order to protect the party against whom the report is directed and whose reputation may be tarnished by a report even if such a report subsequently turns out to be unfounded. The reporting party or whistle-blower should also be protected against any form of reprisal. This will require monitoring the situation to make sure that reprisals are not exercised under some pretence other than the report. The best protection is, however, to keep the identity of the whistle-blower confidential to the greatest extent possible, whether s/he has requested this or not.

It is important for the credibility of the system that the reporting party receives feedback on the follow-up to his/her report. Receipt of the report should be acknowledged as soon as possible, and some feedback should be provided after completion of the investigation. Only victims of a violation of the code of conduct should be informed of the result of the investigation. In other cases, the feedback may be limited to a non-committing confirmation that the matter has been investigated and that appropriate measures have been taken, to the extent required. Such a limited feedback is especially appropriate in cases of anonymous reports if the reporting party has provided an e-mail address under an alias, or if it has been arranged with him/her to call back to obtain feedback or to answer additional questions that may arise in course of the investigation.

Even in large organizations, the number of reports will rarely exceed fifty per month and are more likely to be under twenty. A majority of reports will be irrelevant and can be disposed of summarily, because they are not specific enough or because they do not relate to matters covered by the code of conduct. Many of these relate to purely human resources matters, such as termination or absence of a promotion or of a pay raise. These reports should be referred to the Human Resources Department if they appear to warrant any action. Reports of violations of the company's code of conduct should not open an additional avenue to air such matters unless they raise an integrity issue, such as discrimination, bullying or sexual harassment.

Even though only a minority of reports are relevant, there will be a few matters presenting a real risk for the company which will well justify organizing a reporting system.

Conducting investigations

Investigations should be conducted by the compliance officer or by others under the supervision of this officer. Experience in conducting investigations should be one of the requirements when selecting a compliance officer. Where experience is lacking, training should be provided.

Investigations must be conducted confidentially, involving people only on a 'need to know' basis. If a report is directed at a specific individual, that individual should be informed as soon as the information gathered supports the allegation and s/he should be given the opportunity to defend him/herself.

A record should be kept of all investigative steps. Minutes should be kept of interviews, which should always be conducted in a team of no fewer than and no more than two in order to have a witness (and a record keeper) without overwhelming the interviewee. Interviews should be conducted with fairness and impartiality.

In certain instances it may be necessary to hire outside investigators. They should be required to observe the company's code of conduct and policies when conducting the investigation.

Sanctioning misconduct and taking corrective measures

The investigation should be concluded by a report setting out the facts and assessing them in terms of the code of conduct with a proposal for corrective and/or disciplinary measures. The ultimate decision in this respect should be a joint decision by the compliance officer and management, or by the board of directors or board committee in charge of overseeing the implementation of the code of conduct.

The compliance officer should make sure that any sanctions and/or corrective measures are implemented. Cases of violations of the code and the sanctions or measures to which they gave rise, may be summarized on the company's intranet to illustrate the implementation of the code of conduct for the employees' benefit. This kind of publication should take place some time (for example, six months) after the conclusion of the case and not include any names or any circumstances that might allow the identification of the individuals or location involved. A publication of summary information on violations may also be published on the company's internet to underline the company's commitment to its code of conduct.

Monitoring, reviewing and periodically assessing the programme

An integrity programme is not a static instrument. It needs to be monitored constantly to adjust it to the changing business of the company and to integrate changes in the latter's environment. Its impact also needs to be assessed periodically. Are staff familiar with the programme? Has it become part of the company's culture? Is it a successful influence on staff behaviour? Are clarifications or additional policies necessary?

Keeping the programme alive by constantly remodelling and improving it is an essential element in its success. This is not surprising, since, in devising a code of conduct and an integrity programme, as in other ethical or spiritual endeavours, the path is part of the goal.

Notes

1. *The Foreign Corrupt Practices Act of 1977 ('FCPA'), 15 U.S.C. §§ 78dd–1, et seq.* is accessible on the US Department of Justice website at: http://www.justice. gov/criminal/fraud/fcpa.
2. H.R. Rep. No 95–640 at 4 (1977).
3. *Convention on Combating Bribery of Foreign Public Officials in International Business Transactions*, adopted by the Negotiating Conference on 21 November 1997, accessible on the OECD website at: http://www.oecd.org/ daf/nocorruption/convention.
4. The signatories of the Convention include, as of March 2009 (non-OECD members in italics): *Argentina*, Australia, Austria, Belgium, *Brazil*, *Bulgaria*, Canada, *Chile*, Czech Republic, Denmark, *Estonia*, Finland, France, Germany, Greece, Hungary, Iceland, Ireland, *Israel*, Italy, Japan, Korea, Luxembourg, Mexico, the Netherlands, New Zealand, Norway, Poland, Portugal, Slovak Republic, *Slovenia*, *South Africa*, Spain, Sweden, Switzerland, Turkey, UK, USA.
5. Council of Europe, *Criminal Convention on Corruption*, European Treaty Series (ETS) No. 173, 27 January 1999; and *Civil Law Convention on Corruption*, European Treaty Series (ETS) No 174, 4 November 1999, accessible on the Council of Europe website at: http://conventions.coe.int/Treaty/EN/treaties/html/173.htm and http://conventions.coe.int/Treaty/EN/treaties/html/174.htm.
6. *United Nations Convention against Corruption* (UNCAC), adopted by General Assembly Resolution 58/4 of 31 October 2003 accessible on the United Nations Office on Drugs and Crime (UNODC) website at: http://www.unodc.org/unodc/en/treaties/CAC/index.html.
7. A list of signatories is accessible on the UNODC website at: http://www.unodc.org/unodc/en/treaties/CAC/signatories.html.
8. For the history of Arthur Andersen, see Wikipedia on: (http://en.wikipedia.org/wiki/Arthur_Andersen) and the French site of the Arthur Andersen alumni (http://www.arthuralumni.com/public/association/histoire.html).
9. *Arthur Andersen LLP* v. *United States*, 125 S. Ct at 2134 (citing 18 USC § 1512(b)(2)(A) and (B)).
10. *Arthur Andersen LLP* v. *United States*, 544 US 696 (2005).
11. *The Federal Sentencing Guidelines Manual and Appendices* (2008) is accessible on the website of the United States Federal Sentencing Commission at: http://www.ussc.gov/guidelin.htm.
12. *Business Principles for Countering Bribery*, 2009 edition, is available on the Transparency International website at: http://www.transparency.org/global_priorities/private_sector/business_principles.
13. Transparency International (www.transparency.org) was founded in 1993 and is now a global network including more than ninety locally established national chapters and chapters-in-formation. It is combating corruption in

many ways, including the publication of a Corruption Perceptions Index (CPI) published annually since 2001, and of a Bribe Payers Index (BPI) published to date in 1999, 2002, 2006 and 2008.
14. Social Accountability International (http://www.sa-intl.org/) is best known for its SA8000 certification standard for improving working conditions.

Bibliography

Arthur Andersen LLP v. *United States*, 544 US 696 (2005).

Council of Europe (1999) *Criminal Convention on Corruption*, European Treaty Series (ETS) No. 173, 27 January.

Council of Europe (1999) *Civil Law Convention on Corruption*, European Treaty Series (ETS) No. 174, 4 November.

Organisation for Economic Co-operation and Development (OECD) (1997) *Convention on Combating Bribery of Foreign Public Officials in International Business Transactions*. Adopted by the Negotiating Conference 21 November.

Transparency International (2009) *Business Principles for Countering Bribery.*, available on the Transparency International website at: http://www.transparency. org/global_priorities/private_sector/business_principles.

United Nations (2003) *United Nations Convention against Corruption* (UNCAC). Adopted by General Assembly Resolution 58/4 of 31 October.

United States Department of Justice (1997) *The Foreign Corrupt Practices Act of 1977* ('FCPA'), 15 USC §78dd–1, et seq.

United States District Court, Southern District of Texas (n.d.) *United States of America against Arthur Andersen, LLP*, Indictment (T.18, USC, §1512 (b)(2) and §3551 et seq.).

United States Federal Sentencing Commission (2008) *Federal Sentencing Guidelines Manual and Appendices 2008*.

United States House of Representatives (1977) *Report No. 95–640*, 95th Congress, 1st Session.

United States Supreme Court (2005) *Arthur Andersen LLP* v. *United States*, 544 US 696.

11
The Implementation of CSR as a New Social Contract in Poland

Janina Filek

> By stimulating commerce and development at the bottom of the economic pyramid, multinationals could radically improve the lives of billions of people and help create a more stable, less dangerous world. Achieving this goal does not require MNCs to spearhead global social-development initiatives for charitable purposes. They need only act in their own self-interest.
>
> (Prahalad and Hammond, 2002)

CSR as a new version of the social contract

Since the very beginning, the idea of a social contract has been closely connected with reflection on the problems related to the functioning of society. Therefore, the idea has been referred to occasionally in the hope of, generally speaking, possibly solving the basic problem of human-kind: that concerning the right (according to some) or the optimal (as others imagined) way for society to function.

The idea, similar to all other important political and social ideas, has had a complicated history, with great supporters and equally great adversaries, and it has given rise to many controversies and disputes. The beginnings of the idea can be traced back to the ancient Greeks' disputes concerning the problems of the state. It was only in the thoughts of Thomas Hobbes, John Locke, Jean-Jacques Rousseau and Immanuel Kant that the idea was developed to the fullest extent, and after that surge of interest, was temporarily forgotten. Ever since then, the history of the idea is one of ups and downs: after periods of oblivion, the idea was occasionally remembered and reborn. The idea was reborn most recently in the 1990s. In order to briefly outline the reasons behind the recent interest we should first mention the timeless usefulness of contractual tradition, present since the days of Hobbes and Locke; and second, we should point out the interest in decision theory.

Yet another reason behind the rebirth of the idea of social contract may well turn out to be the idea of corporate social responsibility (CSR).

The subject matter of social contracts

Despite many historical differences, what all social contracts seem to have in common is what they have always been: first, an attempt to find a solution to the dilemma of the governed versus the government; second, an attempt to find a solution to the dilemma of an individual's safety versus that individual's freedom; and third, an attempt to find a way that leads to the welfare of the general public.

The problems that present-day societies have to contend with provoke reflection on whether the current changes, and specifically the issues connected with social and economic nature that result from ubiquitous globalization, are not reason enough to yet again take an interest in the idea of a social contract. Is it time to yet again ask the questions about the way society – global society – functions? Is it time to ask not only about the principles of the functioning of society in the political sphere but also in the economic sphere; in other words, to enquire anew about the principles of the way the free market functions in the context of the realization of one common objective – namely, the common good? Is it the time to enquire again about the legitimacy of those governing or ruling society; not in the context of political power, but with regard to economic power and economic forces. In other words, is it time for a new social contract?

The idea of corporate social responsibility

Judging by the way that the idea of CSR developed, it can be deduced that the reasons behind its coming to existence, and the solutions it offers, are very similar in character to the ones that gave birth to the idea of a social contract.

The recent popularity of the idea of CSR has caused a multitude of definitions to be created. Among the many currently functioning definitions (as of the year 2001), the most interesting and the one that best reflects the subject matter of CSR seems to be the definition according to which CSR is a voluntary obligation of business to contribute to sustainable development in co-operation with the workers, their families, local communities and the whole of society in general; an obligation that leads to improving the quality of life, which, in turn, serves both business and social development (World Bank Report, 2005).

CSR and social contracts

Let us try to examine the questions that have appeared most frequently in the discourse on the naturalness of the social order, or its contractuality, with the solutions the concept of CSR offers, and try to verify CSR's usefulness as a new social contract. The questions that have appeared most frequently concerning social contract, regardless of the political stance of their authors, are as follows:

- What made people abandon a stateless and lawless condition; that is, how did society come into existence? The idea of CSR broadens our knowledge in the area of what society is, what community is, and what brings benefit to the community as companies themselves are micro-scale social communities. The solution offered by CSR consists of the possibility of perfecting the way a company functions (by considering CSR as a new management strategy), which may in turn be translated into better functioning of the company, and consequently, into better functioning of society as a whole.
- How does the law become legally binding? The idea of CSR does not create new concepts here, but broadens our knowledge of the question of the legitimacy of the operation of companies and business circles. The justification for a company's existence is that it caters for the needs of the people, and that a company is a social entity. The solution offered by CSR consists in considering a company to be an active and creative social player.
- What is justice, and what does it consist of? The idea of CSR, though it does not answer these questions directly (and definitely does not settle them in a theoretical sense), seems to broaden our knowledge of the question of what is justice in an economic dimension by showing the wrongs of abuse (for example, the abuse of employees by employers, clients by producers, contractors by hirers), and by promoting actions supporting local communities where there is a shortage of resources. The solution offered by CSR consists of establishing a company's 'obligation' towards stakeholders (understood as groups vitally interested in a company's operations).

The vital element of every social contract that has not been mentioned so far is the law that becomes legally binding on all parties as a result of the contractual agreement. Therefore, many thinkers considered social contract as a root, core and beginning of society understood as a political union (legal and justice union), which has been called *pactum unionis* or *pactum sociale*. In this context, it is worthwhile drawing attention to the meaning of law within the idea of CSR, and, consequently, abiding by the law as a necessary condition for the implementation of the principles of CSR (Filek Janina, 2006), as well as the possibility of creating the law as a grass-roots initiative of entrepreneurs' business organizations. By emphasizing strongly the significance of the law, the idea of CSR refers to moral principles, and consequently encourages reflection on what is a crucial area: namely, on the relationship between law and morality. CSR does it by attempting to establish the range of mutual interaction between law and morality (very important for Kant's social contract). The law, as an element of the contract, must be obeyed by every economic entity, therefore also by companies; otherwise, the social contract loses its force and the area of what is above the law, what is pure morality, remains in some part in the decision-making power of each entity. However, the standards applying to companies result also from the influence of moral culture typical of a given society. Therefore the concept of CSR is undoubtedly a new pact for sustainable social development.

The concept of CSR, as any social contract, is not the aim in itself; nor is it pure theory. The concept was born out of need that had been signalled by democratic societies. If such a need is catered for, and the problems hindering its realization are solved, it will become a permanent element of cultural awareness, as with, for example, the idea of freedom. At present, the concept is not an answer to social demand, because the historical development of economies has been too vigorous (and has not gone entirely to plan, understood as the human plan). For these reasons, the free-market economy (as an area of human activity) has been entangled in many contradictions, such as, for example, that between the economic interests of rich countries and the interests of developing ones. Furthermore, the fast pace of the changes taking place, and their negative results, have threatened social stability. Yet again in the history of humankind, the actions taken by those in power have shown a less than just character of certain solutions adapted.

When treating CSR as a new social contract, its two different levels must be taken into consideration. The first is the level of the economic sphere – a contract between society and entities of the economic world. The latter is the contract between the management of the company and all its stakeholders. As far as the second level is concerned, it can be claimed that those founding a company are repeating the gesture of founding a society, albeit in a miniaturized form.

What we can learn from the authors of classical social contracts

Let us briefly compare the concept of CSR to one of the most widespread concepts of the social contract, namely that of Jean-Jacques Rousseau,[1] without considering the dissimilarity between the spheres being under the influence of the social contract. For Rousseau, it is mainly the political sphere, whereas in the case of CSR it is mainly the economic sphere. However, if, as Hans Jonas noticed, the economic sphere has currently overtaken the sphere of essential activity (Jonas, 1996), therefore becoming the most essential one (frequently even more essential than political activity), it is no surprise that the weight of deliberation on a social contract related to the political sphere has been shifted on to the one related to the economic sphere.

What interested Rousseau was not asking the question (that had already been asked) about the origin of humanity, but rather the question about what can provoke a human being to become who s/he can and should be, in order to fulfil his/her vocation. It was obvious to Rousseau that his contemporaries were not able to fulfil their vocations. It is also the case with CSR; this is a concept originating from a conviction about the imperfection of humankind operating within the economic sphere, and a concept attempting to indicate what actions taken by economic entities will allow those representing them to fulfil their difficult vocation of living in society. The first sentence of Rousseau's *The Social Contract* (Rousseau, 1994) was: 'I intend to examine whether, in the ordering of society, there can be any reliable and legitimate rule of administration, taking men as they are, and laws as they can be.' If we were to treat CSR as a social contract, its preamble could start with the following words: 'We intend to examine whether, in the ordering of the economy, there can be any reliable and legitimate rule of administration, taking humankind as they are, and laws as they can be. For the concept of CSR, such a rule turned out to be the principle of responsibility towards stakeholders' (see Filek, Janina, 2007). The stakeholders have a similar function to the one that *société générale* had in Rousseau's idea.

Rousseau's main problem was finding such a form of community that would defend and protect all its member and their welfare, and thanks to which every person uniting with all others would yet listen only to themselves and would remain as free as they had been before. If we were to consider how the idea of CSR tackles the problem, it could be claimed that, drawing on the impressive achievements of many thinkers (but mainly the existentialists and supporters of the philosophy of dialogue), CSR has 'solved' the problem of retaining both the freedom of the individual and the freedom of an economic entity through complementing the idea of freedom (still remaining within the range of each entity) with the idea of responsibility. The idea does not limit any given entity's freedom, but adds a moral dimension to it, and enables each entity to fulfil its own vocation better through a voluntary choice of action taken in favour of the society.

The aim of introducing the idea of CSR is, as in the case of Rousseau's social contract, protecting freedom and increasing the power of each individual or economic entity. Dedication to society becomes the means of doing this, through aiming at the realization of the common good (even if only to a small extent) in accordance with the principle that Rousseau adopted as well, namely saying that no one is able to improve his/her circumstances at the cost of others.[2] Similarly, in accordance with CSR visualizations, all are able to improve their circumstances by improving the circumstances of others, but at the same time, no one can improve their circumstances at the cost of others without taking significant economic and legal risks.[3] The functioning of society on the basis of the adopted social contract finds its ultimate support in the interests of every individual – as Rousseau wished – or in the interests of every economic entity, alongside the benefit to local communities or the whole society – as the idea of CSR suggests. Referring again to the extract from Prahalad and Hammond (2002) quoted at the start of this chapter: 'By stimulating commerce and development at the bottom of the economic pyramid, multinationals could radically improve the lives of billions of people and help create a more stable, less dangerous world. Achieving this goal does not require MNCs to spearhead global social-development initiatives for charitable purposes. They need only act in their own self-interest.'

The idea of a social contract according to Rousseau cannot contradict any of the natural laws, therefore not only the freedom, independence and equality of particular individuals, but also their dignity. In the concept of CSR, this aspect is also given consideration, which can be demonstrated by two significant documents supporting the idea of CSR: Caux Round Table (1994), or in the United Nations Global Compact.[4]

In Rousseau's concept, the idea of a contract results from an assumption that what is natural is good, and that the historical process of de-naturalization is a negative phenomenon. To the philosopher, destroying the natural balance, which is the result of a clash between the natural needs of a human being, and insufficient capabilities of the individual to satisfy them, leads to the state where support from other members of the society becomes essential. Members of a community can no longer survive without the 'support of their neighbours'. Consequently, common interdependence between people is created, forming the basis for the birth of society in general (*société générale*). Social relations result from the fact that people need one another. However, setting up the first dependencies is a dynamic event and therefore they are entangled in a range of contradictions – for example, a lack of balance between the needs of a human being and the possibilities of meeting these, or, most importantly, contradictory interests between a human being and the society in which he or she lives. A social contract is necessary to minimize them. Rousseau considered the social contract – dictated by nature itself – as a chimera, a speculative construct of philosophers. The foundation for humans uniting into social communities must always be the voluntary permission of the community members (contract) to take on certain obligations and commitments to one another. The concept of CSR is one of the interesting proposals realizing this condition, as within the 'functioning of an economic body' where economic units, economic entities, agree to meet certain legal commitments upon entering the market. Also, as independent and free units, they take additional decisions about commitments beyond their legal obligations to others, to their stakeholders. Beyond the law itself, the units set the boundaries of the contract. Thus, the CSR principles fulfil the conditions determined by Rousseau in the frame of his social contract.

'Man is only separated from the state of nature by his own history which cannot be reversed. In order to remedy the existing evil, one must reckon with history; it is necessary to find a way to remedy evil in "evil itself".' (Baczko, 2002). New solutions can 'repair' society that does not function well, through the elimination of the omissions and weaknesses of old solutions. However, one has to be able to identify and diagnose such weaknesses. It must be remembered that a social contract does not necessarily aim at solving a particular problem, but rather at finding a principle according to which the problems can be solved. Specific solutions are created as a consequence of the adopted principles that form the basis of the contract.

A social contract is in itself the establishment of a new order; the creation, from scratch, of a new social and political organization; the creation of new laws; or an attempt to bring back an older, lost order. The concept of CSR, ever more popular in Europe, has similar aims. It is mainly about putting the relationship between companies and their stakeholders in order in the economic sphere. More and more frequently, it is considered that – apart from the realization of economic aims – a company becomes a small community of people who are already technically bound by the general society; hence, people with individual preferences, with their own unique habits, united by a common need, are still divided by the game of private interests. As such a community, the company undertakes actions within a higher level of community, namely society as a whole, and as a result of the globalization process, within an even higher-level community, namely humankind in general.

Bearing Rousseau in mind, it needs to be noted that the new social idea cannot just enter history in any given moment; each society has its own age that is particularly conducive to the introduction of new laws. The need for a contract surfaces when the political springs are already 'used up'. To paraphrase the thought, it can be claimed that the idea of CSR surfaced when some of the economic springs appeared to be 'used up', or the principles regulating economic activity started to show their destructive power.

The surfacing of the CSR idea can be seen through Hegel's perspective, where vigorously forming capitalism is a thesis, democracy is the antithesis, and CSR – the synthesis in the economic sphere that allows us to overcome the contradiction between the principles and practice of the vigorous (therefore sometimes imperfect) capitalism – and democracy promising us not only freedom, but also equality before the law, and in this way also a certain amount of social justice. In such a case, new principles will be established as a result of the intervention into the course of history of a non-historical factor; namely, a rational, legislative decision, preceded by the adoption of a new social contract. Such a solution reconciles in some sense the conflicting two '*laissez-faire*-isms': Ludwig von Mises's rational one and Friedrich Hayek's evolutionary one.

As mentioned earlier, CSR as a new social contract cannot just be realized at any given moment and place. It can only happen under certain conditions: first, a high economic level; second, the moment when the old solutions are 'used up'; and third, respecting the values upon which a new principle of the functioning of society (or economy) can be created. The surfacing of the idea of CSR, and its popularity, especially in Europe, is not a coincidence. It is here that such an idea would be well received and can 'come true'. This is because of several factors; first, a well-developed free market functions in Europe, which is increasingly showing its imperfect form; and second, apart from the awareness of the necessity of abiding by the law in force, such social values as freedom, equality, fraternity (or solidarity) and tolerance are vital here, and these values form the basis for discovering the principle of responsibility.

However, while enforcing the principles of CSR, it cannot be forgotten that the conditions that must also be taken into consideration are national uniqueness and historical identity, as well as the cultural resources of a given society. Therefore, in very broad terms, it can be stated that the implementation of the idea of CSR alongside the laws promoting these actions must be done as a peculiar synthesis of the natural and the historical.

The principles of CSR, similar to the principles of 'body politic' in the social contract, serve the purpose of obtaining maximum compliance between the interests of a particular individual and the common interest, through combining the individual's sense of being different with the sense of belonging to the community, in the individual's spiritual life. Only those economic entities that show respect for the law and take on voluntarily a certain proportion of social commitments (that the concept of CSR mentions) will have a sense of belonging to community.

The subject matter of CSR, similar to the subject matter of a social contract, is based on the idea of freedom, as it is a voluntary decision by an economic entity that makes the adopted commitments factually binding.

Entering the social contract – as Rousseau states – is an agreement of a peculiar kind, where all participants incur obligations towards one other, and as a result all are bound by obligations towards one another. Rousseau stated 'From this it will be understood that the factor which makes the will general is not so much the number of persons voting, but rather the common interest that unites them, for under this system everyone necessarily submits to the conditions that he imposes on others' (Rousseau, 1994), but at the same time is no less free than before entering the agreement. The principle of responsibility that is fundamental to CSR similarly binds the sides of the agreement without subjugating them to anyone's will in particular, and leaves them as free as they had been before the agreement was made.

A similar analysis can be done by comparing CSR to Locke's or Kant's concepts of a social contract. However, as was mentioned at the beginning of this chapter, all concepts of a social contract have certain elements in common. These elements are also part of the CSR idea. As with any social contract, the concept of CSR not only refers to the law, but also influences the creation of the law. And as in the case of any social contract, CSR takes up and solves (in its own manner) the social dilemma of freedom and safety by increasing the latter without excessively limiting the freedom of an economic entity. On a much smaller scale, CSR takes up the problem of the government understood as the governed–government dilemma, mainly because it is the world of economics, not the world of politics, that is its domain, though some solutions in this area can be found in the concept of a company's obligations towards its employees, or in an increasingly promoted thesis about company as community. As with every social contract idea, CSR takes up the problem of the common good, since CSR is the obligation of business to contribute to sustainable development in co-operation with workers, their families, local communities and the whole society.

The discussion outlined above (very briefly) seems to justify the conclusion that CSR can be the new social contract.

The implementation of CSR in Poland

The factors conditioning interest in and the development of CSR

In short, the idea of CSR surfaces when, on the one hand, there is advanced economic growth, but on the other, the imperfections of this too-fierce economic development appear with increasing frequency, and have serious social consequences. Second, CSR can only be established in societies that represent a high level of law and order, as its foundation is only possible on a permanent basis of law. Third, the condition conducive, if not vital, to its development is the existence of social capital. Fourth, to enable the idea of CSR to develop, a thorough knowledge of the concept in a given society is necessary. And in the fifth place, the idea's actual development is only possible when some institution or organization begins to promote it, as can be seen in the example of the United Kingdom.

The reasons for less interest in the idea of CSR in Poland

It was only in recent years that the idea of CSR began to be discussed in Poland, and then only by a small circle of theorists of business ethics. During the early years, the meaningfulness of the idea was discussed, and its supporters had the job of 'forging' the idea into Polish minds.

It was argued that the concept was possibly an ideological attack on free market principles (see Friedman, 1970; Crook, 2002), and the supporters of the idea frequently had to justify their alleged antipathy towards a free market system. Next, it was argued that CSR was only a temporary fad, and its supporters were forced to refute some very intricate arguments formulated against it. At present, the discussion on CSR is entering the next level of consideration: the level that can be characterized by the question 'What should be done to put the idea into effect for the benefit of all stakeholders'?

In other words, gone are the days of theoretical discussion about the reality of CSR,[5] what it should be implemented for, and of the analysis of the charges against it (see Filek, Janina, 2005), as well as the benefits of introducing it. The time has now come to consider how to implement it within the Polish reality? To answer this question, however, it has to be considered why despite more than a decade's discussion on the idea in the academic environment, the concept of CSR still has not generated any real interest among Polish entrepreneurs.

According to research, it can be demonstrated that around 40 per cent of companies operating in the Polish market (mainly Polish companies), belong to the 'beginners' group (no CSR strategy); 45 per cent of companies (mainly multinational corporations and large Polish companies) belong to the group of 'observers' (uncoordinated operations within the area of CSR); and only 15 per cent of companies (mainly multinational corporations) belong to the 'leaders' group (CSR strategy is included in overall company strategy) (Kuraszko, 2007).

Objective reasons

Before the characteristic reasons for the Polish situation are analysed, it will be worthwhile to mention the problems and lack of clarity that are immanently connected with the idea itself.

Reasons of a methodological nature

One of these reasons is the internal conflict between the economic and social aims of a company, as noted by Friedman (1970).

Another one is the multitude of currently functioning definitions of CSR and their lack of precision, as mentioned earlier. According to some, corporate social responsibility is understood only as charity; while, for others, it belongs mainly to the sphere of public relations. According to some, CSR creates a new, social face of an economy; while others think it is merely another tool with which to fight the competition, or a new marketing strategy. The multitude of definitions characterizing the nature of CSR, as well as the ambiguity related to understanding what it involves, prove that the idea is still in its developmental phase; and if it is only being shaped now, it is not an easy task to determine what its subject matter is, and in consequence, it is not an easy task to enforce it.

The multitude of definitions also creates an additional threat of a mismatch between theorists' expectations and practitioners' actions. Theorists investigating the development of the idea, being up to date with recent debate on the idea, usually think of a more 'advanced' meaning for it; whereas practitioners are usually not able to keep pace with such debate, which in turn means that what is enforced can differ greatly from what theorists expect.

Reasons of a theoretical nature

While the reasons of a theoretical nature that make it difficult to enforce CSR practices, are not typical only of Poland, without their full understanding it will not be easy to differentiate between the reasons that are typically Polish and the reasons connected partially 'with the theory'. Recognizing reasons of a theoretical nature will help greatly in differentiating between what can be considered an objective reason and what is more of a subjective and local character – in this case, the Polish character.

Let us begin with what constitutes, in the light of the theory, the factor founding positive responsibility (see Filek, Janina, 2002), upon which the idea of CSR is built. The following can most definitely be mentioned:

 (i) social expectations (the awareness among the members of society as to what are the responsibilities of particular entities operating within the social life of the country);
(ii) real possibilities of economic entities (the economic state of companies, their ability to implement changes and the level of organizational culture); and
(iii) external circumstances (the economic and social circumstances of a given country, political system or legal system).

These elements are built on the moral idea that determines people's living conditions, and the world that is worth the mankind; the idea that, according to Charles Taylor, forms a moral horizon (Taylor, 1996).

Thanks to this horizon, we, as members of society, can distinguish between what is acceptable ethically and what is not. One of the most important features that form the moral horizon, apart from cultural conditions that are different in every society, is the fundamental question of ethics: how to live? (Filek, Jacek, 2001).

Assuming the above, it is not difficult to see that the implementation of CSR in practice will be the outcome of social expectations, the financial and cultural situation of a company, the economic and social situation of a given country, and the moral awareness of society (social capital). In other words, the implementation of CSR will differ in practice depending on the culture of a given society, its economic and social situation and its level of morality. When analysing the issue of our interest in the theoretical context, it is worthwhile mentioning the 'long-lasting absence' of the idea of assigning responsibility (positive responsibility) to economic entities in economic theories.[6] This undoubtedly has its roots in history. Social ideas surface normally as a response to some important problem that arises in 'grim reality'.

The 'long-lasting absence' of the idea of CSR in economic theories was also caused by the following assumptions made by economists:

- An accidental order theory that stands in opposition to universal responsibility founded on the moral idea of living conditions of people.
- A separatist vision of economic activity as a sphere governed by separate rules.
- Methodological individualism, seeing freedom only through the perspective of individual actions (if there are no common actions, there is no positive responsibility for possible good).
- The assumption about the positivism of the economy that enables the elimination of judgements and ethical notions from the sphere of economics.

Despite economic theory slowly departing from these premises, or complementing them with additional assumptions that help to attach the idea of CSR to the core of economic theory, in Poland's case, there appears to be a significant problem related to economic education. After the period of socialist economic education, the political change caused a strong desire for a 'free market economy', and in consequence the economic theory that was firmly established and present in American course books was hastily adopted as the educational canon. The economic theory taught in Poland is frequently obsolete, and maintains that – to put it briefly – the only aim of business operations is still only to make a profit.

Practical reasons – however, of a rather objective nature

The main reason behind the difficulties in putting CSR into practice is not only the theoretical, but mainly the practical domination of the criterion of efficiency used for the evaluation of business.

Another reason is a commonly experienced difficulty in introducing theoretical ethical principles into practical activities. It is frequently easier to say how one should act rather than to do it every day, in particular when such actions require additional effort and when the temptation to minimize the effort by taking 'short-cuts' appears.

Yet another reason is the social and economic situation, understood as the divergence between social and economic levels of society. The more significant the divergence, the more difficult it is to implement CSR strategy.

The reasons characteristic of Polish conditions

These reasons can be divided into historical/intellectual and material/organizational; however, the division is purely for presentation purposes, as many conditions discussed here are intertwined.

Historical and intellectual reasons

Implementing CSR principles in Poland meets with serious problems as the history of the country has not been particularly conducive to the development of a pro-social way of thinking that refers to the common good. The *liberum veto* principle is a good example of individualist thinking that does not take the common good into consideration. For Polish people, freedom is and has often been more important than the common good, or social good (which is a notion additionally debased by the previous political formation). Polish people as a nation are capable of throwing off any yoke, but much less capable of building a society that cares for all on the ruins of the defeated oppressor. An example of this may be the birth of the 'Solidarity' movement, which crushed the unwanted authority, but whose ideas have yet not been turned into the expected social solutions. The recent protests among particular professional groups hoping to 'snatch' as much as they could for certain circles while ignoring other groups is a clear example of this situation. The problem becomes even clearer when the escalation of the demands of certain circles starts to overlap with the phenomenon of the ever-growing number of socially excluded people in Poland.

There is another historical condition related to the legacy of individualism. Polish people, forced to fight governments that enslaved them, learnt how to oppose 'evil' authority and how to overthrow it. This ability to oppose authority, moulded down the centuries, has remained in the nature of Polish society, and even though the country has finally lived to see a democratically elected government, a part of Polish society still opposes the government. The specific Polish mentality that makes it difficult to implement the idea of CSR in the country, is conditioned by this. By not accepting the laws imposed by 'evil government', the Polish 'learnt' how to elude, or even to reject, almost any law that limits them. A significant part of Polish society does not abide by the law, notoriously eluding or even breaking it. The Polish nation has a problem with obeying any law in force. This undoubtedly differentiates Polish society from other European societies, and makes it difficult to implement CSR principles, as they must be preceded by a rigorous obedience to the law, so that CSR principles do not become just an 'improving of the country's image' or 'a smokescreen'.

Another feature related to the reluctance to abide by the law, which differentiates Polish society from the societies of, for example, Scandinavian countries, is the common consent to elude or break the law in Poland. The average Pole does not protest against those eluding or breaking the law every day, and nor do they see anything wrong in it, as long as breaking the law does not mean any harm to them personally. The average Pole does not have an 'ingrained' respect for the law in the same way as a German or Dutch citizen does; therefore, Poles do not bridle at little dishonesties among their countrymen.

Social and economic conditions

Apart from historical conditions, another difficulty in implementing CSR principles in Polish entrepreneurs' operations is too large a rift between the level of economic development and that of social development. While much has been done in the economic field since the beginnings of the country's transformation, and the pace of economic development is commonly considered to be satisfactory, the same may not be said about social development. Some even consider that it is now more difficult for Poles to operate within the social sphere, by pointing to the problems of unemployment, illegal work, homelessness, ever-growing social stratification, and the increasingly common phenomenon of social exclusion. The poor social situation results in not only grudges and grievances among particular social groups, but also resentment which, in the social context, can result in the impediment of economic development, and in our problem's context can result in unrealistic expectations towards corporate social responsibility; expectations that would be impossible for economic entities to meet.

Another difficulty in implementing CSR principles in Poland are commonly functioning stereotypes concerning running a business, such as: 'You have to steal your first million', and 'Business is a jungle', and those connected with abiding by the law: 'If the law does not state otherwise, I can do whatever I wish' or 'What is not illegal must be ethical' as well stereotypes justifying unethical behaviour – for example: 'Everybody steals', and 'Apart from fish, bribes make everyone bite'.

Other reasons behind a reduced interest in the idea of CSR in Poland are the weaknesses of the country's political sphere, high corruption and significant unemployment, as well as an economic transformation characterized by 'axiological homelessness' and pushing the problems of an ethical nature to the back, in accordance with a Polish saying that states that there is no time to care for the roses when the forests are aflame.

Material and organizational conditioning

The main reason behind a reduced interest in CSR among Polish companies, when compared to their counterparts from Western countries, is their economic situation. Assuming that the implementation of the CSR rules requires the incurring of some initial costs, particularly during the preliminary period and similar to any other investment, then the poor financial situation of Polish companies, compared to the capabilities of Western firms able to implement CSR rules, puts them in a far worse situation. This fact relates to both small and average-sized companies. The introduction of a company code, adopting a suitable strategy based on the analysis of stakeholders' expectations, hiring a CSR expert, the preparation of annual reports, and in particular obtaining suitable certificates, are all costly.

According to the preliminary analysis of CSR implementation in Poland, the use of the tools and the system of CSR management is present in 20 per cent of the analysed companies (of which only one was Polish); only 37.5 per cent have ISO14001[7] implemented; only 10 per cent have the EMAS;[8] only 2.5 per cent have the SA8000 standard;[9] and only 8 per cent have the EFQM[10] certificate (CSR in Poland. Preliminary Analysis (SOB w Polsce. Wstępna Analiza), 2007).

Another reason, stressed by almost everyone, is the low quality of the law. It is imprecise, outdated, ill-adjusted, changing too quickly, and frequently not allowing pro-social conduct.

This reason is closely related to another one – namely, insufficient interest among the Polish administration to propagate CSR ideas or introduce laws and solutions encouraging companies to implement CSR.[11] When asked 'What might encourage companies to engage in more pro-social activities?', about 80 per cent of business operators from small companies and 71.3 per cent from average-sized ones answered that it is the government's policy, bringing the answer to first place in order of importance. It is worth noting that among business operators from large companies, even though this answer was placed first, it was given only 61.8 per cent of votes (Research conducted by Office of Competition and Consumer Protection – UOKiK; see Filek, Janina, 2006). Another reason is that there is still a small consumer movement (compared to the situation in developed countries), which is not putting enough pressure on economic entities. These in turn do not comply with even minimal ethical requirements, such as a common sense of decency (which assumes the exclusion of most illegal acts), or distributive justice (Sternberg, 1998).

Other essential reasons for such little interest in CSR ideas include, first and foremost a lack of knowledge of what CSR is, related faulty education with respect to CSR; and a lack of trust among Polish society with regard to what companies do, originating in the small amount of social involvement among Poles and a weak democratic tradition.

Lack of knowledge

A number of variants can be detailed within the notion of lack of knowledge with respect to CSR. Nearly all the research conducted in Poland, and related to the knowledge of the idea of CSR, indicates that such knowledge is either very weak or quite superficial.

Lack of fundamental knowledge

The first type[12] of lack of knowledge may be described as simple, or fundamental, whereas the second case describes insufficient knowledge for CSR to be implemented. At the category level, CSR is often confused with the ideas of, for example, PR, philanthropic activity or sponsoring.

Lack of economic knowledge

Another variant of the lack of knowledge may be called economic, since it does not concern the subject matter of the CSR idea and the rules arising from it. On the contrary, it involves a lack of knowledge of the actual costs of implementation, and the basic steps to realization. Many entrepreneurs complain about the high costs of such investment, but in fact they are unable to assess it, as well as their lack of ability to determine the economic results of realizing such an investment.

Lack of factual knowledge

Under this heading we shall cover the lack of knowledge regarding the appropriate tools to be used to implement CSR and to diagnose the effects of such implementation. It does not change the fact that many of the business operators observed declare CSR to be useful. They would even often undertake internally uncoordinated CSR-related actions, but only because it is a frequent subject of discussion, and its issues have become a recent kind of fashion.

The lack of factual knowledge is also reflected in the ignorance of solutions used in developed countries – the fact that mainly describes Polish companies; whereas in the case of foreign companies a lack of fundamental knowledge can be explained as the ineffectual and often forceful implementation of certain solutions successful in developed countries, even though such solutions culturally do not fit Polish reality. Evidence of the lack of factual knowledge is demonstrated, for example, by inappropriate treatment of employees, while at the same time attempting to build the company's reputation of being socially responsible.

Lack of philosophical knowledge

The philosophical lack of knowledge may be described as the lack of understanding of the rules underlying the idea of CSR, as well as their philosophical sources. Because of insufficient preparation, many entrepreneurs are unable to understand this idea. They do not understand that every right to act freely bears a responsibility. As Kant would put it, every free action brings responsibility for the results of such an action. As existentialists would put it, every decisive and creative power creates more responsibility, not only for what has been done (negative responsibility), but also for what good (socially) could be done based on the possession of such power (Jonas, 1996).

Lack of historical knowledge

This variant of lack of knowledge relates to the history of the idea of CSR. The lack of historical knowledge creates the danger of an instrumental treatment of this idea, which means using it only as a factor enhancing the company's reputation in the consumers' eyes. What is probably even worse, the idea may become a useful factor for concealing certain irregularities exercised within or by the company. The lack of historical knowledge also favours an argument dangerous for the whole CSR idea, which states its alleged occasional character, based on current fashion. Such an unjustly discrediting argument clearly seems unauthorized and unsupported if only the historical background of the CSR idea is looked at in isolation.

Lack of ethical knowledge

The different kinds of lack of knowledge are to a great extent the result of an imperfect educational process. The most fundamental of their kind, however, is based on a lack of knowledge in relation to the meaning of ethics in social life – hence, a lack of ethical knowledge. All the other varieties of lack of knowledge are primarily a consequence of this basic one. The lack of ethical knowledge is therefore one of the major reasons behind the small amount of interest in CSR in Poland, and as a result its weak implementation in the country. If social responsibility remains an unknown concept, the chances for wide implementation of the whole idea are low.

Diminishing social involvement

When it comes to little interest in CSR, a reason as serious as the lack of knowledge about the area – as I have previously noted – will need to be recognized as weak social involvement of Polish society, or, to be more precise, a decrease of such involvement in recent years. Surprising though it may sound, based on the recent data, the average Pole is less and less preoccupied with social problems. The data in question provide evidence not only for the diminishing voter turnout of the Poles, but also – and what may be equally alarming – they indicate falling interest among Poles to solve social problems by helping those in the greatest need, or even in supporting similar initiatives instigated by others.

Indeed, as a society the Polish nation is able to act occasionally with ultimate dedication – gathering, for example, millions of zlotys year after year during the Great Orchestra of Christmas Charity (Wielka Orkiestra Świątecznej Pomocy) collection. Nevertheless, as research shows, the scope of help granted from Polish citizens to their fellows decreases year after year. According to a report prepared by the Klon/Jawor organization, not only the Poles one of the last on the European list with respect to the number of volunteers undertaking any community aid action, but the volunteer numbers have also decreased (Klon/Jawor Association, 2004 and 2006).

The decrease also relates to the number of donors, as well as members of non-governmental organizations. As such, if the attitude of the average citizen is characterized by a decreasing interest in social problems, the companies operating within Poland cannot be expected to show willingness to solve social problems more than the citizens themselves. All this happens for a very prosaic reason – the fact that most employees of these companies are Polish. If the employees do not demonstrate a pro-social attitude, then Polish business operators will not demonstrate it either, not to mention any foreign managers.

The low level of social initiative among the Poles is closely related to their low level of confidence in one another. The percentage of Poles who trust their compatriots (11.5 per cent) is nearly three times lower than the European average (32 per cent) (Social Diagnosis (Diagnoza Społeczna), a Polish report on public feeling in the country (2007). The low level of common trust among Polish citizens may be a consequence of their low confidence in public institutions and in individuals holding high positions. As a result, the Poles' trust in social actions undertaken by companies is also low (Badziąg, 2007). Polish people do not believe that a company may undertake pro-social activities just because it regards them as its duty. In fact, people tend to treat such activities as a 'smokescreen' for other profitable or barely legal business.

Without doubt, the final reason behind the small amount of interest in CSR is the present economic crisis. Even though it has not struck the Polish economy with all its strength, it has undoubtedly been involved in the postponement, for some time to come, of the ability of its economy to implement CSR ideas.

Therefore, implementation of CSR in Poland will require a substantial amount of work, but it would be wrong to claim that it is impossible.

Notes

1. This part of the chapter is an extract from a more extensive work; therefore, not all of the social contract concepts mentioned above will be analysed here. In order to compare the idea of CSR with the social contract in this text, Rousseau's social contract was chosen.
2. Periodically, economists draw our attention to the fact that operations related to CSR also bring factual material benefits, such as increased company profits.
3. A good example here (that is, an example that shows the mentioned dependence) is the collapse of Enron, whose executives wanted to make profit at the

cost of stakeholders and which ultimately led to everyone's loss: theirs, other stakeholders', and society's.

4. The United Nations Global Compact is a strategic policy initiative for businesses that are committed to aligning their operations and strategies with ten universally accepted principles in the areas of human rights, labour, environment and anti-corruption (see www.unglobalcompact.org/).

5. This does not necessarily mean that deliberations on what CSR is should be abandoned. As with any other idea, this one has also been changing, and will continue to change alongside social development; therefore, it will be necessary occasionally to revert to the original question of what CSR is and what is its role. However, taking into consideration the dialectics of the developmental process, making the theory absolute in any way should be avoided. Despite the fact that at present the theory seems to be the antithesis of former economic rules that were closed to ethical values, it does not mean that the theory, understood as a peculiar 'social institution', will last for ever.

6. In the subject literature, the origins of the CSR idea are traced back only as far as the 1950s. Its surfacing was a response to the problems of the Great Depression of the 1930s which shook the American economy. Howard Bowen's *Social Responsibilities of the Businessman* (Bowen, 1953) is often considered to be the first work about CSR.

7. International Organization for Standardization. A standard for environmental management.

8. Eco-Management and Audit Scheme. A standard set by the European Parliament in 2001.

9. Social Accountability International — Human Rights at Work.

10. European Foundation for Quality Management.

11. In 2005, an Interdepartmental Working Group for CSR was appointed at the Department of Work and Pensions. This, however, does not translate into practice/action on the part of the government. Nevertheless, it must be noted that during the Group's most recent conference, in March 2008, a report was brought forward which depicted the state of works (Conference Working Materials: Support for the Development of the CSR in Poland, 2008), as well as recommendations for further action.

12. The research among students of seven institutions of higher education has shown that 70 per cent of students are not familiar with the idea of CSR, including 40 per cent of students at the Warsaw School of Economics (SGH), and over 80 per cent of students at University of Warsaw (UW). (Report on the research, CSR oczami studentów: Warsaw School of Economics, 2006).

Bibliography

Baczko, B. (1964) *Rousseau: Samotność i Wspólnota* (Warsaw: PWN).

Badanie UOKiK (Office of Competition and Consumer Protection Research) (2006) *Skłonność do angażowania się w działania pro-konsumenckie i pro-społeczne wśród polskich przedsiębiorców.*

Badziąg, A. (2007) *Społeczna odpowiedzialność biznesu a społeczna odpowiedzialność Polaków* (Typescript).

Janina Filek   159

Bowen, H. (1953) *Social Responsibilities of the Businessman* (New York: Harper & Bros).

Caux Round Table (1994) *Principles for Business.*

Crook, C. (2005) 'The Good Company. A Sceptical Look at Corporate Social Responsibility', *The Economist*, January.

Diagnoza Społeczna (Social Diagnosis) (2007) (A report in Polish on public feeling in the country).

Filek, Jacek (2001) 'Pytanie: jak żyć?, jako podstawowe pytanie etyczne', in Jacek Filek, *Filozofia jako etyka* (Krakow: Znak).

Filek, Janina (2002) *O wolności i odpowiedzialności podmiotu gospodarującego* (Krakow: Wydawnictwo AE).

Filek, Janina (2005) 'Jeśli biznesem biznesu jest biznes', *Tygodnik Powszechny* No. 17.

Filek, Janina (2006) *Społeczna odpowiedzialność biznesu. Tylko moda czy nowy model prowadzenia działalności gospodarczej* (UOKiK – Office of Competition and Consumer Protection).

Filek, Janina (2007) 'Między wolnością gospodarczą a odpowiedzialnością społeczną biznesu', in B. Klimczak and A. Lewicka-Strzałecka (eds), *Etyka i ekonomia* (Warsaw: Wydawnictwo PTE – Polish Scientific Publishers).

Friedman, M. (1970) 'The Social Responsibility of Business Is to Increase Its Profits', *New York Times Magazine*,13 September.

Jonas, H. (1996) *Zasada odpowiedzialności* (Krakow: Wydawnictwo Platan).

Klon/Jawor Association (2004) *Wolontariat, filantropia i 1%*. Report, Klon/Jawor Association).

Klon/Jawor Association (2006) *Wolontariat, filantropia i 1%*. Report.

Kuraszko, I. and Rok, B. (2007) *Krytyczne spojrzenie na rozwój społecznej odpowiedzialności w Polsce. Wnioski z badań, prezentacja.* (Warsaw, 15 October).

Prahalad, C. K. and Hammond, A. (2002) 'Serving the World's Poor, Profitably', *Harvard Business Review*, 1 September. Trans. unknown (2007) 'Jak obsługiwać biednych i dobrze na tym zarabiać?', *Społeczna odpowiedzialność przedsiębiorstw* (Gliwice: Wydawnictwo HELION).

Pratley, P. (1998) *Etyka w biznesie*. Trans. M. Albigowski, (Warsaw: M. Gebethner i Ska).

Rok, B. (ed.) (2001) *Więcej niż zysk, czyli odpowiedzialny biznes. Programy, strategie, standardy* (Warsaw, FOB).

Rok, B. (2008) *Wzmacnianie rozwoju CSR w Polsce. Rekomendacje.* Typescript.

Rousseau, J.-J. (1994) *The Social Contract* (Oxford University Press). Trans. Christopher Betts (2002) *Umowa spoeczna.* (Wydawnictwo Antyk, Kęty).

Sternberg, E. (1998) *Czysty biznes. Etyka biznesu w działaniu.* Trans. P. Łuków (Warsaw: PWN).

Taylor, C. (1996) *Etyka autentyczności.* Trans. A. Pawelec (Krakow: Znak).

Warsaw School of Economics (SGH) (2006) Survey report: *CSR oczami studentów.*

World Bank Report (2005) *What Does Business Think about Corporate Social Responsibility?*, Pt II (Washington, DC: World Bank). *Wspieranie rozwoju społecznej odpowiedzialności biznesu w Polsce. Raport zespotkań z interesariuszami* (2008) (Support for the Development of the CSR in Poland. Report in Polish from a meeting with stakeholders, Transcript.

12
Stakeholder Dialogue in Polish Organizations

Barbara Fryzel

Corporate social responsibility and sensemaking[1]

Socially responsible business seems to be the result of profound pressures on firms coming from their organizational environment, including various stakeholder groups. It also seems to be the result of a strong belief that, when opposed, such pressures might become a source of potential threat and risk to the corporate entities. However, when incorporated into company strategy, stakeholders' expectations might become a source of competitiveness and market advantage, which seems to be well grounded in the open systems theory.

Some companies simply include the cost analysis as a key decision-making factor when engaging in CSR activities (Hart, 1997; Russo and Fouts, 1997; McWilliams and Siegel, 2001), proving that socially responsible management does not need to be separated from basic operational economics.

There is a richness of research linking CSR behaviours with financial results of the company (Waddock and Graves, 1997; Wright and Ferris, 1997, McWilliams and Siegel, 2001, Rodriguez and Siegel 2006), introducing the notion of strategic CSR (Porter and Kramer (2006); which might serve as a way of explaining the divergence in the above-mentioned research results, often pointing to a positive, negative or lack of correlation between CSR and profit.

From the operational perspective, the key issue is to differentiate between managerial and social aspects of CSR (Hillman and Keim, 2001). The logical consequence of such an approach manifests itself in a debate on how to manage stakeholder relations, previously categorized against the criteria of importance, urgency and various other factors, as opposed to performing a dialogue with them and building relations based on common values (Charan and Freeman, 1979; Freeman, 1984; Dunham *et al.*, 2006; Hughes and Demetrious, 2006).

The majority of research focusing on instrumental aspect of CSR (Donaldson and Preston, 1995; Jones and Wicks, 1999), seems to favour the context of managing external relations (Freeman, 1984), where stakeholder identification, stakeholder accommodation problems and goal alignment remain key operational questions. Attempts to approach stakeholder dialogue strategies from an operational perspective are still rare (Dunham *et al.*, 2006). For example, Dunham *et al.* promote the view that co-operation with stakeholders should be based on building common values, especially when the symbiosis with a given stakeholder group is significant.

From an operational perspective, both approaches are justified despite being distinct in their ontological background.

The concept of managing stakeholder relations implies treating stakeholders as being strictly external to the company, and possibly as a source of a potential threat. In such cases, managers might be tempted to concentrate on one-sided, asymmetric communication with stakeholders, focusing on designing outgoing messages to suit what the receiver wants to hear, or should hear, which often remains very distant from what the company actually does and how it performs its business.

The concept of building relations based on common values would naturally assume a two-way, symmetric communication – a dialogue, to ensure clear understanding on both sides, and the internalization of stakeholder values (not necessarily expectations) in corporate strategy. While it would not be justified for the company to adopt all stakeholder expectations, simply because it is not possible to accommodate all, often divergent, goals, building a consensus over underlying values and a philosophy of how the surrounding world functions and what is the role of business in it, sounds like a solid background for successful operation, from both a social and a managerial perspective.

An interesting question remains: what is the key factor determining the way of thinking that the company adopts?

Understanding the world around us clearly involves making sense of surrounding events; symbols and the way they are used; discourse and interpersonal relations and so on. In parallel, we construct our reality with everyday interactions and behavioural artefacts. A sensemaking perspective in organizational studies (Weick, 1995), specifically in stakeholder relations, deals with the extent in which stakeholders are involved in corporate decision-making and strategic discourse.

Organizations perform sensemaking constantly in leadership process, when motivating their employees or when constructing their image for the external environment.

Sensemaking theory is based on the assumption that reality does not exist independently from our cognitive structures but is co-constructed by all involved actors. Interpersonal activities and the relations we build, in a sense, precede building formal structures, which proceduralize and standardize behaviours. The extent of stakeholders involvement in the dialogue with the organization defines its sensemaking perspective.

Given the above, corporate social responsibility implemented as long-term relationship building and involving stakeholders in corporate discourse presents itself as another expression of a sensemaking paradigm.

The sensemaking process in organizations (Basu and Palazzo, 2008) consists of three dimensions. How companies perceive themselves is defined as a cognitive dimension. From the corporate culture perspective this may serve as a repository of basic assumptions and deeply grounded values. What companies say about themselves is expressed in the linguistic dimension – above all in formal messages and texts – for example, reports, press releases, advertisements, authorized interviews with corporate senior management and so on.

Last but not least, the conative dimension gives behavioural confirmation of whether the company is convergent with its deeply-rooted beliefs when actually operating and doing business.

In a search for the key factors responsible for the corporate approach to stakeholders, whether it is the instrumental approach with the preference to manage external threats or the relational approach with a preference for long-term relation building, attention is drawn to the cognitive dimension of sensemaking, with its fundamental element – a corporate identity.

It is defined as the differentiating attribute of the organization (Balmer, 1998), consisting of elements that are central to the company and enduring and which describe the way employees identify themselves with the firm. It might serve as a lens through which to perceive the surrounding world (Konecki, 2002) and as such remains very important to studying organizations from the sensemaking perspective.

From the perspective of the question of how identity might determine organizational approach to stakeholder relations, it is the internal dimension of corporate identity that is the most interesting. Being the cognitive scheme for employees and a construct related to internal perceptions, as opposed to reputation and image, which both relate to the external perceptions of an organization – internal identity might be a sensemaking platform which turns organizational values into an approach to stakeholders, manifested in certain communication strategies.

Stakeholders as business partners – corporate identity and cultural background

Corporate identity as part of the sensemaking process in organizations (Basu and Palazzo, 2008) can be individualistic, relational or collectivistic, depending on how the organization locates itself in relation to other market participants. Theoretically, the more an organization perceives itself to be part of a larger social and economic unit, the more attention should be drawn to how it relates to the environment and what is the quality of its relations. In a sense, the greater the focus on the relational aspect, the stronger the inclination towards a dialogue type of communication. Such an approach might be explained by the ontological background. Positioning itself as a market dominator, aiming to beat the competition, involves relations of power and subordinance by definition. In opposition stands the ideology of having a broader social and economic role in the world, a role often exceeding a simple market-only orientated and narrow vision. Such a standpoint tends to equalize relations among the market actors, perhaps positioning the organization more centrally in the social network.[2]

The intensity of stakeholder involvement in the organizational discourse seems to parallel the symmetry of the communication between the parties involved. This intensity, differentiating communication strategy adopted by the company, can be described as the interrelation between factors such as the perceived role of stakeholders; the locus of CSR-related decisions in the company (who decides what is important); definition of the strategic goal of CSR communication; and the strategic task of those responsible for communication (Morsing and Schultz, 2006).[3] It can be imagined that all these factors relate to each other in a certain pattern.

On one side of the continuum, there will be organizations reacting to the specified stakeholder requests for more information, where stakeholders are perceived as a potential support or opposition. In such cases, an organization needs to concentrate on designing an appealing informative message about the positive CSR activities. Such an approach, called by Morsing and Schultz (2006), 'stakeholder information strategy', does not leave much room for any involvement by the stakeholders. Additionally, the fact that the key CSR focus is decided by the top management alone may point to the lack of any strategically in-built systems for approaching CSR, proving that social responsibility has a marginal status of important but ad hoc activities.

On the other hand, there will be organizations that co-construct their CSR strategy within a process of ongoing consultations with stakeholders, where the key task for those responsible for such communication is to create a systemic basis for a regular dialogue. Hence, organizations sympathizing with the instrumental view of managing stakeholders as an outside threat will be more inclined to adopt a stakeholder information strategy, while those adopting the long-term relationship view will most probably engage in stakeholder involvement and dialogue.

As organizations are constructed and managed by people, the attitudes to other market players they present might depend on their own perceived roles in the surrounding environment. The definition of such roles can be analysed through the examination of a corporate identity. Together with the other sensemaking dimensions,[4] the identity implies the character of CSR adopted by the company.

The individualistic identity tends to form aggressive corporate visions focused around outperforming the competition, dominating the market, winning clients and so on. The relational identity, focusing on specific ties perceived by the organization as being critical, expresses itself in the visions related to pleasing the clients or being the best employer, trusted service provider and so on. Finally, the collectivistic identity characterizes organizations which perceive themselves as part of a larger macrocosm, and as such see their roles often as being related to global issues – for example, solving the problem of poverty, reducing social inequalities or preserving the planet and its resources so it is sustained for future generations (Basu and Palazzo, 2008).

Relational and collectivistic identities both locate 'relationship' as the focus of attention. By definition, a relationship is intentional and long-term, and is a reciprocal process which turns the parties involved into a commonwealth of shared interests (Rogozinski, 2006). It might therefore be expected that organizations with such identities will perceive stakeholders as partners in strategy building and will involve them in a dialogue in order to make those relations effective. This may result in adopting the stakeholder involvement strategy model (Morsing and Schultz, 2006). The individualistic identities, where ties to other market players do not have the characteristic of a relationship as defined above, might be more inclined to adopt a simple information strategy, where the main focus is to identify accurately the right group of stakeholders and design a tailor-made message for them.

In a sense, individualistic identities seem to be more focused on themselves, but not necessarily being introverted – they might represent very aggressive, market-orientated firms which simply do not include the well-being of other stakeholders in their value system, at least not beyond their commercial and purely mercantile purpose of the business. Opposed to this are relational and collectivistic identities, where the importance of stakeholders might derive from a difference of perceiving one's own role in the world– that is, corporate vision expressing the importance of global, social problems, such as poverty, improving sanitation in the Third World and so on implies a different value system.

The question here is: is there any connection between corporate identity and a corporate approach to stakeholders, expressed in communication strategies?

The value system of every organization is the more internal cognitive layer upon which organizational cultures are built. Among many available taxonomies of culture, one of the clearest and most simplistic defines clan, market, adhocracy and hierarchy as the basic types (Cameron and Quinn, 2003).

Corporate identity, both as integral part of the sensemaking process and as the interpretative platform for members of organization, resides in an organizational cultural setting and must relate to it in some way. However, it is not explicit, given that two differentiating dimensions here are: stability and control versus freedom of action and flexibility, and internal focus versus external focus on market position.

Having said that, while a hierarchy culture is characterized by strong control procedures and an internal focus towards its own systems and operation procedures, this is most often seen in organizations which, by definition, have a broader role of serving other stakeholders – for example, public administration. Not always, though, such an organization tends to have a regular dialogue with the stakeholders – the evidence of the public unhappy with the service and treatment it gets from the various institutions whose existence is justified by the requirements of public service and the costs covered by the taxpayers, is almost anecdotal.

Clan culture, characterized by internal focus coupled with flexibility and relative freedom, implies that care for people (in this particular case, employees and their families – and including stakeholders) holds a key place in the value system. One might expect a stronger stakeholder involvement in such organizations and as a result, a dialogue-based communication strategy.

Adhocracy and market – both externally orientated, differing from each other only by the extent of the control procedures – both have the potential to represent all previously defined identities.

None of the criteria differentiating the culture types seem to be directly linked to identities.

The question here is: can corporate identity be independent of the organizational culture, and if not, how do both constructs relate to each other?

The practice of stakeholder communications in Polish organizations

The issues discussed encourage us to test whether the synthetic model of communication strategies holds in a given organizational environment, and whether there is a relationship between corporate identities and the adopted model of communication strategies.

A diversity of notions analysed as well as a diversity of perspectives, encourage a tailor-made approach where qualitative methods could be combined with quantitative ones. Such an approach would be justified as the analysis requires an examination of internal perceptions and individual opinions of corporate informants as well as the examination of texts and events, should the linguistic and conative aspect of the sensemaking process be included.

A pilot study was conducted on a small sample of Polish companies' (N = 47) communication strategy to define corporate identities.

The study was carried out on a sample of corporate informants (postgraduate students) who represented various hierarchy levels. Their organizations are drawn from different sectors and represent a diverse range of operations – from local to multinational and global, though the extreme results were excluded from the sample (employment numbers were controlled for). The final sample included mainly locally operating companies (71.11 per cent) represented by informants employed in operational (51.11 per cent), assistance (33.33 per cent) and managerial posts (13.33 per cent).

The cognitive aspect of the sensemaking – corporate identity – was defined through a set of vision statements. Respondents were asked whether, in their opinion, those statements conformed with the philosophy of their company or not.

The pilot survey included three proxy variables defined on the basis of the communication strategies model (Morsing and Schultz, 2006). These were the strategic CSR communication task; the key task of the corporate communications department; and a locus for the identification of CSR focus (that is, which hierarchy level decided what was important).

Additionally, a proxy variable to test the social versus the financial model of the company was included. Respondents were asked to define their views on the scale of the responsibility companies have, in their opinion. Options included responsibility towards shareholders only; responsibility towards shareholders and other primary stakeholders only (that is, employees and customers); and a broad responsibility towards both primary and secondary stakeholders(that is, including local communities, administration bodies, local government and so on).[5]

Organizational culture features were analysed against two dimensional macro criteria based on the Cameron and Quinn model (2003): that is, on the scale of external versus internal focus in organization and flexibility, and freedom versus stability and control. From there a proxy model of culture patterns was developed, defining the culture of support, power, objective and role, respectively.[6]

Perceived role of the business and corporate identities

Of the respondents, 71.43 per cent believe that business should be responsible towards all stakeholders, thus widening the scale of expected involvement of companies far beyond regular operations with primary stakeholders and owners. At the same time, the majority of the tested sample indicated individualistic identity (66.67 per cent), with only 33 per cent pointing towards a relational one. There were no traces of collectivistic identities in the sample. This, to some extent, puts a question mark against the assumed relationship between broad perceptions of the role of business and collectivist identity. It might indicate that while both concepts seem to be relying on the same axiological background, in reality perceptions of one's role and attributed responsibility do not relate directly. It is also likely that, when asked about the responsibility of the business at large, respondents attribute it to other hypothetical companies, not necessarily including their own in such attributions.

Communication strategies

As far as the features of the communication strategies are concerned, the results are as follows: 52.38 per cent suggested that their organizations have relationship building and dialogue as the strategic goal of CSR communication, in contrast to 38.10 per cent of those who believed that it is rather that persuasion and convincing the stakeholders that the actions the company undertakes *do* meet stakeholder expectations. A minority (9.52 per cent) agreed that their organizations have only the provision of information as the key goal of the communication process.

In line with the above, in 66.67 per cent of the cases, relationship building is also defined as the key task of the corporate communication department. The others admit that it is rather the accurate identification of stakeholders (14.29 per cent) or designing an appealing message (19.05 per cent).

In the majority of cases, management makes decisions regarding CSR engagements during the process of consultation with stakeholders (57.14 per cent); 16.67 per cent of organizations perform various market surveys and opinion polls to test the views of stakeholders and make educated decisions on this basis; and 26.19 per cent admit that the focus of CSR is decided purely by the management.

The results of the communication strategies features show little consistency, therefore it seems difficult to attribute a clear strategy type to all cases.

In half of the cases reporting information only (asymmetric) as their key task for CSR communication, it is indeed the management alone who decide on the CSR focus, as expected. Similarly, 57.1 per cent define the communication goal as convincing the stakeholders that activities undertaken are expected and positive, also declare that the CSR focus is decided on the basis of some form of stakeholder survey. Convergence of the communication task defined as dialogue with CSR focused on regular consultations with stakeholders is reported in 66.7 per cent of the cases. It seems likely that there is a slight relationship between the way the company defines the goals of corporate communication and the locus of defining the CSR focus. The more a company is focused on building dialogical relations when communicating with stakeholders, the more the stakeholders are involved in defining how organizations approach CSR.

However, when asked about the main task of those responsible for the corporate communication department, the vast majority pointed to relationship building and dialogue, irrespective of whether the communication process aims at providing information only, or at convincing the stakeholders and ensuring a long-term dialogue.

Taxonomy of cultures

On average, the organizations analysed show features of all four culture types, with a dominance of the support culture. This is accompanied by the perceptions that 'support culture' features should be enforced, while those specific to 'power culture' and 'objective culture' should be reduced. This might be a result of a specific structure of the sample, where there is only a small proportion of managerial positions. One could expect that operational staff and assistants perceive hierarchy and control procedures more as oppressive and unnecessary, compared to the opinions of managers, who need to manage their teams and are directly responsible for results and efficiency.

Relations

The 79.2 per cent of cases reporting that CSR focus is decided in the process of ongoing stakeholder consultations, also report that relationship building and dialogue are the key tasks of those responsible for corporate communication. There seems that there is a weak positive correlation here (rho = 0.324, significant at 0.05) suggesting that organizations that define the key task of the corporate communications department in terms of building a relationship, also define their key CSR focus in the process of regular consultation with stakeholders – that is, they effectively use the relations and have systemic resources available to build them.

In the case of the perceived role of business at large, there seems to be a higher proportion of respondents agreeing with the broad responsibility (primary and secondary stakeholders) in organizations where CSR focus is decided by management on the basis of surveys and opinion polls, or in the process of ongoing social consultations (85.7 per cent and 79.2 per cent, respectively). This is confirmed by a weak positive correlation (rho = 0.295, significant at 0.05). Those organizations with a philosophy of business based on relating to other market players (relational identity) also tend to design a systemic background for reaching out into the environment to learn its views and opinions.

In cases of companies where stakeholder identification and relationship building are the key tasks of those responsible for communication, a larger proportion of respondents also agree with the broad responsibility of the business (66.7 per cent and 82.1 per cent, respectively). This is confirmed by the positive correlation (rho = 0.395, significant at 0.01) between the two variables, suggesting that organizations accepting responsibility for the broader range of stakeholders, beyond the direct relations of corporate ownership, usually describe the job of those responsible for corporate communications in terms of relationship building with the stakeholders – that is, the broader responsibility embedded in the corporate philosophy, the greater the planned stakeholder involvement.[7]

While it seems that it is the stakeholder involvement strategy that dominates in the sample tested, there are no definite relations visible between the features defining those strategies, apart from a weak relationship between the key task of the corporate communication department and the decision-making on CSR strategic focus (rho = 0.292, significant at 0.05).

The latter also seems to be related to the corporate identity (rho = 0.302, significant at 0.05) suggesting that organizations with relational identities tend to involve stakeholders in the process of defining the company's CSR focus, while those that are individualistic would most probably leave that decision unanimously to their top management.

Cultural determinant for stakeholder involvement

A closer look at the cultural environment of the processes analysed provides an interesting background for further research. It might be expected that an organizational culture would stay in a close relationship with the systemic features of management practice and could even determine, or be determined by, some of its aspects.

For example, an objective-orientated organizational culture shows a weak relationship with features of communication strategies – that is, the goal of corporate communication, CSR strategic focus decision-making and the key task of the corporate communication department (rho = 0.363, 0.364 and 0.399, respectively, all significant at 0.05). The same applies to 'role culture'.

It seems that stakeholder involvement in decision-making as well as including dialogue and relationship building in corporate strategies intensifies in parallel to the intensity of 'objective' orientation in corporate culture. It makes perfect sense, given that objective-focused cultures are extravertic and focus on the external environment rather than on the internal one.

The same applies to 'role', which additionally gives the company much more flexibility in reacting to its environment, as role cultures tend to be adhocratic and do not have firm and well-defined systemic procedures for management. Perhaps this flexibility of reaction and lack of many formal procedures is the reason why managers naturally perceive stakeholders as being critical to corporate success and wish to stay closer to the market through profound dialogue with the key actors.

Power cultures show significant relations with defining the goal of corporate communication and CSR decision-making process (rho = − 0.332 and − 0.407, respectively and support cultures do not show significant correlations at all.

Power cultures, in contrast to 'objective' and 'role', seem to play a negative role in introducing stakeholder dialogue – the more formal and power-orientated the culture, the less focus there is on dialogue as the goal of communication and less involvement of stakeholders in the decision-making process.

Interestingly, there is a relatively strong and negative correlation between the objective-orientated and support cultures (rho = -0.597, significant at 0.01), suggesting that those two types are indeed on opposing sides and far apart on a certain continuum.

Some questions for further research

The results described above point to some useful directions of future research, implying the necessity to redefine some of the analysed notions, or the conditions and context of the research process.

The first question relates to the perceptions of business responsibility. The majority of respondents pointed to the broad responsibility of business irrespective of the type of business and the sector in which a given company operates. There also did not seem to be any relationship between the corporate identity and the perception of the scale of business responsibility.

Two possible explanations come to mind. The majority of the respondents represented lower levels of the organizational hierarchy and as such did not participate in formulating the strategy of the company. They also did not have a direct responsibility for generating financial results, and therefore did not experience any direct pressures from shareholders or their representatives. For that reason, their individual perceptions of what the business should be doing in the societal context might originate from pure ideology rather than from the business operational experience, especially in view of the fact that the majority of respondents attended a corporate social responsibility class. In that context, their views might be affected by a kind of 'political correctness'.

Interestingly enough, though, respondents defined the corporate identity of their organizations in individualistic rather than collectivistic terms. Given that respondents' expectations towards the scale of responsibility were very high (responsible towards all stakeholders), this may point to a divergence between the perceptions of what firms should do and what they actually express as their modus operandi. Further conclusions on that issue might be drawn on the basis of qualitative analysis of corporate texts and communications (the linguistic dimension of corporate identity) and the research into stakeholders' perceptions carried out with the stakeholder sample linked to the analysed companies.

The second question relates to the potential correlations between the features defining the CSR communication strategy. It would seem logical that, according to the model proposed by Morsing and Schultz (2006), having one of the feature described would determine others – for example, companies defining their goal of communication only in terms of informing the stakeholders of positive CSR actions would also define the key task of the corporate communication department in terms of designing an appealing message. At the same time, they would locate the decision on CSR focus at their top management levels (information strategy).

At this early stage of (preliminary) research, such relations can be detected only between the definition of the task of corporate communication and the way the CSR focus is decided; that is, the more the corporate communication task is focused on building relations, the more the CSR focus is decided by some kind of stakeholder consultation process.

However, when asked about the main task of those responsible for the corporate communications department, the vast majority pointed to relationship building and dialogue, irrespectively of whether the communication process should provide information only, or whether it should convince the stakeholders or ensure a long-term dialogue. This might indicate that, while corporate communication is in general focused on relationship building, there is a substantial degree of freedom left to those responsible for communication, as to what is the corporate rationale behind those relations. In other words, they might be genuine and dialogue-focused as well as manipulative and aiming at stakeholder consent. This might indicate a potential risk point of inconsistency between strategy and operations.

Pilot research suggests that a relationship between stakeholder involvement and corporate identities might indeed exist and could be dependent on a cultural environment of sensemaking processes. However, to define the nature of those relations, further research should be conducted.

Notes

1. Sensemaking in organizations relates to the set of processes aimed at creating shared meanings and resulting in a common understanding of the experienced situation. People make sense of the events around them as well as of actions taken by other people. They also give sense when they attempt to promote their individual interpretations of the surrounding reality to others.

This is particularly true of organizations as well, where sensemaking provides a cognitive map for its members, enabling them to position themselves within organizational policies, standards and corporate culture.

2. Paradoxically, central position in the network may also be a source of strong power, even though the relations might be weaker. In such cases the power instead of being based on purely economically grounded factors, i.e. current market position enabling manipulating the entry barriers, assets/property ownership enabling to increase entry costs for potential competition, extensive control of related market segments, etc., might be based on access to knowledge and control of the information flow.

3. In the pilot research the model originally proposed by Morsing and Schultz was simplified by excluding the variable of the perceived role of the stakeholders. Due to the fact that majority of the pilot sample consisted of the entry level or/an lower hierarchy staff, it seemed reasonable to limit the questions only to the operational issues. Perception of the role of stakeholders seems much related to the overall strategy the company designs and as such is most likely to be decided by the strategists and managers responsible for the communication. More junior staff employed on the operational posts is not very likely to have such knowledge unless it would be clearly communicated to them by the management. Consistency of the internal communication about CSR in organizations makes an interesting area for future investigations.

4. The other dimensions are legitimacy argumentation used to justify events and behaviours at both the cognitive and linguistic levels, transparency and corporate behaviour (posture, consistency and commitment).

5. The terms 'primary and secondary stakeholders' are used only to conform with the existing literature on the subject – they were not used in the research to avoid potential suggestions on categorization and the importance of the selected stakeholder groups.

6. These relate in the Cameron and Quinn model to clan, hierarchy, market and adhocracy.

7. The variable here is the key task of the department/person responsible for corporate communication, therefore this does not allow us to draw any conclusions on the actual, operational involvement of the stakeholders. The result presented indicates only the strategic assumption of the analysed organization.

Bibliography

Balmer, J. T. M. and Wilson, A. (1998) 'Corporate Identity: There Is More Than Meets the Eye', *International Studies of Management and Organization*, 28(3): 12–31.

Basu, K. and Palazzo, G. (2008) 'Corporate Social Responsibility: A Process Model of Sensemaking', *Academy of Management Review*, 33(1); 122–36.

Cameron, K. S. and Quinn, R. E. (2003) *Kultura organizacyjna – diagnoza i zmiana*, (Krakow: Oficyna Ekonomiczna).

Charan, R. and Freeman, R. E. (1979) 'Stakeholder Negotiations: Building Bridges with Corporate Constituents', *Management Review*, November: 8–13.

Donaldson, T. and Preston, L. (1995)'The Stakeholder Theory of the Corporation. Concepts, Evidence and Implications', *Academy of Management Review*, 206: 65–91.

Dunham, L., Freeman, R. E. and Liedtka, J. (2006) 'Enhancing Stakeholder Practice: A Particularized Exploration of Community', *Business Ethics Quarterly*, 16(1):, 23–42.

Freeman, R. E. (1984) *Strategic Management: A Stakeholder Approach* (Boston, Mass.: Pitman).

Hart, S. (1997) 'A Natural Resource-Based View of the Firm', *Academy of Management Review*, 20: 986–1014.

Hillman, A. and Keim, G. (2001) 'Shareholder Value, Stakeholder Management and Social Issues: What's the Bottom Line?', *Strategic Management Journal*, 22: 125–39.

Hughes, P. and Demetrious, K. (2006) 'Engaging with Stakeholders or Constructing Them? Attitudes and Assumptions in Stakeholder Software', *The Journal of Corporate Citizenship*, 23: 94–101.

Jones, T. and Wicks, A. (1999) 'Convergent Stakeholder Theory', *Academy of Management Review*, 24: 206–21.

Konecki, K. (2002) 'Tożsamość organizacyjna' (Corporate Identity), in K. Konecki and P. Tobera (eds), *Szkice z socjologii zarządzania* (Drafts in Management Sociology) (Łódź: Wyd.Uniwersytetu Łódzkiego), pp. 82–101.

McWilliams, A. and Siegel, D. (2001) 'Corporate Social Responsibility. A Theory of the Firm Perspective', *Academy of Management Review*, 26: 117–27.

Morsing, M. and Schultz, M. (2006) 'Corporate Social Responsibility Communication', *Business Ethics. A European Review,* 15(4): 324–38.

Porter, M. and Kramer, M. (2006) 'Strategy and Society: The Link Between Competitive Advantage and Corporate Social Responsibility', *Harvard Business Review*, December.

Rodriguez, P., Siegel, D., Hillman, A. and Eden, L. (2006) 'Three Lenses on the Multinational Enterprise: Politics, Corruption and Corporate Social Responsibility', *Rensselaer Working Papers in Economics*, April.6

Rogozinski, K. (2006) *Zarządzanie relacjami w usługach* (Warsaw: Difin).

Russo, M. and Fouts, P. (1997) 'A Resource-Based Perspective on Corporate Environmental Performance and Profitability', *Academy of Management Journal*, 40: 534–59.

Weick, K. E. (1995) *Sensemaking in Organizations* (Thousand Oaks, Calif./London: Sage).

Wright, P. and Ferris, S. (1997) 'Agency Conflict and Corporate Strategy: The Effect of Divestment on Corporate Value', *Strategic Management Journal*, 18: 77–83.

13
The Role of NGOs in Promoting Responsible Business Practice

Peter Davis

There can be little doubt that, since the mid-1990s, the activities of non-governmental organizations (NGOs) have done a great deal, both to highlight the impact of the corporate sector on wider social, environmental and ethical issues, and to prompt corporate action on these issues. While it would be too much to say that NGOs gave birth to the corporate responsibility movement, since the mid-1990s, they have most certainly acted as the midwives of the process.

In 1995, Greenpeace activists occupied Shell's Brent Spar oil storage facility in the North Sea as part of their *Protect the Oceans* campaign against ocean dumping. Greenpeace proved to be highly adept media managers, and the iconic images of their activists being hosed with water cannons, and relief teams being flown in by helicopter brought the stand-off to a massive audience. The wider impact on Shell was enormous: spontaneous protests in support of Greenpeace and against Shell broke out across Europe, and some Shell stations in Germany reported a 50 per cent loss of sales and the then-Chancellor Helmut Kohl raised the issue with the UK government at a G7 meeting. Eventually, Greenpeace's campaign, and the public pressure it generated, resulted in Shell agreeing to dismantle and recycle the Brent Spar facility on land. However, the campaign also had a deeper impact on the oil company. Some recipients of funding from the Shell Foundation returned their cheques, and the company was forced to accept that what mattered was not how the company spent its money, but how it earned it.

Nor was Shell's experience with Greenpeace an isolated example. Many companies found themselves and their activities the object of detailed and critical scrutiny by NGOs. The examples are almost too numerous to mention. Clothing companies such as Nike and Gap were on the receiving end of the attentions of anti-sweatshop campaigners;

Shell also found itself attacked by human rights groups for alleged complicity in the extra-judicial killing of Ogoni leader, Ken Saro-Wiwa in Nigeria; and Freeport McMoRan found its activities in Indonesia attacked for allegedly harming the people and environment near their mine.

What was most notable about these campaigns was their sophistication, and they marked a sea-change from the vocal but largely ineffective placard-waving that had typified previous NGO demonstrations. The anti-business campaigns of the late-1990s used a range of tactics and approaches to achieve a very carefully-thought-through strategy. In the case of the Brent Spar, for example, Greenpeace's aim was not to prevent the platform's disposal at sea as such, but rather to affect overall corporate behaviour: as a result of the campaign, member states of the Convention for the Protection of the Marine Environment of the North-East Atlantic announced that de-commissioned oil facilities would in future be disposed of on-shore. As noted above, these campaigns were highly effective at gaining media coverage as a tool for mobilizing public opinion. An Opinion Leader Research poll in early 1996 found that 57 per cent of the British population were aware of the Brent Spar, and more than half of those people supported Greenpeace's position.

However, campaigners also used more innovative tactics to bring companies to book for what they saw as their failings, one of the most interesting of which was the use in the USA of the Alien Tort Claims Act. Originally introduced in 1789, the ATCA was intended to provide a vehicle for those attacked by pirates to be able to claim against those pirates' US-based assets for damage done. Campaigners discovered that this long-unused piece of legislation provided the perfect way to bring companies to court in the USA for alleged human rights abuses in third countries. Companies who have faced ATCA suits include Yahoo (over actions in China), Unocal (Burma) and Chevron (Nigeria). While no company has as yet been found against, the sheer amount of effort and time that defending these actions takes has proved costly to the companies involved. These cases have also proved to have very long tails – the case against Shell for its alleged abuses in Nigeria only came to court in the USA in early 2009.

Assessing the damage that these campaigns do to companies is difficult, simply because the impacts are difficult to calculate. Writing in the *New Scientist* at the end of 1995, Greenpeace UK's executive director, Peter Melchett, estimated that the cost to Shell of the Brent Spar incident, including lost sales, was as much as £100 million (Melchett, 1995: 50–1) However, the impacts probably went further than that.

Shell's strap line used to be 'You can be sure of Shell'. The Brent Spar and Ogoniland campaigns undermined this image of reliability and it seems likely that the company is still feeling the impact of this. The impact of more recent problems with mis-reporting of reserves were probably more marked, since the reservoir of trust in the company had already been severely depleted by the NGO actions. It is certainly the case that, for Shell and others, the sophistication and organization of these campaigns prompted a fundamental shift in how many companies managed their external relationships and the wider impacts of their activities: the phenomenon we now know as corporate responsibility.

Nor has NGO influence proved to be merely a temporary phenomenon; NGO campaigns have continued to be important in influencing both companies and government behaviour. From the late 1990s onwards, campaigners demonstrated at key international meetings such as the G8 and the World Trade Organization (WTO): culminating in the famous demonstrations and 'Live 8' concert surrounding the Gleneagles meeting of the G8 in 2005. The ongoing influence of NGOs has continued to be typified by the development of new and innovative tools and ways of working.

Perhaps the most notable of these has been the emergence, since 2000, of a number of 'multi-stakeholder partnerships' to address facets of corporate interaction within wider society. Though, by definition, these initiatives include corporate and government representatives, the NGO sector has been highly influential in their foundation and operation. The first of these initiatives, begun in 2000, was *The Voluntary Principles on Security and Human Rights*. These provide guidance to companies which are operating in unstable situations. This guidance falls into three categories: risk assessment; relations with public security; and relations with private security. The Principles have been criticized: Business for Social Responsibility commented that 'implementation is difficult because of the lack of tools associated with the Principles ... Some companies may publicly support the Principles, but have no obligation to follow through on stated goals' (Business for Social Responsibility, 2005). However, since 2008, pressure, including from the NGO participants, led to the agreement of a new set of participation criteria covering a range of issues about participation in the Voluntary Principles' process, including minimum requirements for participation, a dispute resolution process, and accountability mechanisms that include the possibility of expulsion. The participation criteria also strengthen the admission procedure. A second example is concerned with the contracts between extractive companies – oil, gas and mining – and their host governments, which typically involve the payment of significant revenues to those countries. The *Extractive Industries Transparency Initiative* (EITI) was established to improve 'governance in resource-rich countries through the verification and full publication of company payments and government revenues from oil, gas, and mining' (see http://www.eitransparency.org/section/abouteiti).

At the heart of the organization are a set of principles centred on the notion that 'belief that the prudent use of natural resource wealth should be an important engine for sustainable economic growth that contributes to sustainable development and poverty reduction' (see http://www.eitransparency.org/section/abouteiti/principlescriteria); and a set of six criteria designed to ensure 'regular publication of all material oil, gas and mining payments by companies to governments.' (see http://www.eitransparency.org/section/abouteiti/principlescriteria).

The rise of the so-called 'fair trade' movement is another example of NGOs adopting novel and inventive ways of having an impact on corporate behaviour. It was the campaign in the 1980s and 1990s against illegal logging in rainforests in South East Asia and Latin America that gave rise to the first certification body, the Forest Stewardship Council, which is 'an independent, non-governmental, not for profit organization established to promote the responsible management of the world's forests' (see http://www.fsc.org/about-fsc.html). Since then, the wider fair-trade movement has become a significant element of retail sales in a number of product areas including tea, coffee and cotton. Certification schemes such as those run by the Fairtrade Foundation and the Rainforest Alliance have become important tools for companies to be able to demonstrate that the goods they are selling meet key environmental, social and ethical standards.

Both the multi-stakeholder partnerships and the fair-trade schemes demonstrate a significant shift in the way in which NGOs interact with the companies whose behaviour they are seeking to influence. Despite campaigning, and 'naming and shaming' companies they perceive to be behaving badly, weapons remain in the NGO armoury, so the game moves on significantly, with these organizations increasingly seeking to work with the corporate sector in order to change existing paradigms. Whether it is by promoting the Voluntary Principles, or certifying a coffee plantation, NGOs are having to get more deeply involved in the detail of how companies operate, and the real challenge presented by dealing with challenges of this sort. This shift also reflects a greater maturity and sophistication on the part of NGOs. In the 1990s, companies routinely reported that NGOs were great at identifying problems, but no use at finding solutions. This has now changed. The development of partnerships between companies, NGOs and governments represents a sophisticated approach to addressing what are effectively complex problems of development.

How to understand this new role

It is therefore clear that, since the mid-1990s, many NGO groups have been able to make their presence felt, and so have had an impact on the policies of companies, on national governments, and on the policies of supra-national organizations. There is evidence that this change is beginning to become institutionalized. In his recommendations for reform of the UN, *In Larger Freedom,* Kofi Annan proposed that the Economic and Social Council 'should serve as a high-level development cooperation forum' (Annan, 2005, para. 176), explicitly incorporating not just UN and state-based organizations, but also civil society and other actors too. His proposal to the Human Rights Council also envisions the involvement of non-state actors (Annan, 2005, paras 181–3).

But how are we to understand this influence? Organizations such as Greenpeace, Amnesty International and Human Rights Watch, as well as countless small groups around the world, have been able to exert more than simply influence: they have demonstrated the power to change attitudes and behaviour on many very important issues. But how are we to understand the new influence of the NGO sector? How does the power that these organizations have demonstrated sit with wider notions of power and influence in international affairs?

For some writers, the impact that NGOs have had is nothing less than a demonstration of the emergence of a vibrant global civil society; a demonstration that the tectonic plates of international governance have definitively shifted. Mary Kaldor, for example, argues that, while the notion of 'civil society' emerged in the context of a state, its usage in the 1970s 'broke that link with the state' (Kaldor, 2003: 586), particularly since, in places like Latin America and Eastern Europe, civil society was defined precisely in opposition to state structures, and advocated global norms such as human rights. As a result, Kaldor argues, 'the new understanding of civil society represented both a withdrawal from the state and a move towards global rules and institutions' (Kaldor, 2003: 588). Amitai Etzioni also argues that civil society is 'a counterweight to a potentially overpowering state' (Etzioni, 2004: 348) In his view, elements of civil society have developed into what he terms 'Transnational

Community Bodies', which he defines as 'groups that have a shared set of beliefs and bonds among their leaders and their staff as well as some of the members across national borders' (Etzioni, 2004: 343). Such groups undertake a number of roles, including the setting of transnational agendas; acting as public interest groups that lobby governments; and the development of transnational values. Such organizations, and the global values they represent, could, he advocates, be the basis of a global state based on the UN. Such an analysis derives, of course, from the interpretation that what we know as 'globalization' has fundamentally altered the way the world operates. This has become one of the most widely-used expressions in the International Relations lexicon (and indeed, also in popular usage) yet is one whose definition, as Mats Berdal puts it, which 'suffers from lack of precision.' (Berdal, 2003: 481). In an attempt to provide some much-needed precision, Jan Aart Scholte, attempts a summary of the various 'conceptions' that are frequently held to be contained within the term, 'globalization' (Scholte, 2005: 15–17). The first notion is 'internationalization': that globalization designates a growth of international exchange and interdependence. The second is 'liberalization', meaning the removal of state-imposed restrictions to create an open and borderless world. Third, is 'universalization' – the creation of a global value system. The fourth facet is the notion that globalization reflects a process of Westernization – in particular, the spread of American values and brands to all parts of the world. Finally, 'globalization' entails 're-spacialization'; the perceived impacts of technological developments, and the sense therefore that, an individual can be in immediate contact with others on the other side of the world.

Many argue that the development of globalization has fundamentally altered, indeed undermined, the role of the territorial state in global governance. David Held, for example, argues that, 'the contemporary phase of globalization is transforming the foundations of the world order, leading away from a world based exclusively on state politics to a new and more complex form of global politics and multi-layered governance' (Held, 2004: 162). Similarly, Anne-Marie Slaughter, for example, bases her proposed new world order on 'disaggregated rather than unitary states', whose building blocks 'would not be states, but parts of states' (Slaughter, 2004: 6).

Others, however, are much more sceptical of the idea of the development of a global civil society, and the claims made by it, and on its behalf, to represent a set of global values, and to act as the basis for a global governance. Chandler calls global civil society a 'fuzzy and contested' topic (Chandler, 2004: 313). He argues that, far from being representatives of an emergent polity, much of civil society in fact consists of activists who are unable to gain any traction in their own societies, so they therefore claim to be part of a 'global movement', which allows them to claim a significance they do not really have. In Chandler's view, therefore, 'the celebration of global civil society would appear to be based less on any emergence of new political forces at the global level than the desire of Western activists and commentators to justify their avoidance of accountability to any collective source of political community or elected authority' (Chandler, 2004: 320). As the proponents of the idea of global civil society are predicating their ideas on the notion that globalization has fundamentally changed the world, so its sceptics doubt how novel, and how much of an impact the phenomenon known as globalization is having. A number of authors question exactly how much of a novelty globalization is, and argue that the developments we have witnessed since the mid-1990s do not represent a revolution in global affairs. Hirst, for example, makes the point that, in the late nineteenth and early twentieth centuries, global trade and migration were much more significant as a proportion of overall economic activity than they are today (Hirst, 1997: 409–25). According to José Antonio Alonso, 'the coefficient of business openness (exports and imports as a proportion of GDP) of rich European countries only returned to 1913 levels in the 1980s' (Alonso, 2000: 350). Others make the point that the impact of the elements of change that are held to constitute globalization is felt by a relatively small proportion of the world's population. Ankie Hoogvelt argues that, when measured in terms of trade, investment and migratory flows, the core of the world economy is less integrated with the periphery than at any time since the Industrial Revolution (Hoogvelt, 2001).

The truth is that, for all the hype about globalization, it is not as revolutionary as many would like to claim, and it has in no way altered the basic structures of international governance, which are, and remain, firmly based on the sovereignty of the territorial state.

For much of the past century, power, and the ability to wield it has been seen as exclusively the preserve of the territorial state – the so-called 'realist' interpretation of international affairs, whose antecedents include the writings of Thucydides, Thomas Hobbes and Machiavelli. It is this realist view of the world that has provided the conceptual underpinnings to the system of global governance which accords primacy and legitimacy to the territorial state. The membership, and indeed the very name, of the United Nations demonstrates that it is individual states which are seen as the basic building blocks of the international community. As Robert Gilpin puts it, 'world politics is characterised by the struggle of national entities for power, prestige and wealth' (Gilpin, 1981). In this paradigm, governance is a 'top down affair, with state-dominated institutions a given' (Ruggie, 1993:151), and other institutions, be they non-governmental organizations, civil society groups or corporations, have no formal role to play in global affairs, save as vehicles for the interests of the states from which they come. The developments we have since the 1980s have certainly seen non-state institutions becoming more influential, but states remain the building blocks of the international community. Power, therefore, and the legitimacy to wield it, therefore lies exclusively with states. One of the twentieth century's foremost realist writers, Hans Morgenthau, argued that the aim of political policy was 'either to keep power, increase power or to demonstrate power' (Morgenthau, 1978: 9). For the neo-realist Kenneth Waltz, international relations is simply a matter of power, and 'its distribution across states, and changes in that distribution' (Waltz, 2003: 36).

For the realists, power is therefore synonymous with political influence, and the military force to back this up. However, in the past century or so there has emerged the notion of 'soft power', which can be interpreted as the influential power that derives from military might. The fact that a smaller state is aware that a larger one has the power to overcome it, then the larger state can usually get its way whilst stopping short of actual violence: the threat of force is sufficient to carry the day. Theodore Roosevelt recognized the importance of this, famously observing in 1903 how important it was to 'speak softly and carry a big stick' (Miller, 1994: 337). During the 2000s, the idea of soft power has been expanded further, and is described by Joseph Nye as arising 'from the attractiveness of a country's culture, political ideals, and policies' (Nye, 2004(a): 254) This type of power, it is argued, assisted the West in defeating the Warsaw Pact in the Cold War. Whatever might have been the relative military strengths of the two sides, the West had the additional soft power that derived from the relative attractiveness of its political and wider culture.

It is perhaps this notion of soft power that best provides a way to understand the nature of the power demonstrated by NGOs and other social movements: that these organizations have gained a legitimacy, and therefore power and influence, from the fact that they espouse values and behaviour that are regarded favourably by the wider society. Such organizations are 'accorded a certain degree of moral authority because of their non-state nature, their substantive expertise, and their positive normative commitments' (Lipschutz and Fogel, 2002: 116).

As Robert O'Brien puts it, while states remain the basic unit of the international system, it is now the case that 'actors other than states express the public interest', and NGOs 'have something [international institutions] need'(O'Brien *et al.*, 2003: 3).

There seem to be two key elements to what this 'something' is. The first is the ability to be able to reflect, and to some extent represent a groundswell of opinion in society on an issue or theme which, for whatever reason, is not being adequately expressed or addressed through 'normal' political channels. Most NGO campaigns revolve around an apparently simple core theme, be that the ills of environmental degradation, the importance of human rights, or the need for more aid to Africa. The reality is, of course, that these issues are immensely complex: the skill of the NGOs lies in being able to crystallize this complexity into a clear call to action – 'Make Poverty History', for example – that appeals to a diverse cross-section of society: what one might term a 'cohering power'. Such a notion of social movements is not new. In the early nineteenth century, the Luddite movement in the UK protested against the increased mechanization of the Industrial Revolution, which they believed was taking away their livelihood. Though their tactics involved destruction of looms and other machinery, there is no doubt that they reflected the real fears and concerns of a significant segment of the population of the time. More positively, the success of the civil rights movement in the USA in the middle part of the twentieth century was based on a widespread sentiment that the racial segregation laws were unjust and needed to be changed. In the same way, the Live 8 campaign built on a broad, but hitherto rather nebulous, public opinion in many Western countries that 'something must be done' to address poverty in Africa.

If NGOs, as the latest incarnation of the concept of a social movement, are not new, what seem to be original are the tactics and tools that such organizations use to achieve their ends. As noted earlier, from Brent Spar onwards, NGO campaigns have grown in sophistication and in the intelligent use of new ways of operating. Old-fashioned demonstrations still have a role to play, but the real teeth of many of these campaigns have come from new tools, the use of ATCA, multi-stakeholder partnerships and the adept use of the media. These approaches have allowed campaigns to gain traction in effecting real change. We might term this 'expressive power'.

However, there is still a need to urge caution. NGOs do not, unlike states, possess power *de jure*. Such power and influence that they do wield stems from the perception that they reflect, and to some extent represent, opinions and values held by the world's publics which in some way states, or state-derived institutions, are not reflecting. Such power is therefore necessarily fragile, and rests on the ability of these organizations to continue to monitor the pulse of popular opinion, and to be able to continue to reflect this effectively. As Joseph Nye makes clear in relation to the soft power of states, it is by no means as durable as hard force. He argues that America's soft power has declined in recent years as the US government has pursued policies that are seen as being harmful to other states and peoples. As a result, American culture and values are no longer seen to be as desirable as once they were, with the result that America's ability to influence international affairs by exercising soft power has consequently diminished: 'anti-Americanism has increased over the past few years and the US's soft power ... is in decline as a result' (Nye, 2004(b): 16).

Surely, therefore, the power exercised by NGOs is similarly fragile, and therefore the rise in the influence wielded by these organizations over recent years is by no means an irreversible process. Indeed, the NGO community is itself already under scrutiny – for example, the NGOWatch website argues that 'NGOs address critical issues ... [and] it is important that they are encouraged to embrace the same standards of transparency and accountability that they demand from governments and corporations' (http:www.globalgovernancewatch. org/about/). There have been a number of examples of NGO activities that have been significantly criticized. The campaign to withdraw from Burma, for example, has been held up as an example of where obliging companies to leave the country may do more harm than good to key populations in the country. In the USA, the anti-sweatshop labour movement has sometimes been criticized as being more interested in preserving jobs in the USA than in improving working conditions in developing economies. Even Greenpeace, whose actions might be said to have started this whole process, were recently described to this author as 'an unaccountable organization based in the Netherlands which is in possession of its own navy!' And this accusation is to some degree true. Unlike many governments, Greenpeace and other NGOs are not elected; few of them are even membership organizations which are directly accountable to their members (if they have any) for their actions. Even companies might actually be said to be more accountable, since they have to produce goods and services that people want to buy, and their directors are directly accountable to shareholders who could, albeit in extremis, vote them out of office at the AGM. NGO power is also necessarily limited. To the extent that this power derives from the ability to reflect wider public opinion, NGOs cannot advocate views that do not enjoy broad support in the wider society. They can therefore only challenge society to limited degree.

Conclusions

There is little doubt that the NGO community has been instrumental in driving corporate actions on responsibility issues since the mid-1990s. However, rather than heralding a new age of global civil society, it is necessary to be rather more sanguine about precisely what has been going on. Despite what the advocates of globalization might like to claim, the changes of the past few years have not altered the fundamental architecture of international governance and power. NGOs have not therefore become powerful in the way that states are powerful: they still lack – in the same way as do companies – *de jure* power and legitimacy. NGO power instead derives from the ability to cohere, express and advocate change based on otherwise unexpressed hopes and fears of the wider society – 'cohering' and 'expressive' power.

Civil society groups therefore walk a very fine line between being in no formal way legitimate, yet deriving legitimacy from the ability to reflect those views in society that society itself does not believe are expressed adequately by governments or other institutions. Like the soft power of states, this power is fragile; it rests on the continued ability to identify relevant seams of public concern. Repeated failure to do so, or advocating the wrong courses of action, would potentially be very damaging. NGOs have therefore been instrumental in promoting responsible business practice: their ability to be able to continue to do so therefore rests on their ability to express society's view of what needs to change about corporate behaviour, and why.

Bibliography

Alonso, J. A. (2000) 'Globalisation, Civil Society and the Multilateral System', *Development in Practice,*10(3–4): 348–60.

Annan, K. (2005) *In Larger Freedom: Towards Development, Security and Human Rights for All. Report of the Secretary-General* (New York: United Nations).

Berdal, M. (2003) 'How "New" are the "New Wars": Global Economic Change and the Study of Civil War', *Global Governance*, 9(4): 477–502.

Business for Social Responsibility (2005) *Learning from the Voluntary Principles on Human Rights*. Notes of BSR Annual Conference breakout group 3 November.

Chandler, D. (2004) 'Building Civil Society From Below', *Millennium: Journal of International Studies*, 33(2): 313–39.

Extractive Industries Transparency Initiative (2004). Available at: http://www. eitransparency.org/section/abouteiti and http://www.eitransparency.org/ section/abouteiti/principlescriteria.

Etzioni, A. (2004) 'Capabilities and Limits of Global Civil Society', *Millennium: Journal of International Studies*, 33(2): 341–53.

Forest Stewardship Council (FSC). Available at: http://www.fsc.org/about-fsc. html.

Gilpin, R. (1981) *War and Change in World Politics* (Cambridge University Press).

Global Governance Watch (2010); available at http:www.globalgovernancewatch. org/about/.

Held, D. (2004) *Global Covenant: The Social Democratic Alternative to the Washington Consensus* (Cambridge: Polity Press).

Hirst, P. (1997) 'The Global Economy: Myths and Realities', *International Affairs*, 73(3).

Hoogvelt, A.(2001) *Globalization and the Postcolonial World* (Basingstoke: Palgrave).

Kaldor, M. (2003) 'The Idea of Global Civil Society', *International Affairs*, 79(3): 583–93.

Lipschutz, R. and Fogel, C. (2002) 'Global Civil Society and the Privatisation of Transnational Regulation', in R. Bruce Hall and T. J. Biersteker, *The Emergence of Private Authority in Global Governance* (Cambridge University Press).

Melchett, P. (1995) 'Green for Danger', *New Scientist*, 148, 23 December: 50–1.

Miller, N. (1994) *Theodore Roosevelt: A Life* (New York: Harper Perennial).

Morgenthau, H. (1978) *Politics Among Nations* (5th edn) (New York: Alfred A. Knopf), pp. 4–15.

Nye, J. S., Jr. (2004a) 'Soft Power and American Foreign Policy', *Political Science Quarterly*, 119(2): 255–70.

Nye, J. S., Jr. (2004b) 'The Decline of America's Soft Power', *Foreign Affairs*, 83(3): 16–20.

O'Brien, R., Goetz, A. M., Scholte, J. A. and Williams, M. (2003) *Contesting Global Governance: Multilateral Economic Institutions and Global Social Movements.* (Cambridge University Press), p. 3.

Ruggie, J. G. (1993) 'Territoriality and Beyond: Problematizing Modernity in International Relations', *International Organization*, 47: 139–74.

Scholte, J. A. (2005) *Globalization: A Critical Introduction.* (Basingstoke/New York: Palgrave), pp 15–17.

Slaughter, A. M. (2004) *A New World Order* (Princeton, NJ: Princeton University Press), p. 6.

Voluntary Principles on Security and Human Rights, The (2010). Available at: http://www.voluntaryprinciples.org/principles/index.php.

Waltz, K. N. (1990) 'Realist Thought and Neorealist Theory', *Journal of International Affairs*, 44 (Spring/Summer): 21–37.

Part IV

Global Issues in Corporate Social Responsibility

14
In Search for a New Balance: The Ethical Dimension of the Crisis[1]

Wojciech Gasparski, Anna Lewicka-Strzalecka,
Boleslaw Rok and Dariusz Bak

Introduction

In his book, *Business Fairy Tales: Grim Realities of Fictitious Financial Reporting* (2006), Cecil W. Jackson quotes the words of Arthur Levitt, the former Chairman of the Securities and Exchange Commission (SEC), who draws attention to the habitual behaviours that lie in the grey zone; that is, between what is legal and what is not. Illusion wins over honesty, continues the cited author; we are witnessing a specific kind of deception. These words seem to be incredibly prescient, considering the crash on the US financial market. Craftiness turns out to be more valuable than integrity. Is this because – in the words of John Hendry (2004) – we live in a bimoral society? Perhaps not everybody, but rather the 'developed' (in terms of what: unreliability or integrity?) societies of highly active economies, though globalization stimulates the attitude of 'getting as much as possible, as fast as possible, in whatever way', which does not have a place of origin and continues to spread to remote places in the world.

The imposed authority

The gradual disclosure of the causes of the crisis forces us to ask this question: why, in such a rationally organized economic system, insured by rating and audit institutions, has the crisis escalated to such an enormous extent? To find an answer, it is worth analysing how the relationship functions between the investor and the institution, based on whose advice we make our investment decisions.

The ethical dimension of the crisis can be expressed in transparency categories. It is not possible to evaluate motivation. Similarly, one cannot indicate the thin line that, once it is crossed, causes precaution to change into greed, and concern for the welfare of the company to become a reason to take extremely risky decisions. Therefore, the only matter that can be subjected to an ethical evaluation is responsibility, which may be described as the instruction to inform economic partners about all possible consequences of their decisions and about the scale of risk that comes with these decisions. The foundation of such formulated responsibility is an asymmetrical relationship between the financial institution and the client. Such asymmetry is normal in any kind of relationship that is established between an expert in a given field and a person that wants to, or is forced to, make use of the services of an expert. Vital elements of these kinds of relationships are: trust, recognizing authority and responsibility.

The expert–client relationship will always be based on some form of trust. Naturally, trust is a multidimensional phenomenon. In the sphere of economic life, a trust formula can be encountered that is the result of a pure economic calculation. I trust, because I know that it is to the disadvantage of the other party to mislead me. I trust, because my thus far positive experience gives me the certainty that future experience will be positive as well. This kind of reasoning can be a foundation of trust in the business sphere, as long as one rather crucial element is present – partnership; that is, a symmetrical relationship between the parties that are both able to evaluate each other's motives and submit them to certain rational criticism. In such a case, both parties consciously accept their share of the risk, or voluntarily resign and look for other partners.

In an asymmetrical expert–client relationship, the above provisions are not met. One cannot evaluate the motives of the expert, because s/he is not a real partner for us. On the contrary, s/he is a representative of a reality that is not known to us. His or her actions are determined by a methodology of his or her domain, which we, as non-experts, are not able to verify or criticize. The only rational way of doing this would be to confront the opinion of the expert with the opinions of other experts; however, this option involves the same unknowns. Therefore, the trust we have in the expert is completely irrational. From the point of view of the client, it can even be described as 'wishful thinking'. We want the expert to be right, because this is of vital importance to our business. We have faith in the expert's competency, because we do not have any other choice. Even if trusting seems to be conscious and free decision to have faith in someone (I can, but I do not have to), in the relationship of expert–client this decision is not a free one.

This determinism carries certain consequences that can be deduced by interpreting the so called Rule of Reciprocity (Cialdini, 1993). If we decide to trust someone, even if it is determined trust, then we expect an appropriate reaction from that person. These expectations aimed at the expert primarily concern his or her professionalism. Prerequisites are adequate technical competencies – that is, the qualification to operate; the instrumental efficiency to make something happen as well as cognitive competencies – that is, the ability to foresee the effects of one's own actions. We assume that the expert has an adequate factual knowledge (on account of which s/he knows that...); procedural knowledge (on account of which s/he knows how...); and knowledge about different life circumstances and social changes, as well as knowledge with respect to the relativism of life goals and values (Pietrasinski, 2001). After all, the trust we put in the expert can be perceived in axiological categories and, according to the rule of reciprocity, we expect the expert to have appropriate axiological standards – that is, the ability to evaluate the effects of his/her own actions in moral terms.

The described competencies can (but do not have to) be a field of expert knowledge. It was noted a long time ago that having a certain degree of knowledge gives the illusive feeling of confidence, regardless of the extent or accuracy of this knowledge. Such a situation is well described by the expression *docta ignorantia* (learned ignorance), introduced in the fifteenth century by Nicholas of Cusa. Five hundred years later, José Ortega y Gasset noticed this to be the effect of a far-reaching specialization and believed it to be a serious social issue:

> The specialist serves as a striking concrete example of the species, making clear to us the radical nature of the novelty. For, previously, men could be divided simply into the learned and the ignorant, those more or less the one and those more or less the other. But your specialist cannot be brought in under either of these two categories. He is not learned, for he is formally ignorant of all that does not enter into his specialty; but neither is he ignorant, because he is 'a scientist', and 'knows' very well his own tiny portion of the universe. We shall have to say that he is a learned ignoramus, which is a very serious matter, as it implies that he is a person who is ignorant, not in the fashion of the ignorant man, but with an the petulance of one who is learned in his own special line. (Ortega y Gasset, 1994)

Including expert knowledge in moral categories is crucial, because every profession or discipline 'happens' in its own axiological context and has its own specific standards and responsibilities. However, the phenomenon here is the list of moral standards that are expected from specialists or experts. Ortega y Gasset accuses the specialist of extending his/her scope of authority into fields where his/her competencies are limited or non-existent. However, this allegation can be extended even further. An expert, because of his/her competencies, can be perceived by his/her environment as a person also competent in other fields, especially when ethical issues arise. This illusion of infallibility can therefore work both ways. From the perspective of society, the expert has a position of authority, which comes with all kinds of moral issues. We generally listen to an expert, however, and when it comes to an authority, we are usually obedient. We do not enter into discussion with an authority, even if his or her opinion clearly is at odds with the knowledge, beliefs and moral feelings of the people submitted to his/her influence.

The above reflections show the specificity of the ethical category of responsibility of experts. It means not only being responsible 'for', but also being responsible 'towards'. Responsibility 'for' implies intellectual reliability, integrity in handling the possessed knowledge and skills. It is a value directed and realized internally; an element of self-discipline. The ethical horizon in this case is limited to the principal – the thinking and acting moral entity. Responsibility 'towards' expands this horizon. Within this range the welfare of other people is also included; that kind of welfare of which the acknowledgement does not merely have a declarative character. In the expert–client relationship, it is the client who is in a subordinate situation. S/he is subordinated and his/her trust is binding and becomes the source of moral duty. In this dimension, responsibility is a moral command to protect the interests of the people whose decisions and actions depend on the knowledge and advice of the expert/authority. Therefore, one cannot make this judgement without claiming increased self-criticism. If we recall the words of the Roman poet Virgil – *Follow the learned man*, we should add *and stay alert*.

The crisis: financial or moral?

The financial crisis showed that violating certain ethical standards becomes dangerous in global terms, for example the lack of responsibility in the mortgage market was one of the causes of the global collapse in the markets. Financial institutions are being accused of carelessness and speculation at the expense of their customers, and their managers of greed and dishonesty. Aggressive marketing and similar advertising of financial products emphasized the positive aspects and concealed the risk involved. The authorities also carry their share of responsibility in the current crisis. Ethical standards related to the norm of complying with financial commitment were forgotten in the frame of liberal bankruptcy legislation and attitudes of moral hazard were favoured. Consumers also contributed to the crisis, by carelessly taking out loans that it was beyond their financial capabilities to repay.

The decision of the American government, and subsequently of the governments of other countries, to supply powerful private financial institutions with multi-billion dollars in capital to prevent them going bankrupt will long remain disputable. This move, which aimed at avoiding a total economic slump, is seen as a fiasco of market fundamentalism. It is seen as a display of a phenomenon that Staniszkis described as the 'internalization of benefits and externalization of costs' (1994: 271), where she referred to the Polish reality of the transformation period. This phenomenon is based on passing the operational costs of private businesses on to the state, and private persons deriving advantage from these operations. Managers in the financial sector receive generous compensations and severance pay; however, the costs of salvaging the financial institutions are incurred by the taxpayers.

Without doubt, the present perturbations in the USA, and consequently the global financial system, will have an influence on the changes in economic doctrines as well as in the practice of management. Neoliberal concepts will lose their status and the role of financial oversight will become increasingly more important. Ethicists will try to understand the phenomenon of responsibility for the results of the actions of credit institutions, which more and more often turn out to be disastrous, both for the individual entities as well as society as a whole. It is therefore valuable to carry out a reconstruction of the place and significance of credit institutions in society.

Even though the essence of loans has not changed over the years, an analysis of the transformation of this institution allows us to reveal certain characteristics that are distinctive at the present time, such as: democratization, depersonalization and diversification. Democratization of credit means that loans currently play a much more significant role in the life of the ordinary citizen than ever before. Some societies in developed countries are described as 'loan societies', because loans have become the standard way of coping financially. In the past, consumer loans were limited to small amounts from a local shopkeeper, say, or by pawning valuables. At the beginning of the twentieth century, banks began to make these kinds of loans on a wider scale. Until recently, only respected and wealthy citizens had access to loans; however, over time, all kinds of people were able to get loans, which they could use not only to buy the means of production, but also a range of consumer goods and services. The consumer boom that took place after the First World War caused a change in the social mentality. The attitude directed towards saving in order to be able to buy certain goods with cash was replaced by the attitude of 'buy now, pay later' (Olney, 1991). The period after the Second World War only reinforced this trend, because years of sacrifice made people hungry for consumer goods and they did not want to wait a long time to get them. An increasingly popular way of fulfilling this need for consumer goods was by means of incurring credits and loans.

The present financial crisis will have an impeding effect on the development of markets and credit instruments, for at least two reasons. First, the 'life on credit' lifestyle has revealed its downside, to individuals as well as society as a whole, and the promotion of such a lifestyle will not in future be as simple as it was previously. Consumer loans can no longer be portrayed as reaching for a level of modernity that has already been reached by some highly developed countries. Second, the decrease in confidence caused by the crisis will add to the tightening of the regulations for obtaining loans and to an increase in the cost, which in consequence will lead to a decrease in the number of borrowers.

Another characteristic of contemporary loans is depersonalization, which means removing the connection to particular individuals (Rona-Tas, 2008). This process began in the second half of the twentieth century. Previously, negotiating a loan implied a direct relationship between borrower and lender. This direct contact created a double commitment. The lender knew personally the person to whom s/he was lending the money, and could judge whether the person was trustworthy, while the borrower committed to borrow from an actual person, who had specific social sanctions at his/her disposal in case of default. Traditionally, loans used to be an individual commitment by an entity and therefore this act of an economic nature was perceived to have moral overtones. Lending was evaluated in religious texts, where the obligations of both sides of the agreement were pointed out. Those who borrowed and did not repay the money were stigmatized, people were told to lend to those in need of help, and imprudent lending and borrowing was warned against.

Nowadays, when the act of lending/borrowing has been deprived of a personal relationship between lender and borrower, institutional intermediaries have come between them. Borrowers have to submit to formalized evaluation procedures and it is the institutions that penalize in case of default. The loan decision is based on official criteria, so personal trust no longer plays a part. The client who deposits his/her money entrusts it not to a person, but to an institution that s/he has chosen based on rational considerations. Personal trust is substituted by a different kind of trust, namely a calculated trust of institutional character.

The widespread risk that is typical in the credit market causes careless and opportunistic behaviour among market participants. Loans are granted without appropriate provisions (the value of property is lower than the value of the loan, for example) and without a contribution from the borrower, and the salaries of loan officers increase with the number of customers gained. Lenders transfer risk by means of the securitization process on to investors who buy credit derivatives. During the risk transfer process, structured investment vehicles (SIVs), credit-rating agencies and investment banks collect the charges; however, they also avoid risk. The lack of transparency of oversight of credit-rating agencies as well as the conflicts of interest caused by them being paid by the issuers contribute collectively to the mechanism of fudging issues of responsibility.

The third characteristic of contemporary loans is the diversification of its form and the continuous appearance of new products. Alongside cash loans and buying on credit there is the option of loan savings accounts and credit cards with a huge variety of different offers that are usually beyond the understanding of the average customer. The vast amount of credit products, their diversity and high level of complexity make it difficult or even impossible to make a rational decision and chose one product over another. This causes customers to make rash decisions, based on emotion, and financial institutions to take advantage of their supremacy of information.

It seems that the above-mentioned characteristics of present-day loans have caused the ethical dimension that was applied previously to fade somewhat. The universal use of this institution in all its forms has strengthened the feeling that the payment obligation is something ordinary, on a daily basis, resulting from the realities of life in the market economy, that it is something imposed by external forces, something that one has not much influence over, and consequently bears limited responsibility for. As a result, people become less and less afraid of stigmatization from their further or closer environment as a result of avoiding repayment of loans, which causes the potential disapproval that would normally induce to fulfil the financial commitment to become meaningless.

However, as research on the ethics of financial commitment (Lewicka-Strzalecka and Bialowolski, 2007) has shown, in the declarative layer, the norm that tells people to repay debt is strongly rooted in the moral conscience of Poles (according to 97 per cent of the respondents, loan repayment is a moral duty) and particular behaviours that violate this norm are strongly condemned. The degree of disapproval is diversified and depends on who is the creditor. The most blameworthy are considered to be the behaviours that cause particular individuals to be harmed, such as a friend, neighbours incurring extra costs, or even the debtor him/herself. However, the behaviours that could damage the welfare of institutions or the broadly defined 'common good' are looked on more tolerantly. The above-mentioned research also revealed that most of the respondents believe that ethical standards concerning loan repayment have deteriorated. Almost 57 per cent of respondents said that previously people used to place more importance on loan repayment, over 9 per cent thought it did not matter, and almost 34 per cent did not have an opinion on the issue.

Depersonalization of credit relationships– that is, a particular individual in the role of creditor being replaced by an institution, weakens the ethical imperative that mandates loan repayment. The motivation to repay debts is now created by the fear of legal sanctions, the willingness to build a positive credit history, and the desire to avoid the negative repercussions of being included in various lists of difficult debtors. The relationships with the institutions are not perceived in terms of ethics, and the civil regulations, which should regulate these relationships, are not yet fully established in developing countries, and they have deteriorated in developed countries. The irresponsibility of financial institutions will only worsen this erosion.

What kind of capitalism: predatory, civilized or responsible?

The capital market has gone through many breakdowns in its history. Each time it has managed to overcome the crisis and rebuild its financial value. Every breakdown in the market is another valuable lesson, both for those who maintain that this is the final crash of that system, as well as for those who do not lose faith in its survival. Also, these days, at a time of another crisis in the financial markets, we hear the voices of those who maintain that nothing has happened, and that it is just the way things go, as well as the voices of those who are already formulating new economic doctrines, new market visions. However, new formulas can be effective only if we can give the right diagnosis of previous events.

It seems that the biggest difference can be seen at the level of diagnosis, describing the principles of the functioning of a free market economy. Everyday discussions that are held on the causes of the crisis are becoming more and more difficult, since various authors perceive the economic reality in completely different ways. Simplifying, we can adopt three basic versions describing the situation that can be encountered currently:

(i) *Predatory capitalism*: the best way to convey this is by using the famous words of the main character of the movie *Wall Street*: 'Greed is good. Greed is right. Greed works.' It is the acknowledgement that, in business, there is no place for ethical behaviour and the main characteristic is a free, unimpeded pursuit of profits.

(ii) *Civilized capitalism*: this can be described as the search for an optimal equilibrium between regulation and self-regulation. One of the forms of self-regulation are obligations of an ethical nature, which are sometimes formulated by means of codes of conduct for employees or for the management staff, but mostly it simply comes down to basic individual integrity.

(iii) *Responsible capitalism*: the basis of this version is the belief that the foundation of every business activity, as well as complying with legal regulations, is the common good. Therefore, every enterprise is an actor on the global scene and has a sense of social responsibility, which causes the enterprise to adjust its management systems to the various expectations coming from all kinds of stakeholder groups.

Those who believe in predatory capitalism, regardless of whether they openly admit this or not, treat the emerging crisis on the capital market as a fairly normal part of the business cycle. If 'the market knows better', then the blame for the current crisis can be laid on the inefficacy of the regulation policy, unjustified opinions given by experts from various rating agencies, speculative activities of hedge funds and so on. Summarizing, this diagnosis leads to the simplest formula: 'capitalism – yes, distortions – no', counting ineffective state regulations, the incompetence of some analysts or investment risk managers, and irresponsibility as distortions. Therefore, this formula suggests a higher level of the narrowly understood professionalism of managers, the search for better risk management models, and the assessment of stock value.

That is why the fear of the 'unprecedented' market interference by governments, which we are currently witnessing, is part of this belief.

It is even being said explicitly that government intervention may deepen the current crisis even further. Since the 'market knows better', then those that are not coping in this market should simply go bankrupt, regardless of the social consequences that come with this. When writing about the story of Enron, Young (2003) observes that the main architect of the fraudulent (called 'creative') accounting techniques that were employed in this firm called himself proudly a believer in the principles of social Darwinism, agreeing with Herbert Spencer that losers deserve no sympathy or regard.

Moreover, according to this version, any regulated business activity disturbs competition, which is the foundation of the natural selection process. So according to the followers of predatory capitalism, any market regulations simply impede the functioning of the market. Therefore, the only conclusion we should draw from the current crisis is that the less regulation there is, the greater the chance of a quick end to the crisis and a further development of the market. The belief that government interference in the economy usually does more harm than good leads the believers of this theory to the conclusion that the scope of legal regulations should be reduced. Consequently, managements of companies should concentrate on the maximization of income; and possibly even lobby for economic freedom, regardless of the social or ecological consequences.

Surely, nowadays in the European market there are not many who believe in the principles of predatory capitalism in its purest form. Most people believe in so-called civilized capitalism. It can take many forms, but there is a general agreement that the coexistence of legal regulations and ethical self-regulation of the behaviour of people working in business is necessary. According to the followers of this vision of capitalism, the system that creates wealth is extremely simple. All that is needed is a moral foundation, economic freedom, private property and limited intervention by administrative regulators. It is the deviations from moral and market standards that influence the condition and survivability of an economic system. Deviations from moral standards include the corruption occurring among business representatives, and deviations from market standards, including excessive government interference.

According to the followers of civilized capitalism it is necessary to introduce such procedures that make unethical behaviour in the market impossible. In this context, the authors of the book *Corporate Governance* write:

> Regulators have two responsibilities – prevention and prosecution. The regulations give honest people rules to play by, and they work for most

people. Greedy, unethical, and dishonest parties, however, are not going to play by the rules. For the errant, there must be consequences for violations – and these have not always been pursued with vigor for a variety of reasons, including lack of staff, political considerations, and incompetence, among others. (Colley *et al.*, 2003)

Therefore, as these authors write, restoration activities should concentrate primarily on the enforcement of existing regulations, fierce sanctions where necessary, and a careful and well-thought-out introduction of new regulations and incentive systems, especially in the area of counteracting unethical behaviour. Primarily, boards should make careful decisions when it comes to hiring people for managerial positions, information transparency and so on, which all depend on the selection of suitable people. If senior board members and senior management are not forthright and trustworthy, there is a high risk that problems will arise.

It should be agreed that integrity, or more specifically, that employees and managerial staff abide by ethical standards, is an important and necessary element of economic activity. However, ethical conduct at the individual level is not enough on its own for the responsible functioning of a company. The entire sphere of corporate behaviour, also on global level, is becoming increasingly important in the contemporary world.

Therefore, civilized capitalism emphasizes the significance of individual ethics, as well as the significance of personal responsibility in the sense of individual philanthropy, such as the sovereign decision of a shareholder to give away part of his/her dividend to social causes. Simultaneously, this form of capitalism expects essential activity from the government, whether it is in, for example, enforcing sanctions for fraudulent behaviour, or in taking responsibility for social and ecological challenges. Therefore, according to this belief, the current crisis in the financial markets is not strictly the result of a lack of adequate regulation, but is above all connected to the unethical behaviour of a section of the active players in this market who were able to find a way around the existing regulations, and thus violating the basic principles of integrity.

It is, however, doubtful whether government administration– that is, market regulating institutions – is able to introduce such a set of rules and system of sanctions that would make attempts at finding a way around regulations impossible. In his book, *The Manager's Book of Decencies: How Small Gestures Build Great Companies* (2007), Steve Harrison discusses the consequences of introducing the Sarbanes–Oxley Act as well as other legal regulations after the disclosure of the affairs at the beginning of the twenty-first century. On the basis of his research over recent years, the author claims that 'we can't create compliant organizations solely by punitive means'. That is why the laws and legal regulations that were created, with the main goal being to educate people about the real threat of punitive consequences, were not sufficient. According to Harrison, the carrot-and-stick method, with the emphasis on the stick, will not work if the organization lacks a genuine will to embrace an ethical culture at all levels of the organization and in all areas of activity. This culture refers to the virtues of citizens and a positive attitude of service. Corporate behaviour – according to Harrison – matters more than it once did. American business is not just a private matter; whether or not businesses succeed has immense implications for the world economy we all share. We have come to expect more from leaders, and we are understandably distressed when they turn out to be scoundrels.

Changing social expectations cause the vision of the current market economy in its specific equilibrium between economic freedom and individual integrity to be substituted more and more often by responsible capitalism. Those who describe the present economy in terms of responsible capitalism acknowledge the obviously vital role of individual ethical behaviour, but place companies in a broader context of social expectations and actions for the sake of the common good, showing in what way these expectations are met in business practice. The diagnosis of the current crisis within the framework of this version leads to the conclusion that the actions of a certain group of businesses, especially from the financial market, were focused on the short-term interest of a narrow group of managers, ignoring the interests of clients, employees and other stakeholder groups, and as a consequence neglecting the matter of creating long-term value for the shareholders, whose shares were bought out by, for example, the government at a very low price. As a result, everybody lost. Therefore, the formula here is obvious: to prevent future crises, social expectations should be met to a greater extent, and entirely new regulations that encourage the putting into effect of such a model should support this style of management. The success of a large enterprise is also the success of all its stakeholders, and bankruptcy affects not only the owners of financial capital.

It can therefore be said that the foundation of the current crisis lies in the capitalism model that does not take into account corporate responsibility. It should, however, be emphasized that describing the functioning of the market in terms of responsible capitalism is not a case of wishful thinking, because more and more companies in the global market, both large and small (however, unfortunately this does not include investment banks, of which the consequences of the crisis are a painful proof), consider in their activity, to a lesser or greater extent, the minimization of negative consequences for society and the maximization of positive ones. This theory is still in a 'pre-paradigmatic phase', as the authors of *Beyond Good Company* (Googins *et al.*, 2007) call it, but it is becoming increasingly common and at the same time increasingly desirable as a new ethos of co-regulation and co-operation between stakeholders.

So, is taking into account corporate responsibility in management solely an individual virtue, an expression of the necessity of the ethical conduct of entities – just as in civilized capitalism – or is it actions that bring benefits to all who serve the common good? One could use arguments in the style of Adam Smith, just as Steven Young does in *Moral Capitalism*, saying that the 'pursuit of self-interest arrives at a common good, a stable equilibrium of mutual benefit' (Young, 2003). However, this is an ideal image that should be supported by, as Young adds: the 'right state of mind' of the business participants and by regulations so that 'self-interest considered upon the whole will lead market players toward socially beneficial outcomes.' One can assume that pursuing this direction will reduce the susceptibility of the market to crises, which destroy social trust, reduce the value of companies and lower the standard of living.

A methodological failure or dishonesty?

Various creators of 'financial products' probably thought that the fall of Enron and the consulting firm Arthur Andersen would cover up misconduct that had been presented as 'innovations', that should merit recognition, because they supposedly stimulated the boom even further until it reached an unprecedented scale. If technical products were created in the same way, products such as planes or bridges, then not a day would pass without numerous construction or transport disasters. Reliable designers/engineers realize that their knowledge is not perfect, so they support their constructions by applying the so called 'security factor'. The value of this factor is reduced with the growth of technical knowledge and the durability of the applied materials. Meanwhile, as Sheldon Krimsky writes, these days conflicts of interest as well as risk are usually 'managed' rather than avoided or prevented (Krimsky, 2004).

Krimsky formulated the title of his book about corruption in science (2004) as a question, because he did not want to allow the thought that the knights of truth (given that scientists should serve the truth) would oppose the mission of a university, research institute or expertise. The word *expert* comes from the Latin *expertus*, which means 'experienced', 'skilful'; *experiti* means *tried out*. Therefore we can assume that an expert knows what s/he is doing, that s/he is a specialist in a given field. Science and expertise – which is a derivative of science, uses science as its reference and is assumed by the social contract within which a professional carries out his work – belong to the domain where success depends on the truth. They depend on facts, hypotheses and on designing and applying reliable methods of finding relevant data to test hypotheses for their validity (Bunge, 1989). Bunge also observes that, in business and politics, falsehood sometimes pays off and only mistakes are punished. The author adds that the contemporary popularity of unrealistic epistemology is an alarming indication of the universal misconception of science.

The authors of textbooks on research methods used in business and management write in a very straightforward manner about the relative ease of presenting falsified research results in that field (Remenyi *et al.*, 2003). These authors reproach scientific institutions for being satisfied with authors' statements, which affirm that the results of the research presented by them are in fact the results of their own work. The confidentiality of business data favours a lack of openness in presenting the details of research, with respect to content as well as applied methods. It is possible to smuggle in methods that are unreliable under the cover of this confidentiality. This stimulates us to pay more attention to the significance of the ethical dimension of scientific activity associated with economic research.

Therefore, who should we trust if all narratives, as they say, would have equal rights? Saying that each of us acts according to his/her own system of values does not solve the problem of ethical theory, of which the fundamental dilemma is defining the principles of choice (Boulding, 1985: 60). Similarly, it is essential to specify a standard for acknowledging research results, project solutions and expertise, and for declaring it to be trustworthy in the sense of the validity of cognitive scientific theory and the accuracy (relevance) of the created solutions. In ethics, the theory is adopted that, among all the possible ways to chose – that is, all the possible systems of values – only one is 'correct' or 'the best'. And that is what we call the ethical system of values. A methodology indicates the best way of explaining/designing, while eliminating other so-called narratives as unauthorized.

Krimsky, being a critic of the corruption of American science – and not only American – writes that 'universities have gone too far: they permit themselves and their faculties to be ridden with conflicts of interest; and through their aggressive support of technology transfer and their liberal acceptance of industry contracts, they compromise the integrity of scientific inquiry and communication. While subfields in medicine and the biosciences have been at the epicenter of these debates, other disciplinary voices can also be heard' (Krimsky, 2004). The current financial crisis provides evidence that this concerns economics and management, as well as the regulation that supports defective contracts, without checking them thoroughly, and which is not free from conflicts of interest.

However, Krimsky remains optimistic, which shows in his comment:

> The moral boundaries of research and publication integrity have been tested, and efforts are underway to reset the moral barometer to a higher level. There are five major stakeholders that are beginning to react to the public's negative attitudes about conflicts of interest in science and medicine. They are the journals, the professional societies, the governmental agencies, the universities, and the nonprofit research institutes. (Krimsky, 2004)

This extract concerns the United States of America, where the Academy of Management adopted the *Code of Ethical Conduct* that applies to all its members. In Europe, the European Science Foundation introduced *Good Research Practice* in the nineties. Recently, the European Commission established the *European Charter for Researchers* and published ethical rules and guidelines for research for the Seventh Framework Programme (Pauwels, 2007). In Poland, despite a number of regulations with respect to ethics,[2] the issue of ethics in scientific research remains a topic that is not included in the debate on the moral condition of Polish society, even though it has been written about many times before (Gasparski, 2001, 2005).

Conclusions

According to Fuller (2004) there are some similarities between the two concepts of economics and the two concepts of morality. The two concepts of economics are, on the one hand, economics based on relationships of exchange between business entities,[3] and on the other, economics that refers to the principle of marginal utility. When it comes to morality, on the one hand there is the morality of duty,[4] and on the other, the morality of aspiration.[5] Economics of exchange has a close affinity with the morality of duty, and the economics of marginal utility is, as it were, the economic counterpart of the morality of aspiration. Comparing, just as Adam Smith did, the morality of duty to the rules of grammar and the morality of aspiration to the rules that critics lay down for the attainment of what is sublime and elegant in composition, Fuller reflects on what advice a legislator would give regarding games with a high stake– to be precise, Jeremy Bentham's so-called 'deep play', which is exactly like the kind of speculation that led to the current crisis in the world of finance, making this world a global casino.

A legislator who acts according to the morality of duty would find that keeping from deep play is a duty, which is also supported by the arguments of marginal utility economics. A legislator who acts according to the morality of aspiration would treat such speculation with contempt. It is more probable that a legislator would act out of the sense of duty, because there is no way through which the law can compel a person to live up to the excellences of which s/he is capable (Fuller, 2004). However, Fuller continues, in one aspect our whole legal system represents a complex system of rules designed to rescue humanity from the blind play of chance. Nowadays we are inclined to ask whether the beliefs of Fuller still apply to the present day, postmodernism and deconstruction being so popular. But do we not convert these deconstructions intentionally into alibis for 'derogation from the rules'?

Fuller encourages acting according to the Aristotelian principles of the golden mean. Because of the default of some higher moral or economic good, we resort ultimately, both in the morality of aspiration and in marginal utility economics, to the notion of balance – not too much, not too little. This notion is not as trite as it seems. It is a characteristic of normal human beings that they pursue a plurality of ends; an obsessive concern with some single end can in fact be taken as a symptom of mental disease. For modern humans, the middle way is the easy way, involving a minimum of commitment. For Aristotle, the golden mean was a difficult road, dangerous to the indolent and unskilful and requiring the same kind of insight as efficient management (Fuller, 2004).

This advice is directed both towards people from the business world and to those from the legal world, but also moralists who sometimes need to be reminded of the virtue of practical realism – in other words, the attitude of eminent people that is restrained for the benefit of the remaining members of society. The characteristics of a practical realist are: a sober view of the world, using currently existing matters as a point of reference; respecting the conditions and limited possibilities of actions; an appropriate setting for a hierarchy of the norms leading to particular actions and plans (Pszczolowski, 1991: 229).

Notes

1. This chapter is a new and abridged version of the paper ready to be printed, in Polish, in 'Prawo-Biznes-Etyka' which will be published by Academic and Professional Press and Kozminski University, Warsaw.
2. *Dobre obyczaje w nauce: Zbior zasad i wytycznych*, Polish Committee of Ethics in Science (Warsaw: PAN, 2002); *Dobra praktyka badan naukowych: Rekomendacje*, edited by Group on Ethics In Science with the Minister of Science and Information. Accepted by the Polish State Committee of Scientific Research of the IV Term, Warsaw 2004; *Dobre praktyki w szkolach wyzszych*, edited by the Polish Rectors Foundation and approved by the Plenary Assembly of the Conference of Rectors of Academic Schools in Poland on 26 April 2007, published in Cracow, June 2007.
3. This was the standpoint of Ludwig von Mises.
4. Morality of duty: 'It lays down the basic rules without which an ordered society is impossible, or without which an ordered society directed toward certain specific goals must fail of its mark' (Fuller, 2004: 3).
5. Morality of aspiration 'is the morality of the Good Life, of excellence, of the fullest realization of human power' (Fuller, 2004: 3).

Bibliography

Boulding, K. E. (1985) 'Etyka i biznes',' in J. Grossfeld (ed.), *Ponad ekonomia* (Beyond Economy: Polish translation) (Warsaw: PIW), pp. 59–69.
Bunge, M. (1989) *Treatise on Basic Philosophy, Vol. 8: Ethics* (Dordrecht: Reidel).
Cialdini, R. (1993) *Influence: Science and Practice* (New York: HarperCollins College Publishers).
Colley, J. L., Doyle, J. L., Logan, G. W. and Stettinius, W. (2003) *Corporate Governance* (New York: McGraw-Hill).
Fuller, L. L. (2004) *Moralnosc prawa* (The Morality of Law: Polish translation) (Warsaw: ABC Publishers).
Gasparski, W. (2001) 'O etyce nauki, techniki i gospodarki (biznesu) przypomnien kilka', in I. Wojnar (ed.), *Dylematy etyczne dnia dzisiejszego i przyszlosci* (Warsaw: ELIPSA Publishers), pp. 116–33.
Gasparski, W. (2005) 'Etyka marketingu – marketingiem etyki', in L. Garbarski (ed.), *Kontrowersje wokol marketingu w Polsce: Tozsamosc, etyka, przyszlosc* (Warsaw: Kozminski University Press, 2005), pp. 205–16.
Googins, B. K., Mirvis, P. H., Rochlin, S. A. (2007) *Beyond Good Company: Next Generation Corporate Citizenship* (New York: Palgrave Macmillan).
Harrison, S. (2007) *The Manager's Book of Decencies. How Small Gestures Build Great Companies* (New York: McGraw-Hill).
Hendry, J. (2004) *Between Enterprise and Ethics: Business and Management in a Bimoral Society* (New York: Oxford University Press).
Jackson, C. W. (2006) *Fairy Tales: Grim Realities of Fictitious Financial Reporting* (Mason, Ohio: Thomson/Texere Group).

Krimsky, S. (2004) *Science in the Private Interest: Has the Lure of Profits Corrupted Biomedical Research?* (Lanham, Md.: Rowman & Littlefield).

Lewicka-Strzalecka, A. and Bialowolski, P. (2007) 'Etyka zobowiazan finansowych i stosunek do upadlosci konsumenckiej' in B. Klimczak, A. Lewicka-Strzalecka (eds) *Etyka i ekonomia* (Warsaw: PTE Press,), pp. 87–108.

Olney, M. L. (1991) *Buy Now, Pay Later. Advertising, Credit, and Consumer Durables in the 1920s* (Chapel Hill, NC: University of North Carolina Press).

Ortega y Gasset, J. (1994) *The Revolt of the Masses* (New York: W. W. Norton).

Pauwels, E. (2007) *Ethics for Researchers: Facilitating Research Excellence in FP7* (Brussels: European Commission).

Pietrasinski, Z. (2001) *Madrosc czyli swietne wyposazenie umyslu* (Warsaw: Scholar), pp. 38–40.

Pszczolowski, T. (1991) 'Wieloaspektowosc realizmu praktycznego' in W. Gasparski and A. Strzalecki (eds), *Logika, praktyka, etyka: Przeslania filozofii Tadeusza Kotarbinskiego* (Warsaw: Learned Society of Praxiology Press), pp. 229–36.

Remenyi, D., Williams, B., Money, A. and Swartz, E. (2003) *Doing Research in Business and Management: An Introduction to Process and Method* (London: Sage).

Rona-Tas, A. (2008) 'Consumer Credit and Society in Transition Countries', in V. Perez Diaz (ed.) *Markets and Civil Society* (New York: Berghahn Books, 2008).

Staniszkis, J. (1994) 'Dylematy okresu przejsciowego. Przypadek Polski' in W. Morawski (ed.), *Zmierzch socjalizmu panstwowego. Szkice z socjologii ekonomicznej* (Warsaw: PWN).

Young, S. (2003) *Moral Capitalism: Reconciling Private Interest with the Public Good* (San Francisco: Berrett-Koehler).

15
Corporate Responsibility in Multi-Stakeholder Collaboration in Social Governance

Aurore Lalucq, Michel Sauquet and Martin Vielajus

Today, much discourse on governance fails to take into account the role of corporations in the construction of social models, nor does it emphasize their potential (or indeed existing) participation in strategies of public regulation. Nevertheless, this question is at the very heart of the Institute for Research and Debate on Governance's (IRG's) reflection, notably within its 'International Initiative for Rethinking the Economy' (IRE).[1]

Three major points will be raised during this chapter: the significance of the word 'governance'; the approach of the IRG in its reflection on governance; and, finally, the role of the economic sphere and the business community in new conceptions of governance.

Governance: the non-linear path of a concept

Starting with the very word 'governance', beyond the plurality of its possible applications, there is a common dynamic behind the use of this term. Whether in the public or the private sector, for the majority of those who employ the word governance, it is effectively and above all used to refer to the decentralization of decision-making – with a multiplicity of actors and locales involved in the decision in question. It refers to the implementation of new and more flexible modes of regulation, based on partnerships between different actors.

The notion itself is certainly not a new one. With its provenance in the French language, the word dates from the political discourse of the Middle Ages, from the term *gouvernement* which it progressively came to replace; the term then disappeared through the centuries before reappearing in the 1970s: referring to the business community through the expression 'corporate governance'. It is therefore in the private sector that the notion re-emerged, referring to a style of corporate management based on articulation between the power of shareholders and that of management. What is at question is the types of actors involved in decision-making within the corporation, and their methods of interaction. At the centre of the corporate rationale, this notion then expands to encompass the question of how employees, suppliers (and all those involved) interact in the collective management of the corporation, and how this features in the general management dynamic.

Subsequently, political and administrative thought borrows the notion of governance from business management in two stages:

- The first stage corresponds to the neo-liberal revolution in the 1980s, which led to a new way of considering politics. While the role of the state was thrust into question (notably in the Anglo-Saxon nations) a 'functional' conception of governance emerged, linked to the rationale known as *New Public Management*. This rationale is based on a minimalist vision of the state, in which it should return to its 'core of its activity', to its 'normal' job, decentralizing and delegating non-strategic functions to other actors, as many large industrial corporations do when faced with globalization. This 'managerial' vision is also often found in state action, in the deeply normative character of the very notion of 'good governance', which is placed at the fore by international financial institutions. This notion effectively involves putting in place a battery of evaluative criteria measuring good and bad types of interaction between society and the state. This is evidently based on a specific democratic model, which is difficult to export in its entirety to countries where very different models of social contract and political culture already exist.
- The second stage came in the 1990s, when a deeper reflection on the role of the 'regulating' state emerged, in the guise of a response to the 'technician's' vision of *New Public Management*. Authors such as Guy B. Peter and Donald J. Savoie, Pierre Calame and Bernard Jouve maintain that the state crisis was not simply of a 'functional' nature – that it was not only symptomatic of the over-burdening of functions, and the weight on the state apparatus, but that it also seriously concerned the conditions of public policy formulation and the condition of the legitimacy of public power.

The IRG's approach to governance, local and global

Despite being open to a number of approaches, and indeed employing them for analysis and comparison, the IRG[2] is fundamentally behind the former conception of governance. A conception which distances itself from *New Public Management* and the somewhat contestable handling of the concept of 'good governance'. In fact, to us, it is important not to limit this concept to the performance of isolated institutions, or to the re-definition of its relative merits. On the contrary, it is necessary to study the interaction within the hierarchy, fields and actors. The rules detailing the organization of 'living together' cannot come from a single decision from each institution (however powerful it might be), and neither can they be subject to the singular principle of lawfulness. They would be much more legitimate if they were the result of a collective drawing-up process, as opposed to being decreed from 'on high'. This process would be informed by research detailing common challenges, according to clearly laid-out, unanimous standards.

Today, the work of the IRG contextualizes itself in this background and focuses on these fundamental questions:

- First, how to construct a mode of governing based not only on the domination of public power, but also on a partnership-centred and multi-actor rationale? What role can private actors play (notably corporations) in this dynamic of collective regulation?
- Second, how to move past conceptions of governance where the legitimacy of power is too often 'regulated' by a lawfulness uniquely incarnated by the state? How to evaluate other actors – their expertise, their authority and their capacity to participate in public decisions? What *de facto* legitimacy have they built in this field?
- Third, how to evaluate the relevance and the efficiency of institutional systems? What is at stake, and which methods must be applied to optimize the tools of institutional engineering and the reform of the state?
- Fourth, how to build an effective system of articulation between levels of governance – from the local to the global? What would allow for a simple distribution of skills and proficiencies, and engender a coherent bond between these scales and levels?
- Finally, in what ways can companies themselves become favoured actors in an improved integration of scales of governance, when faced with the fragmentation and strict apportionment of administrative systems?

This final reflection enables us to underline the idea that governance does not only affect modes of interaction at a national level, but realistically affects each level, subject to the exercise of power.

Thus, today, it is with a certain potency that the notion of 'international governance' has emerged. Through this concept, it is still necessary to question the new position of the state, faced with the increasing need for a transnational regulation and a communal handling of global concerns.

The economic sphere and corporations in new conceptions of governance

The evolution of economic thought regarding governance

Reflections on supranational modes of regulation have given rise to the evolution of economic thought, which is moving towards a use of the concept of governance that is not simply limited to *corporate governance*. The notion of international governance is gradually imposing itself on international economic debates, following a period of mistrust on the part of economists regarding a notion that is often seen as being too vague.

Until recently, authors such as Joseph Stiglitz or Dani Rodrik evoked the notion of international or global governance in order to emphasize the necessity of reinforcing or reforming the function of international institutions.

Their perspective largely advocated the regulation of commercial and financial flux, with particular concern for the equality of states of the North and states of the South in international negotiations. This reflection came within the perspective of an international order which would be little (or not at all) structured by the states themselves.

Yet the importance and the multiplicity of international problems (financial instability, commercial inequalities, environmental problems and so on) the passage of the internationalization of economies to globalization, associated with the loss of sovereignty, difficulties managing market and financial flux, as well as the impossibility of distinguishing national and international regulation have progressively made sectorial management impossible; international problems are thus further state-centred.

In this context, the notion of international governance is improving. For some (Jacquet *et al.*, 2002; Stiglitz, 2004; Lamy, 2005; or even Chavagneux, 2001), it encompasses the following concern: How to govern (globalization) without (a global) government? How to conceive of a new collective action on an international scale, composed of a considerable number of actors from the international scene?

Initially rejected for having been judged too 'managerial', or for representing a challenge to state power, the notion of international governance seems increasingly to breathe new life into the international political economy, by injecting politics into economic considerations.

Private corporations as non-state actors of governance

The emergence of non-state actors (NSA) – notably in institutional discourse – illustrates the integration of private actors as essential interlocutors in today's models of governance. This notion was greatly advanced by the European Commission in 2002 within the development policy of the European Union. The NSA were to become increasingly incontrovertible interlocutors (or decision-making bodies for consultancy), or even operators on the ground.

For the EU, the term NSA refers mainly to not-for-profit civil society organizations, which operate independently. Yet more and more theorists and practitioners of governance extend this notion to all the actors who, in reality, are not part of public power and can (and do) operate in the field of formulating regulations and the organization of society.

Fully supported by the IRG, this notion includes the corporations in a collective of 'non-state actors', which also comprises associations, NGOs and social movements, organizations, suppliers and consumers, trade unions, professional associations, foundations, and even universities and their research departments, think tanks, spiritual movements, the media....

In this ample landscape of actors, certain corporations assume responsibility and demand a growing role in the construction of social regulations. Examples of collaborations between business, public power and other non-state actors in resolving problems where all parties are implicated have occurred in domains as varied as sustainable development, public health or the fight against discrimination and threats to human rights.

How does this current of entrepreneurial participation fit into issues of sustainable development and environmental regulation? Since the end of the 1980s, under widespread pressure from both consumers and public powers, agricultural firms have been increasingly concerned with issues of environmental conservation and are subsequently modifying their strategies to respond to these issues. At times born of regulations or fluctuations in demand from the market (or indeed, sometimes voluntarily), these strategies extend to ensuring the legitimacy of production in the context of the degradation (or exhaustion) of planetary resources.

This entrepreneurial activity is judged in a variety of ways: for some, it aims to impose regulated solutions (without compromising the execution of their activities) while for others, they consider themselves as primary developmental actors who are responsible not only for their participation but also for the negotiation of the conditions of this participation. Whatever judgement can be applied to the foundations of these strategies, it cannot be denied that behaviour is changing, whether it is in the aeronautical industry, in industrial ecology experimentation which could result in the reduction of resources wasted in a given locale and so on. The IRG is particularly aware of these changes, and endeavours to embrace the results.

Where health is concerned, there are examples of attempts at multi-actor collaborations between pharmaceutical laboratories, national administrations, NGOs and trade unions to achieve communal preventative strategies. Taking into account the violent confrontations between pharmaceutical lobbies and patient organizations (or organizations fighting pandemics) in this, a domain so complex, it is extremely important that analysis and evidence from constructive experiences is well displayed.

Finally, in the struggle against discrimination, we can raise the pertinent example of the mobilization of business around the 'diversity charter' to participate in the fight against discrimination at work. This charter was developed within the framework of a dialogue between public power and other actors involved in governance. These examples point to the rising profile (no doubt aided by public opinion and the defenders of social actors) of correct ethical practice in the economic domain, with particular reference to the social responsibility of corporations.

Even so, it is not about considering the active role of these firms in governance simply through 'ethical' initiatives. Obviously, the rationale of these corporations resides overwhelmingly in their profit margins, and we must not underestimate the influence of industrial lobbies at major negotiations concerning climate change, commerce, the information society and so on. Yet it can certainly be stated that in many sectors a new dialogue is being established between corporations, public powers, and the rest of the civil society in the construction of a democratic society. The transition from an attitude of hostility and disregard between corporations and NGOs, to the first efforts at collaboration, seems to be, to us, a promising move towards this new dialogue.

Notes

1. Created and supported by the Charles Léopold Mayer Foundation, the IRE's mission is to encourage the emergence of new proposals in the economic domain. Its work consists in identifying the themes and proposals that call for innovation, have a significant impact on the life of societies and lend

themselves to practical applications. Situated at the point where concrete social and environmental problems intersect with internal questions within economics, IRE has chosen to focus on five major themes: currency and finance; institutional arrangements; the regulation of goods and services; the role of territories; and trade pattern. In all these domains, the IRE wishes to encourage discussions and debate capable of leading to new proposals. To this end, IRE was conceived as a site open to ideological, disciplinary and cultural diversity, and a place of exchange for those who think, act and innovate in the economic domain. IRE has established an online documentary centre (www.i-r-e.org) to bring together and showcase innovative discussions. It organizes and supports seminars and colloquia, hosts an international competition and publishes economic works.

2. The Institute for Research and Debate on Governance is a 'think tank' based in Paris, with an office in Bogota, Colombia. Born of an FPH initiative, its mission is to facilitate debate on governance by delivering expertise, setting up training modules, organizing seminars, and gathering and disseminating documentation (website and publications). The IRG uses methods that are: (i) cross-disciplinary, cross-fertilizing of contributions from specialists in political science, anthropology, economy, lawand so on; (ii) multi-actor, through connecting the realms of academia, national administration, civil society organizations, traditional and religious authorities; and (iii) international and intercultural – by connecting networks of researchers and practitioners from all over the world, the IRG brings out the diversity of cultural responses to issues of governance.

Bibliography

Chavagneux, C. (2001) 'Quelle gouvernance mondiale?', *L'économie politique*, 2001/4(12).

Jacquet, P., Pisani-Ferry, J., Tubiana, L., De Boissieu, C., Cohen, E. and Aglietta, M. (2002) *Gouvernance mondiale*, Rapport du conseil d'analyse économique, La documentation Française, collection les rapports du conseil d'analyse économique La documentation Française.

Lamy P. (2005) *Gouvernance globale, leçons d'Europe*, Gunnar Myrdal Lecture, (Geneva: United Nations Economic Commission for Europe).

Stiglitz J. (2004) *The Future of Global Governance*, IPD Working paper (Columbia University, New York: Initiative for Policy Dialogue).

16
The Fabric of Knowledge: The Role of Large Corporations in Knowledge Production and Dissemination

Laszlo Fekete and Zsolt Boda

Economic and sociological studies, public discourses and governmental blueprints have put particular emphasis on knowledge and information, their production, use and dissemination since the beginning of 1990s. In the age of the 'informational mode of development', as Manuel Castells characterizes our times, knowledge produces more knowledge which, in turn, accelerates growth and productivity (Castells, 1989: 10). Briefly, knowledge and information reconstruct our economic and social realities. Therefore the production, transformation, acquisition, exploitation, spread and distribution of knowledge and information constitute the most important elements of the dynamics of social and economic development. The notions of a knowledge-based economy and society, information society, post-industrial economy, network economy, learning economy and learning society are commonly rooted in the firm belief of the pivotal role of knowledge and information in the course of economic and social development.

The blueprints of the European Union (EU) and the governments of the EU member states habitually attribute some kind of redemptive power to the information and communication technologies in the production, use and dissemination of knowledge and information, which enable our societies and economies to remove long-lasting social and economic difficulties – 'more and better jobs and greater social cohesion' – as well as global environmental problems. Producing increasing amounts of knowledge and reliable information appears to offer the final remedy for the economy and society of the future. The Lisbon European Council of 23–24 March 2000 summarized the strategic goal of the new community policy: 'The shift to a digital, knowledge-based economy, prompted by new goods and services, will be a powerful engine for growth, competitiveness and jobs. In addition, it will be capable of improving citizens' quality of life and the environment' (European Council, 2000, para 8). According to this appraisal of the recent course of development, as the presence of knowledge and information has become increasingly pervasive in all areas of production processes and social formation, the knowledge-based economy and knowledge society extend over all European social and economic spaces. Besides the political aspiration of reforming the scientific and technological policies of the member states, and, more broadly, of transforming the whole European economic and social system for the twenty-first century, European political institutions and national governments regularly appeal to the European business community to increase its private contribution to innovation and R&D in order to create a knowledge-based economy and society. Because knowledge and information are the preconditions for fostering a democratic culture as well as a sustainable economy, European governments regard a knowledge-based economy and society as the outcome of the joint efforts of business and society at large.

In this chapter we confront these propositions with the concept of corporate social responsibility as well as empirical data. In terms of R&D activity, corporations, at least in the information and telecommunications as well as the energy sectors that we examine, do not seem to live up to the expectations of the European policy-makers, which may raise questions about how responsible these companies are. However, the basic documents of corporate social responsibility, such as the EU Green Paper on corporate social responsibility, or the OECD *Guidelines for Multinational Enterprises*, mention, but do not elaborate on the ethical case for knowledge production. We believe that this is a lacuna which should be filled, but we do not intend to do it with this chapter; rather, it aims at raising the issue and introducing some basic dilemmas.

Corporate social responsibility documents on knowledge production

Despite being a recurrent topic of public discourse, knowledge and information are not particularly considered in a comprehensive way; for example, what kinds of knowledge; whose knowledge and information; the acquisition, possession of or exclusion from knowledge and information; the social, economic and cultural conditions of the invention of new knowledge; the control and monopolization of knowledge and information; the perplexity of differentiation between robust and fallible knowledge; the positive and negative externalities of knowledge on the environment; productive versus destructive knowledge;

and the latter's detrimental effect on society and so on. Knowledge in a knowledge-based economy and society is simply regarded as the calculated, unproblematic and effective use of its different – epistemic, technical and practical – manifestations, whose validity claims are robust and well-founded. A knowledge-based economy as the result of the production, use and distribution of more and more knowledge and information is supposed to operate as a self-contained autopoietic system. With respect to social and economic development, knowledge and information are generally assumed to improve economic and social circumstances by creating new resources of growth and increasing overall social welfare. Since knowledge and information appear to generate huge positive externalities, their importance in production processes and social formation is believed to stand firmly without further qualification.

As a result of this belief, there is very little discussion about the significance of knowledge, information, innovation and R&D in corporate business strategies in the basic international documents of corporate social responsibility. The EU Green Paper (European Commission, 2001: 6) merely quotes the political declarations of the Lisbon European Council without providing standards and benchmarks for evaluating corporate performance or stipulating the social and political expectations of the corporate engagements in the production, use and dissemination of knowledge and information. Sustainability is neither considered in the context of the accumulation, distribution and effective utilization of intellectual capital and knowledge assets, nor the environmental consequences of faster economic growth. Meanwhile, the scope and dimension of corporate social responsibility for working conditions, human rights and environmental issues are quite clearly defined a result of extensive government regulations, the commitments of many business organizations, and the evolving civic participation in lawmaking processes and monitoring of corporate compliance with the rules and standards of business conduct. The corporate role of intellectual capital formation on behalf of the whole society is far from being settled, and the relationship between public and private knowledge is at stake.

The Global Reporting Initiative's (GRI) Sustainability Reporting Guidelines (GRI, 2000–2006) stress that the intangible assets such as intellectual capital, innovative ability and investment in R&D have paramount importance for measuring and depicting the value, sustainability and financial prospects of a company; however, they do not rank the production, use and dissemination of knowledge, technology and innovation among the major performance indicators of the productive capacity of corporations. While intellectual capital and knowledge assets are the main sources of the value creation processes, the GRI's Sustainability Reporting Guidelines do not imply any determination of the appropriate level of corporate expenditure on innovation, technology, R&D, or non-financial indicators and support mechanisms for intellectual capital formation. They merely go into details about how to give account of investment grants and R&D grants incurred by government in the economic report of a company. The other elements of intangible assets that are also supposed to be important resources of knowledge economy are not particularly specified (GRI, 2000–2006).

In a similar manner to the above-mentioned documents, the 2000 revision of the OECD *Guidelines for Multinational Enterprises* also sets the general principles and makes official declarations in Chapter VIII concerning the R&D activities of multinational corporations for the purpose of improving the innovative capacities of the host countries, and of contributing to their long-term development prospects, and science and technology policies. The OECD *Guidelines* set out the institutional and procedural mechanism for the investigation of the implementation of these principles. They assign authority to the newly created governmental offices of the OECD member states – the National Contact Points (NCPs) – to supervise and promote the adherence of multinational corporations to the OECD *Guidelines*. The NCPs are entitled to investigate individual cases, to impose sanctions for non-compliance, and to submit an annual report on their activities to the OECD's Investment Committee. However, the OECD *Guidelines* do not contain any standards or benchmarks, and fail to specify what would be the proper measures for compliance – territorial, sector, size, activity-specific and so on. It is hardly surprising that there has not been any sign of communication, analysis, investigation or action carried out by the National Contact Points concerning the implementation of the principles and standards elucidated in Chapter VIII: Science and Technology since 2000. While a few cases have been investigated because of alleged breaches of various chapters of the OECD *Guidelines*, corporate compliance with Chapter VIII has not yet been scrutinized (OECD *Guidelines*, 2001; OECD Watch, 2005: 52).

The lack of a complete enumeration of performance indicators relating to knowledge assets and intellectual capital formation, and their impacts on social welfare, shed light upon theoretical and methodological difficulties. For the reason that intellectual capital and knowledge assets are regarded as a mixture of heterogeneous – narrative and quantifiable – elements in the process of corporate value creation; for example, R&D, information and communications, intellectual property rights, patent portfolios, securities, trademarks and brand names, corporate and managerial culture, human resources, employee training and education, and other kinds of intangible assets that do not depend on physical embodiments, they are susceptible to different interpretations that cause further conceptual ambiguities and quantitative uncertainties. They also frequently lead to the inaccurate description of the economic realities and prospects of corporations (Eustace, 2000; Arewa, 2006: 66–79).

In addition to the above-mentioned theoretical and methodological difficulties of measuring and evaluating private and public investments in intellectual capital and knowledge assets, many experts discuss critically the effectiveness of the voluntary principles and vague standards of these political documents for responsible business conduct in the formation of corporate business strategies and economic decision-making. They are convinced that the positive impacts of policy statements, legally not binding principles and standards on corporate practices are negligible. In brief, policy statements, at most, reflect the political commitments of governments and international political bodies, which may appeal to the public but do not boost private investment in knowledge and information. Few corporations are inclined to incorporate noble social aims into their business strategies if they do not serve their short-term economic interests and payoffs. To determine the veracity of this sceptical view, we shall examine the impacts of the normative pronouncements of these documents on both governmental and corporate strategies and decision-making processes concerning the formation of a knowledge-based economy and society.

From Lisbon 2000 to Barcelona 2002 and later

In spite of the favourable and unique economic climate for social and economic development, the overall economic performance of the EU member states remained meagre during the 1990s. Meanwhile, a few EU countries – especially Finland, Sweden, the Netherlands, Denmark and the United Kingdom – were able to keep pace with the high level of labour productivity and capital intensity growth of the USA, the majority of the EU member states failed to follow the growth patterns of the most dynamic countries and experienced a persistent economic slowdown from the beginning of the 1990s.

The impressive figures of overall economic capital intensity and productivity growth as well as the low levels of unemployment and inflation in the USA were generally attributed to the positive spillover effects of the spread and use of the new information and communication technologies in all segments of economic and social activities which continuously opened up new business opportunities for further technological investments, new products and services, and a higher potential for profit. While the exceptional constellation of the high rates of labour productivity and capital intensity growth as well as the declining rate of unemployment and inflation in the USA during the 1990s recently went through a critical re-examination, the majority of the EU member states were unable to shift their economic and human resources from traditional and medium-level manufacturing industries to high productivity, knowledge-intensive sectors of the economy and to set up a proper institutional structure for managing this economic and social transformation (Alesina and Perotti, 2004: 27–48; Abramovitz and David, 2001). Additionally, aggregate corporate spending on R&D declined in most of the EU member states during the 1990s. Thus capital intensity and labour productivity growth remained stagnant and declining, with a slight increase in the rate of employment, which caused an additional decline in labour productivity in Europe (McMorrow and Werner, 2007: 82–98). As a result of their relatively weak capacity to innovate and the less efficient use of capital and labour in production processes, the majority of EU member states could not capitalize effectively on the emergence and diffusion of the new information and communication technologies. In the context of ambitious political statements made regularly by the European policy-makers about the outstanding importance of the knowledge production, use and dissemination for future growth and social welfare, the decennial downturn of public and private R&D expenditures accelerated from 1991 was particularly disappointing. As a result of misguided economic and R&D policies, the productivity gap between the USA and the EU member states widened further during the 1990s.

The persistent divergence between the economic performances of the USA and the majority of the EU member states during the 1990s was the core reason why the Lisbon European Council of 23–24 March 2000 initiated a comprehensive economic and social policy reform for the following decade. The poor performance of the European economy appeared to mobilize and unite the European policy-makers to act. The Presidency Conclusions enumerated some obvious (and less obvious) social, economic and institutional instruments – such as tax allowances for private investment in R&D; financial assistance and other preferential treatment for innovative enterprises; removing obstacles to the mobility of researchers; community-wide patent protection; an efficient intellectual property rights regime and management; fostering a European network for electronic scientific communications; promoting joint research projects between business enterprises, universities and other public research centres and so on – which were supposed to be the important factors of the production, use and dissemination of knowledge; however, it did not set down specific targets regarding overall R&D expenditure in terms of GDP.

Two years after Lisbon, the Barcelona Summit indicated an exact figure of public and private expenditure on R&D for the EU member states. According to the Presidency Conclusions of the Barcelona European Council of 15 and 16 March 2002, '[i]n order to close the gap between the EU and its major competitors, there must be a significant boost of the overall R&D and innovation effort in the Union, with a particular emphasis on frontier technologies. The European Council therefore ... agrees that overall spending on R&D and innovation in the Union should be increased with the aim of approaching 3 per cent of GDP by 2010. Two-thirds of this new investment should come from the private sector' (European Council, 2002: para. 47).

As well as this voluntaristic proclamation of the European policymakers, comprehensive or country-specific economic studies did not analyse the feasibility of these political objectives and did not outline the necessary steps to be taken in order to reconcile the considerable differences existing between the EU member states' R&D policy preferences, capabilities, and annual expenditures. Because the planning and financing of R&D policy falls mainly into the competence of national governments, and prerogatives are not assigned to the political institutions of the European Union in this policy domain, the European Council left to the EU member states to integrate the main objectives of the Lisbon Strategy into their own growth models, budget planning, execution and management, and national R&D programmes (Alesina *et al.*, 2005: 285–7, 309–10).

As can be seen from the budgetary data of the European Union, the initiatives of the European Council could not scale up very much the accomplishment of the main objectives of the Lisbon Strategy during the following years. In 2000, a budget of €3.63 billion – 3.9 per cent of the EU Budget – was devoted to funding the Fifth European Community Framework Programme (1998–2002) covering research, technological development and demonstration projects, which just about equalled the Intel Corporation's, or Merck Pharmaceuticals' annual R&D expenditures in terms of money. Nor does the budget of the Sixth European Community Framework Programme (2002–6) exhibit a paradigmatic change in the composition of the EU budget standing for declared community-wide priorities; almost the same amount of money – €17.5 billion – was spent over a period of five years to fund and promote the creation of the so-called European Research Area. The Seventh European Community Framework Programme for Research and Technological Development (2007–13) has been a little more generously financed: 5.08 per cent of the EU Budget – a total of €6.8 billion – was devoted to funding common R&D projects in 2009. For all the efforts made by the European Commission in recent years, the redistributive and integrative effects of the use of the EU Budget to fund and promote common R&D projects were quite limited, so the EU member states had to draw on their own political agendas, decisions and financial resources to overcome their long-term underinvestment in this domain, and to accomplish the objectives of the Lisbon Strategy.

The accomplishment of this 3 per cent Barcelona target by 2010 imposes fewer and more manageable burdens on the budgets of national

Table 16.1 Gross domestic expenditures on research and development as percentage of GDP, 2000–8

Country/Year	2000	2001	2002	2003	2004	2005	2006	2007	2008
EU-27	1.85	1.86	1.87	1.86	1.82	1.82	1.84	1.83	1.90
EU-15	1.91	1.92	1.93	1.92	1.89	1.89	1.92	1.93	1.99
Sweden	3.78	4.17	4.27	3.85	3.62	3.80	3.74	3.64	3.75
Finland	3.34	3.30	3.36	3.43	3.45	3.48	3.45	3.47	3.46
Austria	1.94	2.07	2.16	2.16	2.26	2.44	2.46	2.56	2.66
Denmark	2.24	2.39	2.51	2.58	2.48	2.46	2.48	2.55	2.72
Germany	2.45	2.46	2.49	2.52	2.49	2.48	2.54	2.53	2.63
France	2.15	2.20	2.23	2.17	2.15	2.10	2.10	2.08	2.02
Belgium	1.97	2.08	1.94	1.88	1.87	1.84	1.88	1.87	1.92
UK	1.81	1.79	1.79	1.75	1.69	1.73	1.76	1.82	1.88
Netherlands	1.82	1.80	1.72	1.76	1.81	1.79	1.78	1.71	1.63
Luxembourg	1.65	:	1.71	1.65	1.63	1.56	1.66	1.63	1.62
Ireland	1.12	1.10	1.10	1.17	1.24	1.25	1.30	1.31	1.45
Spain	0.91	0.91	0.99	1.05	1.06	1.12	1.20	1.27	1.35
Portugal	0.76	0.80	0.76	0.74	0.77	0.81	1.00	1.18	1.51
Italy	1.05	1.09	1.13	1.11	1.10	1.09	1.02	1.21	1.18
Greece	:	0.58	:	0.57	0.55	0.59	0.58	0.58	:

Sources: OECD, Eurostat.

governments than on the budgets of European business enterprises. That is, public R&D expenditures were not far from 1 per cent of GDP in the majority of the EU member states in 2000. The real problem arises from the fact that the percentage of public spending on R&D in the terms of GDP has not shown any progress in the majority of the EU member states since the Lisbon European Council of 2000. The EU-15 average is still below the 1 per cent target of public R&D expenditures by a significant margin; it was only 0.77 per cent of GDP in 2000, the same as in 2006. Among the most advanced EU member states, only Finland has met the 1 per cent Barcelona target of public R&D expenditure from the outset. Despite of the lack of change in the allocation of budgetary resources to public R&D, the augmentation of national R&D expenditures by 2010, as determined at the Barcelona Summit, hinges mainly on the significant increase in the financial contribution of European business enterprises. Without addressing the appeal of the Barcelona Summit directly to the European business community, the 3 per cent target practically meant that European business enterprises should more than double their efforts at financing their corporate R&D projects by 2010. In brief, alongside many institutional, legal and fiscal impediments that may reflect the EU member states' uneasiness at giving up their prerogatives, their own political preferences and particular budgetary priorities, the lack of innovational capacity in the European economy originates mainly from the quite modest R&D expenditures of the European business enterprises in comparison with their American, Japanese and South East Asian competitors.

While the main objectives of a knowledge-based economy and society were agreed on in Lisbon and Barcelona, the composition of public and private spending on R&D still varies widely across countries. The British government set up a less ambitious schedule in the *Science and Innovation Investment Framework, 2004–14*, published in 2004 for the United Kingdom. According to this document, public and private investment in R&D will rise from 1.9 per cent to 2.5 per cent of GDP by 2014 in the United Kingdom. The authors of this document also expressed their reluctance regarding the feasibility of the fulfilment of the 3 per cent Barcelona target by 2010 (HM Treasury, 2004: 7, 53). Needless to say, the actual R&D figures gave good reason for scepticism. Beyond the most innovative countries, such as Finland and Sweden, only a few EU member states – Austria and Denmark, for example – have made considerable progress in the renewal of their innovation policy and economic performance, and public and private R&D spending since 2000. The commitments of the majority of the EU member states to the targets of the Lisbon and Barcelona European Councils have not been visible in terms of comparative statistical figures so far. To put it in economic terms, the majority of the EU member states allocate less budgetary resources to innovation and R&D than they have officially promised to do since Lisbon and Barcelona. Thus the achievement of the Barcelona target by 2010 seems to be unrealistic for most of the advanced EU member states.

Because the Lisbon Strategy was designed and adopted well before the accession of the Baltic and the Central and Eastern European countries to the EU, neither the Lisbon Strategy nor the Presidency Conclusions of the Barcelona European Council contained specific recommendations, requirements, guidelines or benchmarks for the candidate countries in the field of R&D policy. The European Commission attempted to fill this gap by encouraging the new member states to set up their own long-term policy targets following the Lisbon Strategy in their national reform programmes.

In the new EU member states, public and private R&D expenditures fell significantly short of the 3 per cent Barcelona target in the year of their accession. Meanwhile, the former Baltic, Central and Eastern European countries experienced very high, sometimes double-digit growth rates from the end of the 1990s until mid-2008, but these impressive growth figures did not bring a strategic change in their public and private R&D policies. In the new EU member states, high rates of economic growth have been produced under circumstances of quite low and stagnant R&D spending. As the situation of many latecomer countries, such as the Republic of Ireland, demonstrates, a high rate of economic growth

Table 16.2 Gross domestic expenditures on research and development as percentage of GDP, 2000–8

	2000	2001	2002	2003	2004	2005	2006	2007	2008
EU-15	1.91	1.92	1.93	1.92	1.89	1.89	1.92	1.93	1.99
Slovenia	1.39	1.5	1.47	1.27	1.4	1.44	1.56	1.53	1.66
Czech Rep.	1.21	1.2	1.2	1.25	1.25	1.41	1.55	1.54	1.47
Hungary	0.78	0.92	1	0.93	0.88	0.94	1	0.97	1
Lithuania	0.59	0.67	0.66	0.67	0.75	0.75	0.79	0.82	0.8
Latvia	0.44	0.41	0.42	0.38	0.42	0.56	0.7	0.59	0.61
Poland	0.64	0.62	0.56	0.54	0.56	0.57	0.56	0.57	0.61
Romania	0.37	0.39	0.38	0.39	0.39	0.41	0.45	0.52	0.58
Bulgaria	0.52	0.47	0.49	0.5	0.5	0.49	0.48	0.48	0.49
Slovakia	0.65	0.63	0.57	0.57	0.51	0.51	0.49	0.46	0.47

Sources: OECD, Eurostat.

is not necessarily a corollary to high R&D intensity. The main driver of economic growth in the new EU member states has been rather an imitation of some leading-edge and more medium-level technologies than innovation of these in the course of decade 2000–9. Therefore, during the period of their economic integration into the global economy, the underperformance of R&D intensity did not bring about economic decline, at least in the short and medium term, but imitation is not able to draw these countries nearer to the frontier of innovation.

The current R&D policy of Central and Eastern European countries is a case in point. The weak R&D intensity in Central and Eastern European countries is shown by the fact that only thirteen large innovative corporations – three Hungarian (€110.01 million), four Czech (€77.57 million), two Slovenian (€63.69 million), and four Polish (€53.67 million) – can be found in the European list of the top 1,000 corporate R&D investors in 2008 (European Commission, 2007; European Commission, 2008).

The contribution of these thirteen large innovative corporations adds up to just 0.24 per cent of the €126.36 billion of the total private R&D expenditures of the 1,000 most innovative corporations of the EU. At the same time, the weak innovative ability of the small and medium-sized enterprises cannot compensate for the very low innovative intensities of the large corporations of the Central and Eastern European countries. A lack of 'business angels', developed venture capital markets and private equity funds – a general problem all over Europe – means that innovative small and medium-sized enterprises face the difficulty of obtaining sufficient external finance for R&D. In Hungary, for example, most of the venture capital funds are invested into non-innovative activities. In this respect, the contribution of venture capital and private equity funds to innovative activities is rather weaker in the other Central and Eastern European countries (Karsai, 2006: 1033; OECD 2008: 76–8). The innovative small and medium-sized enterprises have bleak prospects of developing into larger enterprises or to be taken over by a large corporation. To improve their positions in this unfavourable corporate ranking, the governments of new member states usually announce in their national action programme a constant and resolute adjustment to the Lisbon Strategy which can be judged as overconfident and quite baseless considering the past and present experiences of their fiscal and R&D policies.

The Polish Council of Ministers, for example, adopted the National Reform Programme on 8 June 2006, which indicated a significant increase of gross domestic expenditure on R&D, from 0.58 per cent of

GDP in 2004 to 1.65 per cent by 2008. The private R&D expenditure of Polish business enterprises was to be tripled, from 0.17 per cent of GDP to 0.55 per cent in the same period. The Hungarian government submitted to the European Commission in 2006 a less ambitious National Action Programme than that of its Polish counterpart. It anticipated an increase of gross domestic expenditures on R&D from 1 per cent of GDP in 2007 to 1.4 per cent by 2010. Interestingly, the Hungarian government seemed to be less assured of the intentions of the corporate actors who were supposed to increase their private contribution from 0.39 per cent of GDP in 2007 to 0.7 per cent by 2010. By and large, only the Czech Republic, Estonia and Slovenia have been able to produce a noticeable improvement in this domain; they have moved step by step towards the EU-15 average since their accession to the European Union. Consecutive governments in the majority of the new EU member states have regularly redesigned the functions, governance and institutional structure of their national innovation system without achieving a breakthrough or even a modest perceptible advancement in this field since the beginning of the 1990s. One has reason to wonder whether the projects and predictions of these national action programmes are based on reliable figures, comprehensive social and economic analyses, and the sincere intention of the governments to promote a new R&D policy.

Because some of the governments of the new EU member states – in particular, Poland and Hungary – have acted under permanent pressure from the European Commission for fiscal consolidation in recent years, it would be hard to expect them to bring about a radical change in the composition of public spending and institutional structure in order to display the commitment of financial resources to fostering a knowledge-based economy and society during the current intensification of the global downturn. It is to be feared that the recent economic contraction will be intensified by a weak and inappropriate policy response by the governments of the new EU member states concerning R&D policy. Recently, no measures or action plans are visible in the new EU member states that would aid the recovery of the economy through mobilizing and allocating new financial and human resources for innovation, R&D and productivity-enhancing public and private investments. To mitigate the social and economic consequences of the current economic crisis, the limited public resources are used to reduce the economic contraction of traditional businesses such as automotive component manufacture and the construction industry, which are struggling with massive overcapacity worldwide than to invest in knowledge for the fulfilment of a knowledge-based economy and a society project for the future. With regard to recent R&D policy, economic growth in the long term is not sustainable in the new EU member states.

The role of large corporations in research and development expenditure

In this section we shall take a closer look at two business sectors, and examine their R&D activities. We chose information and telecommunications, and the energy sector, for different reasons. Information and telecommunications is considered to belong to the knowledge-intensive sector, so corporate R&D expenditure should be high and ever-increasing. The energy sector was selected because meeting the challenge of climate change would need a significant effort in energy-related R&D investment. One could argue that the corporate responsibility in the given sectors is directly related to R&D activity and spending.

Research and development in the information and telecommunications sectors

The Lisbon European Council of 23–24 March 2000 ascribed outstanding importance to information and communication technology investments in the implementation of its ten-year knowledge-based economy and society project. As it transpired later, the timing of the introduction of the new EU economic and social policy reform of the European Union in the spring of 2000 was quite unfortunate. The significantly overvalued Nasdaq, which was identified with the new economy, and in particular the publicly-traded corporations of the information and telecommunications sectors, in the economic journals as well as the popular press, began to decelerate after 10 March 2000 and crashed a year later, driving hundreds of leading-edge technology and service companies into bankruptcy. After the bursting of the internet bubble, the overall devaluation of share prices at the global level and the decline of corporate earnings made it difficult to retain the asset values of the information and telecommunications corporations, as well as obtaining funding for further technological investments, R&D by means of initial public offering or private stock offering, external equity financing or leveraging. The investors' over-optimistic beliefs about the robust growth potential of intangible asset-based industries and the soaring revenues of their expenditure on intangible investments, which had achieved up to 698 per cent premium of the first day of trading (VA Linux Systems) in the favourable times of the internet revolution, quickly vanished from global as well as European markets. Thus more and more public and private information technology projects were abandoned or postponed indefinitely. Information and telecommunications sectors went through an upheaval over subsequent years, which also badly affected the economic prospects of the newly privatized information and telecommunications corporations in Europe.

However, the knowledge-based economy and society project of the European Union had lost momentum earlier than the turn of the millennium. Because of the slow and hesitant abolition of information and telecommunications monopolies and misguided information and communication policies, most of the EU member states missed a significant opportunity to lay the foundation of a new economy at the beginning of the 1990s. The European Commission had already alarmed the member states by forecasting a dim future for the parochial, monopolistic and state-controlled information and telecommunications markets in a competitive global environment in 1983 (European Commission, 1983: 7). In spite of the economic challenge of the American, Japanese and South East Asian corporations in global information and telecommunications markets, and the social and economic needs of new and value-added telecommunications services in Europe, the rearrangement of public policy priorities was sluggish and suffered about a ten to fifteen-year delay in most of the EU member states.

It is true that many governmental documents and analyses of the EU member states expressed their discontent and fear that information society projects in Europe lag behind the most dynamic countries – the USA, Japan, Canada, the Netherlands and the Scandinavian countries, for example. Despite the proliferation and spread of new communication tools, techniques and technologies causing anxiety, these documents did not propose to follow the developmental strategy of the most dynamic countries – namely, the liberalization and deregulation of the information and communication sectors, the dismantling of state monopolies, the abolition of the parastatal characteristics of information and communication services, and the creation of competitive and platform-neutral markets for contesting product and service providers. The authors of many governmental documents pondered over how to maintain and reformulate the regulatory role of the state with the coming of the information society, and recommended a cautious reorientation of the information and communication policy of the government in its well-established framework.

The governments of the EU member states have, from the mid-1990s, gradually abandoned the idea that the state should set up and finance the development of information and communication infrastructure and services. It had to be conceded that the state did not have the required economic resources, technical and entrepreneurial expertise, and proper institutional and organizational structures at its disposal to provide leading-edge information and communication infrastructure and to command the flow, direction and modes of communication. In this field, the proactive behaviour of the state – namely, predefining social and economic needs, designing, financing and controlling the technical, economic and social preconditions of communications by the state – has become rather dysfunctional and anachronistic.

In spite of the mutual understanding on the surface, the majority of the EU member states attempted to protect the position of their own information and telecommunications monopolies with reference to the main tenet of mainstream economics regarding natural monopoly. According to the economic theory of natural monopoly, because of the large sunk costs, economies of size, scale and scope, and positive network externalities, a single telecommunications service provider can supply the entire market at a lower per unit cost than two or more service providers. The test for natural monopoly is the subadditivity of its cost function. Many economists were convinced, without having a shred of evidence to support this claim, that a monopoly firm could produce the same output for a lower per unit cost than could multiple competitors. If the cost function was subadditive, which they had thought to be the case, a natural monopoly market should be protected from the free entry of other service providers and price competition in order to prevent destructive competition, market failures, higher consumer prices or lower quality of service, and overall social welfare losses (Baumol *et al.*, 1988). In contrast to a natural monopoly market, the outcome of the competitive market would be detrimental for both business and private customers. To sum up, the operation of a natural monopoly can comply with the requirements of productive, techno-logical and allocative efficiencies; while competition cannot yield the best possible outcome in a market that passes the subadditivity test. In the natural monopoly debate, the Schumpeterian view regarding the innovative, technological and entrepreneurial advantages of large monopoly organizations was also recalled. As Joseph A. Schumpeter pointed out with regard to the economic inevitability of the rise of large monopoly organizations:

the perfectly competitive arrangement displays wastes of its own. The firm of this type that is compatible with perfect competition is in many cases inferior in internal, especially technological, efficiency. If it is, then it wastes opportunities. It may also in its endeavors to improve its methods of production waste capital because it is in a less favorable position to evolve and to judge new possibilities (Schumpeter, 1950: 106)

As well as citing the economic arguments that may appear to be compelling, France, Italy, Germany, Belgium, Greece, Spain and Luxembourg challenged the Commission Directive 90/388/EEC of 28 June 1990 on competition in the markets for telecommunications services before the European Court of Justice, questioning the European Commission's competence on the matter of legislating the withdrawal of the special rights granted to national monopolies regarding telecommunications services (*France* v. *Commission*, Case 202/88, [1991] ECR I-1223; *Spain, Belgium and Italy* v. *Commission*, Cases 217/90, 281/90 and 289/90, [1992] ECR I-5833; Burley and Mattli, 1993: 41–76; Verhoeven, 1996: 861–87; Jauk, 1999/2000: 1–113). But the growing indebtedness, for example, in Italy, Spain, France, and later on the candidate countries, impelled the governments of the EU member states to recognize the financial necessity of the privatization of the state-owned telecommunications monopolies to consolidate their excessive budget deficits.

Nevertheless, the later comparative studies about the prices of the competitive and monopoly information and telecommunications markets, and the legal and political barriers to the introduction of new technologies and value-added information services, proved convincingly that as a result of monopoly rents and technological inefficiency the operation of these state-owned monopolies had caused significant social welfare losses (Bortolotti *et al.*, 2001; DotEcon and Criterion Economics, 2003: 8, 49–51).

For this reason, the Lisbon European Council of 23–24 March 2000 placed particular emphasis on the importance of the liberalization of the European markets to improve the productive, technological and allocative efficiencies of the information and telecommunications sectors as well as to realize knowledge-based economy and society projects. As stated in the document, '[f]ully integrated and liberalized telecommunications markets should be completed by the end of 2001' (Presidency Conclusions, I., para. 11, Lisbon European Council, 2000). After a long preparation period, the abolition of the natural monopolies in the European information and telecommunications markets was not as radical as the AT&T antitrust divestiture in the USA in 1984, because the European policy-makers sought to achieve two, in some ways contradictory, objectives – namely, to create a competitive market for multiple product and service providers and strengthen the economic position of the former state-controlled telecommunications monopolies against their global competitors. By the beginning of the 2000s, the process of liberalization had successfully transformed the fragmented and monopolistic European information and telecommunications markets into oligopolistic ones with legal and geographical segmentations which, as it appeared later, could only function with the regular intervention and control of the European and national regulatory and competition authorities. Nevertheless, this delicate arrangement of quasi-competitive markets, and the proactive interventions of the new regulatory and competition authorities in the fields of pricing, access rights, market entry, contracting and so on has brought about the rapid diffusion of new communication technologies, the major improvement and differentiation of services, and a considerable reduction in the prices paid by private and business customers.

As the political presumptions in governmental documents as well as the conviction of the economic advocates of the market fundamentalism show, the privatization of the state-owned corporations was thought to improve the productive, technological and allocative efficiencies of the information and telecommunications sectors. By means of the regular intervention of by the regulatory and competition authorities, the overall trends in the information and telecommunications sectors to some extent confirm the original presumption since the year 2000. While the newly privatized information and telecommunications corporations have experienced hard times, especially in the first part of the 2000s, the privatization and deregulation contributed overall to an increase in their revenues, profitability and productive efficiency. The improvement in operational performance can be attributed to the expansion of new and value-added services, more efficient operations, productivity growth, the reduction of operational costs, outsourcing services, engaging in mergers and acquisitions transactions, selling and leasing back of a property portfolio, and so on.

In this way, the information and telecommunications sectors seem to be properly classified as the most dynamic parts of the economy. However, the statistical data show a declining trend of private R&D expenditures by the privatized telecommunications corporations. Meanwhile, the European telecommunications corporations have increased their revenues significantly; but they have invested less and less money into R&D since their privatization. The basic changes in ownership, corporate governance structure, competitive markets and the regulations themselves do not generate additional incentives for the corporations to increase or at least to keep up their previous R&D expenditures in terms of their revenues since the year 2000. While a few telecommunications corporations, such as Telefónica and the BT Group, tend to inflate the actual figures a little by a loose definition of the notions of R&D, and include marketing research, survey research, software amortization and upgrading, and other overhead costs in the private R&D expenditures in their annual financial reports, the downward trends concerning R&D in the telecommunications sector are inevitable.

A few authors explain this paradox by saying that the new management of the privatized corporations economized on operational costs, and restructured and downsized research facilities, but these structural changes yield higher R&D intensity which is manifested in the growing number of new patent filings and patent citations. They consider the number of new patent filings and patent citations as the proper measure of knowledge spillovers, patent quality, and the diffusion of new technologies (Munari and Sobrero, 2002: 1–28; Munari *et al.*, 2002: 31–53; Munari and Oriani, 2005: 61–91). Unfortunately, European telecommunications corporations usually publish rather vague and inaccurate figures regarding the actual size of their patent portfolios, their new patent filings and patent citations in their annual reports. The patent data of France Télécom, for example, which seem to be quite reliable, or at least less inconsistent when compared with others companies' data, does not prove the above explanation. In addition, European Patent Office data do not confirm the hypothesis that declining and stagnant R&D expenditures may be a corollary of higher R&D intensity after privatization, especially in the field of patentable knowledge, because noticeable increases in patent citations cannot be demonstrated (Hall *et al.*, 2000; Michel and Bettels, 2001: 185–201; Bacchiocchi and Montobbio, 2004; Hirschey and Richardson, 2004: 91–107; Roberts, 2005: 33–38). The growing number of filed patents and patent citations is not a straightforward signal of innovative activity. Besides innovation and commercial exploitation, patents are filed for different purposes without an intention of manufacturing the original ideas; such patent filings are used for building a monopoly position, demonstrating economic strength, blocking competitors from entering a market, leveraging infringement claims, preventing lawsuits, litigation purposes to earn profits and so on. In addition, the vast majority of filed patents are never used because of a lack of economic interest and competitive pressure (European Patent Organization, 2007: 35).

Table 16.3a Revenues and R&D expenditures of the European telecommunications corporations, 2000–8

	2000	2001	2002	2003	2004	2005	2006	2007	2008	Change % 2000/2008
Deutsche Telekom										
Revenue €bn	40.90	48.3	53.7	55.8	57.9	59.6	61.3	62.5	61.7	50.86
R&D exp. €bn	0.86	0.90	0.90	0.90	0.90	0.40	0.50	0.50	0.60	-30.23
Revenue/R&D exp.	2.10%	1.86%	1.68%	1.61%	1.55%	0.67%	0.82%	0.80%	0.97%	-53.75
Telefónica (Spain)										
Revenue €bn	28.48	31.05	28.41	28.4	30.32	37.88	52.9	56.44	57.9	103.30
R&D exp. €bn	0.59	0.59	0.51	0.43	0.46	0.53	0.58	0.59	0.67	13.56
Revenue/R&D exp.	2.07%	1.90%	1.80%	1.51%	1.52%	1.40%	1.10%	1.05%	1.16%	-44.14
France Télécom										
Revenue €bn	33.70	43.02	46.63	46.1	45.28	48.02	51.7	52.9	53.5	58.75
R&D exp. €bn	0.45	0.57	0.58	0.48	0.56	0.72	0.85	0.86	0.90	100.00
Revenue/R&D exp.	1.34%	1.32%	1.24%	1.04%	1.24%	1.50%	1.64%	1.63%	1.68%	25.98
Telecom Italia										
Revenue £bn	28.91	30.82	30.4	30.8	28.29	29.92	31.27	30.9	30.18	4.39
R&D exp. £bn	0.15	0.14	0.12	0.15	0.14	0.12	0.13	0.10	0.08	-46.67
Revenue/ R&D exp.	0.52%	0.45%	0.39%	0.49%	0.49%	0.40%	0.42%	0.32%	0.27%	-48.91
British Telecom										
Revenue £bn	18.71	20.42	18.45	18.73	18.51	18.43	19.51	20.22	20.7	10.64
R&D exp. £bn	0.35	0.36	0.36	0.38	0.33	0.52	0.73	0.69	0.86	248.41
Revenue/R&D exp.	1.84%	1.78%	1.96%	2.03%	1.80%	2.83%	3.73%	3.42%	4.14%	224.53
KPN (The Netherlands)										
Revenue €bn	13.51	12.86	12.78	12.91	11.82	11.94	12.06	12.63	14.60	8.07
R&D exp. €bn	0.057	0.046	0.032	0.023	0.024	0.020	0.017	0.016	0.014	-76.32
Revenue/R&D exp.	0.42%	0.36%	0.25%	0.18%	0.20%	0.17%	0.14%	0.13%	0.09%	-78.09

Table 16.3b Revenues and R&D expenditures of the European telecommunications corporations, 2000–8

	2000	2001	2002	2003	2004	2005	2006	2007	2008	Change % 2000/2008
TeliaSonera (SWE/FIN)										
Revenue SEK bn	54.06	57.20	59.48	82.43	81.94	87.66	91.06	96.34	103.59	91.60
R&D exp. SEK bn	1.56	1.30	1.17	2.54	2.78	2.88	1.84	1.73	1.18	-24.68
Revenue/R&D exp.	2.89%	2.28%	1.96%	3.09%	3.40%	3.28%	2.02%	1.80%	1.14%	-60.69
TDC (Denmark)										
Revenue DKK bn	34.81	41.84	42.01	41.41	43.57	46.59	47.43	39.32	38.82	11.51
R&D exp. DKK bn	0.15	0.17	0.14	:	0.03	0.02	0.01	0.03	0.01	-92.00
Revenue/R&D exp.	0.43%	0.40%	0.33%		0.06%	0.05	0.02%	0.07%	0.03%	-92.83
Telekom Austria										
Revenue €bn	3.81	3.86	3.91	3.97	4.06	4.37	4.76	4.92	5.17	35.78
R&D exp. €bn	0.03	0.02	0.04	0.04	0.04	0.04	0.04	0.05	0.04	47.22
Revenue/R&D exp.	0.74%	0.57%	0.91%	1.08%	1.05%	0.99%	0.87%	0.96%	0.81%	9.40
TP (Poland)										
Revenue PLN bn	:	:	:	18.28	18.53	18.34	18.62	18.24	18.16	-0.66
R&D exp. PLN bn	:	:	:	0.06	0.07	0.06	0.05	0.06	0.06	0.00
Revenue/R&D exp				0.33%	0.37%	0.30%	0.28%	0.33%	0.34%	0.66
Magyar Telekom										
Revenue HUF bn	445.95	547.74	590.59	607.25	596.79	615.05	671.20	676.66	673.06	50.93
R&D exp. HUF bn	1.43	:	:	:	:	:	:	:	0.64	-55.05
Revenue/R&D exp.	0.32%								0.10%	-70.22
Elisa (Finland)										
Revenue €bn	1.24	1.44	1.56	1.54	1.36	1.34	1.52	1.57	1.49	19.37
R&D exp. €bn	0.023	0.036	0.036	0.024	0.017	0.008	0.006	0.008	0.011	-52.17
Revenue/R&D exp.	1.85%	2.50%	2.30%	1.56%	1.25%	0.60%	0.40%	0.51%	0.74%	-59.94

Therefore we side with the view that the stagnant and declining R&D expenditures of the European information and telecommunications corporations are a real phenomenon. These persistent trends fit to the decline in the private R&D expenditures in many sectors of the global economy that began in the 1980s (Sterlacchini, 2006: 5–7.) In the case of the European telecommunications sector, this phenomenon can be attributed to the oligopolistic markets operating under the noncooperative Nash equilibrium situation where the dominant players do not need to, and the less dominant players are not able to, change their business strategies in order to increase their expected payoffs. All players are better off under the current situation; meanwhile, the decline in the private R&D expenditures means that, for society in general, that the production, use and dissemination of knowledge are moving away from the social optimum in the longer term.

Research and development in the energy sector

Humanity is facing a major challenge at present: that of climate change. The rising global temperature may, already in the twenty-first century, cause major restructuring of the global climate, including the distribution of rainfall, the wind direction and the ocean currents. The medium-term and in particular the long-term consequences of climate change are uncertain, but even conservative predictions forecast substantial economic losses and dramatic social effects caused by a rising sea level, accelerated desertification, and other ecological damage caused by altered weather conditions (Stern, 2007; IPCC, 2007). On the more radical side, some experts, such as world-famous biologist James Lovelock, argue that climate change is virtually impossible to stop and that it will soon cause a major catastrophe for humanity as a whole (Goodell, 2007).

The mainstream scientific position, as reflected in the Intergovernmental Panel on Climate Change (IPCC) report or the *Stern Review*, holds, however, that climate change can be stopped and its effects managed – but this needs immediate action from governments, businesses and people all around the world, since climate change is proved to be caused by human activities. According to IPCC estimates, the atmospheric greenhouse gas (GHG) concentration is some 35 per cent higher than it was in pre-industrial times. The atmospheric concentrations of carbon dioxide and methane now exceed by far the natural range in place over the past 650,000 years. Global increases in carbon dioxide concentration are primarily the result of fossil fuel use. In order to stop a global temperature rise of around 2°C, projections imply that global

GHG emissions should peak at some point before the year 2020, and after this a steady decrease of 1–5 per cent per year will be necessary. According to the *Stern Review*, this would cost approximately 1 per cent of global GDP – an important, but affordable, amount, which is much lower than the possible losses and damage caused as a result of climate change. However, given the time needed for developing and adapting new – or already existing, but so far not widely applied – technologies, effective policies must be put in place now.

Currently, energy-related GHG emissions, mainly from fossil fuel combustion for heat supply, electricity generation and transport, account for around 70 per cent of total emissions, including carbon dioxide, methane and some traces of nitrous oxide. Since both the supply of and the demand for energy is still increasing, fighting climate change urgently needs substantial changes in the production and the use of energy. According to the *Stern Review*, without the rapid introduction of supportive and effective policy actions by governments, energy related GHG emissions, mainly from fossil fuel combustion, are projected to rise by over 50 per cent by 2030. Energy efficient technologies and clean energy production methods should be developed further, and renewable energy sources must play an increasing role in supplying much-needed energy. But also, carbon dioxide capture and storage technologies should be developed alongside these and used to reduce the present atmospheric GHG concentration.

Climate change alone would justify a great emphasis on intensive R&D in the energy sector. Energy R&D provides enormous leverage through its ability to furnish technologies that can reduce the costs of complying with emissions reduction and meeting atmospheric stabilization targets. For example, Jae Edmonds, James J. Dooley and Marshall A. Wise demonstrated in 1996 that deploying an advanced generation of cleaner energy technologies around the world would reduce the cost of stabilizing the atmosphere by more than two orders of magnitude over the course of twenty-first century (Edmonds *et al.*, 1996: 71–94).

The European Commission's Strategic Working Group (SWOG) of the Advisory Group Energy (AGE) made an even firmer declaration: 'Although other instruments (such as taxes, subsidies or regulations) may be helpful, by accelerating market diffusion of recently developed energy technologies, SWOG believes that the only route to a sustainable energy system is through new or improved energy technologies that will have to be found through research and development' (European Commission, 2005a: 9).

However, strangely enough, both public and private energy R&D expenditures have been steadily falling since the early 1980s in most of the developed countries. As James J. Dooley and Paul J. Runci pointed out:

> The U.S. federal energy R&D program has fallen by 36% over the 1985–1998 period, a decline of more than U.S. $1.2 billion in real terms from the level in 1990. The energy R&D programs of the European Union declined at a similar rate, falling 37% in real terms over this same period. The deepest reductions were seen in Germany and the United Kingdom, where public investments in energy R&D fell in real terms by more than 73% and 88%, respectively, from 1985 to 1998. The Japanese government might represent the only bright spot, as its investments in energy R&D increased a very modest 1% over the course of this same 14-year period. (Dooley and Runci, 2000: 215–29)

Since just nine OECD countries perform more than 95 per cent of the world's public sector energy R&D and, consequently, nearly all the world's long-term energy R&D. If these countries reduce their R&D efforts, this will have – without exaggeration – a gloomy effect on the world's energy future.

The SWOG position paper argued that '[i]t is SWOG's firm conviction that it is now reckless to maintain such a low level of energy R&D funding. It believes that the level should be restored in real terms to the levels of 25 years ago – that is, increased by at least a factor of four' (European Commission, 2005a: 9).

Since the start of the twenty-first century, after a drop in the 1990s, public energy R&D spending in the OECD countries, including the EU, has more or less stabilized, but has not grown. This might be seen as a problem in itself – given the challenge of climate change – but also because public spending cannot offset the ever-falling private R&D budgets. (Whether public R&D expenditure can effectively substitute at all for the private one is another open question.) The European Commission at least recognizes the depth of the problem: 'Under the 7th Framework Research Programme, annual spending on energy research over the next 7 years at EU level will increase by 50%, but even this will not provide the progress needed' (European Commission, 2007b: 15).

Unlike public R&D expenditure, private spending did not stabilize after the 1990s and continued its downward trend through the 2000s.

In the USA between 1980 and 2005, annual private R&D plummeted from US$4 billion to US$1 billion (Kammen, 2006: 86–93). Major Japanese utility companies reduced their R&D spending by almost 30 per cent between 2000 and 2006 (Sterlacchini, 2007: 1–18). In Europe to energy companies significantly reduced their R&D spending in the 2000s. Alessandro Sterlacchini (2007) argues that between 2000 and 2006 a R&D spending reduction of close to 60 per cent happened in the case of the major European energy companies. Since their sales have practically been stagnating, the R&D intensity of these companies has also fallen by some 60 per cent. Olivier Grosse and Benoît Sévi reviewed a different group of companies, therefore they provide slightly different figures, but the downward trend is undisputable for them as well (Grosse and Sévi, 2005). This means billions of euros are lost for energy R&D. Sterlacchini's and Grosse and Sévi's studies omitted oil companies. Sterlacchini provided data about ENEL, ENI, EDF, RWE, E.ON, Suez-Energy and Gaz de France. Grosse and Sévi's list included: ENEL, EDF, Gaz de France, Scottish Power, British Energy, Edison, Vattenfall, Norsk-Hydro, Union Fenosa, Areva, SUEZ, Scottish and Southern. The difficulties of obtaining reliable R&D data from companies is described by Dooley and Runci as follows: 'The two principal reasons that private sector energy R&D data are hard to come by and interpret are that (a) often companies refuse to report these data, citing business confidentiality concerns, and (b) many national governments simply do not collect information on private sector investments in energy-related R&D' (Dooley and Runci, 2000: 223).

According to data, a number of large energy companies – ENEL, GDF Suez, RWE and E.ON, for example – have stabilized or slightly increased their R&D spending since 2007. Therefore, if we compare the average R&D spending of the companies reviewed by Sterlacchini (2007) for the years 2007–8 to the data of the beginning of the decade, the drop is only about 17 per cent. However, this still means that the R&D intensity of major European energy companies has fallen by almost 50 per cent (see Table 16.4).

The 2008 EU R&D Investment Scoreboard also stresses that since 2007, some large companies in the energy field showed high annual R&D growth rates, and increasing their R&D investment by several times. For example, Royal Dutch Shell increased R&D by 2.2 times and AREVA by 1.7 times over this period. Even higher growth rates are found among some companies in the field of alternative energies. In wind technology, Vestas Wind Systems increased R&D by 2.2 times and Nordex by 3 times. In the solar photovoltaic field, Q-Cells entered

Table 16.4 Revenues and R&D expenditures of the major European energy companies, 2000–8

	2000	2001	2002	2003	2004	2005	2006	2007	2008	Change % 2000/2008
E.ON – Germany										
Revenue €bn	38.37	36.04	35.30	44.11	46.74	56.40	64.09	68.73	86.75	126.07
R&D exp. €bn	0.49	0.51	0.38	0.07	0.02	0.02	0.03	0.04	0.05	-89.07
Revenue/R&D exp.	1.26%	1.42%	1.08%	0.16%	0.04%	0.04%	0.04%	0.05%	0.06%	-95.17
GDF Suez – France										
Revenue €bn					38.06	41.49	44.29	71.23	83.05	118.23
R&D exp. €bn					0.09	0.08	0.09	0.10	0.20	138.82
Revenue/R&D exp.					0.22%	0.20%	0.19%	0.14%	0.24%	9.44
EDF – France										
Revenue €bn	34.42	40.72	48.40	44.92	46.93	51.05	58.93	59.64	64.28	86.73
R&D exp. €bn	0.47	0.40	0.40	0.38	0.40	0.40	0.39	0.38	0.42	-9.66
Revenue/R&D exp.	1.35%	0.97%	0.82%	0.85%	0.84%	0.79%	0.66%	0.63%	0.65%	-51.62
ENEL – Italy										
Revenue €bn	25.11	28.78	29.98	31.32	31.54	35.88	39.02	43.69	61.18	143.67
R&D exp. €bn	0.12	0.10	0.10	0.02	0.02	0.02	0.02	0.03	0.04	-71.37
Revenue/ R&D exp.	0.49%	0.35%	0.33%	0.05%	0.06%	0.06%	0.06%	0.07%	0.06%	-88.25
RWE – Germany										
Revenue €bn	52.00	33.30	46.66	43.88	42.13	39.49	44.26	42.51	48.95	4.90
R&D exp. €bn	⋮	⋮	0.44	0.39	0.11	0.06	0.07	0.07	0.11	-75.86
Revenue/R&D exp.			0.93%	0.89%	0.27%	0.14%	0.16%	0.17%	0.21%	-76.99
Vattenfall – Sweden										
Revenue SEK bn	31.70	69.00	101.03	111.94	113.37	129.16	135.82	143.64	164.55	419.16
R&D exp. SEK bn	0.481	0.564	0.481	0.478	0.529	0.650	0.761	1.015	1.529	217.88
Revenue/R&D exp.	1.52%	0.82%	0.48%	0.43%	0.47%	0.50%	0.56%	0.71%	0.93%	-38.77

Sources: Annual Reports of E.ON, GDF Suez, EDF, ENEL, RWE, and Vattenfall, 2000–2008

the Scoreboard in 2008 for the first time after increasing its R&D by 15.4 times in three years. Whether this is indeed a sign of the end of a long-lasting trend and the beginning of a new one, or is just a momentary fluctuation, limited to a small number of leading-edge companies, is yet to be seen.

With 0.38 per cent of R&D per sale, the European oil, gas and electricity sectors are still classed as being among the Low R&D Intensity sectors and lag behind most of the company on the EU R&D Scoreboard, the average being 2.7 per cent (European Commission, 2007a; European Commission, 2008a). One could argue, however, that the composition of that R&D is also important: maybe both public and private R&D focus more on the challenge of climate change and use the resources in a more efficient way. For example, the number of energy-related patents shows a continuous growth from the end of the 1990s.

Indeed, throughout the 1990s, the importance of energy efficiency grew steadily in public R&D; however, as Dooley and Runci argue, 'perhaps the most significant trend in renewable energy research is the relatively flat budgets of these programs throughout the course of the 1990s, a decade that saw increasing rhetoric from national governments pledging to do their best to reduce carbon dioxide emissions through, in part, the increased use of renewable energy systems' (Dooley and Runci, 2000: 227). Observing the trends from 2000 for both public and private research, Daniel M. Kammen and Gregory F. Nemet stress that neither renewable energy nor energy efficiency have increased their share from R&D spending – but at least, by stagnating, these topics have not lost resources, unlike research related to coal or nuclear energy (Kammen and Nemet, 2005: 84–88).

Energy related R&D is generally considered to exhibit deep problems, not just through its shrinking size, but also by its very nature. Grosse and Sévi (2005) characterize the R&D activity of European energy companies as exploitative. James G. March introduced a distinction between exploitation and exploration in innovation and corporate learning (March, 1991: 71–87). Exploitation happens when a company tries to use its knowledge base it in a more efficient and rational way. Exploitation, if successful, leads to more efficient operation, better quality and reduced costs. By contrast, exploration is about introducing radically new technologies, products and methods of operating – it is about enlarging and changing the knowledge an organization uses and relies upon. Grosse and Sévi argue that not only R&D budgets have shrunk, but the focus of R&D activities have changed towards more efficiency, and a client and application orientated direction, at the expense of basic, explorative research. We shall come back to the possible causes. But let us deal first with the question of energy related patents.

Grosse and Sévi (2005) call attention to a striking contradiction: while corporate R&D spending has been shrinking steadily, the number of energy related patents has increased sharply since the end of the 1990s in both the USA and Europe. This might suggest that perhaps R&D funds are smaller, but better utilized. However, Grosse and Sévi's argument is that the growing number of patents is not necessary a sign of intensive innovative activities, but it rather reflects a new attitude towards the protection of intellectual property rights, not independent from the evolution of the international intellectual property rights regime under the auspices of the World Trade Organization (WTO) (Heald, 2003: 249; Yu, 2006: 369–410). Patents are seen as a strategic resource, as a defence against litigation – or, conversely, as causes to sue other companies. As Kimberley A. Moore puts it nicely, 'Patents may be valuable for defense rather than offense either standing alone or in large numbers. The defensive patenting strategy, like the arms race, focuses on a deterrent theory. Don't sue me on your patents or I'll sue you on mine. This often results in cross licensing' (Moore, 2004: 2). Patenting is also used to increase the value of corporate assets, so the increasing number of corporate patents is not necessarily a sign of intensive R&D activity, but rather of strategic behaviour and asset management (Parchomovsky and Polk Wagner, 2005: 1–77).

Now the causes of this new attitude might be the same as caused the shrinking R&D budgets: deregulation, privatization and liberalization on the energy market. A general observation is that the privatization of previously state-owned companies leads to the reduction as well as the reorientation of R&D activities towards topics with expected short-term benefits (Munari, 2002: 223–32). This was also confirmed for the energy sector: since the energy sector is not a high-tech sector, increased competition leads not towards the intensification of R&D, but towards cost reduction (Dooley, 1998; 547–55). Cost reduction may mean cutting R&D budgets, but also restructuring R&D activities aiming at finding immediate efficiency improvements:

> This conclusion is borne out by our analysis of national (public and private) energy R&D programs ... whereby available data corroborate the assertion that the private sector tends to focus on energy R&D areas that offer the promise of near term payoff (e.g., energy efficiency and conventional fossil power technologies), whereas the public sector focuses on areas that are on average more high risk and

long term (e.g., fusion power, renewable energy). (Dooley and Runci, 2000: 223)

Grosse and Sévi (2005) identified three R&D related strategies under competitive pressure that were not mutually exclusive. One is the above-mentioned reorientation of R&D activities towards short-term objectives. This also means the dropping of R&D topics that are not directly related to the core activity of the company. Finally, companies may try to build strategic alliances, or look for external resources and knowledge to fill the gap between innovation need and financial constraints. The two authors then analysed the possible effects on corporate profitability as well as social welfare in both the short and the longer term (see Table 16.5).

It is obvious that realizing efficiency gains is positive, from both a corporate and a social perspective. If a company utilizes its resources and technology better, or manages to offer new, improved services or better quality for a lower price to its customers, this certainly has positive effects on corporate profitability and stakeholder welfare, and even the environment. However, the other side of the coin is that, by reorientating R&D activities towards short-term objectives, companies may lose a longer perspective on innovation: exploitation may totally prevail over exploration. And this may have a negative effect on long-term corporate competitiveness. It goes without saying that eliminating certain types of research already has potentially negative effects on social welfare in the short run, since knowledge production loses resources and means.

An interesting question is why and how the reliance on external resources, alliances and knowledge import may have negative corporate

Table 16.5 Corporate and social effects of R&D strategies

		Efficiency orientation	Eliminating basic research	Reliance on external resources
Effects on corporate benefits	on the short run	positive	positive	positive
	on the long run	positive	potentially negative	potentially negative
Effects on social welfare	on the short run	positive	potentially negative	neutral
	on the long run	positive	potentially negative	potentially negative

Source: Adapted from Grosse and Sévi (2005: 15).

and social effects. Grosse and Sévi (2005) argue that, while in the short run a reliance on external resources and knowledge may counterbalance the effects of budget cuts, in the long run corporations may become dependent on others and lose their innovative capacity. This may be debated, but the potentially negative effect on social welfare is also raised by a study that modelled the effect of spillovers on knowledge production. As Valentina Bosetti and her co-authors summarized their findings: 'Our analysis shows that international knowledge spillovers tend to increase free-riding incentives and decrease the investments in energy R&D. The strongest cuts in energy R&D investments are recorded among High Income countries, where international knowledge flows crowd out domestic R&D efforts' (Bosetti *et al.*, 2007: 1–26).

To sum up, the energy sector performs rather poorly in terms of R&D expenditures, as it is among the lowest R&D-intensive sectors. While the energy sector was never among the high-tech industries, the sad reality is that energy companies have reduced their R&D spending substantially since the 1980s. Analysts argue that budget cutbacks have been accompanied by a reorientation of R&D activities towards short-term objectives, efficiency improvements and low-risk projects. The main reasons seem to be the intensification of global competition and the deregulation of the energy market. Cuts in R&D activity happened despite the fact that, compared to revenues, R&D expenditures had always been very moderate (well under 1 per cent of total turnover) and large companies had used many other, more effective ways to reduce operative costs, such as laying off employees, outsourcing certain activities, reducing energy losses and so on. The possibility of a global climate catastrophe casts a shadow on the future of humanity, and in order to avoid this happening, a radical ecological turnaround is needed in the way energy is produced, used, and its environmental effects are treated. It is legitimate to argue that corporate social responsibility would imply that large energy companies should devote substantial resources to R&D in order to promote innovation for a sustainable energy system.

Some provisional conclusions

The public and private efforts of building a knowledge-based economy and society steadily fall short of what were agreed in Lisbon and Barcelona in 2000 and 2002. Despite a few EU member states' impressive figures – for example, Sweden, Finland and Austria – public R&D

expenditures have remained stagnant in the majority of the EU member states. The private contributions to knowledge production and innovation, as the two strategic sectors' meagre innovative performances demonstrate, have rather declined and stayed at a very low level during the course of the 2000s. In this respect, the statistical figures for the new EU member states as well as the Central and Eastern European private corporations are particularly disappointing. None the less, the commitments of financial and human resources to promoting a knowledge-based economy and society, strengthening the intensity of innovation, R&D occupies more and more space in the communications and declarations of the major political bodies of the European Union and the national governments, as well as the sustainability reports and corporate social responsibility reports of the corporations. In spite of the substantial gap between the political aspiration and actual achievement, the political communications and documents issued by the European Commission and the European Council regularly have recourse to the Lisbon Strategy as the blueprint of future policy and economic actions (European Commission, 2005b: 24). Recently, the Lisbon Strategy as a brand name of the political ineffectiveness serves as a panacea for economic recovery in time of economic crisis and deep recession (European Commission, 2008b).

If we study the decennial trends of public and private R&D expenditures on the micro and macro levels rather than the hermeneutics of the declarations and the mission statements of the corporate and political actors, we do not run a great risk in predicting that neither the majority of the EU member states, nor the European business enterprises will gear up their R&D investments and innovative intensity to the higher level that would be necessary to achieve the main objectives of the Lisbon Strategy and the 3 per cent Barcelona target by the end of 2010. Thus, the knowledge-based economy and society project still remains a remote and elusive horizon for most of the EU member states.

Apart from the macro problems, this also raises crucial ethical dilemmas at the micro level. According to the phrasing of basic political as well as corporate CSR documents, R&D is taken to be part of corporations' social responsibility; however, the details are far from being explained fully. How should we define the ethical responsibility of corporations in terms of knowledge production, use and dissemination? Our chapter has aimed at raising such basic questions which, we believe, need much more attention from business ethicists.

Bibliography

Abramovitz, M. and David, P. A. (2001) *Two Centuries of American Macroeconomic Growth from Exploitation of Resource Abundance to Knowledge-Driven Development*, SIEPR Discussion Paper No. 01–05.

Alesina, A. and Perotti, R. (2004) 'The European Union: A Politically Incorrect View', *Journal of Economic Perspectives*, 18(4) Fall: 27–48.

Alesina, A., Angeloni, I. and Schuknecht, L. (2005) 'What Does the European Union Do?', *Public Choice*, 123(3): 285–7, 309–10.

Arewa, O. B. (2006) 'Measuring and Representing the Knowledge Economy: Accounting for Economic Reality under the Intangibles Paradigm', *Buffalo Law Review*, 54(1): 66–79.

Bacchiocchi, E. and Montobbio, F. (2004) *EPO vs USPTO Citation Lags*, CESPRI, WP n. 161 (Milan: Bocconi).

Baumol, W. J., Panzar, J. C. and Willig, R. D. (1988) *Contestable Markets and the Theory of Industry Structure*, revd edn (San Diego, Calif.: Harcourt Brace Jovanovich).

Berne, M. and Pogorel, G. 'Privatization Experiences in France', in M. Köthenbürger, H.-W. Sinn and J. Whalley (eds), *Privatization Experiences in the European Union* (Cambridge, Mass.: MIT Press), p. 165.

Bortolotti, B., D'Souza, J., Fantini, M. and Megginson, W. L. (2001) *Sources of Performance Improvements in Privatized Firms: A Clinical Study of the Global Telecommunications Industry*, FEEM Working paper No. 26.

Bosetti, V., Carraro, C., Massetti, E. and Tavoni, M. (2007) *International Energy R&D Spillovers and the Economics of Greenhouse Gas Atmospheric Stabilization*, CESifo Working Paper No. 2151.

Burley, A.-M. and Mattli, W. (1993) 'Europe before the Court: A Political Theory of Legal Integration', *International Organization*, 47: 41–76.

Castells, M. (1989) *The Informational City* (Oxford: Blackwell), p. 10.

Council of the European Communities, The (1988) *Council Resolution of 30 June 1988 on the Development of the Common Market for Telecommunications Services and Equipment up to 1992*, The Council of the European Communities, Brussels (88/C 257/01).

Dooley, James J. (1998) 'Unintended Consequences: Energy R&D in a Deregulated Energy Market', *Energy Policy*, 26(7): 547–55.

Dooley, James J. and Runci, Paul J. (2000) 'Developing Nations, Energy R&D, and the Provision of a Planetary Public Good: A Long-Term Strategy for Addressing Climate Change', *Journal of Environment and Development*, 9(3): 215–29.

DotEcon and Criterion Economics (2003) *Competition in Broadband Provision and its Implications for Regulatory Policy: A Report for the Brussels Round* (London: DotEcon), pp. 8, 49–51.

Edmonds, J., Dooley, J. J. and Wise, M. A. (1996) 'Atmospheric Stabilization: The Role of Energy Technology', in C. E. Walker, M. A. Bloomfield and M. Thorning (eds), *Climate Change Policy, Risk Prioritization, and United States Economic Growth* (Washington, DC: American Council for Capital Formation,), pp. 71–94.

European Commission (1983) *Telecommunications*, Communication from the Commission to the Council, COM (83) 329 final, Brussels, 9 June, p. 7.

European Commission (1985) *Completing the Internal Market*, White Paper, the Commission to the European Council (Milan, 28–29 June), COM(85) 310 final, pp. 30–2.

European Commission (1987) *Green Paper on the Development of the Common Market for Telecommunications Services and Equipment*, Commission of the European Communities, Brussels, COM(87)290.

European Commission (1988) *Commission Directive on Competition in the Markets in Telecommunications Terminal Equipment*, Official Journal, L131, 27 May: 0073–77.

European Commission (2001) *Promoting a European Framework for Corporate Social Responsibility*, Green Paper (Brussels: EC Directorate-General for Employment and Social Affairs).

European Commission (2005a) *Key Tasks for future European Energy R&D* (Brussels: EC Directorate-General for Research Directorate J – Energy).

European Commission (2005b) *Working Together for Growth and Jobs: A New Start for the Lisbon Strategy*, Communication to the Spring European Council, Brussels, 02 February, COM (2005) 24.

European Commission (2007a) *Monitoring Industrial Research: The 2007 EU R&D Investment Scoreboard* (Luxembourg: Office for Official Publications of the European Communities).

European Commission (2007b) *An Energy Policy for Europe*, Communication from the Commission to the European Council and the European Parliament, Brussels, 10 January, COM(2007) 1 final.

European Commission (2008a) *Monitoring Industrial Research: The 2008 EU R&D Investment Scoreboard* (Luxembourg: Office for Official Publications of the European Communities).

European Commission (2008b) *A European Economic Recovery Plan*, Communication from the Commission to the European Council, Brussels, 26November, COM(2008) 800 final.

European Council (2000) *Presidency Conclusions*, Lisbon European Council, 23 and 24 March..

European Council (2002) *Presidency Conclusions*, Barcelona European Council, 15 and 16 March.

European Patent Organization (2007) *EPO Scenarios for the Future: How Might IP Regimes Evolve by 2025? What Global Legitimacy Might Such Regimes Have?* (Munich: European Patent Organisation), p. 35.

Eustace, C. (2000) *The Intangible Economy: Impact and Policy Issues, Report of the European High-Level Expert Group on the Intangible Economy* (Brussels: Commission of the European Communities).

Fekete, L. (2008) 'Public versus Private Domain: Knowledge and Information in the Global Communications Network', *Ethical Prospects: Economy, Society and Environment*, 1: 175–92.

France v. *Commission*, Case 202/88, [1991] ECR I–1223.

Froomkin, M. A. (2003) 'Habermas@discourse.net: Toward a Critical Theory of Cyberspace', *Harvard Law Review*, 116: 782–96.

Goodell, J. (2007) 'The Prophet of Climate Change: James Lovelock', *Rolling Stone Magazine*, 1 November.

GRI (2000–2006) *Sustainability Reporting Guidelines* (Boston, Mass./Amsterdam: Global Reporting Initiative).

Grosse, O. and Sévi, B. (2005) Déregulation et R&D dans le secteur énergetique européen, Cahier No. 05.07.59 (Montpellier: Centre de Recherche en Economie et Droit de l'Energie).

Guibault, L., Westkamp, G., Rieber-Mohn, Th., Hugenholtz, B., van Eechoud, M., Helberger, N., Steijger, L., Rossini, M., Dufft, N., Bohn, Ph. (2007) *Study on the Implementation and Effect in Member States' Laws of Directive 2001/29/EC,* Amsterdam Institute for Information Law: University of Amsterdam.

Hall, B. H., Jaffe, A. and Trajtenberg, M. (2000) *Market Value and Patent Citations: A First Look,* NBER Working paper No. 7741(Cambridge, Mass.: NBER).

Heald, P. J. (2003) 'Mowing the Playing Field: Addressing Information Distortion and Asymmetry in the TRIPS Game', *Minnesota Law Review,* 88: 249.

Hirschey, M. and Richardson, V. J. (2004) 'Are Scientific Indicators of Patent Quality Useful to Investors?', *Journal of Empirical Finance,* 11(1): 91–107.

HM Treasury, Department for Education and Skills and Department for Trade and Industry (eds) (2004) *Science and Innovation Investment Framework,* 2004–2014. (London: HM Stationery Office).

IPCC (Intergovernmental Panel on Climate Change) (2007) *Fourth Assessment Report,* 2007. Available at: http://www.ipcc.ch.

Jauk, W. (1999/2000) 'The Application of EC Competition Rules to Telecommunications – Selected Aspects: The Case of Interconnection', *International Journal of Communications Law and Policy,* 4: 1–113.

Kammen, D. M. (2006) 'The Rise of Renewable Energy', *Scientific American,* 295(3): 86–93.

Kammen, D. M. and Nemet, G. F. (2005) 'Reversing the Incredible Shrinking Energy R&D Budget', *Issues in Science and Technology,* 22(Fall): 84–8.

Karsai, J. (2006) Kockázati tőke európai szemmel: A kockázati- és magántőkeipar másfél évtizedes fejlődése Magyarországon és Kelet-Közép-Európában', *Közgazdasági Szemle,* LIII(November): 1033.

McMorrow, K. and Werner, R. (2007) 'An Analysis of EU Growth Trends, with a Particular Focus on Germany, France, Italy and the UK', *National Institute Economic Review,* 199, 82–98.

March, J. G. (1991) 'Exploration and Exploitation in Organizational Learning', *Organization Science,* 10(1): 71–87.

Mayer, F. C. (2000) 'Europe and the Internet: The Old World and the New Medium', *European Journal of International Law,* 11: 149–50.

Michel, J. and Bettels, B. (2001) 'Patent Citation Analysis: A Closer Look at the Basic Input Data from Patent Search Reports', *Scientometrics,* 51(1): 185–201.

Miller, E. S. (1993) 'Some Market Structure and Regulatory Implications of the Brave New World of Telecommunications', *Journal of Economic Issues,* 27:19–39.

Moore, K. A. (2004) *Worthless Patents,* George Mason Law & Economics Research Paper No. 04–29, George Mason University, Arlington, Va., p. 2.

Munari, F. (2002) 'The Effects of Privatization on Corporate R&D Units: Evidence from Italy and France', *R&D Management,* 32(3): 223–32.

Munari, F. and Oriani, R. (2005) 'Privatization and Economic Returns to R&D Investments', *Industrial & Corporate Change,* 14: 61–91.

Munari, F. and Sobrero, M. (2002) *The Effects of Privatization on R&D Investments and Productivity: An Empirical Analysis of European Firms,* FEEM Working paper No. 64 (Milan: Fondazione Enrico Mattei) 1–28.

Munari, F., Roberts, E. B. and Sobrero, M. (2002) 'Privatization Processes and the Redefinition of Corporate R&D Boundaries', *Research Policy*, 31: 31–53.

OECD (Organisation for Economic Co-operation and Development) (2008) *Reviews of Innovation Policy: Hungary* (Paris: OECD), pp. 76–78.

OECD Guidelines (2000) *The OECD Declaration and Decisions on International Investment and Multinational Enterprises: Basic Texts* (Paris: OECD).

OECD Watch (2005) *Five Years On: A Review of the OECD Guidelines and National Contact Points* (Amsterdam: SOMO – Centre for Research on Multinational Corporations).

Parchomovsky, G. and Polk Wagner, R. (2005) 'Patent Portfolios', *University of Pennsylvania Law Review*, 154(1)(November): 1–77.

Race, T. (1993) 'Interface: People and Technology, Testing the Telecommute', *New York Times*, Technology section, 8 August.

Roberts, S. (2005) *Guide to Measuring the Information Society. Working Party on Indicators for the Information Society* (Paris: OECD), pp. 33–8.

Schumpeter, J. A. (1950) *Capitalism, Socialism and Democracy,* 3rd edn (New York: Harper & Row), p. 106.

Spain, Belgium, and Italy v. *Commission*, Case 217/90, 281/90 and 289/90 [1992] ECR I–5833.

Sterlacchini, A. (2006) *The R&D Drop in European Utilities: Should We Care About It?,* DRUID Working paper No. 06–19.

Sterlacchini, A. (2007) 'Minding the R&D Drop of European Utilities: Relevance, Explanations, Remedies', Paper presented at the International Conference on Innovation and Competition in the New Economy, Milan, May 4–5, pp. 1–18.

Stern, N. (2007) *The Economics of Climate Change: The Stern Review* (Cambridge: Cambridge University Press).

Sweet, A. S. and Sandholtz, W. (1997) 'European Integration and Supranational Governance', *Journal of European Public Policy*, 4(3): 299.

Verhoeven, A. (1996) 'Privatisation and EC Law: Is the European Commission "Neutral" with Respect to Public Versus Private Ownership of Companies?', *International and Comparative Law Quarterly*, 45(4): 861–87.

Yu, P. K. (2006) 'TRIPs and Its Discontents', *Marquette Intellectual Property Law Review*, 10(2): 369–410.

17
The Role of Corporations in Shaping Employee Values and Behaviour

Stefan Dunin-Wąsowicz

Introduction

When forming a company, many entrepreneurs rationally, or even just instinctively, form the nucleus of a company value system and normative code of behaviour. Later, to facilitate transmission during the company growth, these systems and codes become more or less formalized. Together with the compensation and benefits package, they are offered to employees as additional value differentiating one employer from another. Despite the apparent similarity, corporate cultures and value systems differ from each other substantially. The formal value system typically puts forward such virtues as focus on customer, mutual respect, responsibility, trust and profit. The latter is often justified as the precondition of sustainability and growth of the company. These lists of company 'commandments' attempt to make behaviour uniform by laying their corporate structure over the employee's own beliefs and value systems. As long as a company operates in its home country, the similarity of these structures based on common experience of the market and education system is in some way reinforced. Implemented in a different environment, however, this creates tension and a parallel informal hierarchy of values and beliefs.

Corporate formal value systems respond principally to the needs of the company's founders and top management to diffuse their sense of doing business. They are directed as much to the creators of the system as to the recipients. Formal top-down systems are frequently perceived, especially by new employees, as being artificial and meaningless. But over time in the corporation, the employees progressively substitute the company's values for the original value systems brought in from their extra-corporate life. This process leads to a modification of their identity, with good short-term but potentially negative long-term consequences for both employees and the corporations themselves.

The creation of value systems – their origins and impacts on corporate growth

Corporate value systems have different origins but typically we can trace them back to the inspirational founders and their structure of values and purpose for being in business. At the creation of the company there is always an insight, either about customer needs or about a particular technology that will meet customer needs better than one offered by the competition. At an early stage the founders also set up, more or less consciously, a way of working together. Frequently, this is correlated closely with their personal culture and value system. The energy and stress level at the formation of the company crystallize the rules of behaviour as well as tolerance levels for deviations from the emerging standards. We 'will' and we 'will not' are then defined as the basis for the culture of the company. Take Michelin, for example – a world leader in the tyre business founded in Auvergne, France, at the end of the nineteenth century: from the start, the company drew on a culture of sincerity and reliability, devotion to quality and solidarity typical of the region of the founder. Another example is Hewlett-Packard (HP), the world-renowned information technology corporation created originally in the Bay Area of California in 1939, was strongly influenced by the engineering culture of Stanford University grounded in the profound belief that people will do well as long as the conditions have been created for them to do so. And a third example is Philips, the global name in lighting and electronics which even today carries a culture of free commerce combined with legendary Dutch agility and business sense. In all these and many other multinational corporations we find elements remaining of the initial inspiration.

During the second half of the twentieth century, most of the companies with a dominant market share in their area of business in their home country, crossed borders and became multinational. This process required the companies to localize their products, but also to translate their working methods and culture into an exportable commodity. This process forced them to more-or-less formalize their value systems and to develop the process of transmission. The most natural way was to send expatriates to carry out the 'evangelization' and to make sure that the processes were executed within the norms of their home country, and that the people selected, hired and promoted displayed characteristics compatible with the core model. As the process of formalization and transmission continued, the core system began to be affected by the feedback process, modifying to some extent the corporate culture to the so-called transnational level.

The acceleration of this process could be seen in the 1990s. The integration of the elements of the value system imported from abroad was more-or-less successful depending on the integration capability of the corporation, correlated to some extent with the existence of such capability in the home country. Several stylized facts suggest that American companies tended to integrate and adapt the corporate culture faster and more easily than a European or Japanese one.

Formalizations of the value system initiated by top management resulted in various combinations of normative values orientated either externally or internally. External values, such as customer satisfaction or shareholder return, were intended to provide a reference system that is handed to employees as guiding principles to drive their decision-making and actions. Placing customer satisfaction at the top of numerous corporate lists reminds the employees to keep in mind continuously the customer perception of the results of their activities. Listing shareholder value highlights the expectation of delivering returns on compensation, assets and the work environment. Under internal values we shall find predominantly values such as respect, trust and teamwork, perhaps expressed in a different order and form, but all centred on the need to create and sustain co-operative, conflict-free, productive work relations. All these values have in common their purpose of supporting the company's performance. Even those that in declarative manner would indicate citizenship or social responsibility, in reality are meant to support the company objectives instrumentally. What is striking when analysing formalized value systems is their apparent similarity and idealistic character. But this is only an impression. Since none of them state explicitly the value hierarchy nor provide actual guidance on how to handle the intertemporal trade-offs, they will differ in practice. Frequently, long-term customer satisfaction may remain in conflict with short-term shareholder returns. And respect and trust are placed in jeopardy because of the lack of reciprocity or misconduct. Hence the actual value system which makes employees abide by the objectives of the corporation, or not, is much more strongly influenced by the way these conflicts are managed and resolved than by formal statements of values. This in turn is influenced by examples and rules provided by the informal system. Consequently, the company culture itself is a combination of normative values offered as a model to follow and day-to-day practice. The latter is strongly influenced by the way that the company addresses the employee's identity and conflicts of loyalty, which will be discussed at the end of the chapter.

In parallel with the formal value systems within each company, we can observe the deployment of a formal code of conduct which provides practical guidance to the employees of 'dos' and 'don'ts'. These codes are typically focused on relations with customers and suppliers, and are intended to protect companies from liabilities resulting from wrong and/or illegal practice as well as preventing an appearance of conflict of interests. In contrast to value systems, these codes and standards are more the result of accumulated bad experiences and litigation than from the visionary intent of the founders and top management. Here, again, the practice may create a cognition dissonance; hence, in some cases what is not acceptable internally may be tolerated externally. Codes of conduct are documented and enforced by the company in the form of a business code. These rules describe what is permitted and what is not in relations with customers, partners and suppliers, and are regularly audited. The level of coverage of formal rules of conduct and behaviour is, however, relatively low compared to a large number of informal rules. These unwritten internal rules on how to handle particular situations: for example, underperformance or conflicts, how and where to share information, what is acceptable or not in terms of language, and relations within the hierarchy will influence the internal atmosphere and company culture more strongly than anything else. It important to stress that these rules also provide both employees and managers with guidelines on how to advance in the hierarchy and how to reach personal development goals within the corporation. They are exemplified by corporate moral authorities and defined internal role models, and something we could call circles of initiation. Since they are not transmitted uniformly, their existence may lead also to multiple identities. Consequently, the employees may define their 'belonging' as 'we, the members of a given country entity' or, 'we, the members with a given function' and these in addition to corporate identity.

How does the transmission of value systems and codes take place? Let us focus on the rules of hiring, evaluating and firing in a given corporation. Of course, the Human Resources Department will define the set of rules such as the competence model, required skills, evaluation criteria and so on, and will deploy them in a more-or-less disciplined way. In practice, the way that employees are hired and evaluated will depend much more strongly on the degree to which the managers see the employees in terms of their own values and individual perceptions of what is right and what is wrong.

Managers tend to hire the people who are similar to themselves; namely, displaying similar behaviour, ways of thinking and acting. Consequently, we can observe a process of 'adoption' of the new employees based on this similarity. This process reinforces the company's value system.

The evaluation process will to a large extent tend to do the same. In addition to objective measures of performance, it is the level of adaptation of the company's values as well as formal and informal rules that will be evaluated and will have a strongly effect on the employees' further advance within the corporation.

The ability to change becomes more and more a value on its own. In many corporations the most valuable characteristics of an employee will be his/her flexibility, easy adaptation to change, and mobility. The sooner the employee adopts such an attitude, the faster the will the company be able to adjust to changing market requirement and competitive pressure. The sooner the employee immerses him/herself in the company's way of doing business, the more chance he will have to increase his/her level of authority and compensation.

The corporate informal rules of behaviour are strongly correlated and exemplified by the way a given corporation handles information. Typically, there are two circuits: the official one, structured and driven by hierarchy; and the informal one, driven to some extent by seniority and sometimes by groups of interests built around functions or entities. In the first, primary information exchange relate to strategy decisions, product and services development, and financial results. In the second, the information relates to the motivation of people, their interests, promotion and career moves. The internal competition for power and compensation introduces bias into the free information exchange, hence all corporations attempt to limit this by setting up a more-or-less formal system of management development and succession. There are numerous examples which demonstrate that no matter how well a corporation manages internal competition it will have a severe impact on information exchange and consequently also on corporate performance in the market place.

To summarize, each corporation deploys a more-or less-formal system of corporate values, codes of conducts and ways of doing business. In addition, within the corporation we can observe the creation of informal rules of behaviour exemplified by internal moral authorities. The different origins of the informal systems make these quite diverse, even within same corporation. The internal rules of behaviour are reinforced by the way employees are hired, evaluated and fired, as well as how information circulates within the company. The latter depends to a large extent on how internal competition is handled by introducing more or less bias, and in turn having an impact on decision-making and corporate performance.

The tension – sources and impacts

Let us now focus on another aspect of the formation of employee values and behaviours; namely, on the confrontation of an original systems with the values practised within the corporation.

Employees join corporations at different stages of their lives, and at different levels of social and political maturity. Depending on how intense their professional experience was prior to joining, and also on how active their social and private life, the adaptation will take place faster or slower. Certainly, the motivation for advancement will play an important role in the integration and adoption of the company culture. This process is not without discoveries and compromises. Even if the hiring process is geared to identifying the cultural compatibility of an employee with the company's culture and ambition, in practice it is only in the following months that the employee discovers the informal system of values and rules and starts to compromise. If we were to define as a source of individual identity the fact of belonging to a number of communities, such as family, local community and so on, the professional identity is principally shaped by belonging to a company. There are interactions between these identities, and every individual consciously or unconsciously tends towards an internal synthesis. The process of modification of an individual identity comes from a confrontation between the original mix of identities with the corporate value system and rules of conduct. If being, for example, an 'IBM-er' or any similar term becomes more attractive through peer comparison, we would notice a switch in the hierarchy of identities. That is particularly true if the original identity is weak or is relatively detrimental to the feelings of pride and self-esteem. It is no an accident that many senior executives of multinational corporations are first- or second-generation immigrants who find in the corporation a new home and source of value. Their motivation to become well accepted within the corporation is strong and compensates for lack of acceptance and status.

The process of the adoption of the corporate culture and ways of behaving is not without anxiety. There are three typical situations worth analysing. One occurs in the context of a developed market, when an employee moves from one corporation to another. Second, demonstrating a different dynamic and leading to some extent to a different outcome, takes place in the context of emerging markets. Last but not least, we look at the post-acquisition situation, where employees are forced to confront the culture of the acquiring company and the newly imposed identity.

In mature market economies, corporate identities demonstrate many similarities; hence, for an employee, the first stages of integration are fairly easy. This is not to say that there is no tension, and no flashbacks and returns to the previous experience. The process of adoption of new rules may sometime lead to initial discomfort. At the same time, the departure from the previous identity will be facilitated by the wish for advancement and integration. Some corporations ease the transition by valuing previous experience and showing more tolerance. Some will call for a fast and definitive shift. But such integration does not mean necessarily embracing the formal corporate value system. Even in very advanced global corporations, national and site identities persist. This is articulated by internal country or site groups with shared interests and subcultures. The corporate and subcorporate national identities coexist and employees will define themselves as corporate but also as local entity members. This situation may create a conflict of loyalty in situations of adverse economic conditions, when the sustainability and role of a given entity is challenged. Typically in such a situation, the management will split into two camps – one playing up the overall corporate interests and abandoning the local identity, and the other will continue to defend it. After the acceleration of the creation of global corporate functions and business lines, this tension became even stronger. The site restructurings and closures, conducted sometimes among dramatic internal struggles, continued to forge larger and larger groups of managers forced to depart from their local identity and to become entirely devoted to the global corporate interests.

In the context of emerging markets, the confrontation of the imported value systems and rules of behaviour creates even more tension and discomfort. There will be early adopters and convinced corporate employees who are willing to quickly embrace the corporate identity. The cultural distance is, however, so large that in most of the subsidiaries a specific dividing line will appear. On one side of that line will be employees willing to have double identity playing both roles with greater or less ability and living in a permanent conflict of loyalty. On the other side there will be groups of employees remaining in passive resistance. Their strength and source of self-esteem will come from negating the imported culture and hierarchy of values, leading to non-identification with the subsidiary objectives, and underperformance.

Numerous corporations are conscious of the persistence of such a dividing line and its economic consequences. Many do not realize its real importance, or do not know how to change it effectively.

The third situation causing identity tension take place in the context of post-acquisitions. Here, in addition to the typical factors occurring in the case of employee-driven change, frustration surfaces, emanating from the negative emotion of being traded. In the two cases discussed above, an employee had to demonstrate free will in joining a given corporation, in the post-acquisition situation such a decision is made without his/her consent. The new shareholders and their culture are imposed on the employee, thus creating an additional impediment to fast adoption. There is a large body of literature on acquisitions which list this factor of one key reason for failure. This would suggest how strong the corporate identity factor has become compared to others. Opposition to a new identity can in fact be so strong that it leads not only to passivity but also sometimes to irrational departures. It also proves how dangerous it may be for a company when its employees' identities are associated too strongly with the corporate value system and internal culture. In that case it causes a substantial deterioration in an employee's capability to adapt, and, as we shall see later, his/her long-term performance.

Identity sterilization and its consequences

It is in the apparent interest of each corporation to switch the hierarchy of employees' identities to stimulate a higher degree of loyalty. That is particularly true for higher-level managers, from which more and more devotion to the corporation is demanded. Corporations use different tools to achieve such objectives. As mentioned earlier, the first is the hiring process, which is managed not only to acquire technical skills but also to secure a minimum cultural compatibility. Should the corporation identify business aggressiveness as high internal value it will seek to employ individuals who demonstrate this. Should it be innovation that is desired, it is the record of creativity of the potential employee that will be particularly valued. Not all of the characteristics of an employee can be detected during the interview process. Many important sources of his/her identity and motivations remain hidden. Some of them will reappear only later, sometimes several years later.

Over time, the process of adoption of the corporate value system and rules of behaviour crowds out the original value system, first pushing it to the informal level and creating a situation where the identities split. Over time, though, if the integration capability of the corporate value systems is limited, the employee will be forced to become more a more corporate member and less and less a member of his/her original constituency. For many, this process will be to a large extent unconscious. The first area in which the identity shift has an impact is the on the employee's family life. Corporations are becoming more and more conscious as to how this may cause a deterioration in both the employee's and the managers' performance. In fact, an imbalance between an employee's professional and private life has become one of the focuses of human resource departments, and rightly so. This imbalance leads in the long term to a substantial deterioration in employees' energy and motivation. Once the pursuit of corporate objectives starts to dominate the employee's life entirely, the corporate role s/he is playing is transferred progressively and played also within the family. In the majority of cases that is intolerable for other family members, and leads sooner or later to energy-consuming conflicts, and ultimately to rejection and isolation. This process for many individuals reinforces the corporate identity alone. A similar process takes place in terms of transfers of behaviour and roles into other constituencies: peer groups, local communities, social and cultural circles. As mentioned earlier, the higher the level of an employee in the hierarchy of the corporation, the more strongly this phenomenon will occur. For higher managers, this process frequently leads to the total replacement of the original communities s/he used to belong to by new one composed in extreme cases exclusively by his/her professional circle. Through this, the corporate culture and ethics become increasingly isolated from the general social and cultural environment. At the same time, the corporate value system itself becomes more and more vulnerable, since it is evolving without the control and influence of the external constituencies. This is, in fact, one of the major traps of globalization, and it prefigures the fall of a given corporation unless adequate counter-measures are put in place.

The balance between the need for employees' total devotion and loyalty, and the imperative to maintain his/her base in the original constituency may in the future become a critical factor of success for a transitional corporation. And that is not about balancing the employee's time spent on different activities. The numerous 'life balance' programmes in existence in corporations tend to address this in too instrumental a way. Their focus is rather on the energy balances than on issue itself. The issue is about the richness and completeness of the employee's identity. It is about the strength of his or her nutritional linkages with the social environment providing the renewal of his/her energy and motivation.

It is about constant evaluation by non-corporate communities of his/ her moral and ethical standing and resulting self-esteem. It is about to what extent the employee is able to maintain access to non-corporate sources of creativity and engagement.

Are there ways of avoiding 'the sterilization' of the corporate value systems and putting them outside the context of values shared by the social environment? The impetus of the original value system injected by the company founders and executives is enough to support the expansion of the company for a certain time. Their impact will depend on how strong and how differentiated and attractive it was at the beginning. It can and is renewed by new executives taking on the responsibility for expansion in downturns.

Frequent renewals are not necessarily the answer, though. Even the best value proposition may be subject to devaluation by enforcing a unique corporate identity and culture as the assumed pre-condition of performance. To avoid the ultimate destruction of the effectiveness and the appeal of the company value system and culture, the corporation must permanently monitor the formation of the informal systems, and any evidence of adoption tensions must be acted upon. The formation of the informal value systems and codes is in fact a healthy symptom of resistance to the top-down driven homogenization. Wherever such systems appear they lead to the creation of intra-company circles within which employees and managers have something else in common apart from just belonging to the corporation. The substance of this sharing is centred around the values that did not make it to the top of the corporate list and are not recognized or practised as such, whether they be local solidarity, forms of professional associations and codes, or even religious and ethical values. Their emotional importance must not be undervalued, and neglecting it in the name of a corporate-performance-driven system damages the same performance objectives.

An adequate response is, first, the recognition of the diversity of individual values and the importance of individual identities. The corporation that would want to do so would need to reverse the formation of its value system from top-down to bottom-up. That is not to say that the performance objective would need to be abandoned or eased. In fact, the opposite will happen. Allowing employees and managers to fully express their identities and their personal values will reinforce their engagement and motivation.

18
Big Business: A Driving Force for Civic Virtue

Montserrat Herrero

The authority–property dialectic in industrial society

A dialectical tension between authority and property marked the crisis in England in the seventeenth century. This dialectic was a touchstone for understanding the problems that arose during a crucial period in social history, read in both economic and political terms (Pocock, 1985: 67).

Even at the time, the emergence of a bourgeois class as a force in wealth generation prompted suspicion that the common good of the political community was not the sole prerogative of those who had until then made it their concern, on the objective basis of territorial possession; rather, the good of the political community was also susceptible to the force of production driven by the free play of the established – if always reconcilable – interests of individuals. Changes to the way in which property is organized should, as a matter of consequence, prompt changes to the way in which political authority is framed.

A reading of G. W. F. Hegel's writings at Jena a century later discloses his recognition of this fact: to a certain extent, industrial society makes freedom possible; it is a crucial stage in the free development of consciousness. At the same time, however, in so far as it may spark an imbalance in the dynamic of family life, 'civil society' and the state, this process may also be a disruptive force. That is, the free play of private interests would appear to banish moral and political concerns from its sphere of action and influence. Given that the open exercise of freedom in civil society is fully realized only when it is grounded in the context of state politics, the theoretical impetus of Hegel's political philosophy is to reconcile moral, economic and political logic. If civil society is excluded from the political sphere, freedom labours under the constant threat of conflict. As Hegel pointed out in the *Philosophy of*

Right, para. 182ff., this is because in civil society as such – that is, civil society in itself, not as it is ordered towards the state – the individual is a combination of natural necessity and freedom, whose relations with others are a function of the individual's own particular interest. The content of such relations, Hegel noted in the same work, para.183, is the individual's selfish interest. Only through the institution of the state does the citizen – the *bourgeois* – overcome such selfish interest.

In his argument against the manufacturing industry in 'Notes on the State of Virginia' (Jefferson, 1787: 17) (published a century earlier), Thomas Jefferson endeavoured to warn of a similar danger. The manufacturing system puts political virtue at risk. The risk involved is similar to that found in the institution of slavery: the generation of dependence and control. Manufacturing undermines the foundations of self-government, making an authentic and solid conception of freedom impossible. Jefferson sees no profit or political freedom in the commercial society brought about by the manufacturing industry. Thus, in his chapter 18, he writes: 'Dependence gives rise to vigilance and venality; it smothers the seed of virtue and shapes the tools that serve the designs of ambition ... The strength of the republic is preserved by the customs and spirit of the people, whose degeneration is a cancer that soon infects the heart of its laws and constitution.'

Jefferson defends agriculture in the face of new forms of work. His interest is not prompted by agriculture in itself; rather, the focus of his concern is the virtue produced in the heart of the two institutions that are dependent on agriculture as an economic activity: the family and the district. In the last analysis, Jefferson's position is representative of the struggle that has come to define the eighteenth century, described by Pocock as the struggle between the Roman patriot, self-determining in the field of civic activity, and the individual in a society composed of private investors and professional governors (Pocock, 1985: 69).

The land-owning aristocracy had effectively disappeared as a political force by the twentieth century, to be replaced by a new aristocracy of business and finance which remained ignorant of specifically political issues – with the exception of those political concerns that might have a direct bearing on their own interests. The gap opened in earlier times between private interests and the common good appeared to have been institutionalized in a structural way.

Liberal democracy rests on a shared consciousness as the political framework that preserves the separation between property and authority. On the basis of a negative conception of freedom as lack of interference – defined as such by Thomas Hobbes in chapter 15 of *Leviathan*, (Hobbes, 2007: 145) and echoed in contemporary political philosophy in the work of Isaiah Berlin – liberalism frames politics as a means by which private interests may be safeguarded. The business sector clings to this idea of privacy, regards the public sphere as the field of play of the state and the means of communication, and legitimizes political power only when it might enhance private economic profit. Thus the public sphere is structured in terms of a division of functions: politicians provide a secure framework in which businessmen may help people to acquire wealth. This division of roles sustains the opposition between property and authority in an institutional way – a relationship which functions as a *complexio opositorum* in the liberal paradigm. The opposing forces need one another.

Civil and private virtues

The authority/property division provoked the opening of a deep social divide between the private and public spheres, and as a result, the exclusive definition of private virtues, bourgeois virtues with regard to work, and public virtues, from which private individuals were exempt. Such division was a matter of profound concern to Jefferson.

This distinction comprises the difference between private interest and the common good. Jefferson's view of the dependence involved in the manufacturing system as being harmful to virtue rested on the idea that the individual could not seek out the common good for himself in such a process; rather, he was dependent on the action of others in control of the common good. In brief, virtue is harmed because 'self-government' is relinquished. Echoing Jefferson, it may be said that civil virtue is – by definition – self-government; that is, the absence of any need for external coercion in carrying out a common good (Herrero, 2006: 130).

In exercising his or her freedom, in the absence of any external coercion, the individual may safeguard his/her own self-preservation without difficulty; that is, defend his/her own interests – a limited definition of private virtues. However, to work for the common good, the good of society as a whole or a given community within it, calls for external coercion of some form. This description would appear to comprise the view of the world among those who interpret the relationship between authority and property, state and civil society, politics and ethics, private virtue and civil virtue in dialectical terms.

This dichotomy rests on a view of the human being as exercising his/her freedom above all in defence of his/her own interest in self-preservation; that is, a freedom that has no need of the presence of others, involving only the use of others. A significant question arises in this regard: how might civil virtue be engendered in such a context? The response to this question offered by modern philosophy since the institution of the modern state is insufficient: an act of external coercion cannot give rise to civil virtue. Once the family – the classical locus, along with the 'district' to which Jefferson deferred – has been compromised by the tyranny of economic forces, where in the contemporary political context is education in civil virtue to be carried out? The institutions of a liberal democracy cannot give rise to the virtue on which they depend if they are to be grounded as parts of an authentic, self-governing political community.

The 'atomized' individual, so often the subject of debate in contemporary political philosophy, feels free in so far as s/he sees him/herself as owner and master of his/her own person and capacities. Independence of any will other than one's own, which is often read as the individual's capacity for material possession, appears to have become definitive of a human being. In the liberal context, the common, public good is nothing more than an agglomeration of individual interests and preferences. A progressive increase in corruption at all levels of institutional life is the most obvious consequence of this way of understanding the public sphere.

The global context

Globalization may be defined as the general trend towards the integration of national economies. In this new context, 'big business' comprises multinational companies. Hence the social benefits or political dysfunctions such companies may effect have a global, and not merely local or national, impact. The trend towards globalization also encompasses liberal democracy itself, though with a great deal more difficulty than in the field of business administration. In this context, the global reach of liberal democracy serves only to amplify the problems and contradictions of the economic-political system. The relativization of state sovereignty – at least during times of peace – may be regarded as a threat, since the common good is stripped of the protection of the state, its historic guardian; or as a sign of hope, if the necessary corrective on the force of privatizing individualism is seen as issuing from another source.

It goes without saying that the need to strengthen the role of the state – as a national or multinational entity – in the control and redistribution of wealth might also be argued, as is the case in the 'cosmopolitan' school of thought (*cosmopolitanism*) in contemporary political philosophy (Shapiro and Bilmayer, 1999).

However, this line of argument might also tend towards a paradigm shift; that is, in Michael J. Sandel's terms, towards 'a political economy of citizenship', as opposed to a 'national political economy' (Sandel, 1996: 60). For Sandel, this new framework of organization would involve a shift from the nation state model to a model of large political spaces, undoing in the process some of the old principles on which the nation state is based – such as, for example, the principle of sovereignty (Sandel, 1996: 74). A global economy calls for global government, which in turn requires the establishment of transnational political institutions.

Although a number of international tribunals have been established, political globalization is still some way off. Instead, multinational companies function as real political agents (Sison, 2003: 163), with political government as such following in their wake. Multinational companies are nowadays more efficient than states in the provision of public goods. While security or defence may not be the prerogative of a multinational company, the company does not exact taxes or exercise exchange control. Nevertheless, such companies have taken on many of the roles once associated exclusively with the state: diplomatic relations between countries; the design of aid, welfare and education programmes, including research and development; the provision of products and services as part of sustainable development; salaries and benefits for workers, including pension funds and social security payments; contributions to technical development and progress; and adding value to shareholder investment. To a certain extent, it may be said that multinational companies function as welfare states, thus enabling the survival of the values of liberal democracy – that is, they contribute to the legitimization of the political culture.

Nevertheless, instances of political corruption are commonplace. The alliance between economics and political government, the interrelationship of states and multinational companies, is also fraught with significant risks.

For that reason, the question posed by Jefferson at the dawn of the industrial era cannot be ignored: how may the political and economic sphere be extended in a way that does not undermine civic virtue? Businesses have an important role to play in this regard.

Big business as a driving force for civic virtue and corporate social responsibility

The latter view prompts the following question: what might the source of civic virtue be in a global liberal society? Given that property is the basis of modern freedom, the answer to the questions formulated above would appear to be *a non-individualist organization of property whose principal institution is big business* is the condition that enables the emergence of civic virtue. The sense of property must be strengthened in the twenty-first century if a new social cohesion of individual interests and wills is to be guaranteed. In industrialized nations, big companies have consolidated their position as the decisive, representative and constitutive institutions in society (Drucker, 1993: 50).

In contrast to Jefferson's observation of the functioning of the manufacturing industry, technological development and the emergence of a business culture may allow big business to be framed as a space where the virtue on which democratic institutions depend is based.

This approach involves an analysis of the socio-political status of both business itself and the business class; that is, the degree to which property, work and dialogue – the keystones of any political society – are shared in business (Alvira, 2008: 63); or, in other words, what relationship between the figures of worker and citizen might be discerned in the business context.

In *The New Realities*, Peter Drucker (Drucker, 1989) points to the changes that took place at the beginning of the twentieth century: modern society is a society of workers who neither exploit others nor are themselves exploited; who, as individuals, are not capitalists, but who are collectively, through their savings and investments, the owners of the means of production; who are at the same time both superior and subordinate, both independent and dependent; who are free to move, but who require the structure of an organization so as to be in some way efficient. Companies are the organizations that perform this role of social catalyst.

Drucker is one of a number of thinkers who attribute great significance to big business as a political (as well as economic) institution. In so far as it guides the efforts of a group of individuals towards a common goal, a business is a political institution; moreover, and this is the key point in Drucker's argument, the business grants the individual both status and function (Drucker, 1947: 112). Status involves social recognition, and thus gives rise to a sense of belonging. In practice, a number of the benefits enjoyed by the individual in his/her status as citizen derive from his/her status as worker: social security measures, access to an adequate level of acquisitive power, and equality of opportunity. Seen in this light, business provides a neat distillation of the citizen's rights. Thus, one way in which the private activity of business has public significance is in relation to the framing of citizenship, but it is not the only one. In terms of the national economy, *business deter-mines specific economic policies to a large extent,* and gives rise to economic decisions and measures that have a direct bearing on the common good. A small number of big businesses, for example, may set limits on salaries and prices.

At the same time, *the business is the specific place in which each citizen experiences the principles of general social order in a visible way.* Social order cannot be lived in the abstract; it is lived in a real closeness to others. The individual's position in a community of workers – that is, in a business – is a microcosm of the structure of society as a whole. Similarly, the network of relationships formed in this business micro-cosm is reflected in an amplified way in society. Thus the habits and potential of each person are shaped by his/her shared experience of the business setting, which may be, as a result, the best way of acquiring the culture of democracy – self-government in the context of a struc-tured plurality of organizations. In relation to the state, business is an autonomous institution. The power and function of business do not derive from the state; its organization and goals are not dependent on the established political and legal order. Business has its own nature, functioning in accordance with its own laws; business is self-governing within the wider form of government exercised by the state.

In so far as it co-ordinates the activity of a collective of individuals, business provides each worker with *a social experience of his/her time.* The relationship of dependence between the activity of some and the activity of others gives rise to a sense of community and belonging that far outstrips anything that might be generated on the basis of shared territory or nationality.

Moreover, every individual carries out his or her *professional career* – that is, his/her service to society – in a business. The feudal system was replaced by the class system, and the classes by the professions; profes-sional status has not yet yielded to income-level. The framework of social distinction, inherent in every society, is nowadays a framework of pro-fessional distinction. A business is increasingly regarded as an inter-pro-fessional association. Different professional workers are brought together in the business setting, to work towards a common goal in the service of society. In a certain sense, business shapes the personal development of every individual; and thus, to a certain extent, is also the space in which the ethical dimension of the individual's experience evolves.

Moreover, the business is also a *governmental organization.* An inter-nal order based on authority and subordination – that is, a network of power relations – underwrites the organization of production. Thus a measure of social power pertains to business. Good business organization and government work in tandem with political power. As a result, the balance of production of goods, generation of profits and social expectations in relation to the common, public good should be borne in mind by all big businesses.

The business's public dimension, which Drucker refers to as social, community and political responsibility (Drucker, 1989: 56), should not be confused with the implementation of specific political measures – as in, for example, support for a particular social group. The primary social responsibility of the business is to do its work well, to carry out the activity that constitutes its service to society without laying claim to goals beyond its specific remit. No institution should act outside its sphere of competence or work against the current of its own proper function.

In this context, the global political world need not be framed as a world populated by individuals whose conflicting concerns for their own interests are to be regulated by a global legal system and police force. Instead, a civilized global world may be a union of distinct units, defined in terms of shared experience (property, interests and goods) rather than shared territory – a union that may give rise to a sense of obedience and order which is much more efficient in practice than any police force engaged in the prosecution of infringers of a law. To share power is to attribute responsibility. A wide and complex world, such as the one in which we live, calls for the exercise of responsibility on the part of many people, who are capable of bringing order to a decentralized and, at the same time, integrated world, a world in which all may live in peace.

To accept corporate social responsibility involves acceptance of the principle that a business does not exist solely for the benefit of its shareholders, but for the good of other stakeholders as well. To use the terms of political philosophy rather than business administration, each business is a small community within civil society, not merely an isolated unit of economic production. Big business is integral to civil society; hence, big businesses should reflect on the most authentic and significant contribution they could make to the common good. To my mind, and in light of the central line of argument articulated in this chapter, the greatest good that big business may foment in society as a whole is civil virtue, going far beyond simple compliance with official standards of corporate social responsibility.

Bibliography

Alvira, R. (2008) 'Lógica y sistemática de la sociedad civil', in R. Alvira, N. Grimaldi, and M. Herrero, *Sociedad civil: la democracia y su destino*, 2nd edn (Pamplona: Eunsa), pp. 63–83.

Drucker, P. (1947) *Big Business. A Study of the Political Problems of American Capitalism* (London: William Heinemann).

Drucker, P. (1989) *The New Realities: In Government and Politics, in Economics and Business, in Society and World View* (New York: Harper & Row).

Drucker, P. (1993) *The New Society* (New Brunswick/London: Transaction).

Hegel, G. W. F. (1995) *Grundlinien der Philosophie des Rechts* (Hamburg: Meiner, 1995). For an English translation of this work, see H. B. Nisbet, *Elements of the Philosophy of Right* (Cambridge University Press, 1991).

Herrero, M. (2006) 'Qué puede significar bien común en la sociedad pluralista contemporánea', *Revista Empresa y Humanismo*, 9(1): 127–40.

Hobbes, T. (2007) *Leviathan* (Cambridge University Press).

Jefferson, T. (1787) *Notes on the State of Virginia* (London: Stockdale).

Pocock, J. G. A. (1985) *Virtue, Commerce and History. Essays on Political Thought and History, Chiefly in the Eighteenth Century* (Cambridge University Press).

Sandel, M. (1996) 'America's Search for a New Public Philosophy', *The Atlantic Monthly*, 277(3): 62–76.

Shapiro, I. and Bilmayer, L. (1999) *Global Justice* (New York: New York University Press).

Sison, A. J. G. (2003) 'Cuando las empresas actúan como gobiernos', in M. Herrero, *Sociedad del trabajo y sociedad del conocimiento en la era de la globalización* (Madrid: Pearson-Prentice Hall), pp. 153–67.

Index

Key: **bold** = extended discussion or term highlighted in the text; f = figure; n = note; t = table.

Abacha, General   98(n3)
abortion   105, 113
academia   ix, x, 60
Academic and Professional
    Press   205(n1)
Academy of Management (AOM/
    USA)   xi, 203
accountability   90, 94, 114(n3), 116,
    181
accounting techniques   198
accounts 'off-the-books'   125, 128
adhocracy   165, 166
advertising   7, 162, 192
aeronautical industry   212
Africa   41, 90, 183
agents   **104–5**, 114(n8–9), 128
Agip   92, 93
agriculture   89, 95f, 259
    farmers   115(n17)
Albania   36(n4)
Alexeev, M. V.   98(n1), 98
Alien Tort Claims Act (ATCA/USA,
    1789)   176, 183
allocative efficiency   **77–8**, 229
Alonso, J. A.   181, 185
ALTER-EU   53
Alvira, R.   x, xii, **xvii, 9–15**
Amato, G.   83, 86
Amnesty International   179
Ancient Greece   9, 138, 204
Anderson, S.   85, 86
Annan, K.   179, 185
anthropologists   37(n14)
anti-Americanism   184
anti-corruption legislation/rules   21,
    121–2, 136(n1–7)
Anti-Fraud Office (OLAF/EU)   55
AOL   84

arbitrage   72
Areva   237
Argentina   136(n4)
aristocracy   259
Aristotle   204
Armenia   36(n4)
arm's-length principle (Weber)
    18–21, **24–9**, 30 32, 34, 35(n2),
    36–7(n8–14)
arms manufacturers   79
Arthur Andersen LLP   **122**,
    136(n8–10), 137, 201
arts   **26–7**, 37(n10)
Asia   41, 101
AT&T anti-trust divestiture (USA,
    1984)   229
Athenians   9
Attac   53
audit committee   129
auditors   189
Australia   82, 136(n4)
Austria   50–1t, 136(n4), 221t, 222, 242
authoritarianism   25, 34, 35
autocracy   7
automotive component
    manufacture   225
axiology   153, 167, 191–2
    see also values
Azerbaijan   36(n4)

Bak, D.   **xvii, 189–206**
balance sheets   42, 82
    economic, societal,
    environmental   40
Balkans   32, 35, 38
Banfield, E.   37(n20)
Bangladesh   110
banking   70, 82, 119, 127

bankruptcy 69, 193, 198, 200, 226
Bar rules (lawyers) 61
Barcelona European Council
　(2002) **220**, 221–2, 223, 242
bargaining power 108
barriers to entry 81, 82, 113, 173(n2)
Barroso, J. M. 58
Basu, K. 164, 173
BBC 'political bias' 6–7
Belarus 36(n4)
Belgium 50–1t, 136(n4), 221t, 229
Bellamy, C. 83, 86
Bentham, J. 204
Berdal, M. 180, 185
Berlin, I. 260
Beyond Good Company (Googins *et al.*,
　2007) 201, 205
Bialowolski, P. 195–6, 206
Bielecki, J. K. x, xii, **xvii**, **3–8**
big business x
　'determines specific economic
　　policies to large extent' 264
　driving force for civic virtue
　　(chapter eighteen) xiv, **258–66**
　driving force for civic virtue and
　　CSR **262–5**
　global context **261–2**
　political authority-property dialectic
　　in industrial society **258–60**
　see also corporations
bimoral society (Hendry) 189, 205
biosciences 203, 206
biotechnology 111
BMW 53
board of directors 39, 105, 123–5,
　128, **129**
Boda, Z. xiv, **xvii–xviii**, **214–47**
'body politic' 146
Boel, F. 62(n2)
Bogota 213(n2)
Bolsheviks 4
Booth, P. xiii, xviii, **99–116**
borderless world 180
Bosetti, V. *et al.* (2007) 242, 244
　Carraro, C. 244
　Massetti, E. 244
　Tavoni, M. 244
Bosnia-Herzegovina 31
'bounds of power' 86

Bowen, H. 158(n6), 159
BP 81t
Braithwaite, J. 17, 37(n16), 37
brands 68–9, 72, 84, 180, 218
Brazil 136(n4)
Brent Spar 175, **176–7**, 183
Bribe-Payers Index (BPI, 1999–)
　137(n13)
bribery 101–5, 112–13, 121–3, **124–5**,
　128, 131, 136–7(n12–14), 153
British Energy 237
British Telecom 231, 232t
broadcasting **6–7**
Bruszt, L. 37(n21), 37
budget deficits 229
Bulgaria 35, 36(n4), 49, 50–1t,
　136(n4), 223t
Bunge, M. 202, 205
bureaucracies 27, 30, 32, 35
　see also public officials
'bureaucratic-authoritarian'
　system 28
Burma 176, 184
business xiii, 31, 95f, 114(n6), 202,
　203, 260
　government–society–business
　　relations x
　'governmental organization' **264–5**
　interaction with academia ix
　international 72, 73
　new research perspectives xii
　R&D 225
　social contribution 106, 114–15(n11)
　start-up costs (Lima) 102
'business angels' 224
business cycle 197
business dilemmas **105–6**,
　114–15(n10–11)
　environment, property rights,
　　corruption **112–13**
　'first-round' versus 'second-round'
　　effects 106
　prices: 'unjustly' high **110–12**
　prices: 'unjustly' low **110**
　wages: 'unjustly' high and 'unjustly'
　　low **107–9**
'business economy' 100
　perceived problems (roles of owners
　　and agents) **104–5**, 114(n8–9)

Business Fairy Tales (Jackson, 2006) 189, 205
Business for Social Responsibility 177, 185
business partners 130
  selection (exercise of due diligence) **131**
  stakeholders as **163–6**, 173(n2–4)
Business Principles for Countering Bribery **124–6**, 136–7(n12–14)
business schools 41, 73
buyers and sellers 8, 78

Calame, P. 208
California 249
Cameron, K. S. 167, 173
Cameron/Quinn model 167, 173
Canada 62(n1), 136(n4), 227
capacity-building 95, 97
capital 71–4, 79, 101–3, 106–9
  financial 200
  international 89
capital intensity 218–19
capital market 196
capital productivity 73
capitalism 19, 25–6, 100, 115
  'civilized' **197, 198–200**, 201
  dialectics 145
  moral 206
  popular criticisms 107
  'predatory' **197–8**
  'responsible' **197, 199–201**
  type **196–201**
  see also state capitalism
carbon dioxide 53, 234, 235, 239
Carraro, C. 244
cartels 80, 115(n21)
Castells, M. 214, 244
Catholic Catechism 100–1, 105, 109, 115
Catholic social teaching xiii, **99–116**
  'welcomes business' **100–1**
  see also Christianity
Caux Round Table (1994) 143, 159
Cavanagh, J. 85, 86
Centesimus annus (CA) (John Paul II, 1991) 100, 114, 115, 116
Central and Eastern Europe (CEE) 4, 6, 17, 32–3, 243

post-Soviet 7
research and development 223t, **223–6**
central planning 106
centre–periphery 74, 181
certification schemes 178
chairman (corporate) 129, 130
Champlin, D. 84, 86
Chandler, D. **180–1**, 185
Charles Leopold Mayer Foundation 212(n1)
  'FPH initiative' xxv, 213(n2)
Charles, R. 107, 108, 115
checks and balances 4, 17, 18, 23, 26, 27, 33, 35, 120
Chevron 81t, 92, 176
Child, G. 83, 86
chief executive officer (CEO) 107, 125, 130, 132
  compliance programmes **129**
child labour 106, 110, 114(n10), 116, 131
Chile 136(n4)
China 16–17, 176
Christianity/Christians 9, 99, 105
  Protestant ethic 20
  see also religion
Church of England 96
Church of Scientology 49
churches 14, 15, 60
'circles of initiation' 251
Citizens Against Government Waste (US-based) 84
citizens' rights 31
citizenship 31, 263–4
civic virtue/civil virtue 260, 261
  big business as driving force **262–5**
civil law 105
civil rights movement (USA) 183
civil society xi, xiv, xv(n2), 13–14, 17–18, 21, 23–4, 31, 33, 38, 41, 49, 54, 95, 182, 185, 212, 213(n2), 258–60, 265
  'dignity of democracy' 12
  global 179, 185, 186
  global (sceptics) **180–2**
  interaction with government and MNEs viii–ix
  not-for-profit organizations 211

civil war   90, 92, 185
civilization
   'purely transactional'   74
clan culture   165–6
clans   28
class system   264
clientelism   20–1, 24, 27, 32
clients   19t, 68, 164, 200
'climate change'   **234–5**, 239
coal   239
Code of Conduct for Commissioners
   (European Commission,
   2004)   54, 63
Code of Ethical Conduct (US Academy
   of Management)   203
Code of Good Administrative
   Behaviour (European
   Commission)   54
codes of conduct   43, **123–36**, 153,
   197
   'can be dangerous'   113
   desiderata   **128–9**
   formal   251
   investigations   133–4, **134–5**
   lobbyists   **55–62**
   made part of employment
      contract   130
   translation   130
   transmission   251–2
   see also   compliance
coefficient of business openness
   181
coercion   260
coffee   110, 178
cognition dissonance   251
'cohering power'   183, 185
'cold societies' (Weberian sense)   18,
   19, 20
Cold War   182
Coleman, J.   32
Colley, J. L. *et al.* (2003)   198–9, 205
   Doyle, J. L. 205
   Logan, G. W.   205
   Stettinius, W.   205
common good   xii, 12–13, 42–4, 74,
   97, 104–5, 106, 110–11, 139, 143,
   147, 151, 196, 259–60, 264–5
   contribution of companies   **14–15**
   democracy and   **9–10**

fiction   **10–11**
   public–private distinction and
      22–4, 36(n5–7)
Common Market   79
common will   9–10
common–particular pairing   **10–11**
communication strategies model
   (Morsing and Schultz)   167
communism   16, 25, 28, 35, 35(n1)
   legacies   34
communities (local decline)   86
community   **10**, 145, 146
   nature   140
   sense of   84
Community of Cross of Nails
   (CCN)   91
community development
   sustainable   94, 95, 95f, 97
community protection   90
community regeneration   114(n3)
companies/firms
   affiliated   68, 80, 81
   ATCA suits (USA)   176
   conative dimension   162
   contribution to common
      good   **14–15**
   criminal liability   123–4
   CSR versus financial results   160
   economic versus social aims   148
   extractive contracts   178
   financial and cultural
      situation   150
   foreign   155
   indigenous   103
   individual   5
   justification   140
   'large enterprises'   3
   'named and shamed'   178
   Polish   148, 155
   Polish (poor financial
      situation)   153
   Polish (practice of stakeholder
      communications)   **166–71**,
      173(n5–6)
   Polish (stakeholder dialogue)
      160–74
   political donations   8
   public versus private sector   14
   publicly listed   68

role in democracy 12–13
self-perception (cognitive
 dimension) 162
self-regulation 119
small 78, 79, 153, 154
'smaller' 129
social versus financial model
 167
voices 39–46
way of thinking (determining
 factor) 161
'company as community' 147
company size 62, 153, 154
Compendium (Pontifical Council for
 Justice and Peace) 104, 111,
 114(n10), 115(n12), 116
compensation [recompense] 112
competition 109, 114(n11), 148,
 198, 230
 global 242
 imperfect 78
 increased 240
 perfect 67, 228–9
Competition Appeal Tribunal xiii
competition law xiii, 76–87
 Framework Directive (2002/21/
 EC) 83
 regional and national 77
 relevant market 84
competition policy 87
 implications of economic
 power 83–5
competitive advantage ix, 74, 103
 'market advantage' 160
competitive pressure 231, 252
competitiveness 87, 114(n3), 160,
 241
competitors 44(n1), 81, 83, 163,
 164, 173(n2)
complexio oppositorum 260
complexity 88–9
compliance 119
compliance officer 129–30
 investigations 134–5
 providing guidance 132–4
 sanctioning misconduct and taking
 corrective measures 135
compliance programmes 123–5,
 136–7(n11–14)

communication (internal and
 external) 129, **130**
implementation 126–7
implementation in multinational
 organizations xiii, **119–37**
issuing the policy 127–9
levels of responsibility **129–30**
monitoring, reviewing,
 assessing **135–6**
CONECCS xxiv, 55
confidentiality 128, 133–4, 134–5,
 202, 237
conflict-intensity 95, 95f
conflicts of interest x, 128, 201, 203,
 251
conflicts of loyalty 254
Congress of Berlin (1878) 90
Conoco Phillips 81t
Conrad, R. F. 98(n1), 98
Conradt, M. 49, 63
conscience (properly-informed) 112,
 113
consequentialism 90
conservation 100, 164
Conservative Party 7
constitutions 4, 16, 48, 259
construction sector xi, 225
consultants/consultancies 59, 60f,
 131
consumer goods 194
consumers ix, 39, 69, 78, 83, 110,
 113, 114(n6), 154, 156, 193
contract enforcement 101, 102, 103,
 114(n6)
contract law 30–1
'controlling feedback loops'
 principle 72
Convention for Protection of Marine
 Environment of North-East
 Atlantic 176
corporate behaviour xii, 12
corporate bonds 70
'corporate citizenship' xiv
corporate communication/s xii, 39,
 40, 43, 170, 172, 173(n6)
 key task 167, 169
corporate and community goals
 alignment xiv
corporate criminal liability 127

corporate culture   xv(n3), 39, 43, 97,
    108, 119, 127, 162, 173(n1), 200,
    248, 256
  ethical   123
  'exportable commodity'   249–50
  objective-orientated   170–1
  'power'-orientated   170–1
  proxy model   167
  'role'-orientated   170–1
  'support'-orientated   171
  taxonomy   **165–6**
  top-down homogenization
    (resistance)   257
  transnational level   250
  uniform trans-national
    standards   120
corporate dialogue   xiii–xiv
corporate discourse   162
Corporate Europe Observatory   52–3
corporate governance   99, 114(n2),
    116, 207–8, **210**, 230
Corporate Governance (Colley *et al.*,
    2003)   198–9
corporate growth
  impact of value systems   **249–53**
corporate identity   162, 172
  collectivistic   164, 165, 167, 171
  versus communication strategy
    model   166
  connection with corporate
    communication strategies   165–6
  and cultural background   **163–6**,
    173(n2–4)
  individualistic   164–5, 167, 170,
    171
  linguistic dimension   171
  perceived role of business and   **167**
  relational   164, 165, 167, 169, 170
corporate learning
  'exploitation' versus 'exploration'
    (March)   239, 241, 246
corporate lobbying
  democracy and   **xii, 1–63**
corporate power   **xiii**, 17, **65–116**
  global   85, 86
  practical aspects   xiii
corporate size   78–9
corporate social responsibility
  (CSR)   x–xvi, 12, 39, 99, 105,

    112, 114(n3, n9), 115(n22), 164,
    171, 173
  big business as driving force   **262–5**
  'can be the new social
    contract'   147
  communication   163, 173(n3), 174
  communication strategies   **167–8**,
    172
  compared to Rousseau's concept of
    social contract   **142–7**,
    157–8(n1–4)
  current corporate
    communication   40
  definitions (ambiguity)   **148–9**
  dialectics   145
  'economico-legal'   **41–2**
  energy sector   242
  EU Green Paper (2001)   215, 216,
    245
  factors conditioning development
    147
  focus   167–70
  Friedman (1970)   84, 86
  global issues   **xiv, 187–266**
  idea/definitions   **139–40**
  implementation   150
  information strategy   172
  instrumental aspect   161, 162, 164
  knowledge production
    (documents)   **215–18**
  level of interest (Poland)   **147–8**,
    158(n5)
  'long-lasting absence'   150
  managerial versus social
    aspects   160
  methodological problems   **148–9**
  multi-stakeholder collaboration in
    social governance   xiv, **207–13**
  new social contract: 'two
    levels'   141–2
  'new version of social contract'
    138–9
  NGO influence   **175–86**
  origins of idea   158(n6)
  practical problems (objective
    nature)   **151**
  problems   **148–51**, 158(n6)
  relational approach   160–1, 162,
    164

relationship-building 168, 169–70, 172, 173(n6)
and sensemaking **160–3**, 172–3(n1)
and social contracts **140–2**
strategic 160
surfacing of idea 145–6, 147, 158(n6)
taxonomy of cultures **168–9**
theoretical discussion 148, 158(n5)
theoretical problems **149–51**, 158(n6)
theorists' expectations versus practitioners' actions 149
VBEs **67–75**
voluntary principles 178
corporate social responsibility: evolving principles **41–3**
corporate value systems
American versus European/ Japanese 250
formalization 249–50
informal 250–3, 255, 257
integration capability 250, 256
origins; and impacts on corporate growth **249–53**
tension (sources and impacts) **253–5**
tensions 248
transmission 251–2
corporate world: 'single voice' **39–46**
corporations
CEE 224, 243
core activity 241
decision-making 208
economic power xiii
EC's lobby register 59
French 40
governance (new conceptions) **210–12**
hiring 253
internal [staff] competition 252–3
internal standards xv
performance indicators 216–17
performance-driven systems 250–4, 257

political legitimacy xiv
reliance on external resources 241t, 241–2
responsiveness to social concerns **xiii–xiv**, **117–86**
role in knowledge production/ dissemination **214–47**
role in shaping 'employee' values xiv, **248–57**
role in R&D expenditure **226–42**
rules of hiring, evaluating, firing **251–2**
sources of power xiii
see also MNCs
corruption x, xii–xiii, **4–6**, 7, 11–12, 17–22, 24, 28–35, 36(n6), 37(n13), 37, 43, 90, 92–7, 101–2, **112–13**, 120–1, 153, 261–2
'classic definition' 25
see also Transparency International
Corruption Perception Index (CPI, TI, 2001–) 137(n13)
2008 edition **36(n4)**
cosmopolitanism **261**
cost-recovery (rapid) 89–90
cost-reduction x, 240
cotton 178
Court of First Instance 83–4
Coventry Cathedral 91, 98
credit **193–6**
credit-rating agencies 82, 189, 195, 197
creditors 30–1
crime 29, 41, 119, 122, 124, 131
criminal law 105, 123, 126
Crook, C. 148, 159
cross-licensing 240
culture xv, 17, 32, 120, 184, 213(n2), 254
corporate identity **163–6**, 173(n2–4)
national 182
political 35
currency 100–1, 213(n1)
customers 40, 44(n1), 83, 167, 248–51
Cyprus 50–1t
Czech Republic 49, 50–1t, 136(n4), 223t, 224, 225

Daimler-Benz   53, 79
data deficiencies   69, 237
Davis, P.   xiv, **xviii**, **175–86**
Davis, S.   91, 95, 96, 96f, 98
de Gaulle, C.   6
de Soto, H.   **101–2**, 115(n15), 115
de-differentiation   29, 37(n13)
'dead capital'   101
decision theory   139
decision-making   207, 208, 218
deconstruction   204
'deep play' (Bentham)   204
default   194
defence contracts   102
Della Porta, D.   37(n15), 37
Deloitte   122
Dembinski, P. H.   **xiii**, **xviii**, **67–75**
democracies
    European and Anglo-American   14
    'general' versus 'particular'
        interests   **3–4**
    market-orientated   33–4
    semi-consolidated   34
    see also   dialectics
democracy   xiv–xv, 90, 119, 141,
        152, 212, 215, 264
    and common good   **9–10**
    and corporate lobbying   **xii**, **1–63**
    dignity   **12**
    direct   20
    'key paradox'   xii, 3
    'organic or corporative'   12
    private interests and   **3–8**
    role of companies   **12–13**
    'universalistic foundation'   10–11
democracy, networks of power, and
        trust   xii, **16–38**
    'clear message'   35
democratic community fiction   **10–11**
democratization (of credit)   **193–4**
démos (Greek, 'peaceful group of
        individuals')   9
    'world demos'   xv
Denmark   36(n4), 50t, 50, 51t,
        136(n4), 218, 221t, 222, 233t
dependence   259, 264
dependencies   26
depersonalization (of credit)   193,
        194–5, 196

depersonalized/personalized
        relationships   21, 29
deregulation   227, 230, 240, 242
Deutsche Telekom   232t
developed countries   110–12, 120,
        128, 141, 154–5, 189, 193–4, 196,
        253, **254**
    'emerging markets'   **254–5**
    'high-income countries'   242
    'industrial society'   68, **258–60**
    'industrialized nations'   263
    North-South (global divide)   **70–2**,
        74, 210
    political authority-property
        dialectic   **258–60**
    'Triad countries'   70
    see also   G7; OECD
developing countries   141, 196
    ethical dilemmas for large
        corporations   **99–116**
    'highly-indebted countries'   73
    institutional framework   **101–3**,
        114(n4–7)
    'less-developed countries'   112
    'low-income countries'   111
    'low-wage countries'   ix
    MNCs in   **103–4**
    'poorest countries'   67, 73
    'Third World'   21, 165
    'under-developed countries'
        99–116
    working conditions   184
development   179
development aid   93
    'aid organizations'   96
dialectics
    common-particular, public-private
        (chapter two)   xii, **9–15**
    democracy   xii, **9–15**, 145
    developmental process   158(n5)
    political authority-property
        (industrial society)   **258–60**
Diamond, L.   33, 37(n18), 37
differentiation   38
'dignified livelihood'   109, 115(n14)
discrimination   211, 212
dishonesty   **201–3**
distance/proximity distinction
        18–19, 21

distributional efficiency **78**
district, the 259, 261
diversification (of credit) 193, **195**
'diversity charter' 212
dividends 199
docta ignorantia (learned
  ignorance) **191–2**
donors
  specificity of benefit expected **8**
  wealth 7
Dooley, J. J. 235–7, 239–41, 244
Doyle, J. L. 205
Drucker, P. 263, 265, 266
due diligence 125, 126, 130
  selection of employees and business
    partners **131**
Dunham, L. *et al.* (2006) 161, 174
  Freeman, R. E. 174
  Liedtka, J. 174
Dunin-Wasowicz, S. xiv, **xviii–xix**,
  248–57

E.ON 237, 238t
East India Company 88, 94
Eastern Europe xii, 179
  democracy, networks of power, and
    trust **16–38**
Eco-Management and Audit Scheme
  (EMAS, 2001–) 153, 158(n8)
economic development ix, **152–3**,
  214, 216, 218
  see also social development
economic education 150
economic freedom 115, 116
Economic Freedom of the World (Fraser
  index) 103
economic growth 13, 35, 37(n21),
  86, 103, 223–4
  environmental consequences 216
economic power
  absence of unequivocal
    definition 82
  competition law, economic
    evaluation, policy
    implications xiii, **76–87**
  'corrosive nature' 85
  global platform 80
  measurement xiii, 76–7, **80–3**
  perspectives **77–80**

political dimension 79
social responsibility of VBEs xiii,
  67–75
  uncontested definition lacking 77
  see also political power
economic sphere 141–2, 145
  corporation in new conceptions of
    governance **210–12**
  'separate rules' (assumption) 150
economics 8, 11, 67, 77, 115(n15),
  147, 150–1, 213(n1), 228
  evolution regarding
    governance **210–11**
economics of exchange 203–4
economies of scale/scope 68, 76, 78,
  81, 228
Economist Intelligence Unit 102
economy 16–18, 21, 23
  national 28, 68
  regional 68
  sustainable 178, 215
Eden, L. xii
EDF 237, 238t
Edison 237
Edmonds, J. 235, 244
education 14, 156, 248
efficiency **73**, 74, 81, 88, 94,
  100, 123, 133, 151, 169, 230,
  239–42
  economic **77–8**
elections 18, 25, 90, 92
  voter turnout 156
electorate x, xv(n2)
electricity 239
electronic mail 133, 134
Elf 92
Elisa (Finland) 233t
elites 17, 18, 24, 25, 28, 33–5,
  37(n14), 95
  negative effect of MNCs on local
    governance **90–1**
empiricism 69, 115(n12), 215
employees ix, 26, 39–41, 44(n1),
  106, 114(n6), 124–6, 128, 135,
  140, 155, 157, 162, 165, 167,
  200, 208, 218
  corporate obligations 147
  selection (exercise of due
    diligence) **130–1**

employers   26, 103, 109, 114(n6),
    115(n13), 123, 140, 164
    see also management
employers' associations 56, 63(n3)
employment   ix, 70, 71f, 71, 95, 101,
    103, 108–9, 166
    'full employment' ix
    'job creation' 85
    'illegal work' 152
    MNCs 'net job destroyers' 85–6
empowerment 95–7
ENEL   237, 238t
energy sector   82, 95f, 102, 215,
    245
    R&D   226, **234–42**
    R&D expenditure (private
      sector) **236–42**, 246, 247
    R&D expenditure (public
      sector) **236**, 239, 240
    R&D spillovers 242, 244
ENI 237
Enron   82, 122, 157–8(n3), 198, 201
entrepreneurs   141, 155, 248
entrepreneurship   31, 76, 102
environment
    business   106, 109
    corporate   135, 162–3, 170, 248
    economic   73, 106, 149–51
    legal   120, 149
    natural   92, 104, 111–12, 128,
      175–6, 178, 183, 211, 214–16,
      241
    organizational   160
    political   149
    social   73, 149–51, 256–7
environmental management (ISO
    14001) 153, 158(n7)
epistemology 202
equality   16, 19, 30, 146
'equitable commercial
    exchange' **111**
Erhard, L.   79
Ernst & Young (EY)   xi, 122
Estonia   36(n4), 50–1t, 136(n4),
    225
ethical dilemmas   xiii, 132
    corporations **99–116**
ethical dimension of global economic
    crisis (2008–)

imposed authority **189–92**
'methodological failure' versus
    'dishonesty' **201–3**, 205(n2)
search for new balance   xiv,
    189–206
ethical nobility 13
ethics   xv, 12, 15, 54, 60, 75, 126–8,
    147, 150, 153–4, **156**, 178, 212,
    215, 243, 256–7, 260
    challenge to MNCs **122–3**
    'ethos of efficiency' **72–4**
    'ethos of humanism' 74
    'good ethics is good economics' 53
    tests of conduct 127
ethnicity   31, 90, 91, 96f, 122
Etzioni, A.   179–80, 186
Eucken, W.   79, 81, 87
Eurobarometer   49, 50–1n, 51, 52n
Europa website 58–9
Europe   xi, 41, 72, 87, 90, 92, 145,
    146, 175, 181, 198, 240
    energy R&D expenditure (private
      sector) 237, 246, 247
    values-based approach **126–7**
European Charter for Researchers
    203
European Commission   47, 53–7,
    62(n1), 63(n3), 63, 83, 113(n1),
    221, 223, 225, 227, 243, **244–5**
    lobby register (2008–) **58–61**
    lobby register rules (first revision,
      2009–) **61–2**
European Commission: 'Advisory
    Group Energy' (AGE): Strategic
    Working Group (SWOG) 235,
    236
European Commission: Directive
    90/388/EEC (competition/
    telecommunications) 229
European Community Framework
    Programme (Research and
    Technological Development)
    Fifth (1998–2002) 220–1
    Sixth (2002–6) 221
    Seventh (2007–13) 203, 206, 221,
      236
European Council   56, 58, 59, 243,
    245
    see also Barcelona; Lisbon

European Council: Criminal and
Civil Law Conventions on
Corruption 122, 136(n5), 137
European Court of Justice 84, 229
European Foundation for Quality
Management (EFQM) 153,
158(n10)
European Institute of Public
Administration (EIPA) 62(n1), 63
European Parliament 47, 56, 61,
158(n8)
regulation of lobbyists 57–9
European Parliament: Committee on
Constitutional Affairs 57
European Patent Office 231
European Research Area 221
European Single Market 48
European Transparency Initiative
(ETI, 2005–) xii, 47–63
main areas of action 54–5
origins and purpose 53–5
proposed rules for monitoring
lobbies 55–6
European Union 23, 34, 87, 211,
214, 219, 228
competition policy 77, 83
'competition vendetta against US
business' 84
direction 52, 52t
energy R&D programme 236
EU-15 221t, 222, 223t, 225
EU-27 221t
innovation effort 220
integration 85
lack of transparency 49–53
law 47, 48
lobbying (at Brussels) 47–63
new members 7, 17, 27, 35,
225–6, 243
new members (R&D policy) 223
optimism versus pessimism 52,
52t
telecommunications corporations
(R&D expenditures, 2000–8)
232–3t
trust 52, 52t
European Union: Budget 221
European Union: R&D Investment
Scoreboard 237, 239

Europeanization process 34
evil 144, 152
exchange relationships 102
existentialists 143, 155
experiti (L) 202
expert knowledge 191–2
expert–client relationship 192
'partnership' element 190
experts
'illusion of infallibility' 192
expertus (L) 202
exploitation 106, 108–9, 110,
115(n21), 263
'expressive power' 183, 185
externalities 8, 114–15(n11), 216,
228
Extractive Industries Transparency
Initiative (EITI, 2004–) 178, 186
Exxon Mobil 80, 81t, 92

'fair trade' 110, 115(n16), 115, 178
fair trial 4, 63(n3)
fairness/justice 13, 108, 127
Fairtrade Foundation 178
familialism 27, 30, 32, 37(n13)
family 14, 15, 21, 26, 28, 30, 34, 41,
104, 106, 122, 140, 147, 165, 253,
256, 258–9, 261
Federal Sentencing Guidelines 127
feedback process 250
Fekete, L. xiv, xix, 214–47
Filek, Jacek 150, 159
Filek, Janina xiii, xix, 138–59
'finance following the vote' 6
financial crisis *see* global economic
crisis (2008–)
financial impropriety 82
financial institutions 90–1, 192, 195
asymmetrical relationship with
clients 190
bail-outs 193
economic power 86
irresponsibility, 196
Finland 49, 50–1t, 57, 136(n4), 218,
221t, 222, 233t, 242
expenditure on R&D (percentage of
GDP, 2000–8)
'first-order' vision 42
fiscal consolidation 225

fiscal prudence   114(n5)
food supply   84, 111
Foreign Corrupt Practices Act (FCPA/
   USA, 1977)   121, 136(n1–2)
foreign direct investment (FDI)   ix,
   x, 70, 72
Forest Stewardship Council   178,
   186
Fortune 500 (1954–)   69
fossil fuels   234–5, 240
founders (corporate)   251, 257
France   12, 23, 36(n4), 50–1t, 90,
   136(n4), 221t, 229, 238t, 249
  French people   9
  French Revolution   3, 4, 22
France Télécom   231, 232t
Fraser Institute   103
fraternity (solidarity)   146
fraud   xiii, 55, 198, 199
'free economy'   100, 104, 106
  'free-market economy'   141, 146,
     148, 150
  see also   market economy
free speech   4, 6
free trade   72, 111, 116
free will   255
free-riding   242
freedom   19, 21, 30, 146, 150, 258,
   263
  negative conception   259–60
  political (major problem)   8
  relationship with private
     property   16–17, 35(n1), 38
freedom of association   23
freedom of contract   101, 108
Freedom House   36(n4), 37(n17–19)
freedom of individual   10, 12, 22,
   24, 100
  versus freedom of economic
     entity   143
  versus individual safety   139
  protection against state
     intrusion   16
  see also   individual rights
Freeman, R. E.   174
Freeport McMoRan   176
Friedman, M.   84, 86, 115, 148,
   159
Friedman, R.   115

friends/friendship   19t, 21, 25,
   28–30, 38, 196
  instrumental or utilitarian   37(n14)
Frost, B.   78, 79, 86
Fryzel, B.   xiii–xiv, xix, 160–74
Fukuyama, F.   29–30, 37
Fuller, L. L.   203, 204, 205
'fully fledged economicism'   74
'functioning of economic body'
   144
fusion power   241

G7 meeting   175
G8 meeting (Gleneagles, 2005)   177
Galbraith, J. K.   83
Gap   175
gas   28, 82, 178, 239
  liquid natural gas   91
Gasparski, W. W.   xiv, xix–xx,
   189–206
Gaz de France (GDF)   237, 238t
GDP   103, 235
  R&D target   220
  world   69–70, 70, 71f
General Counsel (smaller
   companies)   129
general elections   6
'general interest'   3, 4, 6, 23
General Motors   81t, 81
'general politics'   12
general public   25, 55, 139, 165
'general will' (Rousseau)   3, 4, 5, 11,
   146
Georgia   36(n4)
Germany   21, 36(n4), 50–1t, 51,
   79–80, 81, 85, 136(n4), 152, 175,
   229, 238t
  energy R&D programme   236
  expenditure on R&D (2000–
     8)   221t
Geroski, P.   82, 87
'getting things done'   25, 29, 32, 34,
   38, 90
gifts   126, 128
Gilpin, R.   182, 186
global economic crisis (2008–)   x, 42,
   86, 127, 157, 225
  diagnoses   196–7
  ethical dimension   xiv, 189–206

'financial' versus 'moral' **192–6**
responsibility 192–3
global economy/world economy x,
74, 200
VBEs versus poorest countries
70–2
weight of VBEs **67–70**
Global Policy Forum 80, 81n
Global Reporting Initiative
(GRI) 216–17, 245
globalization x, 25–6, 28, 67, **72–4**,
75, 103, 116, 139, 145, **180–1**,
185–6, 189, 208, 210, 256, **261–2**
concept 'suffers from lack of
precision' (Berdal) 180
definition 261
political 262
golden mean (Aristotelian) 204
'good connections' 24–5
'good governance' 18, 20–1, 35, 101,
112, 209
normative character 208
good will (Kant) 10
goods (products) and services ix,
40–2, 68–9, 72, 76–9, 85, 100,
184, 194, 213(n1), 214, 219, 252,
262
Googins, B. K. *et al.* (2007) 201,
205
Mirvis, P. H. 205
Rochlin, S. A. 205
governance xiii, 33, 38, 74, 90, 92,
96, 178
evolution of economic
thought **210–11**
global xv, 180
international 179, 185, **210–11**
levels 209
multi-layered 180
new conceptions (economic sphere
and corporations) **210–12**
non-linear path of a concept
207–8
political and administrative 208
poor **91**
private corporations as non-state
actors **211–12**
proneness to weakness 94
'top-down' 182

weak 89
see also 'good governance'
governed-government dilemma 139,
147
governments xi–xii, xv(n2), 5, 22,
32, 34, 44(n1), 73, 78, 85, 86, 90,
92–7, 100, 102–3, 106, 115(n22),
120–1, 152, 154, 158(n11), 167,
177–80, 184–5, 193, 199, 200,
215, 217, 222, 224–5, 227, 229,
234, 237, 239, 243
comparative weakness as
regulators x
disempowerment 96
dysfunctional 109
global 262
infantilization **93–4**
interaction with large MNEs
viii–ix
revenues (oil, gas, mining) 178
'unprecedented' market
interference 197–8
grace (supernatural) 12
Great Depression (1930s) 158(n6)
Great Orchestra of Christmas Charity
(*Wielka Orkiestra Swiatecznej
Pomocy*) 156
Greece 49, 50–1t, 136(n4), 221t, 229
greed 190, 197, 199
Green Construction services xi
greenhouse gas (GHG) 234–5
Greenpeace 53, 175–6, 179
'unelected' 184
grey areas
legal-illegal 189
right-wrong 126–7
Grimaldi, N. 15
Grosse, O. 237, 239–42, 246
Gwartney, J. 102–3, 115(n15), 115

Hammond, A. 138, 143, 159
Harrison, S. 199–200, 205
Hayek, F. von 8, 79, 145
Hayoz, N. xii, xx, **16–38**
health/healthcare 41, 95f, 111, 211
hedge funds 197
Hegel, G. W. F. 145, 258–9, 266
Held, D. 180, 186
Hendry, J. 189, 205

Heritage Foundation   102, 116
Herrero, M.   xiv, xx, 15, **258–66**
Hewlett-Packard (1939–)   249
hierarchy   165–7, 169, 171, 251
High Level Working Group on
    Common Register and Code of
    Conduct for Lobbyists   58–9
Hillman, A.   xii
Hirschman, A. O.   36(n6), 38
Hirst, P.   181, 186
'historical majority'   4
Hobbes, T.   34, 138, 139, 181, 259,
    266
Hoffmann-La Roche Ltd   84
homelessness   104, 152
honour   13, 15(n1), 90
Hoogvelt, A.   181, 186
'horse-trading'   xii, 3
hotlines   133
House of Lords   90
housing   102, 104
Houston   122
Hübner, Ms   62(n2)
human resources   43, 125, 218, 251,
    256
    policy adaptation   **131–2**
human rights   **11**, 20, 25, 98(n3),
    124, 176, 179, 183, 185, 211,
    216
Human Rights Watch   179
humanist lobbies   48–9
humankind/human beings   138,
    141–2, 144–5
    creativity   100
    dignity   100
    'hundred friends countries'   25
Hungary   36(n4), 49, 50–1t, 136(n4),
    223t, 224–5, 233t
Hurley, S.   81, 87

IBM   253
Iceland   136(n4)
ideal type   19t, 35(n2)
identity
    hierarchy   253, 255
    national   254
    professional   **253–4**
identity shift   256
identity sterilization   **255–7**

identity tension
    developed economies   253, **254**
    emerging markets   **254–5**
    post-acquisition situation   254, **255**
illiteracy   115(n17)
image   162–3
imported wealth   **89–91**
'imposed authority'   **189–92**
independencies   26
India   88, 102, 109
indigenous weakness
    accelerated by imported wealth or
        natural resources   **89–91**
'indirect employers'   110, 115(n18)
individual rights   **4**, 6
individual totality   **13–14**
individualism   151–2
    'antithetical to moral nobility'   **13**
individuals   xv(n3), 9, 258–9, 263
    ethical behaviour   200
    rich   8
Indonesia   176
industrial ecology
    experimentation   212
industrial era   262
Industrial Revolution   183
industry   89
inequality   37(n20), 107
    empirical evidence
        questioned   115(n12)
    social   164
inflation   219
information asymmetry   42, 105,
    108–9, 110, 115(n17), 168,
    173(n2), 195
information and communication
    technologies   72, 214
    research and development   **226–34**
    spillover effects   219
information society   214
'informational mode of development'
    (Castells)   214
information-handling   252–3
information-sharing   251
ING Group   81t
initial public offering   226
innovation   85, 212(n1), 215, 217,
    224, 242, 255
    national systems   225

insider trading 128
Institute for Research on Governance
(IRG, Paris) 207, 212, **213(n2)**
approach to governance **208–10**
fundamental questions **209**
institutions 21, 23–4, 30–5, 53, 157,
165, 185
effectiveness 20
EU 54, 57
EU (transparency) 50t
governmental x
inefficiency (versus regime
type) 33–4
national (transparency) 51t
performance 32
relevance and efficiency 209
state-derived 184
structure 225
transnational political 262
transparency 49, 50t
under-developed countries **101–3**,
114(n4–7)
instrumental social capital
(Coleman) 32
insurance funds 105
intangible assets 216–18, 226
integrity 127, 131–2, 135–6, 189,
192, 199–200
research and publication **202–3**,
206
Intel Corporation 221
intellectual capital 216–18
intellectual property **110–12**,
115(n20–1), 220, 240
intellectuals 40
Inter-service Working Group 55
Interdepartmental Working Group for
CSR (Poland, 2005) 158(n11)
'interdependence links' 72
interdependencies 73–4
interest groups ix, 22–3, 54–5
definition 47–8
interest representation
definition 56, 62–3(n3)
'interest representatives' 56
specific categories **61**
'interference' 27–8
Intergovernmental Panel on Climate
Change (IPCC) 234

'internalization of benefits,
externalization of costs'
(Staniszkis) 193
International Centre for
Reconciliation (ICR) 91, 92, 98
international companies in places
of instability: issue of mutual
capture xiii, **88–98**
approaches to solutions **94–7**
chapter purpose/structure 89
empowerment and its
problems **95–7**
summary of issue **94**
International Competition Network
(ICN) 83
International Finance Corporation
(IFC) 68
international financial
institutions 208, 210
International Initiative for
Rethinking the Economy
(IRE) 207, **212–13(n1)**
International Relations 180
neo-realism 182, 186
power and influence 179
'realist' interpretation 181, 186
'internationalization' 180
internet 40, 58–9, 82, 130, 133, 135
bursting of bubble (2001) 226
interviews 135, 162, 255
intra-company charging 90
intranet 130, 133, 135
investment 69, 102, 114(n6), 181,
225
ethical pressures 92
external 89–90
investment banks 195, 201
investment pressure
negative effect of MNCs on local
governance 89–90, 98(n1)
investors 40, 42, 44(n1), 68, 102,
105, 226, 259
'ethical' 108
Iraq War 6–7
Ireland 50–1t, 136(n4), 221t, 223–4
Irwin, D. 103, 116
ISO 14001 (environmental
management) 153, 158(n7)
Israel 136(n4)

Italy   37(n20), 49, 50–1t, 81, 136(n4),
    221t, 229, 238t
Italy: Antitrust Authority   79

Jackson, C. W.   189, 205
Jacobins   3–4
Japan   72, 81, 136(n4), 222, 227,
    236–7
Java   88
Jefferson, T.   259–60, 262–3, 266
Jews   9
John Paul II   100, 114, 116
joint ventures   125, 128, 131
Jonas, H.   142, 159
Jouve, B.   208
judicial independence   4, 103
judicial system   31
justice   30, 140

Kaldor, M.   179, 186
Kallas, S.   58, 62(n2)
Kammen, D. M.   239, 246
Kant, I.   10, 138, 141, 146, 155
Kaser, K.   37(n14), 38
Keeley, T.   115(n20)
Keynes, J. M.   79
Khodorkovsky, M.   18
kinship   30
Kis-Katos, K.   106, 115(n19), 116
Klon/Jawor organization   156–7,
    159
Knoedler, J.   84, 86
knowledge   11
    public versus private   216
    spillovers   231, 242
knowledge-based economy   214–17,
    225–7, 229, 242–3
knowledge-intensive sectors   219
knowledge assets   217–18
knowledge production   243
    CSR documents   **215–18**
knowledge production/dissemination:
    role of corporations (chapter
    sixteen)   xiv, **214–47**
    chapter purpose   215, 243
    empiricism   215
Kohl, H.   175
Korea (South)   136(n4)
KPN (Netherlands)   232t

Kramer, M. R.   xi
Krimsky, S.   **201–3**, 206
Kulczyk, J.   5

Laborem exercens (LE) (John Paul II,
    1981)   110, 116
labour   71–2, 76, 103, 106, 109
labour market   x, 28
Labour Party   5
    UK Government (1997–2010)
    6–7
laicism   **14**
laissez-faire
    'rational' versus 'evolutionary'
    145
Lalucq, A.   **xx–xxi, 207–13**
Lamoureux, P. A.   115(n18), 116
land   102
language   53
láos (Greek, 'people')   **9**
large corporations: ethical
    dilemmas in under-developed
    countries (chapter nine)   xiii,
    99–116
    chapter purpose   99
    context   99
Larger Freedom (Annan, 2005)   179,
    185
Latin America   41, 178, 179
Latvia   36(n4), 49, 50–1t, 223t
law   ix, xi, 6, 42, 43, 77, 100–1, 128,
    140, 142, 145–7, 152–3, 204,
    259
    'low quality' (Poland)   154
    Nazi Germany   80
    relationship with morality   141
    unjust   113
    see also   natural law
law firms   59
Lawson, R.   102–3, 115(n15), 115
lawyers   19t, 56, 63(n3)
    lobby register (EC)   **61**, 62
Layard, R.   20
leadership   162
learning economy   214
legal systems   26–7, 28, **101–2**,
    115(n11), 149, 204, 265
    international ranking   **103**
    politicized   17

legal–illegal distinction 29, 37(n13)
legalism 126
legality 48
legislation/legislators viii, 110, 128
legitimacy xiv, 182, 185, 208, 209, 262
Lehman Brothers 82
Lenin, V. I. 4
letting agency (property) 104
Leuenberger, M. 36(n7)
Levi, M. 29, 38
Leviathan (Hobbes) 259, 266
Levitt, A. 189
Lewicka-Strzalecka, A. **xxi, 189–206**
liberal democracy 4, 9, 27, 33, 86, 259–61
'liberal modernity' 25
liberalism 22
liberalization x, 35, 180, 227, 229–30, 240
liberum veto principle 151
licence fee (broadcasting) 7
Liedtka, J. 174
'life on credit' 194
Lilico, A. 111, 116
Lisbon European Council (2000) 214–16, 226, 229, 245
Lisbon Strategy (2000–) **219–22**, 223–4, 242
  'brand name of political ineffectiveness' 243
Lithuania 36(n4), 49, 50–1t, 223t
Live 8 (2005) 177, 183
loan repayment 196
loan savings accounts 195
'loan societies' 193–4
lobby/lobbies
  definition 47–8
  EU versus purely national (differences) 48
  funding 60
  industrial 212
  monitoring (proposed rules) **55–6**
  self-regulatory approach 55–6
  types 48
lobby register (European Commission, 2008–) **55–62**
  financial information **62**
  rules (first revision, 2009–) **61–2**

scope **61**
  voluntary approach 61, 62
lobbying xiii, **47–63**, 17, 180
  definition 56
lobbyists 22, 131
  common register **59**
  funding information 57, 58
  'in-house' 59, 60f
local communities ix, 44(n1), 93, 140, 147, 167, 253, 256
Locke, J. 138, 139, 146
Logan, G. W. 205
Lovelock, J. 234
Luddite movement 183
Lugard, Lord 90
Luhmann, N. 37(n13), 38
Luxembourg 50–1t, 136(n4), 221t, 229

Machiavelli, N. 181
Macquarie Bank 82
macroeconomics xiv, 12, 67, 86
'mafia gangs' 102
Magyar Telekom 233t
majority interests 3, 4
'Make Poverty History' 183
Malta 50–1t
management **104–5**, 114(n9), 120, 123–4, 129, 132, 140, 142, 161–2, 164, 168–70, 172, 173(n3), 193, 198–203, 208
  'employees' [seems to mean 'management' here] **248–57**
  flexibility/adaptability 252, 255
  identity and conflicts of loyalty 251
  local (versus global corporate identity) 254
  multiple identities 251
  professional experience 253
  social and private life 253
  values and behaviour (role of corporations in shaping) **248–57**
Manager's Book of Decencies (Harrison, 2007) 199–200, 205
manufacturing 72, 102, 219, 231, 259, 260, 263
March, J. G. 239, 246
marginal utility (principle) 203–4

market economy   34, 100, 108, 109,
    114(n8), 200
  institutional background
    (absent)   101
  see also   'free economy'
market forces   17, 73, 100
market fundamentalism   193, 230
'market knows better'   197–8
market power   76, 80
  proxy for 'economic power'   82–3
  traditional measures
    (limitations)   83
market share   78, 249
market surveys   168, 169
market transformation   76–7
marketing   39, 68, 99, 149
markets   8, 21, 22, 24, 34, 40, 68,
    72, 84–5, 108–9, 160, 163, 165–6,
    248
  competitive   230
  global   114(n3), 201
  idealized   67
  informal   28
  'insider-outsider'   106
  perfectly competitive   77, 78
  quasi-competitive   230
  see also   monopolies; oligopoly
Massetti, E.   244
Méan, J.-P.   xiii, **xxi**, **119–37**
means of production   100, 194,
    263
media   xv, 31, 33, 35, 39–41, 47, 51,
    59, 121, 127, 131, 175, 176, 183,
    211
  'broadcasting'   **6–7**
  companies suspected of
    misconduct   **122**, 136(n8–10)
  'press'   52–3
  private sector   7
  public sector   **6–7**
Melchett, P.   176, 186
Melich, A.   xii, **xxi–xxii**, **47–63**
Merck Pharmaceuticals   221
mergers (and acquisitions)   69, 75–7,
    79, 85, 230
  identity tension   254, **255**
'meso-economic' field   69
methane   234, 235
methodological failure   **201–3**

methodological individualism   150
Mexico   136(n4)
Michelin   83, 249
microeconomic theory   12
microfinance   41
migration   181, 253
military force   182
militias   90, 91, 92, 96f
mining   112, 176, 178
minority interests   23
Mirvis, P. H.   205
Mises, L. von   145, 205(n3)
modernity/modernization   25–28, 30
Moghul Empire   88
money   14–15, 114(n5)
money laundering   95f, 119
monitoring   54, 124–6, 130, 133–4
  compliance programmes   **135–6**
  lobbies (proposed rules)   **55–6**
  lobbyists   **56–7**
monopolies   76, 78, 109–12,
    114(n11), 227, 230, 231
  'natural'   228–9
monopoly rents   81, 229
monopsony   108–10, 115(n13)
Montegrano (Italian village)   37(n20)
Moody's credit agency   82
Moore, K. A.   240, 246
Moral Capitalism (Young, 2003)   201,
    206
moral categories   191–2
moral crisis   **192–6**
moral horizon (Taylor)   149–50,
    159
morality   xv, 105, 198
  relations with law   141
morality of aspiration   203–4,
    205(n5)
morality of duty   203–4, 205(n4)
Morgenthau, H.   182, 186
Morsing, M.   163, 172, 173(n3), 174
mortgages (sub-prime)   82, 192
Mortreuil, L.   xii, **xxii**, **39–46**
motivation   39, 43, 189, 252, 255–7
motor vehicle sector   80
Mulgan, G.   36(n8), 38
multi-actor rationale   209, 213(n2)
multi-disciplinary approach   xi,
    213(n2)

multi-national corporations
  (MNCs) 88, 95–6, 101, 148, 166,
  217, 249, 253, 261–2
  changing environment of
    international business 121–3, 136
  conditions of employment (better
    than those offered by indigenous
    companies) 103
  distinctive features 120–1
  ethical challenge 122–3
  'fifty-one of largest economies in
    world' 85
  headquarters 39, 93–4
  implementation of compliance
    programmes 119–37
  legal challenge at the example of
    anti-corruption legislation
    121–2, 136(n1–7)
  media challenge 122, 136(n8–10)
  negative effects on local
    governance 89–91
  'net job destroyers' 85–6
  networked holdings 81
  'no clear definition' 120
  operating in under-developed
    countries xiii, 103–4
  parent companies (responsibility
    within groups) 81, 87
  'penalized for economic
    success' 84
  self-interest (Prahalad and
    Hammond) 138, 143
  share of world trade 81
  top ten 80, 81t
  'transnational corporations'
    (TNCs) 80, 81t, 120
  see also subsidiary companies
multi-national enterprises
  (MNEs) 215
  'critical role' viii
  terminology 68
multi-stakeholder partnerships
  (2000–) 177, 178, 183
'mutual capture' 88–98

naira 89, 92
NASDAQ crash (2001) 226
Nash equilibrium situation
  (non-cooperative) 234

nation 10
nation-state 262
National Contact Points (NCPs)
  217
nationalistic movements 9
natural law 103, 113, 143–4
  see also rule of law
natural resource curse 89–91, 98
  vulnerability of governance (Niger
    Delta) 91–4, 98(n2–7)
natural resources xiii, 43, 97, 178
Nazi Germany 80
Nemet, G. F. 239, 246
neo-colonialism 96
neo-liberalism 193, 208
Netherlands 20, 50–1t, 51, 136(n4),
  152, 184, 218, 221t, 227, 232t,
  249
network economy 214
networks
  civic 34
  personalized 20–1, 34, 35
networks of power xii, 16–38
New Economy xii
New Public Management 208, 209
New Realities (Drucker, 1989) 263,
  265, 266
New Scientist 176, 186
New Zealand 36(n4), 136(n4)
NGOWatch website 184
Nicholas of Cusa 191
Niger Delta xiii, 98(n2)
  context 91–3, 98(n3–7)
  natural resource curse (vulnerability
    of governance) 91–4, 98(n2–7)
  oil company response and
    failure 93
  peace and sustainable
    development 95, 95f
Nigeria 89, 90, 97, 102, 176
Nike 175
nitrous oxide 235
non-business corporations 114(n8)
non-governmental organizations
  (NGOs) xi, xiv, 7, 15, 48, 53, 56,
  57, 59, 60f, 60, 74, 92, 124, 157,
  211, 212
  campaigning sophistication 175–7
  criticism 184

non-governmental organizations –
　continued
　'lack *de jure* power and
　　legitimacy' 185
　'new role' **179–85**
　novel and inventive
　　campaigning 178
　power 'limited' 184–5
　role in promoting responsible
　　business practice (chapter
　　thirteen) xiv, **175–86**
　soft power **182–4**
　soft power (fragility) 184, 185
　sophistication 178–9
　tactics 176
　tactics and tools (new) 183
'non-market environment' viii, xi
non-profit organizations **13**, 56, 211
non-state actors (NSA) **211–12**
Nordex 237
Norsk-Hydro 237
Norway, 36(n4), 136(n4)
'Notes on State of Virginia' (Jefferson,
　1787) 259
nuclear energy 239
Nye, J. S., Jr. 182, 184, 186

O'Brien, R. 183, 186
'objective culture' 169
objectivity 10, 11, 15
Oceania 41
OECD
　energy R&D 236
　guidelines for MNEs 215, 217, 247
　see also post-industrial
　　economy 68, 214
OECD: Anti-Bribery Convention
　(1997) 121–2, 136(n3–4)
OECD: Investment Committee 217
Office of Competition and Consumer
　Protection (Poland) 154
officials (civil servants) 32, 33
　abuse of power 30
Ogoni 9 (murdered 1995) 93
Ogoni people 91, 176
Ogoniland 89, 177
oil 28, 91, 98, 175, 176, 178, 239
　crowding out of non-oil
　　economy 92
　see also Niger Delta

oil companies 89–90, **92–7**, 237
ójlos (Greek, 'people') **9**
old-boy networks 20, 21, 24, 34,
　122–3
oligarchy 3, 7
oligopoly 79, 81, 83, 230, 234
open systems theory 160
Opinion Leader Research 176
opinion polls 168, 169
opportunism 22, 23, 29, 195
Oracle 84
ordoliberals 79–80, 85
organization and management
　studies xi
organizational conditioning
　(Poland) **153–4**, 158(n7–11)
organizations xv(n3), 56, 57
　international 73
　supra-national 179
Ortega, B. 85, 87
Ortega y Gasset, J. **191–2**, 206
ORTF 6
Oswalt-Eucken, I. 79, 87
outsourcing/off-shoring ix, 230,
　242
owners **104–5**, 114(n8–9)

pactum sociale/pactum unionis 141
Palazzo, G. 164, 173
palm oil 89, 91
parliaments 4, 33
patent citations 231
patent quality 231
patents 110–12, 115(n20–1), 218,
　220
　'causes to sue other
　　companies' 240
　'defence against litigation' 240
　energy-related 240
　'sign of strategic behaviour and
　　asset management' 240
patrimonialism 36(n6)
patronage (sponsorship) 13, 154
patronage cultures
　negative effect of MNCs on local
　　governance **90**
pay 93
　'asymmetric rewards' 96, 97
　'bonus payments' 131
　see also salaries; wages

peace **10, 14**, 95f
peer groups 256
pensions 93, 105, 262
people of God **9**
Peoplesoft 84
perception 166, **167**, 169, 183–4
  business responsibility **171–2**
Peritz, R. 76, 78, 84, 87
personalism xii, 20, 30, 32, 35
personalized versus de-personalized
    relations 18–19, 19t, 24, 29, 35
Peru 102, 114(n7)
Peter, G. B. 208
'petrostates' 28
pharmaceuticals 111, 116, 212
philanthropy 39, 41, 154, 199
  'charity' 148
Philips [corporation] 249
philosophers 144
philosophy **155**, 205, 261
philosophy of dialogue 143
Philosophy of Right (Hegel) 258–9
Pipes, R. 35(n1), 38
planet Earth 164
Pocock, J. G. A. 259, 266
Poland xi, xiii–xiv, 5–7, 9, 36(n4),
    49, 50–1t, 136(n4), 193, 196,
    233t
  CSR (level of interest) **147–8**,
    158(n5)
  R&D 224–5
  R&D expenditure (2000–8) 223t
  scientific ethics 203, 205(n2)
  social involvement
    (diminishing) **156–7**
  stakeholder dialogue **160–74**
  stereotypes *re* running a
    business 153
Poland: Council of Ministers 224
Poland: CSR implementation **147–8**,
    158(n5)
  factors characteristic of Polish
    conditions **151–7**, 158(n7–12)
  historical and intellectual
    factors **151–2**
  material and organizational
    conditioning **153–4**, 158(n7–11)
  as new social contract **138–59**
  social and economic
    conditions **152–3**

Poland: Department of Work and
    Pensions 158(n11)
Poland: Group on Ethics in
    Science 205(n2)
Poland: National Reform Programme
    (2006) 224–5
police 32, 265
Polish character 149
Polish language 205(n1), 205–6
political associations 22, 36(n5)
political authority-property
    dialectic **258–60**
political communication 23
political community **11**, 258
political correctness 40, 171
political donations **4–6**, 8
  corporate versus individual 5
  general principles **7–8**
  individual (upper limit) 6
  transparency 5
'political economy of citizenship'
    (Sandel) 262
political games **39–46**
political influence **4–6**
political logic (Western society)
    13–14
political parties 8, 23, 33, 56, 90
  corrupt 121
  one-party rule 17
  in opposition (to government)
    18, 33
  social democratic 5
  state financing 6
political personalism syndrome
    16–38
political power 25, 27, 34, 35,
    36(n6), 76, 80, 85, 91, 95–6, 139,
    185, 209, 265
  'good' and 'bad' 36(n8), 38
  'lies exclusively with states' 182
  see also economic power
political society (keynotes) 263
political system 16, 149
politicians (corrupt) 121
politics xi–xiii, 10, 17–18, 20, 26,
    28, 31–2, **74**, 142, 147, 153, 208,
    260
  autonomy xv
  'constitutive element' **13**
  generalized distrust 22

politics – *continued*
  informal 21
  injected into economic
    considerations 211
  normative conception 22
  'state' versus 'global' 180
Pontifical Council for Justice and
    Peace 100, 104, 107, 112, 116
populism 3, 33, 35
Populorum progressio (PP) 107,
    115(n12), 116
Porsche 53
Port Harcourt 91
Porter, M. E. xi
Portugal 50–1t, 136(n4), 221t
'positive responsibility' 150
'positive secularism' 49
post-communism 24, 33–4, 37(n18),
    37
  see also transition contexts
post-graduate students 166
post-industrial economy/society 68,
    214
  see also developed countries
post-modernism xii, 204
post-war era (1945–) 72, 79, 194
poverty 67, 73, 89, 92, 95f, 101–3,
    106, 164–5, 178
  'preferential option for poor' 111
power *see* energy sector; political
    power
'power culture' 169
power relations 163, 173(n2), 265
practical realism (virtue) 204
Prahalad, C. K. 138, 143, 159
pressure groups 55
  EC register (2008–) 59
  VBEs 73
price/s 42, 81–2, 105, 228, 230, 241,
    264
  competitive 85
  fair 115(n17)
  predatory 82
  'unjust' 107
  'unjustly' high 110–12,
    115(n20–1)
  'unjustly' low 110, 115(n16–19)
  world market 28
PricewaterhouseCoopers (PwC) xi

primary products
  'fair price' 106
principal-agent problem 104,
    114(n9)
private corporations
  non-state actors of
    governance **211–12**
private equity funds 224
private interests 258–60
  and democracy (chapter one) xii,
    3–8
  versus public interests 35
'private law enforcement' 102
private life 256
private property 4, 100–3, 110–11,
    114(n6), 198
  not necessarily
    'individualized' 102
  relationship with freedom 16–17,
    35(n1), 38
private sector ix–xii, 7, 16–17, 77–8,
    207–8, 240
private sphere viii, xii–xiv
private stock offering 226
privatization 227, 229–31, 240, 244
procurement 102, 128
production (accelerated) 89–90
productivity x, 70, 103, 107, 109,
    225, 230
  US-EU gap **218–19**
  VBEs versus poorest countries
    71–2
productivity gap 67
professional associations 57, 59, 151,
    211, 257
professional career **264**
professionalism 191, 202
professionals 55, 59, 60f
professions 49
profit 11, 13, 15, 25, 40, 41t, 74,
    107, 219, 265
  investment in R&D 78
  'social responsibility of business'
    (Friedman) 84, 86
profit maximization 111–12, 198
profit motive 88, 104–5, 111,
    114(n3), 131, 151, 157–8(n2–3),
    159, 197, 206, 212, 231, 248, 260
profit signal 106, 114–15(n11)

profitability 69, 230, 241
  illusory 82
  indication of economic power
    (limitations) 81–2
promotion 131, 134, 252
property 76, 262–3
  non-individualist
    organization **263**
  sale and lease-back 230
property rights 101, 104, **112–13,**
  114(n3, n11)
Protect the Oceans campaign 175
protest 9
proximity versus arm's-length
  relations **24–9, 36–7(n8–14)**
public administration 20, 27, 32,
  53, 165
  meritocratic (Weber) 19t, 21, 27,
    35(n2)
public affairs consultancies 60, 62
public authorities 56, 60
public goods 262
public interest 84–5, 86
public officials/civil servants 21, 47,
  121, 132
  see also bureaucracies
public opinion 120–1, 128, 131,
  175–6, 183–5, 212
  corporate influence xv
public power 208, 209, 211, 212
  legal or illegal use 19t
public relations (PR) 148, 154
public sector ix, 8, 16–17, 77, 207,
  240–1
  media **6–7**
public service/s 27, 36(n6), 100
public spending 225
public sphere viii, xii–xiii, xiv, 260,
  261
public–private distinction **11,** 18,
  19, 19t
  absence of clear-cut border 21
  and common good **22–4,** 36(n5–7)
Putin, V. 7, 37(n12)

quality of life 140, 215
quasi-authoritarianism 28, 34,
  37(n14)
Quinn, R. E. 167, 173

'radius of trust' **30,** 32
Rainforest Alliance 178
Rasch, W. 37(n13), 38
're-spacialization' 180
real world/reality xv(n3), 11, 16, 42,
  67, 85, 119, 148, 150, 155, 161–2,
  167, 172(n1), 183, 190, 193, 195,
  197, 242
  reconstruction 214
'recognizing authority' 190
regime type
  versus institutional
    inefficiency 33–4
'region-specific' issues 7
Regulating Conflicts of Interest for
  Holders of Public Office in EU
  (EIPA, 2007) 62(n1)
regulation viii, xv, 5, 21, 22–3, 27,
  44, 77, 100, 109, 115(n11), 121,
  197, 198, 207, 209, 210
  failure 86
  state-induced (inefficiency) xv
  see also self-regulation
regulations 27, 42, 199–201, 203,
  216, 231
regulators 39, 40, 74, 110, 198–9
'regulatory state' x, 8, 208
Reiser, M. 29, 30, 38
relationship-building (CSR) 162–5,
  167–70, 173(n6)
religion 12, 14, 60, 90, 194
  see also Catholic social teaching
renewable energy 235, 241
  'most significant research
    trend' 239
reports (violations of codes of
  conduct) **132–4**
  anonymous 133, 134
  feedback 134
reputation 119, 122, 131, 133, 155,
  156, 162–3
Rerum novarum (1891) 108, 116
research and development 69, 76,
  78, 111, **214–47,** 262
  basic 241t
  corporate expenditure 222
  large corporations **226–42**
  national action programmes
    225

research and development – *continued*
  national expenditure (percentage
    of GDP, 2000–8)   221t
  private sector   243
  public expenditure   222
  public sector   242–3
  strategies (Grosse and Sévi,
    2005)   241, 241t, 246
  tax allowances   220
research methods   202
resource allocation   73, 76
respect   9, 19, 250
responsibility   99, 114(n3), 124–7,
    129–30, 143, 150, 155, 192, **197**,
    198–9, 215
  ethical evaluation   190
  fudging   195
  political   265
responsibility principle
  'fundamental to CSR'   146
Responsible Business Forum (FOB/
    Poland)   xi
responsible business practice   (role
    of NGOs)   xiv, **175–86**
retail sales   178
risk   177, 190, 193, 195, 197, 199
Road to Serfdom (Hayek, 1944)   8
Rochlin, S. A.   205
Rodriguez, P.   xii
Rodrik, D.   210
Rok, B.   **xxii, 189–206**
*Role of Large Enterprises in Democracy
    and Society* (this book)
  analytical perspectives   xii
  further research   **xiv–xv**
  Krakow meeting (2007)   xi, xii,
    xv(n1), xvi
  purpose   xiv
  structure   **xii–xiv**
Romania   35, 36(n4), 50–1t, 223t
Roosevelt, T.   182
Rose, R.   25, 32, 33, 37(n18), 38
Rothstein, B.   20, 29, 30, 33, 38
Rousseau, J.-J.   3, 138, **142–7**,
    157(n1)
rule of law   16, 19, 23, 27, 29, 33–5,
    103–4, 145
  absence   101
  'due process'   4

'law and order'   147
  see also   law
Rule of Reciprocity   191
rules of conduct   253
'rules of market'   42
rules-based approach (USA)   **126–7**
'ruling coalition'   3
Runci, P. J.   236, 237, 239, 240–1,
    244
'Russia Inc.'   17
Russian Federation   7, 25, 28, 33–4,
    36(n4), 37(n20), 38
  society 'extension of state'   17–18
  'Soviet Union'   32
  state power   17
  trust in institutions   33, 38
RWE   237, 238t

Sachs, J. D.   98(n1), 98
salaries   42, 264
Sales, A.   23, 38
sanctions   **135**, 199
Sandel, M. J.   262, 266
Sarbanes–Oxley Act   200
Saro-Wiwa, K.   98(n3), 176
Sauquet, M.   xiv, **xxii, 207–13**
savings   70, 101, 194
  borrowing and saving   114(n6)
Savoie, D. J.   208
scandals   31–2
Scandinavia   18, 19–20 152, 227
Scholte, J. A.   180, 186
Schultz, M.   163, 172, 173(n3),
    174
Schulze, G.   106, 115(n19), 116
Schumpeter, J. A.   228–9, 247
science   26–7, 28, **201–2**, 206, 217
*Science and Innovation Investment
    Framework 2004–14* (UK
    Government, 2004)   222, 246
Scott, A.   xiii, **xxii–xxiii, 76–87**
Scottish Power   237
Scottish & Southern   237
Securities and Exchange Commission
    (SEC/USA)   121, 122, 189
'security factor'   201
self-employment   110
self-esteem   253, 254, 257
self-government   259, 260, 264

self-interest 22, 24, 201
self-regulation 126, 197, 198
sensemaking xii, 165, 172, 173
  conative aspect 166
  cognitive aspect 166
  CSR and 160–3, 172–3(n1)
Sensemaking in Organizations (Weick, 1995) xv(n3), 174
separation of powers 31
separatism 10–11
Serbia 36(n4)
Sévi, B. 237, 239–42, 246
shareholder value 74, 114(n3), 250, 262
shareholders ix, 15, 39, **42**, 44(n1), 84, 92, **104–5**, 114(n9), 123, 167, 171, 184, 199, 200, 208, 255, 265
  dissenting individuals within donating organizations 5, 7
Shell
  cost of Brent Spar incident 176
  'how company earned its money' 175
  image of reliability undermined 177
  mis-reporting of reserves 177
  'Royal Dutch Shell' 80, 81t, 92, 237
Shell Foundation 175
Shell Petroleum Development Company (SPDC) 92, 93
Shlapentokh, V. 33, 38
shocks (economic) 89
short-termism 91, 200, 240–2, 250
Siegel, D. xii
significant market power (SMP) 77, 83–5
Singapore 36(n4)
Slaughter, A-M. 180, 186
slavery 259
Slovakia 36(n4), 50–1t, 136(n4), 223t
Slovenia 36(n4), 50–1t, 136(n4), 223t, 224, 225
small businesses 79, 80, 102
  'local stores' 86
  'SMEs' 224
Smith, A. 22, 201, 204

Smith-Hillman, V. xiii, **xxiii**, **76–87**
Social Accountability
  International 124, 137(n14), 153, 158(n9)
'social action' 105
social audits 93
social capital 21, 22, 29, 34, 37–8, 147, 150
social class
  'bourgeois class' 258, **259**
  'bourgeois virtues' 260
  'middle class' 37(n12)
  'plebs' 9
  'proletariat' 4
  see also workers
social cohesion 214, 263
social contract/s xiii, 202, 208
  classical (lessons) **142–7**, 157–8(n1–4)
  CSR and **140–2**
  identification of principle according to which problems can be solved 144
  'new version' (CSR) **138–9**
  Poland **138–59**
  subject matter **139**
Social Contract (Rousseau) 142
social Darwinism 198
social development **152–3**, 158(n5), 214, 216, 218
  sustainable 141
social exclusion 152, 153
social expectations 149, 150, 200
social governance xiv
  multi-stakeholder collaboration **207–13**
social history 258
'social institution' 158(n5)
social involvement **156–7**
social justice/injustice 40, 145
social network 163, 173(n2)
social order **264**
social power 265
'social responsibility' 114(n2)
Social Responsibilities of Businessman (Bowen, 1953) 158(n6), 159
social security payments 262
social stratification 152
Social and Structural Funds 48

social welfare   76, 216, 217, 229, 241,
    241t, 242
  'public welfare'   22
socialism   150
socially responsible investment
    (SRI)   89, 92, 94, 97
societal action   39, **41**
société générale (Rousseau)   142, 144
society/societies   xiii, xiv, 3, 12–15,
    24, 119, 142, 145, 264
  'cold' versus 'warm'   21, 30
  commercial   259
  depersonalized   20
  'extension of state'   17–18
  global   139
  government–society–business
    relations   x
  inegalitarian   20
  modern   25
  'no real' (Alvira)   14
  normative conception   22
  origins   140
  personalized ('warm')   20
  'radius of trust'   **30**
  warmer   32
  Western   **13–14**
sociology   90
Socratic philosophy   **14**
soft law   xv
'soft power'   **182–4**, 186
  fragility   184, 185
solar photovoltaic field   237–9
solidarity   19, 30, 34, 104, **113**,
    122–3
Solidarity (Poland)   151
Sollicitudo rei socialis (SRS)   107,
    115(n12), 116
sophistic rhetoric   **11**
soul (Socratic)   **14**
South Africa   136(n4)
South-East Asia   32, 178, 222, 227
Spain   50–1t, 59, 136(n4), 221t,
    229
speculation (financial)   204
Spencer, H.   198
spillovers   69, 219, 231, 242, 244
staff   127, 128, 169, 173(n3)
  guidance from compliance
    officer   **132–4**

reports (violations of codes of
    conduct)   **132–4**
  see also human resources
stakeholder communications
  Polish companies   **166–71**,
    173(n5–6)
stakeholder dialogue in Polish
    organizations   xiii–xiv, **160–74**
  further research   170, **171–2**,
    173(n3)
stakeholder information strategy
    (Morsing and Schultz)   163, 164
stakeholder involvement   164
  cultural determinants   **170–1**
stakeholder welfare   241
stakeholders   viii–ix, **42**, 43, 44(n1),
    55, 95, 140, 142, 144–5, 153,
    158(n3), 159, 197, 200, 203,
    265
  as business partners   **163–6**,
    173(n2–4)
  collaboration in social
    governance   **207–13**
  ethos of co-regulation   201
  primary and secondary   167, 169,
    173(n5)
standards   xv(n3), 173(n1)
Stanford University   249
Staniszkis, J.   193, 206
Stark, D.   37(n21), 37
state, the   x, 30, 31, 64, 138, 193,
    209, 228, 258–61
  against civil society   **13–14**
  intrusion into individual
    freedoms   16
  involvement in economy   25
  and market ('supposed
    separation')   **11**
  minimalist vision   208
  'new position'   210
  involvement in economy   25
  performance   33
  'political absolute'   13
  principal task   101
  roll-back   8
  soft power   185
  territorial (undermined)   180
  totalitarian   22
  weak   17, 24

state capitalism 16–17
state ownership 8
state sovereignty
  loss 210
  persistence **181–3**
  relativization 261
state–society dichotomy xii, 16, 26
Statoil 92
Sterlacchini, A. 237, 247
Stern, N. 234–5, 247
Sternberg, E. 104, 114(n2, n8), 116, 154
Stettinius, W. 205
Stiglitz, J. 210, 213
stigma 194, 195
stock markets 68, 69
stockholders 40, 44(n1)
strategic alliances 241
'Strategy and Society' (Porter and Kramer, 2006) xi
structured investment vehicles (SIVs) 195
Stubb, A. 57
sub-contractors 128, 131
Sub-Saharan Africa 89, 91
subjectivity 10
subsidiarity 90, 97, 100
subsidiary companies 68, 78, 80–1, 84, 87, 120, 254
  failure of parent company to control **93**, 93–4
  see also VBEs
subsistence 102, 109
Suez-Energy 237, 238t
suppliers 81, 106, 110, 113, 125, 128, 131, 208, 251
  'providers' 40, 44(n1)
supply 106
supply and demand 108, 110
support culture 168–9
Sustainability Reporting Guidelines (GRI, 2000–6) 216–17, 245
sustainable development 40, 43, 94–7, 114(n3), 140–1, 147, 178, 211, 215, 262
sweatshops 175, 184
Sweden 36(n4), 49, 50–1t, 136(n4), 218, 221t, 222, 233t, 238t, 242
Switzerland 20, 21, 48, 136(n4)

Tantawy, B. M. De xv(n1)
Tanzi, V. 21, 34, 35(n2), 38
Tavoni, M. 244
taxes/taxation ix, 5, 14, 27, 28, 97, 115(n11), 262
taxpayers 165, 193
Taylor, C. 149–50, 159
TDC (Denmark) 233t
TEC Article 82 (now Article 102 TFEU) 77
technical efficiency **78**
technical products (versus financial products) 201
technology 216–17, 249
technology transfer 103, 111, 203
Telecom Italia 232t
telecommunications 80, 82, 102, 215
  R&D **226–34**
  R&D expenditure 230–1
Telefónica 59, 231, 232t
Telekom Austria 233t
TeliaSonera 233t
territorial possession 258
terrorism 10
Tesco 87–8
Thatcher, M. 5
think tanks 56, 59–60, **61–2**, 211
'third-party enforcement' **30–1**
Thomson Financial Database 69
'Three Lenses on MNE' (Rodriguez *et al.*, 2006), xii
Thucydides 181
Tilly, C. 79, 87
time 90, 95, 95f, 193, 256
  15th century 92
  17th century 119, 258
  18th century 88, 259
  19th century 12, 22, 88, 89, 92, 181, 183, 249
  20th century 22, 181, 183, 194, 249, 259
  21st century 102, 200, 215, 234, 235, 236, 263
  future 14–15
  future generations 44(n1), 164
  history 79, 139, 144–6, 150–2, **155–6**
  Middle Ages 207

Time-Warner   84
Tocqueville, A. de   22, 23
Total (oil company)   81t
totalitarianism   4, 22, 34
totality   **13–14**
'*tout est pourri*'   12
Toyota   81t
TP (Poland)   233t
trade   70–2, 111, 115(n21), 120, 181,
   213(n1)
   see also   'fair trade'; free trade
trade associations   56, 59
trade unions   55, 56, 59, 63(n3), 124,
   130, 211, 212
   dissenting individuals within
      donating organizations   5, 7
   individual   **5**
trademarks   218
training   124–6, 129–30, **132**, 133–4,
   218
   e-training   132
transition contexts   18, 32, 34
   see also   post-communism
translation   130
'Transnational Community Bodies'
   (Etzioni)   179–80
transparency   xiii, **11**, 48, 97, 189,
   195, 199, 202
   lobbying   **49–53**
   NGOs   184
Transparency International
   (1993–)   20, **36(n4)**, 92, 124,
   136–7(n12–13)
tribalism   90
trust   **16–38**, 44, 93, 127, 164, 177,
   190–2, 194–5, 201, 248, 250
   EU   52, 52t
   extended or generalized among
      strangers   29–30
   generalized   19, 20, 30–1, 32, 34
   irrational   190
   'personal' versus 'calculated
      institutional'   195
   personalized   19
   Poland   157
trust–distrust distinction   19, **29–34**,
   37(n15–19)
   institutionalization of distrust   31,
      37(n17), 37

truth   202
Tupy, M.   27, 37(n11)
Turkey   136(n4)
TVP   xxvi, 7
tyranny of majority   23

Ukraine   7, 32–3, 36(n4)
unemployment   96f, 152, 153, 219
   hidden   106–10
   'lay-offs'   242
UNIAPAC   xxvi, 41
unintended consequences   88–9, 93,
   244
Union Fenosa   237
United Kingdom   50–1t, 51, 87, 90,
   109, 136(n4), 147, 176, 183, 218
   energy R&D programme   236
   England   258
   expenditure on R&D (percentage of
      GDP, 2000–8)   221t, 222
United Kingdom
   Government   114(n3), 175, 222,
   246
United Kingdom Government:
   DTI   70, 75
United Nations   180, 181, 185
   UN Conference on Trade and
      Development (UNCTAD)   68,
      70, 75
   UN Convention Against Corruption
      (UNCAC)   122, 136(n6–7)
   UN Economic and Social
      Council   179
   UN Global Compact   143, 158(n4)
   UN Office on Drugs and Crime
      (UNODC)   136(n6–7)
United States of America   14–15, 22,
   36(n4), 47, 48, 62(n1), 72, 75,
   82, 87, 92, 93, 119, 133, 136(n4),
   150, 158(n6), 176, 183, 200, 203,
   218–19, 222, 227, 240, 266
   anti-trust policies   77
   corporation law   84–5
   energy R&D expenditure (private
      sector)   237
   federal energy R&D programme
      236
   financial crash   189
   rules-based approach   **126–7**

weakness of party system   17
US Department of Justice   84
US Federal Sentencing
  Guidelines   **123–4**, **125–6**,
  136(n11)
US Government   184, 193
US Supreme Court   122, 138(n10)
universalism   20, 35(n2)
'universalization'   180
universities   x, 202–3, 211, 220
University of Buckingham   115(n20)
University of Warsaw   158(n12)
Unocal   176
user-charges   115(n11)
Uslaner, E.   20, 29, 30, 37(n20), 38

VA Linux Systems   226
value chains   68
value-added   69–70, 75, 107–8,
  217–18, 230
values   xiv, xv, 27, 124, 145–6, 161,
  163, 165, 191
  American   180, 184
  'employees'   **248–57**
  ethical system   202
  global system   180
  transnational   180
  universalistic   29–30, 32, 37
  wider society   182
  see also   axiology
values-based approach (Europe)
  126–7
Van Den Bergh Foods Ltd   83–4
Vattenfall   237, 238t, 238n
venture capital markets   224
very big enterprises (VBEs)
  accountability   **72–4**
  characteristics   68
  data deficiencies   69
  economic power and social
    responsibility   xiii, **67–75**
  empiricism   69
  golden age (1980s–)   72–3
  non-financial   69
  organizational innovators   **73**
  and poorest countries (gap)   **70–2**
  quantitative evidence   69, 71
  self-regulation (insufficiency)   67
  speed of innovation   **69**

stock market capitalization   69–71
structuring power   **72–4**
trans-border networks   68
weight in world economy   **67–70**
  see also   big business
Vestas Wind Systems   237
vicious cycles
  'infantilization of
    governments'   **93–4**
  'maladministration'   31, 37(n15)
Vielajus, M.   **xxiii**, **207–13**
Vietnam   103
violence   88, 89, 92, 95, 212
  threat of force   182
Virgil   192
virtue/s
  bourgeois   260
  civil and private   **260–1**
  political   259
vocations   142, 143
voices of enterprises and political
    games   xii, **39–46**
*Voluntary Principles on Security and
  Human Rights* (2000–)   177, 186
volunteering   24, 156–7, 159

wages   72, 105–6
  'agreed' versus 'just'   109
  'excessive'   **107**
  high   109
  just   108
  market rate   109
  'unjust'   **107**
  'unjustly' high and 'unjustly'
    low   **107–9**, 115(n13–15)
Wall Street (motion picture)   197
Wallström, Ms   62(n2)
Walmart   (Wal-Mart Stores, Inc.)   78,
  80, 81t, 81, 85–7
Walton, S.   87
Waltz, K.   182, 186
Warner, A. M.   98(n1), 98
Warsaw: Kozminski
    University   205(n1)
Warsaw Pact   182
Warsaw School of Economics
    158(n12), 159
Washington: White House press
    office   47

wealth-creation   ix, 41–2, 78,
    114(n3)
Weber, M.   19t, 20, 30
Weick, K. E.   xv(n3), 174
Welby, J.   **xxiii, 88–98**
welfare state   16, 20, 23, 27
West, the/Western society   114(n6),
    115, 182
  political logic   **13–14**
Western Europe   6
Westernization   180
Whetstone, L.   115(n16), 115
whistle-blowing   124, 125, 133–4
White Paper on European
    Governance (2006)   54, 63
wind technology   237
Wise, M. A.   235, 244
wishful thinking   190, 200–1
Wolf, M.   115(n15), 116
Woods [initial/s n/a]   107
work–life balance   256

workers   86, 108, 124, 140
  'social experience'   **264**
working conditions   128, 137(n14),
    216
World Bank   102
World Business Council for
    Sustainable Development   xv(n1)
World Investment Report (UNCTAD,
    2008)   80, 87
World Trade Organization
    (WTO)   177, 240
WorldCom   82
'Worst Conflict of Interest' award   53
'worst lobbyist' award   53
written constitutionalism   **11**

Yahoo!   176
Yeltsin, B.   7
Young, S.   198, 201, 206

zoning laws   81